SIMONE WEIL: UTOPIAN PESSIMIST

Also by David McLellan

ENGELS
KARL MARX: Early Texts
*KARL MARX: His Life and Thought
KARL MARX: Selected Writings
KARL MARX: The Legacy
MARX
*KARL MARX: Interviews and Recollections (*editor*)
MARX: The First 100 Years
IDEOLOGY
*MARXISM AFTER MARX
*MARX BEFORE MARXISM
*MARX'S *GRUNDRISSE*
*THE THOUGHT OF KARL MARX
*THE YOUNG HEGELIANS AND KARL MARX
*MARXISM AND RELIGION
*SOCIALISM AND MORALITY (*editor, with Sean Sayers*)

*Also published by Macmillan

Simone Weil
Utopian Pessimist

David McLellan
Professor of Political Theory, University of Kent at Canterbury

MACMILLAN

First published 1989

Published by
THE MACMILLAN PRESS LTD
Houndmills, Basingstoke, Hampshire RG21 2XS
and London
Companies and representatives
throughout the world

Typeset by Wessex Typesetters
(Division of The Eastern Press Ltd)
Frome, Somerset

Printed and bound in Great Britain at
The Camelot Press plc, Southampton

British Library Cataloguing in Publication Data
McLellan, David, 1940–
Simone Weil: utopian pessimist.
1. French philosophy. Weil, Simone, 1909–1943
I. Title
194
ISBN 0–333–48707–9

For Jane

'To write the lives of the great in separating them from their works necessarily ends by above all stressing their pettiness, because it is in their work that they have put the best of themselves.'—Simone Weil
(OC, II, p. 351)

Contents

List of Maps

List of Plates

Preface

The aim of this book is to introduce the reader to the life and thought of Simone Weil. Chapters 4 and 9 contain complicated material and deal almost exclusively with her thought. They can be omitted by those who want more or less straight biography. But Weil herself wished to be judged by her writings and I have tried both to give them adequate space and, as far as possible, to let her speak for herself in her own limpid and elegant prose. The book will have served its purpose if it sends the reader back to the writings of its extraordinary subject. To this end, I have appended a fairly extensive bibliography, as the piecemeal publication of Weil's work is rather a maze.

My debts to previous writers in this field are obvious, particularly to Simone Pétrement's two-volume biography of her friend, which remains indispensable as a rich and detailed source-book. I am also grateful to those who knew Simone Weil and have been willing to share their impressions with me: Joseph-Marie Perrin, Anne-Marie Reynaud, Maurice Schumann, Albertine Thévenon, Gustave Thibon and André Weil. The comments and criticisms of the following have helped me improve my manuscript: Gabrielle McLellan, Stephanie McLellan, Jane Petzing, Anne Seller and David Standley. Bob Towler offered generous support and encouragement. Jean Gil's efficiency and good humour were indispensable in getting the book through its final stages. And finally I wish to thank Florence de Lussy of the Bibliothèque Nationale, Paris, for being such a pleasant and enthusiastic guide to the manuscripts of Simone Weil deposited there.

DAVID McLELLAN

Acknowledgements

The author and publishers wish to thank the following who have kindly given permission for the use of copyright material:

Oxford University Press, for *Selected Letters*, *Selected Essays*, and *Science, Necessity and the Love of God*, all translated by R. Rees.

Routledge & Kegan Paul, for *Oppression and Liberty*, trans. A. Wills and J. Petrie; *Formative Writings*, trans. D. McFarland and W. Van Ness; *The Need for Roots*, trans. A. Wills; and *Notebooks*, trans. A. Wills.

Virago Press, for *Simone Weil: An Anthology*, ed. S. Miles.

Pantheon Books, for S. Pétrement, *Simone Weil: A Life*, trans. R. Rosenthal.

I am also grateful to Professor André Weil for permission to reprint the photographs from his collection.

Every effort has been made to trace all the copyright-holders, but if any have been inadvertently overlooked the publishers will be pleased to make the necessary arrangement at the first opportunity.

List of Abbreviations
(Full publication details in Bibliography)

A	*Attente de Dieu*
C	Jacques Cabaud, *Simone Weil. A Fellowship in Love*
CO	*La Condition ouvrière*
CS	*La connaissance surnaturelle*
EHP	*Ecrits historiques et politiques*
EL	*Ecrits de Londres*
FLN	*First and Last Notebooks*
FW	*Formative Writings*
GaG	*Gateway to God*
GG	*Gravity and Grace*
IC	*Intimations of Christianity*
IPC	*Intuitions pré-chrétiennes*
LP	*Letter to a Priest*
MILES	*Simone Weil: An Anthology*, ed. Sian Miles
NB	*Notebooks*, 2 vols
NR	*The Need for Roots*
OC	*Oeuvres complètes*
OL	*Oppression and Liberty*
P	Simone Pétrement, *Simone Weil: A Life*
P, I, II	Simone Pétrement, *La vie de Simone Weil*, 2 vols
PSO	*Pensées sans ordre concernant l'amour de Dieu*
PT	J.-M. Perrin and G. Thibon, *Simone Weil As We Knew Her*
SE	*Selected Essays*
SG	*La source grecque*
SL	*Selected Letters*
SNL	*Science, Necessity and the Love of God*
SS	*Sur la science*
SWNYL	Jacques Cabaud, *Simone Weil à New York et à Londres*
WG	*Waiting on God*

Prologue

He entered my room and said: 'Poor creature, you who understand nothing, who know nothing. Come with me and I will teach you things which you do not suspect.' I followed him.

He took me into a church. It was new and ugly. He led me up to the altar and said: 'Kneel down.' I said 'I have not been baptised.' He said: 'Fall on your knees before this place, in love, as before the place where lies the truth.' I obeyed.

He brought me out and made me climb up to a garret. Through the open window one could see the whole city spread out, some wooden scaffoldings, and the river on which boats were being unloaded. The garret was empty, except for a table and two chairs. He bade me be seated.

We were alone. He spoke. From time to time someone would enter, mingle in the conversation, then leave again.

Winter had gone; spring had not yet come. The branches of the trees lay bare, without buds, in the cold air full of sunshine.

The light of day would arise, shine forth in splendour, and fade away; then the moon and the stars would enter through the window. And then once more the dawn would come up.

At times he would fall silent, take some bread from a cupboard, and we would share it. This bread really had the taste of bread. I have never found that taste again.

He would pour out some wine for me, and some for himself – wine which tasted of the sun and of the soil upon which this city was built.

At other times we would stretch ourselves out on the floor of the garret, and sweet sleep would enfold me. Then I would wake and drink in the light of the sun.

He had promised to teach me, but he did not teach me anything. We talked about all kinds of things, in a desultory way, as do old friends.

One day he said to me: 'Now go.' I fell down before him, I clasped his knees, I implored him not to drive me away. But he threw me out on the stairs. I went down unconscious of anything, my heart as it were in shreds. I wandered along the streets. Then I realised that I had no idea where this house lay.

I have never tried to find it again. I understood that he had come for me by mistake. My place is not in that garret. It can be anywhere – in a prison cell, in one of those middle-class drawing-rooms full of knick-knacks and red plush, in the waiting-room of a station – anywhere, except in that garret.

Sometimes I cannot help trying, fearfully and remorsefully, to repeat to myself a part of what he said to me. How am I to know if I remember rightly? He is not there to tell me.

I know well that he does not love me. How could he love me? And yet deep down within me something, a particle of myself, cannot help thinking, with fear and trembling, that perhaps, in spite of all, he loves me.

[Written by Simone Weil in Marseilles, Spring 1942 (NB, pp. 638f), and accompanied by the note: 'The beginning of the book, the book which contains these thoughts and many others.']

The France of Simone Weil

The Paris of Simone Weil

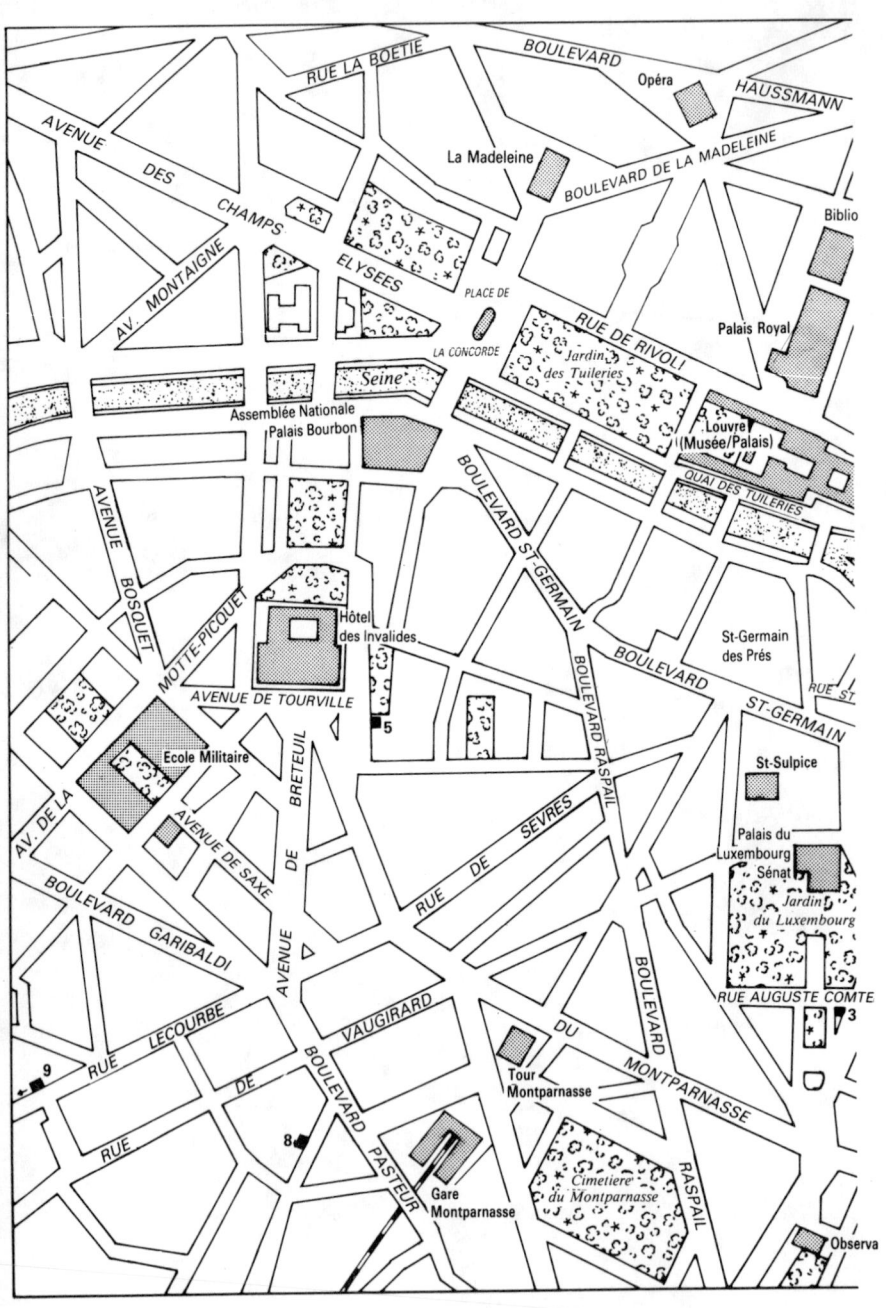

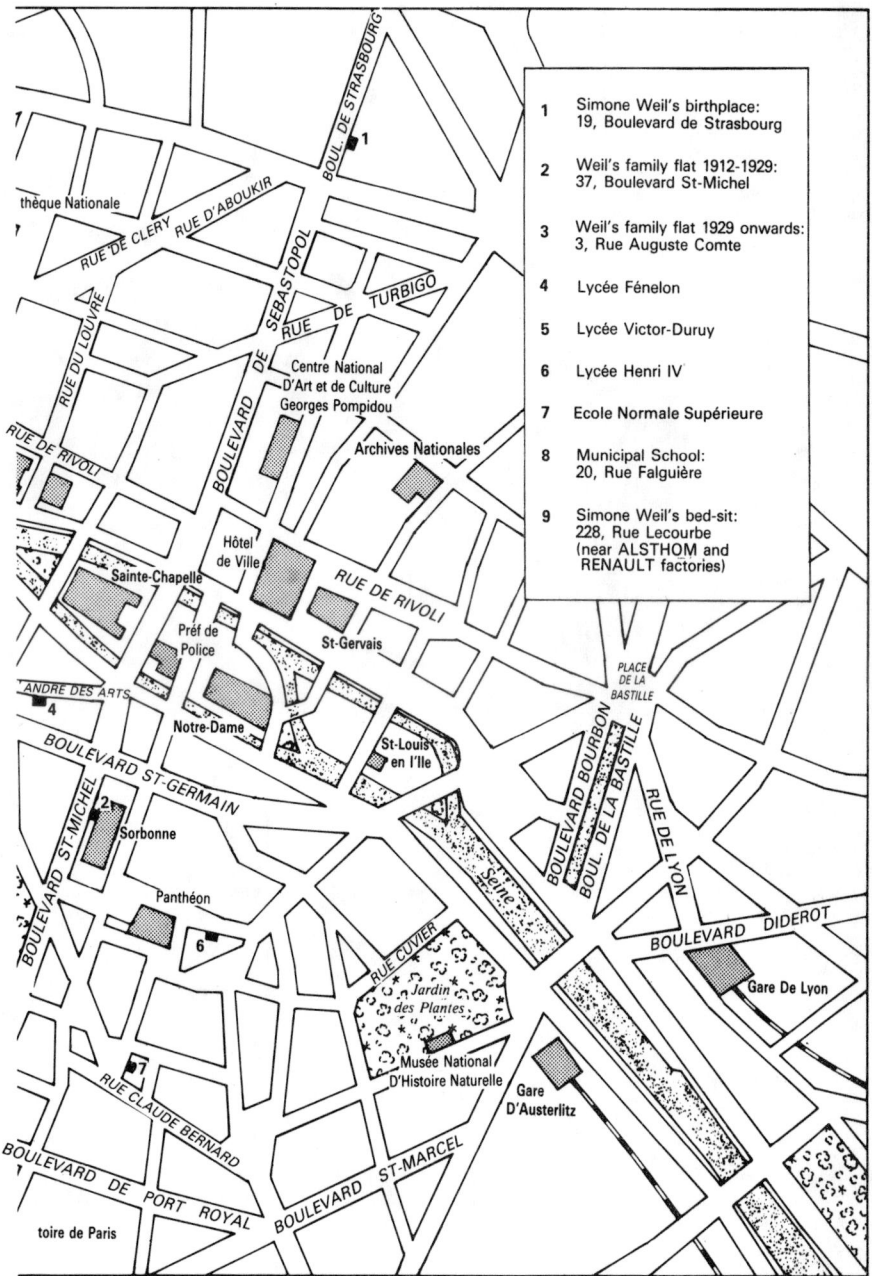

1   Simone Weil's birthplace:
    19, Boulevard de Strasbourg

2   Weil's family flat 1912-1929:
    37, Boulevard St-Michel

3   Weil's family flat 1929 onwards:
    3, Rue Auguste Comte

4   Lycée Fénelon

5   Lycée Victor-Duruy

6   Lycée Henri IV

7   Ecole Normale Supérieure

8   Municipal School:
    20, Rue Falguière

9   Simone Weil's bed-sit:
    228, Rue Lecourbe
    (near ALSTHOM and
    RENAULT factories)

Introduction

'Her intelligence, her ascetism, her total commitment, and her sheer courage – all these filled me with admiration; though I knew that, had she met me, she would have been far from reciprocating my attitude. I could not absorb her into my universe, and this seemed to constitute a vague threat to me.' (Simone de Beauvoir, *The Prime of Life*, Penguin, 1965, p. 126)

From her birth in Paris in 1909, to her lonely death in a sanatorium in Ashford, Kent in 1943, Simone Weil lived only thirty-four years. She had published only a few articles and was known only to a small circle of friends. Yet some consider her the greatest spiritual thinker that the West has produced this century. At the same time, some have found her off-putting, even repugnant. Certainly there are few lives which involve as much paradox as hers: born into a comfortable bourgeois family, she became a fanatical supporter of the proletariat; a pacifist, she fought in the Spanish Civil War; a Jew, attracted to Christianity, she refused to join the Church because of its adherence to the Old Testament; she wrote a lot – and beautifully – about love, but abhorred all physical contact with her fellows; her outlook on life and politics was sombre, even pessimistic, yet she was ever ready to propagate utopian schemes for the reformation of society; finally, she abjured her splendid gifts by refusing existence itself and her death was caused, at least partially, by self-starvation.

There are several reasons for these paradoxes. Weil's writings are addressed to very different audiences – revolutionary syndicalists, Catholic priests, Resistance leaders – and thus differ considerably in tone and style. Much of her most important work is contained in her *Notebooks* and is often aphoristic and allusive. Moreover, like her teacher Alain, she preferred the essay form and seemed deliberately to avoid any systematic exposition of her ideas. Most importantly, there have seemed to many to be two Simone Weils: an early political activist and a later mystical thinker. This fragmentary impression was enhanced by the piecemeal and posthumous publication of her writings. And contradictory assessments of her extraordinary and bizarre personality (let alone her scatty life-style) have coloured – often unduly – appreciations of her thought. With the material currently available, however, a fuller picture and the appreciation of a deeper coherence both in her life and in her thought is possible. There is also a deep coherence, more than with most writers, *between* her thought and her life. This is partly because she was astonishingly quick to put her principles into practice and partly because she was also an extremely *practical* thinker whose ideas tended to spring from the situations in which she found herself: militant trade unionism, factory work, her brother's passion for mathematics, her direct contact with nature as a farm labourer, the people she happened to meet, her own physical sufferings – all are essential ingredients to even her most spiritual writings. Whether it was Berlin, Barcelona, Billancourt or London she had an instinct for being in the right place at the right time and for discerning by a supreme effort of unprejudiced attention, and her unique blend of Plato and Marx, the underlying reality of what was happening.

Weil herself saw her thought as a consistent whole. As she wrote in one of the last letters to her parents: 'I have a sort of inner certainty that there is within me a deposit of pure gold which must be handed out. It is indivisible, and whatever is added to it becomes part of it. And as it grows it becomes more compact. I cannot distribute it piecemeal' (SL, p. 196). But the very striking character of her life and the pithy nature of her writings means that she has been more often quoted piecemeal than studied at length. Her disparate works, always written in the most beautifully lucid prose, have too frequently been used to reflect personal preoccupations or points of view. It is only a complete picture which can avoid the extremes of hagiography or the annexation of Weil to particular established positions. In fact, she remains unclassifiable – and therefore perpetually unsettling. Her trenchant judgements have managed to alienate both Left and Right and most orthodox religion. Many will think that they have never read anyone with whom they have alternately agreed or disagreed so violently. But whether we think of her as a twentieth-century saint or condemn her as a self-absorbed dreamer, few can refuse to recognise her genius, the challenge her life poses to so many of our own preconceptions, and the unerring instinct with which she managed to go straight to the heart of the problems of our time. As she herself remarked: to be always relevant, you have to say things which are eternal.

1
Paris: Childhood and Adolescence

'We do not obtain the most precious gifts by going in search of them but by waiting for them.' (WG, p. 56)

It is striking how many of the traits of Simone Weil's extremely angular personality were established early in her childhood. According to her mother, when she was scarcely three she refused the present of a ring from one of her cousins with the words: 'I don't like luxury.' When she was five she fell off a donkey and hurt herself badly: she insisted on remounting immediately. On hearing, at the same age, from a Syrian student that he was not treated on the same footing as French students, she exclaimed: 'Well, *I* think you are a true-blooded Frenchman.' When an old doctor kissed her hand in the same year, she cried and asked for water to wash herself. Two years later, she shocked one of her uncles, who was complaining that soldiers at the Front were not receiving their parcels, by suggesting that the generals purloined them. When the same pompous old man was lauding the simplicity of the Italian aristocracy by recalling how an Italian Marquis used to address his old nurse with the familiar *tu*, little Simone asked pointedly whether the nurse addressed the Marquis in the same manner. And the varied attitudes to their Jewishness among her immediate forebears was an early influence on her subsequent repudiation of any Jewish identity.

Simone Weil's ancestry was Jewish on both sides. Her middle name was Adolphine after her mother's father Adolphe Reinherz, who, like his wife Hermine, came originally from Galicia. They settled for a time in Russia where they enjoyed a more than comfortable life-style with seventeen servants. Simone's mother Salomea (usually shortened to Selma) was born there in Rostov on the River Don in 1879, three years before they moved to Antwerp, where Adolphe Reinherz continued his highly successful import–export business and acquired Belgian nationality for himself and his family. The Reinherz household, with three children in addition to Salomea, was extremely cultured: Adolphe wrote poetry in Hebrew and had a fine collection of Hebrew books; Hermine was a talented pianist. Both were free-thinking in matters of religion and unattached to any particularly Jewish practice. Adolphe died in 1906; his widow came to live with her daughter and was part of the Weil household until her death in 1929.

Simone's father, Bernard Weil, came from a family long established in Alsace, in which Jewish faith and practice was much more in evidence. Bernard's father, Abraham, had married twice: when his first wife died leaving him four children, he married her sister Eugénie with whom he had another three, of whom Bernard was the eldest, born in Strasbourg in 1872. Most of the family, including the widowed Eugénie, settled in Paris. Eugénie was strictly orthodox and would follow her daughter-in-law into the kitchen on her regular visits for Sunday lunch to make sure that all was kosher. She preferred to see her grand-daughter dead, she said, rather than married to a non-Jew. This attitude left her son with a strong antipathy to the religious and cultural aspects of Judaism: he was a convinced atheist and had a fund of anti-Semitic jokes.

Bernard and Selma Weil were a harmonious couple who enjoyed a comfortable life-style. Bernard was a competent and respected doctor in general practice. An anarchist in his youth and an adherent of the Radical Party in his middle age, he was a gentle, self-effacing man who worried about details that were insignificant to most. He said little, joked self-defensively and, while always extremely frank, went out of his way to accommodate others. He kept his own counsel and his undoubted generosity was always exercised with a rather ironical detachment; he was accustomed to defer to his wife in all matters except those which involved his professional expertise. Selma Weil by contrast was assertive, even domineering. She had wished to study medicine but had been prevented from so doing by her father. Extremely cultivated, sensible and intelligent, she transferred her ambitions to her children. She was energetic and indefatigable, constantly inquisitive, always ferreting out information, the better to guide and control. Her influence was made all the more effective by the fact that she was, at the same time, articulate, persuasive and charming.

The Weils were married in 1905. Their son André was born in May of the following year and Simone three years later on 3 February 1909 in the family apartment on the Boulevard de Strasbourg, just south of the Gare de l'Est. Although she was healthy at birth, her mother developed appendicitis when Simone was six months old and the baby became ill herself. Weaning was extremely difficult, the baby lost weight and one doctor even declared that she would not live. Every day her mother took her, with André and the maid, on the tram to the Luxemburg Gardens in the hope that the fresh air would do her good; but she remained decidedly sickly for a whole year. Then at the age of three and a half the child herself developed a lengthy appendicitis, eventually underwent an operation and had to stay weeks in the clinic convalescing. It was an experience which gave her a life-long aversion to doctors.

While in the clinic her mother read her the story of Golden Mary and Tar Mary. The heroine of the story is sent by her step-mother into the forest: she arrives at a house where she is asked whether she wishes to enter by the Golden Door or the Tar Door. She replies modestly: 'The Tar Door is good enough for me', and is covered by a shower of gold. Her step-mother, seeing her bringing back the gold, sends her own daughter on the same quest. But she chooses the golden door and is covered in tar. This story, Weil said later, influenced her whole life.

By the summer of 1913, Simone's health had returned to normal. The family moved to a large apartment (where they remained until 1929) at 37 Boulevard St Michel just down from the Sorbonne and near the Lycée Montaigne where André was due to start school. André told his sister everything he learned in his class. Their chattering about astronomy on the tram caused one woman to get off, indignantly declaring that she could not stand children reciting like parrots. Simone was extremely attached to her brother, imitated him, and followed him everywhere. He was evidently his mother's favourite and she was already also encouraging Simone towards what she considered the manly virtues. As she wrote to a friend in the summer of 1914: 'I do my best to encourage in Simone not the simpering graces of a little girl but the forthrightness of a boy, even if this must at times seem rude' (P, p. 28). Simone Weil spoke later of the misfortune of her being born a woman and seemed determined to ignore her gender. The ill-placed remark of a family friend that the two children represented Genius and Beauty made Simone all the more determined to neglect the latter and pursue the former. At the same time, she developed an aversion to physical contact that was already prevalent in the family owing to their excessive fear of microbes. Selma Weil did not like the children to be kissed, careful washing of hands before meals was mandatory, and André would even open doors with his elbow to avoid contaminating his hand. Little Simone took all this very much to heart and frequently refused to do something, saying: 'I can't, because of my disgustation.'

On the outbreak of war in August 1914 there began four years of peregrination for the Weil family who moved no fewer than seven times as they accompanied Bernard Weil in his various postings. This meant that both children had very little formal schooling until the end of the war. Bernard Weil's first posting was to a typhoid hospital at Neufchâteau to the west of the Vosges. Officers were forbidden to take their wives with them, but the whole family, including mother-in-law, moved to Neufchâteau and, to keep up appearances, took up separate lodgings. On their frequent walks in the plateau of the Haute-Marne, they could hear the roar of the guns at the Front a few miles to the east. When Bernard fell ill and Selma went to visit him, the landlady would knock on the ceiling whenever she saw a uniform approach and Selma would hide in a cupboard until the coast was clear. But the family's lodging proved too conspicuous and they had to move further away from the town centre. When Simone discovered, during the move, that the parcel her brother was carrying was heavier than her own, she sat down in the snow and refused to budge until she was given one of equal weight. It was at Neufchâteau that she learned to read – as a surprise New Year present for her father. André taught her secretly: when their father was in the room they would hide under the dining-room table to practise. By 1 January 1915 she was indeed word perfect.

Bernard Weil's illness developed into bronchitis and he was sent to Menton on the Côte d'Azur to convalesce. His children spent their days there scrambling up and down the corniche among the wild flowers. Simone put her newly-acquired skill to good use: she learned most of Cyrano de Bergerac by heart and would declaim whole passages with André. In April, Bernard Weil was posted to Mayenne to the south of Normandy; here the family rented a house with a marvellous rose garden where they stayed for the following eighteen months. Both the children had rather desultory private lessons. While André developed a precocious passion for solving quadratic equations, Simone transferred her enthusiasm for Cyrano to patriotic poetry and committed to memory long passages from Déroulède. She was also extremely obstinate. Her mother wrote of her at six years old: 'She is indomitable, impossible to control, with an indescribable stubbornness that neither I nor her father can make a dent in. She stands up to us with an aplomb and assurance that are by now rather comic (my husband can't keep from bursting into laughter in the middle of one of these scenes) but that, if continued, will be distressing' (P, p. 13). Although slow at writing (her hands were slightly misshapen and disproportionately small) Simone was devoted to her books and soon had whole scenes of Racine and Corneille by heart. She and André had both adopted a soldier at the Front to whom they wrote regularly and sent all their rations of chocolate.

In the Autumn of 1916, Bernard Weil was posted to Algeria and his family returned to Paris. Simone and André took to going out without socks in order to harden themselves. Their mother could not prevail upon them to dress sensibly and they further embarrassed her by saying aloud on the tram: 'I am cold, I am cold. Why won't our parents buy us any socks?' They both had a term at the Lycée Montaigne before their father, who had once more fallen ill in Algeria, was posted for six months to Chartres, where his family were again able to join him. In September 1917, he was moved to Laval, where they remained until Bernard Weil was demobilised in January 1919 and they could return definitively to Paris. Simone was able to begin regular schooling at the girls' lycée in Laval. Her teachers were pleased with her progress but her mother continued to worry:

In certain things Simone still has some trouble catching up, since she worked quite irregularly the past year. What troubles me somewhat is that I can see she is always inclined to doubt and mistrust herself. Even when she knows the lesson she always has the nervous fear of failing to remember it. I fight this tendency as much as I can, because I am afraid she will suffer from it later on. (P, p. 16)

At the end of the school year, however, she was top of her class. The following year a severe influenza epidemic persuaded their parents to keep both children at home and give them private lessons.

When they were finally re-established in Paris, Simone, now ten years old, began the classic career of the high-flying French intellectual by attending one of the best Parisian schools, the Lycée Fénelon. The atmosphere of such establishments has been well described by a recent author:

The lycées are built on the model of a convent: entrance from the outside gained through a single door, august and guarded, interior courtyards around which are distributed the classrooms and study areas, and a rhythm of life which, even for the day pupils, is based on the requirements of the boarders. Each day comprises on average five hours of lessons and three of private study, and the word 'class' refers both to a place and a group. The pupils do not traipse about throughout the school as they do today. The methods of teaching are still inspired by the *ratio studiorum* of the Jesuits: homogeneous classes, individual competition, with regular tests given to measure the diligence of the pupils and solemnly composed essays to judge their excellence. This framework, apparently very rigid, gives the pupils a lot of personal freedom: in fact, obedience is only to external rules, and there is no effort to influence or attract the pupils.[1]

At first Simone was extremely unhappy since she could not understand, still less accommodate herself to, the discipline of such a large establishment. But she soon settled down and attended the Lycée happily, if intermittently, for the next four years. Although two years younger than the average age of the class, she was in many respects precocious and excelled in all subjects except drawing and cartography in which she scored a resounding zero. As one of her class-mates remembers:

. . . in subjects such as French, literature, history, she left us behind. We had the impression that she came from somewhere else and had a thought-process that was not of our age or milieu. She seemed to be someone who had lived much more and she must have felt somewhat isolated among her friends since her own preoccupations were so different from theirs. (P, 1, p. 46)

She became the centre of a small closely-knit group of friends who read poems together, acted plays and formed an Association of Knights of the Round Table devoted to redressing wrongs and exercising charity. Her dress was also slightly medieval: she liked to wear a sort of brown cape that was later to become her favourite garment, and kept her bare feet in sandals even in winter.

During her first year at the Lycée Simone began to be interested in politics. The Russian revolution made a favourable impression on her and she called herself a Bolshevik. She would have joined a march of the unemployed down the Boulevard St Michel if her parents had not headed her off. As she herself said later, 'While only a child, in everything that I read or heard tell of, I always put myself instinctively, by indignation rather than pity, in the place of all those who suffered constraint' (EHP, p. 109). She was extremely upset by the Treaty of Versailles, signed in June 1919, which seemed to her to be informed by a desire to humiliate the conquered.

She continued to be absorbed in her books. Pascal, whose *Pensées* she was later to rival with her own, was her favourite author; and she devoured the novels of Dostoievsky. She talked incessantly with her brother of whom she could be very protective: there was a great row when she refused to lend him her copy of Racine because (as she admitted much later) it contained passages about sex that she felt might shock him. Nevertheless Simone would not yield even to him over something she thought unfair, and this often led to fights. These sibling battles would be conducted noiselessly, lest they be separated by their parents who could come across them locked in silent combat, white-faced, tearing at each other's hair.

From October 1920 to October 1922 Simone only attended the Lycée for one term and had private lessons at home. When she eventually returned to the Lycée, she suffered a serious crisis of confidence. This was partly brought on by her having a teacher whose main aim in life seemed to be to belittle her pupils. But she also felt irredeemably inferior to her brother. André had passed the *baccalauréat* brilliantly the previous year and in the summer of 1922 had gained admittance to the highly competitive Ecole Normale Supérieure when only just sixteen years old. This exemplified the kind of intelligence that Simone felt she could not emulate. 'I didn't mind', she wrote later, 'having no visible successes, but what did grieve me was the idea of being excluded from that transcendent kingdom to which only the truly great have access and wherein truth abides. I preferred to die rather than live without that truth' (WG, p. 17). Out of this despair she developed a conviction that was to be central to all her later thought:

After months of inner darkness, I suddenly had the everlasting conviction that any human being whatsoever, though practically devoid of natural gifts, can penetrate to the kingdom of truth reserved for genius, if only he longs for truth and perpetually concentrates all his attention upon its attainment . . . under the name of truth I also included beauty, virtue, and every kind of goodness . . . the conviction that had come to me was that when one hungers for bread, one does not receive stones. (WG, pp. 17f)

Armed with this conviction, she passed the *baccalauréat* in French the following year, and in October 1924 transferred to the Lycée Victor-Duruy to prepare for the rest of the *baccalauréat*. Her main interest was in philosophy and Fénelon had an inferior teacher, whereas philosophy at Victor-Duruy was taught by René Le Senne, one of the leading philosophers of the time, an absolute idealist with a particular interest in psychology. Le Senne said that Simone Weil was one of the most brilliant pupils he had ever taught and the philosophy class frequently consisted in a dialogue between the two of them. Simone disliked the upper-class atmosphere of Victor-Duruy, but she made there two close and lasting friendships: the first was with Suzanne Gauchon who later married the sociologist Raymond Aron; the other was with Suzanne's best friend Edwige Copeau who became a Benedictine nun and Superior-General of their missionary section. Simone was undoubtedly interested in religion and attended, out of curiosity, some meetings organised by one of their teachers who was a recent convert to Catholicism. But it was politics rather which held her interest and she was often to be seen at school with the Communist daily newspaper *L'Humanité* underneath her arm. During the summer of 1925 Simone spent a lot of time talking to employees of the hotel where the family was holidaying. She told them that they were overworked and should form a union. The other guests did not approve.

Meanwhile, in June 1925, she had passed the *baccalauréat* and finished her formal schooling. Six years as a student lay ahead of her before she began her career as a teacher. As she passed from girlhood, her personality was already well-formed along many of the lines that were to impress themselves so firmly on her later thought and action. The influence of the war had turned her into an active pacifist and her instinctive sympathy with the constrained already led her to side with the most deprived sections of society and to refuse to identify with groups with whom she might share a common interest. Her love of nature had been developed by the family's penchant for country holidays and walking: she would drop anything to gaze at a sunset for as long as it lasted. She already possessed a fierce individuality and a passion for thinking things out for herself with rigorous logic. Unable to tolerate even the whitest of lies, she was devoted to the truth. She was naturally inquisitive about everything, ambitious for her own life and anxious to fulfil it in as many directions as possible. At the same time as desiring so strongly communion and friendship, she maintained her dislike of physical contact with people and was enclosed in a radical isolation that inspired a distance in even her strongest attachments. Drawn so uncompromisingly towards the absolute and ideals of purity, she could never be content with the merely relative. It was only her amazing courage and resolution that enabled her actually to pursue the path of rectitude that she had so early and so clearly mapped out for herself.

2
Paris: Student Days

'Never forget that you have the whole world, the whole of life, before you . . . And that, for you, life can be and ought to be more real, more full, and more joyful than it has perhaps ever been for any human being . . . Don't mutilate it in advance by any renunciation. Don't allow yourself to be imprisoned by any affection.' (FLN, p. 18)

With the *baccalauréat* successfully behind her, Weil, now sixteen years old, transferred in October 1925 to the top class of the Lycée Henri IV. These classes (known colloquially as *cagnes* and only opened to girls two years previously) existed largely to prepare pupils for the entrance exam to the elite and highly selective Ecole Normale Supérieure, the Mecca of all those wishing to pursue a high-flying academic career. Henri IV was situated just behind the Panthéon and a few hundred yards from the Weil home in the Boulevard St Michel. Incorporating the ruins of an old convent, its classical quadrangles had something of the air of an Oxford college: together with Louis-le-Grand, it was the most prestigious of the Parisian lycées. Weil's life-long friend and fellow-pupil at Henri IV, Simone Pétrement, recalled the appearance of the new student as follows:

A small, thin face, which seemed to be devoured by her hair and glasses. A fine-boned delicate nose, dark eyes that looked out boldly, a neck that strained forward and gave the impression of a burning, almost indiscreet curiosity; but her full mouth gave one a feeling of sweetness and good nature. Looking at them carefully, her features do not lack charm and even beauty; it was a face at once insolent and tender, bold in asking questions but with a timid smile that seemed to mock itself. But what about those heavy, rather forbidding eyeglasses or that air of always enquiring, knowing, judging? Her charm remained hidden from most people, who saw in Simone only a totally intellectual being. Her body was thin, her gestures lively but also clumsy. She wore clothes with a masculine cut, always the same outfit (a kind of suit with a very wide skirt and a long, narrow jacket), and always flat-heeled shoes. She never put on a hat, which at this time in the upper middle class was very unusual. All this made for a singular personality that evoked the image of the revolutionary intelligentsia and that, for this or some other reason, had the power

11

to irritate many people, sometimes to the point of fury, and still does
irritate them. (P, p. 26)

Weil followed courses in French, English and history; but her main
interest was philosophy where her teacher was the famous Alain, who
had more influence on the development of her thought than any other
of her contemporaries.

The subject that Weil intended to profess – philosophy – was then in
a state of flux. In the late nineteenth century philosophy in France had
become an almost exclusively academic pursuit. After the First World
War the influence of Bergson's creative evolutionism was on the wane;
the positivism so popular in Anglo-Saxon philosophy never really had
the same appeal in France; and existentialist ideas had yet to make their
impact. In so far as there was a philosophical orthodoxy in France in
the 1920s, it was a sort of rational idealism.[1] Distrustful equally of mere
appearances and of intuition or revelation, this rational idealism tried
to steer a course between the dictates of authoritarian religion which
was too conservative and backward-looking and the shallowness of a
simple positivism which was itself being undermined by the progress
of science.[2] Although the influence of Kant was evident, that of Descartes
on French philosophy, culture, and even style was, after three centuries,
as strong as ever. Among the classics, it was Descartes who, together
with Plato, exercised an abiding influence over Weil, for whom the right
use of the mind was both of supreme importance and also possible for
everyone who was willing to exercise the requisite quality of attention.

More immediately, however, Weil was guided by the ideas of her
philosophy professor at Henri IV, the captivating and slightly enigmatic
Alain, the most celebrated philosophy teacher of the Third Republic.
Alain (whose real name was Emile Chartier) presented his pupils with
a view of the world which left a profound impression on them while at
the same time being difficult to summarise. Indeed he rejected any idea
of system and his favoured vehicle was the short essay or *Propos*, dealing
with a single highly specific question or event, of which he published
thousands during his lifetime. Alain himself concentrated on style and
approach more than originality of doctrine. A radical in politics, he had
been an active defender of Dreyfus and, although an ardent pacifist,
had enlisted in the war as a simple foot-soldier as an act of solidarity –
an example Weil was to follow later in Spain. An essayist, therefore, as
much as a philosopher, he was also a great classicist, and denied that
there was any progress in philosophy, and had no time for historical
detail. His aim was to re-think the great tradition of Plato and Descartes
in the light of Kant, whose ideas had been transmitted to him by his
own philosophy teacher, Jules Lagneau, for whom Alain conserved an
unbounded admiration.

There were, nevertheless, several continuous themes running through Alain's philosophy. In the tradition of Plato and Descartes, Alain held to a strong separation between mind and matter. Mind was *in* the world but definitely not *of* the world; and only a mind which knew itself to be utterly distinct from the world could perceive correctly. Alain attributed great importance to perception which he conceived to involve taking an active stance towards the world which, faithful and pure, awaited the activity of mind to understand its relationships, to make it coherent and common to all. Hence the importance that Alain attached to geometry: no-one could properly perceive a cube without some understanding of its geometry. Art and manual labour were also disciplines which greatly aided perception of the real. The main obstacles to correct perception were all the passions and the imagination that were not subject to reason. But the correct use of reason was to a large extent a matter of will-power and Alain added to Descartes's *ego cogitans* the emphasis on will to be found in Rousseau. Reason must be willed and exercise of the will demanded courage and self-reliance – the will to will. Feelings and emotions were functions of the body and, as such, could be accepted or resisted by the mind like other physical facts. Thus Alain had that ambiguity towards religion characteristic of a Feuerbach or a Renan. God was not an entity which could be said to exist, but rather the summation of all values, a model of perfection to which we should conform. Profoundly anti-clerical, Alain nevertheless found a deep moral sense in what he regarded as the myths of Christianity. In politics, Alain thought the citizen's main duty was to prevent strong government: since all power corrupted, it was not a question of reforming government, but of enfeebling it. Although no socialist, he sided with the proletariat, the imperatives of whose life-style had, he thought, prevented them from succumbing to the illusions of ambition and power to which the bourgeoisie were so prone. In his supreme individualism, his distrust of all authority, his truculent acquiescence in the *status quo*, Alain reflected the radicalism of the provincial *petit bourgeois* and the small farmers who constituted the backbone of the Third Republic.[3]

Alain's influence was not only due to his being very much a man of his time; he was also a supremely gifted teacher; and in the France of that time the influence of philosophy teachers on their pupils was enormous: Alain himself spoke of his own teacher, Jules Lagneau, as 'the only god he ever recognised'.[4] A bachelor until his retirement, when he married his secretary, Alain devoted himself to his writing and to his pupils, whom he always treated as adults and with studied formality, addressing each as 'Monsieur' or 'Mademoiselle' and never by name. He was a great encourager and always on the look-out for some positive sign of quality in his pupils' work. School, for Alain, was a society of equals, a sort of haven of reason between family and society.

In his class, no-one was presumed to be more intelligent than anyone else: it was all a question of will-power and the main obstacle to be overcome was laziness. Application was the key and Alain encouraged his pupils to write optional short essays on large white sheets of paper, never to cross out anything, but only to add and select, good writing being the key to good thought. In many ways, Alain was distinctly old-fashioned. He set great store by handwriting – it was no accident, he claimed, that his own master, Lagneau, had the best handwriting he had ever seen – and, in his class, Weil changed her own handwriting from her previous scrawl to a precise, rounded, laboured writing that was to remain with her for the rest of her life. Alain was extremely punctual, finishing his lessons sometimes in mid-sentence if the bell had rung; and, above all, he would emphasise the importance of reading and studying the classics, both philosophical and literary, on the grounds that everything had already been thought but it was up to each generation and individual to reappropriate the tradition in their own mind and manner.

Alain's chair at Henri IV had previously been occupied by Bergson and Brunschvicg and he remained there for twenty-four years. Many of the most brilliant young minds of the 1920s were drawn to his style of thinking: Merleau-Ponty and Maurois were much influenced by his teaching; Raymond Aron admired his 'unadorned sincerity and ever-renewed desire for truth';[5] Maurice Schumann, future Foreign Minister under de Gaulle, began his life-long friendship with Weil in Alain's class; Sartre chose not to become a pupil at Henri IV to avoid Alain's influence, but nevertheless attended his lectures, as did his comrade-in-arms Paul Nizan, soon to become the most incisive of the Communist intellectuals of the 1930s. For the writer Jean Prévost, Alain was, 'the only man who has never disappointed my unbounded adolescent expectations . . . faced with him, we only thought how to understand him, how to follow him, how to anticipate him; his class returned to him a reflection of himself'.[6] The student probably most profoundly influenced by Alain was Simone Weil, who arrived in his class in 1925 when he was at the height of his reputation. Sitting in the front row, one of only three girls in a class of thirty, she listened to him for six hours every week and submitted to him an exceptionally large number of short essays as well as the obligatory dissertations. Her indignant opposition to the prevailing social order and her enthusiasm for the cause of the underdog found a ready echo in Alain's teaching, which developed the lucidity and strength of her expression. There was, as she herself said, a part of Alain's thought that remained always with her.[7]

During her first year at Henri IV, Weil's main interest seems to have been in the area of human action and morality, as evidenced by two remarkable essays that she wrote for Alain. In the first, entitled *Grimm's Fairy Tale of the Six Swans*, she recounted the story of a young woman whose six brothers have been changed into swans. In order to have them changed back into their true selves, she has to make six shirts from white anemones while keeping absolutely silent. This takes her six years, during which she marries a king and is accused by her mother-in-law of murdering her children. Not being able to reply, she is condemned to death and is on the point of being executed when the six swans arrive: she throws the shirts on them and they are transformed. The lesson that Weil drew from this story was that 'pure abstention is active . . . the only force in this world is purity; everything that is without admixture is a piece of the truth . . . the only force and the only virtue is to abstain from action' (OC, I, pp. 58f). It was a sentiment that she could equally have voiced at the end of her life. In the second, longer essay, entitled *The Beautiful and the Good*, Weil identified the good with an act of free will by which the individual conformed to the moral law, an act which could also be beautiful. An example of such an act, for Weil, was Alexander's famous refusal of the helmetful of water that one of his soldiers had brought him when the army was marching through a desert. When Alexander poured the water on the ground, his action was apparently useless and wasteful. In reality, however, this ceremonious renunciation of Alexander created a solidarity with his soldiers whose thirst had been removed by the striking act of their leader. The moral was that

> to save the world it is enough to be just and pure; which is expressed by the myth of the Man–God who redeems the sins of humanity by justice alone without any political action. We must therefore save in ourselves the spirit of which external humanity is the myth. Sacrifice is the acceptance of suffering, the refusal to obey the animal in ourselves, and the will to redeem suffering humanity by voluntary suffering. Every saint has poured the water away; every saint has refused all happiness which means being separated from the sufferings of humanity. (OC, I, p. 71)

Duty to oneself, therefore, coincided with duty towards humanity and consisted in a self-mastery which enabled one freely to choose to share the common lot.

These high moral considerations were complemented by Weil's essays (of very variable quality) in more strictly philosophical matters. Weil saw an intimate link between will and thought in that perfect freedom coincided with perfect knowledge. This knowledge did not consist in immediate contact with physical phenomena but in getting at the intelligible structure of the world as in the example of Lagneau's cube:

although we never *see* all the sides and angles of the cube simultaneously, we know that it is the cubic form which determines the variations of the apparent form. The principal vocation of humanity was not to see and to touch, but to understand. Hence the almost mystical veneration that she felt for plane geometry and mathematics since they contained no perspective and seemed the path to that 'pure perception' that she later said was her aim when seventeen years old. The world itself, existence, was unknowable except as a 'continual presence' underlying our ideas of time and space: 'Everything can change in the world; the world will not abandon us. It will always be there, faithful and pure. In a sense, that is all that we can say about it.' This world, this alien existence, was necessary, otherwise the mind would have no object about which to think. But the mind's role was to think of the world as completely different, as pure indifference and pure necessity. In these tentative and often rather obscure philosophical essays Weil was obviously heavily indebted to her teacher, Alain, as she was also in her enthusiasm for poetry, myth and legend as a supplementary approach to reality. Her attitude to Christianity was a particular example of this: she showed considerable sympathy for Christianity and particularly Catholicism as a source of various beautiful sayings and ceremonies, but not as an object of religious faith. As she wrote later:

> As soon as I reached adolescence I saw the problem of God as a problem of which the data could not be obtained here below, and I decided that the only way of being sure not to reach a wrong solution, which seemed to me the greatest possible evil, was to leave it alone. So I left it alone. (WG, p. 29)

For the young Weil, God was simply a name for human aspirations.

To her philosophy studies Weil devoted enormous time and effort. In 1927 she won the school's philosophy prize and her teacher was generous in his praise. At the end of her first term he wrote: 'She has cogency, lucidity, and often wit and distinction in her powers of analysis. Her overall perspectives are less clear; she has to learn how to construct a coherent argument. She already shows an inventive mind and much may be expected of her' (P, 1, p. 41). And his farewell, prescient comment was: 'An excellent pupil; a rare strength of mind, wide culture. Will succeed brilliantly if she does not embark on obscure paths. In any case, she will attract attention' (P, 1, p. 97). In her subsidiary subjects, however, her teachers were less than enthusiastic. In French, she 'aims for too much originality, even *eccentricity*'; in English her teacher wrote that she was 'irregularly present in body and even more irregularly in spirit. Profits from the lessons in proportion . . . seems resolved to get as little from the class as possible, and succeeds'. And her history teacher saw her as 'an intelligent girl who visibly feels herself to be above history' (P, I, p. 100). More than one teacher saw her as a disruptive element in class and she was certainly a thorn in the flesh of the school authorities. On one occasion she was suspended from school for a week for illicit smoking; on another, when the Vice-Principal had decided to separate the girls from the boys in class, Weil put up ironic placards saying 'Women's Section' and 'Men's Section' and came to blows with him when he tried to remove them.

On many of her fellow-pupils, too, Weil made an unfavourable impression. Alain himself referred to her as 'the Martian', which he explained later as meaning that 'she has nothing in common with us and sovereignly judged us all'. Perhaps he was also thinking of H. G. Wells's Martians, who were all brain and eyes. To one of her fellow-pupils she was quite simply 'undrinkable'.[8] To another, Jacqueline Cazamian, she had 'a sort of "archangelic" character, a transcendence of intellect which admitted no compromise either physical or emotional. Never had so sparkling a soul seemed less incarnate' (P, I, p. 70). As a student Weil seems to have been less 'human' than in later years, when she was more willing to share her desires and her troubles. Her friend Simone Pétrement, who probably knew her better than anyone else at this time, wrote that many people when first confronted with Weil had

the impression that some element of common humanity was missing in her – the very thickness of nature, so to speak. Indeed, one senses that many of her old classmates, when they finally read her writings, were surprised to discover that she was so human. I myself was astonished by the incredible sensitivity she revealed. Certainly, when it came to generosity, a concern and pity for others, nobody has ever denied that she had these qualities, and in the highest, most selfless forms. In this sense, she was more human than anyone else. But what was hard to believe was that she had the ordinary human frailties. One might even think that she didn't have the same needs or the same desires as others, that she was not wounded or hurt by the same things. She forbade herself all weakness with such firm determination that one could mistake for a peculiarity of her nature what was in truth a product of her will . . . in plain fact, she was a strange mixture of coldness and passion; on the one hand there was in her something reasonable, rigorous, calm, and slow, while, on the other, there were lively, often awkward, often naive and charming impulses, together with a blaze of enthusiasm and long moments of violent indignation. But it was precisely in her sensitivity that she could seem different from most people, no doubt because to a rare degree she seemed to forget all personal interest or desire and became excited only for noble causes and with no concern for herself, giving rein to her violence solely for the general welfare and the truth. In a sense, her pride was great, but she was not thin-skinned; she was not concerned about wounds to her feeling of self-esteem, and even sought out those who did not like her. She seemed without resentment or anger for everything that involved only herself; she did not try to please and consequently was not timid in her relations with her class-mates. Even her clumsiness seemed to spring from the fact that she was not made out of the same crude materials as the rest of us. She was truly different in the sense that she was already well above the common level, owing to the purity of her emotions and the strength of her character even more than to her intentions. (P, pp. 27ff)

For all her peculiarities, Weil formed several close relationships at Henri IV, in particular with René Château, Jacques Ganuchaud, and Pierre Letellier, with whom she would sit for hours in cafes and sometimes ramble around Paris all night. She also occasionally went to the Sorbonne where she was to sit the exams for the BA in philosophy as part of her preparation for the Ecole Normale Supérieure. Simone de Beauvoir met her there:

> She intrigued me because of her great reputation for intelligence and her bizarre get-up; she would stroll around the courtyard of the Sorbonne attended by a group of Alain's old pupils; she always carried in the one pocket of her dark-grey overall a copy of *Libres Propos* and in the other a copy of *L'Humanité*. A great famine had broken out in China, and I was told that when she heard the news she had wept: these tears compelled my respect much more than her gifts as a philosopher. I envied her for having a heart that could beat right across the world. I managed to get near her one day. I don't know how the conversation got started; she declared in no uncertain tones that only one thing mattered in the world today: the revolution which would feed all the starving people of the earth. I retorted, no less peremptorily, that the problem was not to make men happy, but to find the reason for their existence. She looked me up and down: 'It's easy to see you've never gone hungry', she snapped. Our relationship did not go any further. I realised that she had classified me as 'a high-minded little bourgeoise', and this annoyed me . . .[9]

When the results were declared in the summer of 1927, Weil was top of the list with de Beauvoir second.

Successful at the Sorbonne, Weil at the same time failed the entrance exam to the Ecole Normale Supérieure, largely owing to her poor performance in history, and returned to Henri IV for a third year. Immediately after her exams, during the summer of 1927, she spent several weeks in Normandy near the farm of the Letellier family at La Martinière. She worked long hours in the fields during the harvest, causing an exhaustion that she was to recall years later while working in the Renault factory. She would pick up heaps of thistles with her bare arms. When Pierre's elder brother Michel urged her to leave them for the harvesters to collect she replied: 'Why them and not me?' She also clashed with him over the treatment of the farm labourers: she tried to persuade them that their conditions were unacceptable, but he said that this kind of talk only made them more miserable. Half in love with Pierre, she was also attracted by what she had learnt of his father, Leon Letellier, who embodied her ideal of the unity of mental and manual labour: the son of small-scale farmers he had left home at sixteen to travel the world as a deep-sea sailor before returning to the school benches at the age of thirty to become a pupil of Alain's beloved teacher Lagneau and later take up farming again. Leon Letellier had died in the previous year. A selection of his writings was being put together for publication and Weil spent long and happy hours at the farm copying them out. She drafted out a few pages of a possible article on Letellier in whom she admired the fact that

> he formed perhaps the one idea that can only be got by application, the idea of the individual conceived as supreme value. He always loved the work to be accomplished more than himself and every human being more than any work . . . work was never in his eyes a necessity imposed by God as a punishment, but, for himself, a duty towards society, for others, a means of salvation. (OC, ɪ, p. 116)

She also wrote, for herself, a fine psychological analysis of the irascible Michel who was in charge of the family farm.

When back in Paris, Weil was once again absorbed by her studies and, in particular, taking her history more seriously. At the same time she was keen to put her ideas into practice. Indeed, her sanguine conviction that 'all human beings, however mediocre their intellect and their talents, can, if they apply themselves, know everything that is within the compass of humanity' (OC, ɪ, p. 177) led straight on to her social criticism and her efforts in workers' education that were to occupy so much of her time during the following decade. An opportunity was provided by Lucien Cancouet, a fellow-soldier of Alain's during the 1914–18 war, who worked on the railways and was active in the trade union movement. He was anxious to provide courses for railway workers who wished to gain promotion or simply to broaden their horizons. Together with some of Alain's pupils, he formed a Social Education Group which held its sessions, continuing for several years, in the municipal school in the rue Falguière. Weil's lectures there were less successful than those of her friends: although the railway workers liked her well enough, her ideas were often too bold and paradoxical. Weil also began in 1927 to develop her abiding interest in politics. The Kellogg Pact outlawing war was being signed in Paris. Like Alain, who considered war a more immediate road to slavery than any form of capitalism, she was a strong pacifist and, with her same friends Château and Ganuchaud, joined the newly-founded group Volonté de Paix (Will for Peace) which met at the Quaker Centre in rue Guy de la Brosse. She distributed their magazine, persuaded her parents to help, and went round sticking up their posters. Although a reader of the Communist Party newspaper *L'Humanité* (as well as a devotee of the satirical *Canard Enchaîné*), she never joined the Communist Party, which maintained a fairly liberal attitude towards its intellectuals until the very end of the 1920s and, in 1926/7 in particular, saw an influx of intellectuals into its ranks. But she would certainly have described herself as a Communist in the broader sense.

For most of the last term she absented herself from Henri IV (the school was under the impression that she was ill) to stay with a friend of her mother's who ran a girls' boarding school near Bordeaux. She worked furiously on the history which had let her down so badly the previous year. She almost missed the examination entirely, having forgotten to enter her name as a candidate and only a direct appeal to the Minister got her special permission to sit. In the event she succeeded brilliantly: out of 218 candidates for entrance to the Ecole Normale Supérieure, 29 were admitted, with Weil in sixth place.

The Ecole Normale Supérieure, where her brother André had been a student and where she was to spend the next three years (1928–31), was a very special place. It was originally founded as part of the Napoleonic organisation of the higher education system to provide a training college for lycée teachers in arts and sciences. During the nineteenth century the Ecole Normale became the most prestigious of all French educational establishments, since its fiercely selective entrance examination distinguished it from universities which were, in principle, open to all who had passed the *baccalauréat*. Raymond Aron, who entered the Ecole Normale in 1924, said that he had never before seen so many intelligent people together in so small a space. At the turn of the century, under political pressure for its growing radicalism, it was affiliated to the Sorbonne, but remained the premier institution preparing students for the *agrégation*, the highly competitive examination which gave students who passed it access to top teaching posts in schools and, increasingly, universities.[10] In 1847, it had moved to a site in the rue d'Ulm only a few hundred yards from the Lycée Henri IV and the Sorbonne and the Weil's family flat. For all its prestige, the buildings were extremely dilapidated: it had been used as a hospital during the war, the roof leaked, there was no central heating or running water, and the food was appalling. In a novel set in 1928, the year of Weil's entry, Nizan described the Ecole Normale:

> It is a large square edifice dating from the time of Louis-Philippe; its centre is a courtyard with a cement-lined pond in which goldfish moved lazily; between the windows was an exemplary frieze of great men; a cold smell of institutional soup lingers in the glassy corridors; a naked man dying against a wall and offering a stone torch of which no one wishes to relieve him symbolises the dead of the war.[11]

From this mixture of monastery and barracks emerged a string of students who were later to become famous. From Taine, Bergson and Jaurès in the nineteenth century to Sartre, Nizan, Aron, Pompidou and Merleau-Ponty in the mid-1920s, the Ecole Normale aimed, together with its great rival the Ecole Polytechnique, to provide the Republic with its ruling elite.

In some quarters the Ecole Normale Supérieure had the reputation of being a hotbed of political radicalism and subversion. But a wild and independent spirit characterised only a relatively small minority and they were not especially political. Mainly former pupils of Alain, these young men were fairly brutal in their conduct and were accustomed to shout 'Thus pissed Zarathustra' as they threw water-bombs from the top of the stairs on those returning in dinner-jackets from a night out.[12] As this implies, it was very much a young man's world: women had only been fully admitted to the Ecole Normale Supérieure in 1927 and Weil was the only woman in her year. Since she was not a boarder and, having already obtained the BA, had no exams in her first year, her contact with the Ecole Normale was intermittent. Indeed, she continued to write essays for Alain and attend his classes at Henri IV, where she had already become a legend to the next generation:

> We were told of the esteem in which she was held by the Master; we already recognised her genius, but our feelings of admiration were mixed with irony. We recounted the reply which she had given to a Sorbonne examiner that the proof that the earth became less warm towards it centre was that you put bottles in a cellar in order to cool them. We recounted her anger every time she was told – to wind her up – of an unbelievably stupid question in the entrance examination to the school. (P, I, p. 142)

Two former pupils of Alain, Michel and Jeanne Alexandre, had started in 1921 a journal entitled *Libres Propos* in which many of Alain's own famous *Propos* appeared. It was here in the summer of 1929 that Weil published her first two articles.[13] They both reworked subjects that she had been meditating for some time. The novelty was the central place she now gave to the idea of *work*. In the first article, entitled *Concerning Perception or the Adventures of Proteus*, Weil recounted the Homeric myth of Proteus, a sea-god of ancient Greece who had the gift of assuming any shape he wished. Proteus is a stand-in here for the age-old problem of correct perception: 'We all', she wrote 'learn to perceive between the ages of one and four and all our life, through science, culture, art and work, we merely commemorate this first revolution' (OC, I, pp. 134f). For Weil, the Protean impressions that the external world made upon the mind were not to be brought to heel by reflection alone, whether it was that of the geometrician or the physicist. The concept of space was essential to perception and it was work that provided an understanding of space. On Weil's definition, work was a sort of indirect action: work, as opposed to reflection, persuasion or magic was a series of actions which had no direct relation:

> Thus for a man who takes refuge in a cave and wishes to block the entrance with a large rock, necessity dictates first of all that the movements that permit him to do this have no relation to the spontaneous movements that, for example, cause him to fear ferocious beasts, and are even their direct opposite. (OC, I, p. 125)

So, 'a workman who ceaselessly experiences the law of work can know much more both about himself and the world than the mathematician who studies geometry without knowing that it is also physics and the physicist who does not accord their full value to geometrical hypotheses. The worker can get out of the cave, the members of the Academy of Sciences can only move among the shadows' (OC, I, pp. 136f). And the conclusion: 'Geometry, as perhaps all thought, is the daughter of workers' courage' (ibid.).

The rather forced and awkward argument of this article reflected Weil's desire to integrate manual labour into her previously more abstract philosophical considerations. Her experience in the fields of the Letellier farm in 1927 and her contact with the workers in the rue Falguière had obviously made a strong impression on her. And in the summer of the following year she had planned to join her friends Château and Ganuchaud in doing some navvying in Liechtenstein for the Civilian Service, a pacifist and charitable organisation founded by the Swiss Pierre Ceresone as a counterpart to military service – a plan she abandoned on being told that the role of women was confined to the kitchen. However sexist its operations, Weil approved the principle of the Civilian Service which she saw as establishing a relationship between work and peace: 'The idea which negates war is the idea that the individual human being has more value than anything else in the world . . . I cannot know the value of the individual human being without experiencing my own value and I can only do that in so far as I act. Only work makes for peace.'[14] In 1929, she spent August and September staying with an aunt in Jura and digging potatoes for ten hours a day. 'What I like about this place', she wrote to her parents, 'is that I have become friendly with the people who live here. The work, the fairs, the fêtes are just opportunities for fostering this friendship by sharing their life' (P, 1, p. 149). Her reflections on these experiences were continued in the second article that she published in *Libres Propos*. It was entitled *Concerning Time* and consisted in an analysis, in the style of Alain, of Kant's view of time as an *a priori* form of thought. For Weil, time was 'this separation between what I am and what I want to be, such that the only path from myself to myself is work, a relationship between myself and myself that is forever being undone and that only work can tie togther again' (OC, 1, p. 143). The law of time was, therefore, 'the law according to which work is the only means of passing from project to accomplishment' (OC, 1, p. 325). Since the world was composed of objects that were simply juxtaposed without any necessary connection, 'it is only by the trial of work that space and time are presented to me, always together, time as the condition, and space as the object, of any action; the law of work prescribes, with regard to my action, that it has duration, with regard to the world, that it is extended' (OC, 1, p. 145). And the conclusion: 'Let us awaken again to the world, that is, to work and perception, while still having the courage to observe this rule . . . to lower our body to the rank of a tool, our emotions to the rank of signs' (OC, 1, p. 147).

Weil was also interested in extending the implications of these rather obscure, if stylish, philosophical reflections into more concrete areas. In notes that were probably destined for lessons at the Social Education Group, she asked: if, for example, the body was but a tool, did it not follow that wages should be equal? For it would obviously be unjust to pay any reaper more than another simply because he or she had a sharper scythe. As long as human beings simply moved matter about, there was no problem; but the expanded division of labour meant that some people moved other *people* about. And with the rise of education, perhaps the greatest power in the present age, the situation was radically altered; for it produced an elite who claimed privilege in the name of science, a word which

> pronounced in the right place, places the individual who uses it in the small number of those who have the right to decide, while the ignorant crowd, the mass, in other words the people, find themselves pushed aside. If the people recogise that the elite have every right to

push them aside, all that remains is to believe in the elite, to obey it, and hope for its benevolence. (OC, i, p. 254)

To this problem, which was to occupy her much in the years to come, Weil as yet saw little solution except in acquainting the workers with the principles of true science. Increases in the standard of living were of themselves no answer. The slavery of American workers in car factories was not compensated by car ownership: workers remained slaves – with cars. Weil also pursued the question of the relationship of laws and rights to power in another essay for Alain. She rejected the notion of Spinoza that measured right by power. For rights were neither of the world (which was simply as it was) nor of the mind (which, being sovereign, could not be given rights) but in the interaction between the two which she once again located in the idea of effective work which alone could found a theory of rights (cf. OC, i, pp. 258f).

These reflections of Weil on power, work, and equality accompanied a continuing political and educational commitment. She increased her teaching work with the railwaymen in the rue Falguières and as soon as she arrived at the Ecole Normale she threw herself into the growing campaign against the compulsory preparation for military service that was in force there. This preparation enabled the students to become officers during their period of military service, which was also thereby shortened. René Château drew up a petition asking that the preparation be made voluntary, the idea of those signing being that they would then be ordinary soldiers during their military service and avoid both the bestowal of privilege and the unwelcome task of commanding. This was very much in the spirit of Alain who gave his unqualified support to the petition, as did Weil who, although as a woman not directly affected, was the most energetic in collecting signatures. Almost half the students signed and there was an outcry in many of the Paris newspapers who spoke of 'gangrenous anarchy' and demanded immediate sanctions against such delinquents. The Ministry rejected the petition and the authorities at the School were severely embarrassed. The same group of students also tried to enlist the League of Human Rights in their pacifist cause. They joined the XIVth section of the League with a view to putting pressure on its Central Committee which was presided over by Victor Basch, Professor of Philosophy at the Sorbonne, to oppose the increase in defence expenditure proposed in the 1929 budget. Weil herself joined and persuaded her parents to do likewise, together with the railway workers from the rue Falguières. A motion was passed pressing for immediate disarmament negotiations with Germany following the evacuation of German territory and the modification of the more humiliating aspects of the Treaty of Versailles. The full congress of the League in April rejected the motion, though it did adopt a few of its points. Another petition Weil tried to get together was against Chiappe, the notoriously brutal Prefect of Police in Paris, who had ordered the preventative arrest of those organising the traditional May Day demonstration. On rushing off to the Sorbonne to collect signatures, the first person she ran into was Victor Basch himself. He signed with good grace after giving her a long lecture on the impropriety of beginning the petition 'We, Students and Teachers . . .' rather than the other way round. The same Chiappe's men actually knocked Weil down during another pacifist demonstration to welcome back Aristide Briand on his return from Geneva.

With the authorities of the Ecole Normale Weil was as little popular as with those at Henri IV. To the sociologist Célestin Bouglé, the Director of Studies and later Principal, she was a particular *bête noire*. During question time after a lecture of his on patriotism, Weil stood up and read without commentary from a speech by Poincaré in 1912 which seemed to recommend the possible invasion of Belgium. Bouglé simply looked at his watch and said: 'It's 12 o'clock; time for lunch.' The reply became a catch-phrase among the students, repeated with the appropriate tone and gesture when anyone was at a loss for a reply. On another occasion, Weil got a donation of twenty francs for the unemployed from Bouglé, on condition that it remained anonymous. She immediately pinned a piece of paper on the notice board, saying: 'Follow the example of your Director. Give anonymously to the unemployment fund' (C, p. 37). Nor were many of her fellow-students very fond of her. However close she might be to some of the ex-pupils of Alain, many found her extremely off-putting: 'We tried to avoid her in the corridors because of the blunt way she had of confronting you with your responsibilities by asking for your signature on a petition . . . or a contribution for some trade union strike fund.'[15] Her curious clothes, her awkward gait, her staccato, nasal, monotone speech were all the butt of hostile jokes. Bouglé referred to her as 'the categorical imperative in skirts'. To clinch an argument, she had a particular cutting horizontal gesture of the arm as though separating irrevocably the higher from the lower. Above all, said one of her friends, she loved to stir up dirt, to uncover anything she thought suspect. But she had a softer side as well. She took great pains to be reconciled to her grandmother who died of cancer during her first year at the school. Madame Reinherz had never concealed her thorough disapproval of her grand-daughter's life-style. During the months before her death, however, Weil visited her frequently, reading aloud to her and insisting that her friend Simone Pétrement come and play the piano.

The students at the Ecole Normale spent most of their second year writing a long dissertation for the Diploma in Higher Studies. Weil's preliminary sketches show that she initially envisaged a very broad discussion of the problem of knowledge in Plato, Kant and Descartes, but narrowed it down to the topic of *Science and Perception in Descartes*. Her dissertation director was Leon Brunschvicg, Professor of the History of Modern Philosophy at the Sorbonne and the most powerful figure in the French philosophical establishment of his day. Brunschvicg was a neo-Kantian idealist who linked the spiritual development of humanity to progress in mathematics and the physical sciences. Weil did not consult him much while writing her dissertation: Brunschvicg was a professional and a mandarin, and her more personal approach to the subject matter was not such as to appeal to him.

Although the title of her dissertation might seem rather narrow, Weil wrote an introduction setting the topic in a larger context. Looking at the history of humanity's search for knowledge, Weil found that from earliest times human beings had not been content with the perception of their senses but had imagined an elite of priests and kings to have access to a superior form of knowledge. With the revolutionary discovery of geometry by Thales of Miletus, the long history of modern science had begun. The question that Weil now asked was what status to give to the successors of Thales:

> Must we submit blindly to these thinkers who see for us, as we used to submit blindly to priests who were themselves blind, if lack of talent or leisure prevents us from entering their ranks? Or, on the contrary, did this revolution replace inequality with equality by teaching us that the realm of pure thought is the sensible world itself, that this quasi-divine knowledge that religions sensed is only a chimera, or rather, that it is nothing but ordinary thought? Nothing is harder to know, and at the same time nothing is more important for every man to know. For it is a matter of nothing less than knowing whether I ought to make the conduct of my life subject to the authority of scientific thinkers, or solely to the light of my own reason; or rather, since I alone can decide that, it is a matter of knowing whether science will bring me liberty or legitimate chains. (FW, p. 32)

(This question was, in essence, the same that she had asked herself when fourteen years old: whether only people of genius had access to the realm of truth.) The answer to this question, she continued, was made all the more difficult because scientists themselves seemed to be divided on the question of whether their theories, which were becoming increasingly abstract and algebraic, were linked in any way to the world of everyday perception and experiment. To determine whether this was indeed the case, she proposed to look at the foundations of modern scientific method in the work of Descartes.

The first part of Weil's dissertation was a textual analysis of Descartes's works in an orthodox style replete with quotations from the Latin originals. Weil began by assembling passages from several of Descartes's central works to show that he was indeed rightly seen as the founder of modern science in that, 'refusing to trust the senses, Descartes puts his trust in reason alone, and we know that his system of the world is the triumph of what is called the *a priori* method' (FW, p. 37). By putting ratios which involved mathematics and algebra at the heart of the old physics and geometry, Descartes had given modern science an abstract analytic basis. On this, the orthodox, accepted interpretation of Descartes, modern science had always essentially been what it was in the twentieth century and it had to be accepted as such or abandoned altogether. But Weil then went on to claim – against received opinion – that there were other passages in Descartes which presented a very different picture. This other Descartes had a realistic side to his thought, was interested in the applications of science, and considered perception to be the beginning of science. Real science was simply the correct use of reason, and open to all. The conclusion of the first part of the dissertation was that Descartes appeared to contradict himself, and the solution was not to be found in examining his texts but in 'becoming, at least for a time, a Cartesian', which was to be open 'to doubt everything, and then to examine everything in order, without believing in anything except one's own thought in so far as it is clear and distinct, and without trusting the authority of anyone, even Descartes, in the least' (FW, p. 54). And Weil then went on to imagine what such a fictitious Cartesian might have said.

Thus the second, and larger, part of the dissertation aimed at nothing less than a re-thinking of Descartes's *Discourse on Method* in the more personal style of his *Meditations*. Like Descartes, Weil began with a systematic doubt: sensations, feelings of pleasure and pain, even abstract mathematical ideas – all these appeared at first to be arbitrary and possibly the product of illusion. What was *not* the product of illusion was the power consciousness had to doubt these appearances. 'As soon as I reject an idea, even if it should be the idea that I am, at once I am . . . and through this power of thinking – which so far is revealed to me only by the power of doubting – I know that I am' (FW, p. 59). Thus for Descartes's 'I think, therefore I am', Weil substituted the more active 'I have power, therefore I am.' But her power over her own thoughts was extremely limited; so there must be something external to her to do the limiting.

Having thus established the bare existence of her mind and an external world, Weil turned to the nature of the link between them:

Although I cannot create a single one of my thoughts, all of them – from dreams, desires, and passions to reasoned arguments – are, to the extent that they are subject to me, signs of myself; to the extent that they are not subject to me, signs of the other existence. To know is to read this double meaning in any thought; it is to make the obstacle appear in a thought, while recognising in that thought my own power. (FW, p. 63)

This 'knot of action and reaction that attaches me to the world' Weil called 'imagination' – a faculty which opened a passage-way into the world for the mind. For, in addition to feelings and sensations, imagination presented her with the idea of number, order and the principles of geometry. How could perception unite these two sides of the imagination? In the key passage, Weil wrote:

I am always a dual being, on the one hand a passive being who is subject to the world, and on the other an active being who has a grasp on it; geometry and physics help me to conceive how these two beings can be united, but they do not unite them. Can I not attain perfect wisdom, wisdom in action, that would re-unite the two parts of myself? I certainly cannot unite them directly, since the presence of the world in my thoughts is precisely what this powerlessness consists of. But I can unite them indirectly, since this and nothing else is what action consists of. Not the appearance of action through which the uncontrolled imagination makes me blindly turn the world upside down by means of my anarchic desires, but real action, indirect action, action conforming to geometry, or, to give it its true name, work. (FW, p. 78)

Her conclusion was thus the same as that in her previous essays on perception: 'Now I recognise that the two kinds of imagination, which are found separately in the emotions and in geometry, are united in the things I perceive. Perception is geometry taking as it were possession of the passions themselves, by means of work' (FW, p. 79). Perception united to work was like a blind person's stick: it was the essential link between the mind and the external world. Body and tools (and industry itself) were simply geometrical concepts rendered material. Thus:

workers know everything; however, when their work is done, they do not know that they had all wisdom in their possession. And so outside of effective action, when the body, in which past perceptions are inscribed, is relieved from the necessity of exploration, human thought is given over to the passions, to the kind of imagination that conjures up gods, to more or less reasonable-sounding arguments received from others. That is why mankind needs science, provided that instead of imposing its proofs it is taught in the way that Descartes called analytic, that is, in such a way that each student, following the same order he would follow if he were methodically to make discoveries himself, may be said less to receive instruction than to teach himself. (FW, pp. 85f)

Philosophical reflection on Descartes's themes thus ended in the conclusion that work alone was the only value that could give existence a meaning. And the question that she had posed at the beginning of her dissertation on the relation of science to equality was answered: science, properly conceived, was merely correct perception and was thus, in principle, open to all. And this answer also laid the philosophical basis for her subsequent commitment to radical politics.

The dissertation was not well received by Brunschvicg; Weil herself admitted that the second part of her dissertation contained ideas that were 'daring' and even 'rash'. He gave Weil a mark of eleven out of twenty, almost the lowest possible mark without actually failing the piece of work. On meeting Brunschvicg soon afterwards, Alain is said to have teased him by saying: 'Ten out of twenty![16] Simone deserves zero out of twenty or eighteen out of twenty, but that, never! Would you like to know why you gave her ten out of twenty? Because she is Jewish' (C, p. 38). Brunschvicg was Jewish himself and there is no evidence that he either favoured or disfavoured Jewish students. But he was opposed to Alain's whole approach to philosophy, and Weil's interpretation of Descartes was even more personal and ahistorical than that of Alain. Brunschvicg found Weil's linking of mathematics and geometry to perception and bodily movement much too materialist. As an idealist, he saw perception as something erroneous and misleading which was to be supplanted by the abstract models of science. He was also something of an expert on Descartes (on whom he was to publish his own book a few years later) and disagreed strongly with Weil's attempt to enlist his writings in her effort to demonstrate a continuity between perception and science. But, however antipathetic it may have been to Brunschvicg, Weil's dissertation did form a preliminary sketch of much of the philosophy which was to be the context of her later thinking. Its rather florid style (typical of much academic philosophical writing of that time) is tentative and obscure compared to her later works, but the interest in mathematics, geometry, and the relation of mind to the network of causal necessity contained in the universe forms the starting-point of her famous *Notebooks*.[17]

One of the most obvious differences between Weil's early philosophical writings and her later *Notebooks* is the different conception of God. In the dissertation, God is conceived of very much in the manner of Descartes, of whom Pascal said that he needed God simply to set the world in motion and then be forgotten. The true God of Descartes was, for Weil, 'not the God of the theologians, but rather that which ensures me against theology; it is what is infallible in myself' (OC, pp. 342f). Her friend Simone Pétrement had become an enthusiast of the ideas of St Augustine and Pascal which gave priority to the grace of God over the liberty of human beings. Weil would have nothing to do with this Jansenism of her friend, being firmly on the side of Descartes: '"You would not look for me if you had not already found me" says the God of Pascal; this formula can be considered as the formula of every religion. But the God of Descartes, in order to find him I only need to stop looking' (OC, p. 340). It was not that Weil was hostile to religion. But her agnostic upbringing had afforded her a more tolerant and detached attitude than many of her friends. Religion and morality were closely linked in Weil's mind and the concept of God served as no more than an ideal model of knowledge and liberty.

Weil's last year at the Ecole Normale was spent studying hard for the *agrégation*. She established a time-table covering every hour of the day, not forgetting the lessons she was to give at the rue Falguières. The scope of her proposed reading can be grasped from the following plan (P, p. 69):

To study thoroughly: Aristotle, Bentham, Schopenhauer and Nietzsche.

To brush up on: the Stoics, Epicureans, Skeptics (Montaigne), and Descartes, Pascal, Rousseau, Proudhon, Comte, Lagneau, Marx and Tolstoy.

To review carefully: Machiavelli, Hobbes, Leibnitz, Wolf, Bergson, Schelling, Fichte, Hegel and Lenin.

To review quickly: Plotinus, the Middle Ages, Bacon(?), Malebranche, Voltaire and Encyclopedists.

To study systematically: the Pre-Socratics, the Sophists, Socrates, Plato, Locke, Hume, Berkeley, Spinoza, Kant and Maine de Biran.

To learn by heart in the third trimester: scientific morality (sociological, psychological and biological – Metchnikov); independent morality (Belot, Rauh . . .).

Get hold of Rey's textbook of logic and morality that is used in *cagne* (and a little idiotic general philosophy?)

It was during this year that the violent headaches began that were to plague her all her life. Although their origin was never diagnosed with certainty, they seem to have been due to a viral sinusitis which followed on a heavy cold caught when she failed to wrap up after an energetic sports session – she did a lot of running and jumping at the Ecole Normale and even joined a rugby team. But the headaches did not prevent her success at the *agrégation*. The results were always difficult to predict (Sartre had failed at his initial attempt and had been placed first the following year) and Weil was not sure that she had passed. In the event, out of the 107 candidates, eleven passed (Lévi-Strauss was third) and Weil was placed seventh.

As a successful *agrégée*, the next question was where she would teach. She had intended to get a job as a manual worker but abandoned the idea because of the growing unemployment. Instead, she asked the Ministry to place her in an industrial town or port such as Le Havre. But the Ministry decided to bury her in Le Puy in the heart of the Massif Central. Weil protested and asked if she might not instead be sent to Valenciennes, an industrial town near the Belgian border where she had learned that a post had just become vacant: but the Ministry insisted. Bouglé was delighted: 'We'll put the Red Virgin as far away as possible so that we won't hear any more of her.' But he had seriously underestimated the resilience of his former pupil.

The France in which Simone Weil emerged from her student years was one of tranquil confidence. The time she spent at Henri IV and the Ecole Normale coincided with the height of France's prosperity. Britain might be plagued with unemployment and a sterling crisis but France in the mid-1920s seemed to be the most successful country in Europe with her hold on extensive colonies in North Africa and Indo-China as yet undisturbed. There had been a slight hiccup in 1924 with the electoral victory of the Left and consequent financial and monetary crisis, but Poincaré's return to power had quickly stabilised the franc and both France's economic expansion and political stability seemed assured. Internationally, too, an era of peace appeared to be dawning under the aegis of the League of Nations. With Briand proposing the creation of a United States of Europe, the recent war could be seen as an unfortunate interruption of the established order which had now finally been restored. Even at the end of the 1920s, with America about to be shattered by economic crisis, with Stalin about to unleash the terror of collectivisation in the Soviet Union, with Germany on the brink of civil war and Italy overtaken by Mussolini's Fascists, France was still a haven of political order and economic well-being.

These 'years of illusion'[18] were interrupted by the accelerated crisis that began to appear at the end of 1930, a year mid-way between the end of the First World War and the beginning of the second and which marked a crucial turning-point in French society. In the following decade the basis of economic organisation, political institutions and intellectual life were fundamentally shaken. Between 1931 and 1933, as Weil began her teaching career, the dreams of the 1920s were cruelly dissipated and the tranquil Indian summer succeeded by a harsh and violent winter. As the Wall Street crash with its aftermath finally began to affect France, all indices of production fell dramatically, as did living standards among the workers, while unemployment figures climbed rapidly to near 20 per cent. Economic crisis brought with it political disarray, with governments falling rapidly and cabinet posts being rearranged in a continuous game of musical chairs. No government had the longevity, the will-power or even the economic knowledge to take the drastic measures necessary to cope with the crisis. The parliamentary system itself was threatened by movements of the right and the left which drew their inspiration from other countries coping apparently more successfully and which could count on considerable support from a disaffected and bewildered population. At the same time, the position of France in Europe declined. The internal difficulties and divisions weakened French foreign policy and France found herself vacillating and incapable of adopting a coherent attitude in the face of the rise of authoritarian regimes elsewhere.

The economic and political crisis of France in the 1930s naturally had a profound effect on the intellectual life of the country. The 1920s had indeed seen a revolt against the patriotism and conformism of postwar society. As the truth about the senseless slaughter of 1914–18 emerged, the anti-hero replaced the hero, pacifism became well-established, and young people were more inclined to enthusiasm about trade union struggles than about military prestige. In literature, the 1920s had encouraged an approach that was keen on psychological introspection, on novels such as those of the early Malraux and Saint-Exupéry which told of departures to distant and exotic places, on metaphysical speculation far removed from humdrum social concerns. As Simone de Beauvoir put it:

The literature of those days was presenting this negative attitude as a positive ethical system. It was turning our disquiet into a crusade; we were seeking for salvation. If we had renounced our class, it was in order to get closer to the Absolute. So immoralism was not just a snook cocked at society; it was a way of reaching God. Believers and unbelievers alike used this name. According to some, it signified an inaccessible presence, and to others, a vertiginous absence; there was no difference, and I had no difficulty in amalgamating Claudel and Gide; in both of them, God was defined, in relationship to the bourgeois world, as the *other*, and everything that was other was a manifestation of something divine.[19]

The continuing influence of Proust, Gide and Valéry preserved Paris as the intellectual capital of Europe. Intellectual curiosity was unbounded, non-conformist, self-indulgent, an end in itself as yet unaffected by the storm that was to break over Europe.

Weil came to intellectual maturity just at the turning-point of the inter-war years. From the 1920s, through Alain, she inherited her pacifism, her rationalism, her individualism. But the world in which she had to exercise them was very different. The 1930s brought an atmosphere of total crisis and disarray.[20] The change of tone was sudden and profound. In literature, the emphasis was now on the serious and the concrete, pondering anxiously over the problems posed to human destiny by a grimmer conception of politics and history. In the words of Mounier:

> An age was coming to an end. The dazzling age of the post-war literary efflorescence of Gide, Montherlant, Proust, Cocteau, and surrealism was becoming a firework that fell back into itself. It had expressed its age with a splendid elan; but it had not brought to humanity the light of a new destiny. The disappointment left by these guides without stars, orchestrated by distant cracks from Wall Street, led their successors to reflect on the destinies of a civilisation which seemed still capable of brilliancy, but at the price of a sort of profound decline. The generation of the 1930s was to be a serious generation, grave, occupied with problems, anxious for the future. The 1920s had been dominated by a literature of the most gratuitous sort. The following decade was to devote itself to research in the spiritual, philosophical and political realms.[21]

In philosophy, too, the old certainties were disappearing. Classical rationalism was undermined in physics by quantum theory which seemed to destroy the bases of traditional determinism, and in psychology by the growing attention paid to Freud who appeared to reduce the role of reason to that of mere rationalisation. And from Germany the existentialist thought of Heidegger put the whole of the western European philosophy in question. Even that traditional bastion of stable conservatism, the Catholic Church, began to modify its opposition to the society to which the revolution of 1789 had given birth and initiated a profound intellectual and spiritual renewal. With the condemnation by Rome in 1926 of the extreme Right-wing *Action Française*, many Catholics detached themselves from the monarchist position. Several of the religious orders began to be actively engaged in social and political questions. And the formation of the Jeunesse Ouvrière Chrétienne (Young Christian Workers) and other Catholic Action movements heralded the involvement of lay Catholics in a similar direction. In politics, the waning of the influence of the *Action Française* meant a re-drawing of boundaries on the Right. On the Left, the situation was even more serious: there was a choice between the growing rigidity of a Communist Party which had completed its Bolshevisation by 1924 and the reformist Left paralysed by its involvement in the parliamentary politics that were to prove incapable of solving the multiple crises. It is also worth remembering that, for all her active participation in politics, Weil never enjoyed the right to vote: women were only enfranchised in France in 1944.

The 1930s in France were a harsher version of the 1960s. The disaffection of young intellectuals with what Mounier called 'the estab-lished disorder' was profound and all encompassing: 'For those who were not around at the time, it is difficult to imagine the spirit of revolt which pitted the intellectual youth – Maurrassian, Marxist, Christian – against a world of hypocrisy which horrified them.'[22] There were several themes running through this revolt, themes which were to be found on both sides of the political spectrum. The most evident was a strong critique of capitalism. An economic system which had produced the crash of 1929 and all the subsequent dislocations and misery had to be replaced. But the critique went further than the current economic malaise which was seen merely as a symptom of a civilisation which had profoundly mistaken the nature and destiny of human beings. The combination of liberal-parliamentary democracy and a capitalist econ-omic system resulted purely and simply in a plutocracy where money was king and everything was for sale. Thus, secondly, the middle of the inter-war years saw a revolt against materialism and a questioning of the nineteenth-century conceptions of inevitable progress. The words of Péguy were frequently quoted: 'The revolution will be a moral revolution or it will not happen at all.' The causes of the current crises lay at a deeper level than economics: they were in human beings themselves and in the kind of doctrines and conceptions that had allowed such an economic system to develop. Materialism, rationalism, determinism were corrosive of genuine moral and spiritual values. Such corrosion could only be remedied by a spiritual revolution which thoroughly subverted the values of existing society. Only by being psychological and metaphysical as well as economic and political could the moral revolution achieve the total restructuring that was imperative.

In addition to its broad anti-capitalism and anti-materialism, the revolt of the young concentrated on three more specific areas. Firstly, they were imbued by a profound hostility to the economic developments taking place in the United States, which was seen as the apogee of the modern world to which they were so much opposed. For them, America represented the rule of industry and banks. The American cancer (the title of a popular book of the time) consisted in a set of abstractions which reduced human beings to the status of machines to produce and consume in a society built on artificial credit and speculation governed solely by the measure of profit. The assembly lines of Ford and the time and motion innovations of Taylor had led to a division of labour and mechanised rhythm of work that robbed those engaged in it of any initiative and of any satisfaction apart from their pay packets. The enthusiasm for such films as Chaplin's *Modern Times* and René Clair's *A Nous la Liberté* reflected this view of the United States as victim of a frenetic productivism which standardised and dehumanised both work and leisure. Secondly, there was much criticism of the parliamentary and party political system that seemed, particularly under Tardieu, to be bent on turning France into a second America. Worse, the parliamentary system seemed to the young quite incapable of dealing with the growing crisis. With cabinet succeeding cabinet ever more rapidly, there could be no continuity of policy. Politicians themselves were parasites feeding off a corrupt system rocked by a number of scandals. Nor could the parties themselves be instruments of renewal since they merely presented abstract, politicised solutions which avoided the real issues and put electoral advantage above all other considerations. Lastly, many young intellectuals of the early 1930s were imbued with a negative attitude towards the state. The defence of the human person against the impersonal structures of state power became a common preoccupation most consistently articulated by Mounier's review *Esprit*. Influenced by Sorel and Proudhon, these thinkers opposed the centralising and socialising tendencies of the state whose artificial and colourless bureaucracy they contrasted with the rich variety of individuals and natural groups and communities.

The atmosphere of 1930 was thus thoroughly contestatory. It was clear to those who criticised the *status quo* that the solution was not to be found in prevailing political attitudes. Their ambition was to go beyond Left and Right, to by-pass both capitalist disorder and communist oppression. They wished to relativise politics by appealing, like Proudhon and Péguy, to a higher spiritual order. They thus developed an anti-politics which, strong on negation, was not equally clear as to what should replace the present sorry state of affairs. The alternative proposed was vague. They did not go much further than an exaltation of the value of the unique human person over the abstract individualism of 1789, the advocacy of decentralisation internally and of federalism for Europe as a whole, and an interest in the problems of technology and a reform of the labour process that would leave scope for personal initiative. These laudable aspirations were soon overtaken by the necessity of choosing between more immediate options. The threat posed by Fascism inside France and the establishment of the Popular Front government, together with the outbreak of the Spanish Civil War and the rise of Hitler, led to a polarisation between Left and Right. One theme, however, continued to hold sway. A broadly pacifist stance in international affairs continued to influence many French intellectuals up to the Munich crisis of 1938. Although bellicose attitudes began to increase on the Left in the mid-1930s, the catastrophe and absurdity of the 1914–18 war and the injustice of the Versailles Treaty which followed it made an impression so profound that many intellectuals of the most varied political persuasions were even prepared to come to terms with the Vichy regime rather than contemplate the consequences of total war.

Much of this intellectual climate was assimilated by Weil – but by no means all. Like so many of that very small young academic elite in Paris, particularly those of a philosophical bent, she felt the sense of mission, of vocation, of responsibility, of the necessity to become *engagée*. She adopted the enthusiasm for radical, even utopian, solutions for which the turbulent circumstances of the time seemed to call. At the same time, she was imbued with the pessimism of the two decades which saw the seeds sown by the ending of one disastrous world war giving birth to a second world war that was expected to be even more destructive. She agreed with the prevailing rejection of materialism, with the critique of capitalism as wasteful and oppressive, with the questioning of modern methods of production and the nefarious uses to which science was being put, with the view of the shallowness and incapacity of the political institutions of the Third Republic to cope with the crisis, and with the antipathy to the growing power of the centralised state.

All these themes inform both *Oppression and Liberty* of 1934 and *The Need for Roots*, written a decade later, in the last year of her life. But, at the same time, she differed from most of her contemporaries in remaining a rationalist: she stayed faithful to the spirit of Descartes and never lost her confidence in the ability of the human mind to attain objective knowledge of itself and the world. So far from rejecting traditional philosophical approaches, she found in the Greeks many of her models for intellectual and social activity. Thus, although in many ways a pessimist, she did not fall prey to the nihilism that many found unavoidable and even attractive. Nor did she really form part of any of the innumerable groups that sprang up in response to the crisis. Whereas most of the leading Left intellectuals were in some way 'fellow-travellers' of the Communist Party,[23] Weil was implacable in her opposition to contemporary communism. She was too much an individualist ever to join any organisation. Even her conception of the role of the intellectual was to foster the demise of intellectuals as a distinct group by working, in the context of the profoundly anti-intellectual anarcho-syndicalist movement, for a society in which the distinction between mental and manual labour would be abolished. And finally, she rejected the various personalist currents so popular at the time, preferring, again from the Greeks, a metaphysic that viewed as sacred the impersonal factors that human beings had in common rather than the personal ones which distinguished them. Like so many intellectuals of the age, she found her path obstructed,[24] but the negotiation of these obstructions led her into ways that were peculiarly her own. Beginning her public life very definitely on the Left, she conserved many of the characteristic sympathies of the Left but failed to find any group that could properly articulate them. Her growing interest in religion led her to adopt a vantage point that was transcendent and thus allowed full scope both to her utopian politics and to the radical individualism of Alain that she had learned so well.

3
Le Puy: Teacher and Anarchist

'I have always regarded dismissal as the natural culmination of my career.' (C, p. 67)

During the three years from late 1931 to late 1934, as France plunged deeper into crisis, Weil combined her career as a lycée philosophy teacher with trade union militancy. Steadfast in her devotion to her teaching and her pupils, she was not surprisingly at loggerheads with the educational administration and changed schools annually. She was also in constant motion politically: early enthusiasm for trade union activity gave way to a growing frustration with all forms of working-class organisation, a frustration which prompted the writing of her great work on *Oppression and Liberty* and culminated in her pivotal decision to interrupt her career and take up factory work.

To any young revolutionary, the Communist Party was an inevitable attraction. The Russian revolution had, together with the First World War, been the supreme political event of Weil's childhood; and, indeed, she claimed to have been a Bolshevik at the age of ten![1] Although she later maintained that she had never been favourably inclined towards the Communist Party, she did toy with the idea of joining it and even drafted a letter of application (P, p. 47). Curiosity led her to attend several Communist Party cell meetings. And, *pour épater les bourgeois*, she often made a show of reading *L'Humanité* and talking loudly about 'Moscow gold'. More seriously she declared that, 'if I could be shown that socialism could be built in a single country, I would join the Party immediately and would never leave it' (P, p. 125). But it became increasingly clear to her that the Soviet Union was as far removed from socialism as it could be and she soon came to regard it as an even greater enemy than capitalism.

If the Communist Party was an impossible context in which to imagine anyone as individualist and naturally rebellious as Weil, revolutionary syndicalism, by contrast, would appear as her natural home. This movement embodied an exceptionally strong feeling for the particular and peculiar nature of the working class and for its outlook born of experience as disinherited and exploited. Its followers preached as complete a break as possible from existing society. As against social democracy, they had no time for the institutions and practices of parliamentary party politics; and as against Marxism–Leninism, they gave pride of place to the culture and solidarity of the workers founded on their experience *as* workers. In place of the party, whether parliamentary or Leninist, they held to the *syndicat* or union as the vehicle for working-class emancipation. Before leaving Paris for Le Puy, Weil had made contact with the militant trade unionists who gravitated round the bi-monthly review *La Révolution Prolétarienne*. This group, although of very little influence even in left-wing circles, included impressive personalities such as Pierre Monatte, founder of the pre-war *Vie Ouvrière*, and Alfred Rosmer, Trotsky's future secretary, men who represented what was left of a tradition of French revolutionary syndicalism going back through Sorel, who had mixed Bergson's process philosophy with class struggle to produce the myth of the general strike, as far as Proudhon the father of French anarchism. Although they had been largely instrumental in founding the French Communist Party in the years immediately following the Bolshevik revolution, most revolutionary syndicalists had left it (or been expelled) by 1924.[2] This rump had established *La Révolution Prolétarienne* to help preserve the working-class movement from the twin dangers of reformist collaboration with the bourgeois state and submission to the Moscow-orientated dictates of the Communist Party. The libertarian revolutionary anarchism of *La Révolution Prolétarienne* appealed to Weil as an open-minded forum in agreeable contrast to the strait-jacket of party political organisations. She described the journal as 'the only revolutionary journal which publishes historical studies of the first order on social questions' (P, p. 185) and used it to publish most of the signed articles which were to appear during her lifetime.

Given her enthusiasm for the ideas of *La Révolution Prolétarienne*, it was inevitable that Weil should be a source of trouble and anxiety to the educational authorities.[3] She had arrived at Le Puy on 30 September together with her ubiquitous mother who even accompanied her to the pre-term interview with the headmistress of the girls' lycée where she was to teach philosophy. In the space of two weeks, Selma Weil had found her daughter two flats, talked a fellow-teacher, Simone Antheriou (who later married the philosopher Georges Canguilhem), into sharing with her, paid the rent, hired two maids in succession, and bought her daughter a whole new wardrobe. But Madame Weil's excellent dispositions did not last for long: returning after two months, she wrote to André:

The place is freezing, no heating – and it's been three or four below zero for several days. The bed wasn't made – after great difficulty I found the sheets. No provisions; and I had just enough to pay for a glass of water. And I couldn't even get angry with the poor trolless, who is so good and affectionate to me; but she hasn't the slightest idea of anything, and since S. Antheriou's departure a dozen days before my arrival, she has been living like this, without a maid, without heat, eating at noon at a restaurant and in the evening making herself potatoes or cocoa with water. And the disorder! For the last eight days of my stay here I've been slaving from morning to night to get things into a halfway decent state! (P, p. 91)

And the ascetic disarray of this life-style did not diminish over the months and years. It was not helped by her decision not to heat her room because, she thought, the unemployed could not afford to heat theirs, and to live on the equivalent of the dole, giving the rest of her money to strike funds. The only thing in plentiful supply was books: Weil liked to spread the larger volumes open on the floor and crawl myopically from one to another when conducting her research.

Meanwhile the school term had started. Weil taught some Greek, the history of art, a special option of her own choosing on the history of science, and (her main task) a philosophy class of some fifteen girls preparing for the *baccalauréat*. Four of these girls recorded their impressions of their teacher:

She was not an ordinary kind of teacher. She gave herself to her pupils, putting her knowledge and time completely at their disposal. Thus when one of us could not sit the *baccalauréat* because she knew no Latin, she suggested immediately teaching it to that student – free of charge, of course. She was concerned about our material needs. We would see her arrive one day carrying with great difficulty twenty or so books that she had taken the trouble to order and pay for in advance so that we could benefit from the deduction the bookshops gave to teachers.[4]

Although her lessons undoubtedly held the attention of her pupils, her superiors were in some doubt as to their effectiveness, given her disregard both for the curriculum and for the use of set books. The school inspector admired her teaching but predicted, with devastating accuracy, that only two of her pupils would pass their *baccalauréat*.

Although unstinting in her devotion to her teaching duties, Weil began also to get involved in the social problems of Le Puy. Despite its genteel bourgeois atmosphere, in December 1931 the effects of the Depression began to produce labour unrest even there. The only public assistance available in Le Puy to the increasing number of unemployed was a subsistence wage in return for breaking stones. And since this activity took place in the Place Michelet in front of the lycée, it is not surprising that Weil soon got involved. A group of unemployed meeting at the Labour Exchange decided to send a delegation to the home of Dr Durand, the mayor, with certain requests. Failing to get any satisfaction, they attended a council meeting the same evening, reported by a local conservative newspaper, *Le Mémorial*, as follows: 'The room, usually deserted, particularly at such an hour at this time of year, was suddenly packed by men in their working clothes led in a squad by a suffragette, a person still young who marshalled her group with smiling authority' (P, p. 94). When the mayor refused to discuss their requests on the grounds that they were not on the agenda, they retired, noisily but peaceably, to the Labour Exchange.

This event caused quite a stir at Le Puy. Teachers were considered government functionaries and were therefore not expected to criticise the authorities. Weil, who had herself spoken up on behalf of the unemployed at the council meeting, was summoned the next day to the office of the school inspectors. They had received a police report and wished to know whether she had been the leader of the demonstration, whether – possibly the real scandal – she had gone to a cafe with the workers afterwards, and finally whether she had actually shaken hands with one of the stone-breakers on the Place Michelet. Weil made her opinion of this kind of harassment clear in an article she wrote for the newspaper of the local teachers' union:

> The national university administration lags several thousand years behind human civilization. It still lives under the caste system. It regards certain people as untouchables, just as the backward populations of India do. There are people with whom a teacher at a lycée can, at a pinch, associate within the secrecy of a well-locked room, but on no account should the parents of her students see that teacher shaking hands with them on Place Michelet . . . We demand from the administration a precise ruling, indicating exactly under what conditions each category of the teaching profession has the right to associate with the members of the various social classes. (P, p. 97)

Evidently, she was not to be intimidated. On 21 December, together with two of the unemployed, she called again on Dr Durand to make sure that their complaints *were* on the agenda of the next council meeting. That meeting, which Weil also attended, was just as fruitless as the first. A fortnight later, however, the situation became more serious. A strike was called among the stone-breakers, with pickets to discourage those who wished to continue. Weil's own account of her participation is as follows:

> The headmistress went into a panic and wanted to barricade the lycée. As for myself I had been urgently summoned to the office of the

school inspector of the region, so I came out of the lycée at four, saw and spoke to the strikers for about five minutes, then set off quickly for the office of the inspector. Just at that moment the police arrived; hence the accusation of my running away. When I got out of the inspector's office, I went to the Labour Exchange. Coming out again to run an errand, I was greeted by a cop, who grabbed me by the arm and led me to the police superintendent, who, with the graciousness typical of his kind, asked me when I intended to quit agitating in Le Puy. He then informed me that he was fed up with it; accused me of being a ringleader; and announced that five or six of my friends would be sent to summary police court, and perhaps me too. That was all. Of course I answered him as he deserved. (P, p. 101)

The authorities in Le Puy were seriously disturbed. Weil was attacked in the press, the mayor called again for her dismissal and she was summoned, for the second time, to the Rectorat of Clermont-Ferrand where Rector Jarre tried to persuade her to accept a post elsewhere, holding out Saint-Quentin, with its proximity to Paris and its heavy industry, as a bribe. Weil stood her ground. She had not done anything criminal and she had strong support from nine of her colleagues, who published a letter protesting at the infringement of her liberties, and from her pupils, who persuaded their parents to send a unanimous endorsement of Weil as a teacher to the Ministry of Education who also received a telegram of support from her union. She even gained the approval of her old teacher, Alain, who remarked: 'Who else but she could start a strike among the unemployed!' (P, p. 106).

For a time it looked as though things would calm down. The mayor suggested that the municipality might pay those employed temporarily on public works a wage of 25 francs a day. He quickly changed his mind, however, when there were no more demonstrations. The lesson for Weil was clear. As she wrote in a stinging rebuke published on behalf of the committee for the unemployed:

Perhaps it is better this way. Between the unemployed and the ruling class there are only relations of force. These relations of force are sometimes disguised by the public powers with fine appearances; sometimes, they are left naked, and then they educate the working class more effectively than anyone ever can. Perhaps someday the working class will thank them by showing them that it has learned its lesson. (P, p. 110)

This view was somewhat vindicated on 3 February when there was a further march through the city and a demonstration outside the mayor's house. His reply was to ban all further demonstrations. But the unemployed assembled at the Labour Exchange in order to renew their demands. *Le Mémorial* wrote:

> The demonstration was preceded by a meeting at the Labour Exchange. Mlle. Weill [sic], red virgin of the tribe of Levi, bearer of the Muscovite gospels, indoctrinated the wretches whom she has led astray. Then, after having formed them in ranks for the procession, she assigned them as their objective the house of the mayor, who had the good fortune to be serenaded. In the musical part of the programme, the 'Internationale' and the 'Carmagnole'; such a programme gives the political keynote of this movement; for it can now be seen quite clearly that it is only a political movement – Communist, to be precise. (P, p. 114)

Having apparently reached a climax, the unrest at Le Puy subsided as quickly as it had started, with the local authorities conceding a large part of the strikers' demands: employment, better working conditions, and increased wages.

While these events were happening in Le Puy, and in keeping with her enthusiasm for *La Révolution Prolétarienne*, Weil had been making a weekly trip of 40 miles to Saint-Etienne, a larger, more industrial town with much more working-class activity than in the quiet Le Puy, chiefly famous for its Romanesque cathedral and its lace-making. What interested her most was the possibility of exploring her ideas in the context of trade union activity and, most, immediately, the effort to heal the split in the French trade union movement.

This movement, in which Weil was to become an active participant for the next two years, was extremely complex and bore little relationship to the fairly clear demarcations that emerged in France after the Second World War. Following the legalisation of trade unions in 1884, revolutionary syndicalism had been the backbone of the movement and a real force in French political life. The dual impact of the First World War and the Bolshevisation of a large part of the Marxist world in the early 1920s reduced revolutionary syndicalism to little more than a rump: the main trade union organisation, the Confédération Générale du Travail (CGT), had supported the war effort and the revolutionary syndicalists had broken away in 1917 to found the Comités des Syndicalistes Révolutionnaires which had contributed to the foundation of the French Communist Party and its parallel Communist trade union organisation, the Confédération Générale du Travail Unifiée (CGTU). The paradox that the most anarchist-inclined part of the working-class movement had helped to found the most centralised and authoritarian party in history was resolved when the revolutionary syndicalists were expelled from the French Communist Party in 1924. The weakness caused by this disarray, which was to last until 1934, was compounded by the fact that the various trade unions had, in any case, only managed to enrol about 10 per cent of the work-force.[5]

The pressure to achieve some sort of unity came naturally from the revolutionary syndicalists who felt ill at ease, both in the over-cautious and reformist CGT and in the Bolshevised CGTU. Even before leaving for Le Puy, Weil had accompanied Cancouet, in September 1931, to the 21st Congress of the CGT where the possibility of unity was one of the main debates. Militants from both the two larger trade union organisations gave themselves the title 'Committee of 22' and put forward a motion advocating their fusion. Although this was defeated by a large majority, there was agreement that unity should be pursued 'from below' through co-operation between individual members and branches.

As a syndicalist sympathiser, Weil was not favourably impressed by the CGT which was, she thought, putting collaboration between classes before collaboration between unions. In an article on the congress she wrote: 'The advantages that the syndicalist leaders boast of having obtained through their collaboration with governmental organizations do not seem to be a gain so much as a bone thrown to people in a period of prosperity.'[6] Nevertheless, on arrival at Le Puy, she threw herself into bringing about trade union unity from below, wishing to unite the party political independence of the CGT with the more militant attitude to class struggle of the CGTU. A united and intransigent class struggle was at the forefront of her preoccupations. Such a class struggle should be accentuated in times of crisis which was caused, she claimed, following the theory of Louzon, one of the editors of *La Révolution Prolétarienne*, by a fall in the rate of profit due to lack of labour rather than by overproduction. It followed that it was useless for workers to mitigate their struggle against capital. On the contrary:

> There is no point in trying to find a remedy for the crisis, something that could only be done with the assent and under the domination of the ruling class. The only thing that should be done is to organize the struggle immediately. Considering its present degree of decomposition, the regime can only subsist because the lack of unity, good organization, and clear ideas keep the working class in its present state of weakness. (P, p. 89)

In fact she put this desire for unity into practice by herself joining both the national union of primary school teachers, which belonged to the CGT, and also the union of secondary school teachers which, although non-communist, was in the CGTU. She arranged meetings between trade union representatives in Le Puy where, as she wrote to her parents:

> We are in the process of bringing together all the working-class elements in the town, without distinction, including the Communists. Moreover, a relationship has been established between the Confederated and United railroad men, both secretaries being partisans of unity and sympathizing with the Twenty-Two. The funniest thing about it is that neither of them knows the other man's name. It has taken my arrival from Paris for them to get into contact with each other. (P, p. 86)

The inter-union meeting was a success and various rules to avoid friction and enhance co-operation at a local level were drawn up. Commenting on this meeting in an article written for *L'Effort*, a journal of the Lyon building workers' union, she wrote:

> One must respect the existing trade union organizations, which are the most precious conquest of the working-class movement; and one must realize unity without the support of these organizations or even, in many instances, in spite of them. This seemingly insoluble problem must be solved by the working class, or else it will be condemned to disappear as a revolutionary force. (P, p. 87)

This singling out of bureaucracy as one of the main reasons for the failure of the working-class movement was a theme that was to occupy a central place in Weil's later writings. Even before she had written the article, however, the annual congress of the Communist-dominated CGTU had rejected any move towards unity. The Committee of 22 broke up, which gave Weil the opportunity to express her disdain for the role played by political parties in the class struggle, as follows:

> Experience has shown that a revolutionary party can effectively, according to Marx's formula, take possession of the bureaucratic and military machinery, but not in order to smash it. For power really to pass into the hands of the workers they would have to unite, not through the imaginary ties created by the community of opinion, but through the real ties created by the community of productive function. (P, p. 76)

This profound mistrust of all forms of political party was also to remain a constant theme in her writings.

Weil had also been active in inter-union meetings in Saint-Etienne. Her friends in *La Révolution Prolétarienne* in Paris had recommended that she go and see there Urbain Thévenon, a school-teacher who was assistant secretary of the Loire branch of the CGT. His wife Albertine, also a schoolteacher, is said to have described Weil's surprising arrival as follows:

> The Thévenons then lived at Saint-Etienne on a busy, populous street in an apartment whose vestibule was one of those long, dark hallways customary in houses in the old working-class districts. Simone rang the bell. Albertine went to open the door, one hand wrapped in a sock she was darning. Simone asked, 'Is Monsieur Thévenon in?' When Albertine said he was, Simone shoved her aside with a thrust of her shoulder and before Albertine had time to close the door and turn around, she had already rushed down the hallway and stepped into Thévenon's room where he was surprised to see her suddenly appear.[7]

In spite of this abrasive beginning, Weil became a firm friend of both the Thévenons. What attracted her most to Saint-Etienne, however, was the possibility of giving evening classes to the workers.

A tradition of working-class self-help in education was well-established. The idea of working-class education was given organisational form by Ferdinand Pelloutier (1868–1901) who had tried to make education one of the main functions (together with the training of skilled workers and the finding of employment) of the growing network of Labour Exchanges that he was instrumental in creating, a network which remained integral to the whole syndicalist movement.[8] So-called 'popular universities' had been started before the war but had proved a failure. Weil herself, while still at the Ecole Normale Supérieure, had given lessons to railway workers and it was this mission that she wished to continue at Saint-Etienne, which offered a good opportunity to expand such activities. A workers' college had already been started there in 1928 and Thévenon was one of those in charge. Under the auspices of the Trade Union Committee for Unity, a series of French lessons was started in early December, with another series on political economy that she shared with Thévenon. These lessons were particularly directed towards the miners, but their success was limited and she was disappointed that these lectures did not have as much effect as she had anticipated: eight enrolled for political economy and only two for the French.[9] Nevertheless she pressed on, getting up on Sundays at 4.00 a.m. to make the three hour journey to Saint-Etienne, hauling along with her a suitcase full of books for the miners which she paid for with the supplement to her salary to which her *agrégation* entitled her. In March, in response to a request from some workers, she began giving lessons on Karl Marx in Le Puy. A touching letter from a young carpenter to whom she gave geometry lessons is evidence of the enthusiasm of some of her pupils:

> I have reviewed the circles on the basis of the demonstrations you have given me . . . In the three lessons I had with you, you have given me almost all the elementary facts of geometry: it is a pity that I cannot see you more often, for I would have ended by becoming a truly learned person. What was really marvellous about it is that I remember almost everything you taught me, even though I could only grasp about half of it; and that with you as the teacher I was never bored for a second; and these few instants exalt all the noble thoughts that inhibit me. If I could see you more often, I would make double progress, intellectual as well as moral . . . (P, p. 124)

Weil explained her commitment to workers' education in an article she wrote for *L'Effort* in December 1931. It was most important, she wrote, 'to distinguish, among the attempts at working-class culture, those that are conducted in such a way as to strengthen the ascendancy of the intellectuals over the workers, and those conducted in such a way as to free the workers from this domination' (P, p. 87). In primitive societies it was command of language that had given priests their power and

> this domination of those who know how to handle words over those who know how to handle things is rediscovered at every stage of human history. It is necessary to add that, as a group, these manipulators of words, whether priests or intellectuals, have always been on the side of the ruling class, on the side of the exploiters against the producers. (P, p. 88)

But the conclusion was not some kind of *Proletkult* derisive of 'bourgeois' culture: on the contrary the workers must prepare themselves 'to take possession of it, as they must prepare themselves to take possession of the entire heritage from previous generations. Indeed, this act of taking possession is the revolution' (P, p. 88). And the work at Saint-Etienne was a first step in this direction:

> In the eyes of Marx, perhaps the most important conquest of the proletarian revolution should be the abolition of what he calls 'the degrading division of work into intellectual and manual work'. The abolition of this degrading division can and must be achieved, and we must prepare for it now. To this end we must, first of all, give the workers the ability to handle language, and especially the written language. (P, p. 88)

Alain had defined the bourgeois as essentially the persuader who dealt (linguistically) with other human beings and not with material objects and had also believed that the workers possessed a latent Aesopian wisdom which only needed education to become articulate. Combining these two views, Weil believed that the emergence of an educated proletariat could ultimately prove socially explosive.[10]

Weil's attitude here is also reminiscent of Lenin's early opponents – the Russian Narodniks or Populists of the 1860s and 1870s who aimed at a kind of cultural revolution by going 'among the people' – in this case the peasantry – and making available to them the cultural achievements of past generations. Weil was certainly enthusiastic about her contacts with workers: in her room at Le Puy she put up on the wall the photo of a worker she referred to as a 'big tough' and remarked 'that's my kind of man!' (C, p. 52). According to Albertine Thévenon:

> Simone tried to integrate herself with them. It was not easy. She sought their company, sat at their tables in the cafes to eat or play belote, she followed them to the cinema, during their holidays, asked them to take her to their homes on the spur of the moment without telling their wives first. They were a bit surprised by the attitude of this young woman who was so well-educated, who dressed more simply than their wives and whose preoccupations seemed to them extraordinary. But they liked her and their meetings with 'La Ponote' [a term of affection for an inhabitant of Le Puy] were always friendly.[11]

It may be doubted how well Weil managed to integrate herself into working-class life, and most of her comrades probably regarded her as no more than a 'big hearted mascot' (C, p. 52). Thévenon himself reproached her with 'only spending in the places which interested her just enough time to extract the information and particulars necessary for her to understand the world of the workers'.[12] But at least Weil wished for more than lectures and conversations with workers. She wished to share their work experience. After much resistance she managed to get to go down a small mine at Sardou, owned by an acquaintance of Thévenon, where she was allowed to wield a pneumatic drill. Of this experience he wrote: 'This machine is not modelled on human nature but rather on the nature of coal and compressed air, and its movements follow a rhythm profoundly alien to the rhythm of life's movements, violently bending the human body to its service . . .' (P, p. 122). And she drew a fundamental conclusion:

> It will not be enough for a miner to expropriate the companies in order to become the master of the mine. The political and economic revolutions will become real only if they are extended into a technical

revolution that will re-establish, within the mine and the factory, the domination that it is the worker's function to exercise over the conditions of work. (P, p. 122)

This idea that any revolution in society would have to be a revolution in the nature of productive forces themselves, as well as in their ownership, was to preoccupy her in the years to come.

But Weil was more aware than most that the possibility of any fundamental change in social and economic circumstances was becoming more and more dependent on the international situation; and that the key to this was what was happening in Germany. She had previously made brief visits to Berlin. Her attention was focused anew by Trotsky's *What Now?*, which she reviewed for *Libres Propos*. Trotsky's stark formulations appealed to Weil. The disastrous legacy of the Treaty of Versailles meant, she considered, that the crisis was at its sharpest in Germany where the problem could be simply posed as *Fascism or revolution*? And it was Germany which was called upon to resolve this problem for the whole world. So with the school year in Le Puy finished, she set out for Berlin at the end of July and soon found a room with a working-class family in Neukölln. Her aim was to get to know the life of the German workers which she considered 'of vital importance for us also' since 'our greatest hope lies in this German working class, the most mature, the most disciplined, the most cultured in the world; and in particular in the young workers of Germany' (EHP, p. 150). The articles she wrote for her friends in France give a marvellously vivid and clear-sighted view of Germany on the eve of the Nazi take-over.

Her first impression of Berlin was that it was surprisingly calm. Her parents were more worried than ever at their daughter's antics and she wrote to reassure them:

As for Berlin, it is at the moment the quietest city in the world. Everyone is in a state of expectation and no one expects anything serious to happen before the autumn . . . You scarcely see any uniformed Nazis in the street and they behave like anyone else. You can read in the morning newspapers that there have been some violent incidents here and there, rather in the same vein as you read that there have been so many car accidents. Rival newspapers do not clash in the underground and the trams, politics is not discussed. There are no more street battles. Nothing indicates an exceptional situation, except this same calm which is, in a sense, tragic. (P, p. 131)

Apart from the unexpected tranquillity, Weil's imagination was immediately struck by the comradeship, courage and lucidity of 'this magnificent young German working-class youth which goes in for sports and

camping, sings, reads, and organises sports for children' (EHP, p. 124).
She reported enthusiastically:

> In these young, bronzed women workers, in these young working
> men with feverish eyes and hollow cheeks who can be seen striding
> along the streets of Berlin, you continually sense, underneath both
> the sadness and the apparent insouciance, a seriousness which is the
> opposite of despair, a fresh and continuous awareness of the tragic
> destiny which is theirs. (EHP, p. 151)

In this idealised picture Weil's combination of Rousseau's romanticism
with the courage of the Stoics makes out of German working-class youth
an anticipation of the free, universal human beings of socialism.[13]

And the same enthusiasm extended to the maturity and discipline of
the German working class as a whole. But in spite of their 'unbelievable'
cultural level, the workers were condemned to passivity: 'The workers
are simply waiting for the time when all this will crash down on them.
The very slowness of the process increases the demoralization. Courage
is not lacking, yet the occasions for struggle don't present themselves'
(P, p. 132). For the effect of the crisis was to destroy the boundaries
between public and private: 'The German worker or petit bourgeois has
no corner of his private life, above all if he is young, which is not
touched or threatened by the economic and political consequences of
the crisis' (EHP, p. 147). Whereas a lesser economic crisis might leave
some hope for individual effort and enterprise, the depth of the crisis
in Germany was all-pervasive:

> No one can even imagine any effort that could be made to take his
> fate back into his own hands that would not take the form of an action
> affecting the structure of society itself. For every German, at least in
> the working class and petty bourgeoisie, good or bad prospects
> concerning even the most intimate aspects of private life are immedi-
> ately formulated, above all if he is young, as prospects concerning
> the future of the regime. (EHP, p. 148)

Such a situation might be justifiably called 'revolutionary'. Why then was
there no revolution? To the psychological explanation of hopelessness
induced by the effects of mass unemployment Weil added two other
weaknesses which inhibited effective action by the working class.

Firstly, the number of white-collar workers had been swollen beyond
all reason by the untrammelled expansion of capitalism in the 1920s.
Whether in work or unemployed, they were both disinclined to make
common cause with manual workers, because of social prejudice, and
less capable of self-reliance, because of the nature of their work.

Secondly, those who *were* in work, whether white-collar or manual, had something to lose and felt threatened by a reserve army of unemployed almost as numerous as the work-force itself, whose presence allowed employers to sack the more revolutionary-minded workers with impunity. These divisions, Weil insisted, simply compounded the tragic torpor induced by long-term unemployment:

> This life of idleness and poverty, which robs skilled workers of their skill and the young of any possibility of learning a trade, which deprives the workers of their dignity as producers, which after two, three, or four years finally leads – and this is what is worse – to a sort of sad tolerance – this life is no preparation for assuming responsibilities in the whole system of production. Thus the crisis constantly brings new ranks of workers to class consciousness, but it also constantly pulls them back again, as the sea brings in and pulls back its waves. (FW, p. 99)

True to her teacher, Alain, Weil placed responsibility for this situation on the leaders rather than on the masses. For the impotence of the working class was further reinforced by the attitudes and policies of the three political parties – Nazis, Social Democrats, and Communists – which claimed to be promoting some form of socialism and between them amassed some two-thirds of the electorate. The Nazis found their support among a few intellectuals, a large mass of the lower middle class, clerks, peasants, and the unemployed attracted by the prospect of food or money offered by party institutions. The contradictory policies of the Nazis were simply 'an ensemble of confused feelings held together by incoherent propaganda' (EHP, p. 130). High prices for agricultural produce were promised in the countryside and cheap food in the cities; the spirit of struggle and self-sacrifice appealed to the more romantic among the young, the prospect of violence and massacre to those with more brutish instincts. A reactionary nationalism, inflamed by resentment at the Versailles settlement, appealed to the 'socialism of the trenches'; but the main achievement of Nazi propaganda was, by pretending that German capitalism was Jewish, to present their nationalism as anti-capitalist and attract thereby all those who were dissatisfied with 'the system'. In this they were at one with the Communists, just as they shared with the Social Democrats a programme of state capitalism and enjoyed an ambiguous relationship to big business, each thinking to use the other for its own ends. And the only thing which unified these disparate ideas and social groups was the visible *force* of the Nazi party, a force which 'is glaringly apparent everywhere – in the parades of uniformed men, in the acts of violence, in the use of airplanes for propaganda. All these weak elements fly towards it like moths to a flame' (FW, p. 106).

The Social Democrats (SPD) were, according to Weil, too compromised by their own past to be effective defenders of the working class. Throughout the prosperous years of the Weimar Republic they had been submissive to the state and integrated into its authority structure – and the experience of the Weimar Republic was such that few would mount the barricades to defend it. In effect, the Social Democratic Party was little more than the mouthpiece of the trade unions, whose considerable funds, invested in state institutions, bound them to the government with chains of gold. And these unions, she wrote, 'are *above all* associations for mutual welfare. They could be dragged along by the masses like dead weights, but that is all' (P, p. 137). Since members of the SPD were mainly those who still had jobs, they were wary of causing any further dislocation of the economy. Moreover the whole Social Democratic organisation was oligarchic and bureaucratic: however impatient the younger members might be, the older ones felt that, contrary to Marx, they had an awful lot to lose besides their chains. If, as Weil insisted, the choice was between revolution or Fascism, the SPD was incapable of deciding.

What, then, of the supposedly really revolutionary party, the Communists? 'I have lost', she wrote to the Thévenons on her return from Germany, 'all the respect that, in spite of myself, I still felt for the Communist Party' (P, p. 137). The weaknesses of the Communists were partly structural: 80 per cent of their members had been in the Party for less than two years; and 80 per cent again were young and unemployed. This accentuated the split with the SPD (which had enrolled the bulk of those who had work) and also meant that the Communist Party was outside the economic system, parasitic upon it, and forced into agitation. But these weaknesses were compounded by the leadership's obsessive hatred of the Social Democrats, a hatred which led it into three suicidal policies. Firstly, the Communist Party considered the Social Democrats to be their main enemy and preached a united left 'from below' (which simply meant trying to poach members from the SPD) rather than making common accord with the Social Democrats against Hitler. Secondly, their propaganda was strongly tinged with nationalist colours, blaming Versailles rather than capitalism for Germany's economic crisis and accusing the SPD of being 'traitors to the fatherland'. And, thirdly, they were quite willing to make common cause with the Nazis (as in the Berlin transport strike of November 1932) in order to defeat the SPD. And this Alice-in-Wonderland politics[14] was reinforced by the iron inner-party dictatorship, which simply handed orders down from above, and the obedience of both action and thought to the imperatives of Moscow. In all this, Weil was concerned to stress the similarities between the

Nazi and the Communist parties: when Nazi and Communist workers argued, she had the impression that they were hard put to it to find some real point of disagreement. But it was the Nazis who, by playing on the apprehensions of big business, inevitably had the upper hand. Indeed, in her view, in spite of their electoral success in November 1932, 'the facts have shown that the power of the Communist Party, when it has to rely on its own strength and when it is a question of real action, is precisely nil' (EHP, p. 144). And her conclusion was pessimistic:

> So that is the situation of the seven-tenths of the German population who yearn for socialism. Thanks to Hitlerite demagogy, the politically unconscious, the desperate, and those who are ready for any adventure have been recruited as soldiers to fight a civil war in the service of finance capital; the prudent and level-headed workers have been handed over by Social Democracy, tied hand and foot, to the German apparatus; and the most fervent and resolute proletarians have been kept powerless by the representatives of the Russian state apparatus . . .
> On the eve of such a battle, facing the formidable economic and political organizations of capital, the gangs of Hitlerite terrorists, and the machine guns of the Reichswehr, the German working class is alone and bare handed. Or rather, one is tempted to wonder if it would not be even better for it to be bare handed. The instruments that it forged, and that it thinks it holds, are in reality in the hands of others, in the defence of interests that are not its own. (FW, pp. 144f)

Weil's articles on Germany were crucial in her re-evaluation of the revolutionary potential of the socialist movement.[15] They were also an impressive display of keen political instinct and analysis reminiscent in their general perspective of Rosa Luxemburg. But, of the major Marxist thinkers of the time, it was to Trotsky that she felt closest. Indeed, she had met Trotsky's son, Lev Sedov, in Berlin and agreed to take out of Germany a suitcase full of his father's papers: at the border crossing-point she passed it over to her mother as someone less likely to attract official attention. It was partly Trotsky's image of an isolated, powerless but heroic exile that appealed to her, but also his ability 'to pass coolly in review all the elements of any situation and still maintain this analysis which is both conducted with an irreproachable theoretical honesty and orientated completely towards immediate action' (EHP, p. 117). She also shared with him the dualist approach which issued in the harsh alternative: revolution or Fascism. Where she parted company with Trotsky was in his view of Fascism as simply a tool in the hands of capitalist interests: Hitler was, for her, more manipulator than manipulated. Neither could she accept Trotsky's 'superstitious attachment' to the Bolshevik party or believe that the situation would be radically improved if only the members of the 'Left Opposition' could gain control – however much she admired their individual courage and tenacity. Nor did Weil share Trotsky's long-term optimism. The editors of *La Révolution Prolétarienne* had cut out the last sentence of one of her articles which ended: 'But who can tell if such a struggle would not end in the defeat which has hitherto crushed all spontaneous uprisings?' (P, p. 139). She summed up the difference with characteristic clarity:

> Insurrections of the order of the Commune are admirable, but they fail (true, the proletariat is much stronger than it was then; but so is the bourgeoisie). Insurrections of the October 1917 type succeed, but all they do is reinforce the bureaucratic, military and police apparatus. And at this moment nonviolence *à la* Gandhi seems simply a rather hypocritical species of reformism. And we do not yet know any fourth type of action. (P, p. 147)

Weil's 'active pessimism' was born out by events: by the time her last article had gone to press, the Reichstag fire had given Hitler the opportunity to seize total power.

Throughout 1933 the situation in Germany was at the forefront of Weil's attention. She wrote: 'If I could have a wish, I would fly there straight away' (P, p. 138). Instead, she found herself teaching philosophy in the girls' lycée in Auxerre. When signing her request for a transfer, she had been promised the more industrialised town of Saint-Quentin. But the Ministry of Education finally decided otherwise and placed her in this picturesque town on the borders of Burgundy and the Ile de France, only three hours from Paris by train. Her mother was just as helpful and omnicompetent as at Le Puy, accompanying her daughter on the first visit to the headmistress, and finding and furnishing her small flat above a cafe on the outskirts of the town – though, on her mother's departure for Paris, Weil rolled up the carpets and installed a decidedly more Spartan atmosphere.

The social climate at Auxerre was much more bourgeois than at Le Puy and Weil found her pupils, many of whom were daughters of army officers, nice enough but little interested in the ideas she was expressing. Her relations with the administration were bad: according to the headmistress, she would deliberately turn her back when addressed, only attending the school for her classes, and read a Russian newspaper throughout the compulsory teachers' meetings as though deliberately cultivating everyone's disfavour. To a colleague who was canvassing her vote on some school matter, she responded: 'No, I'm the head of a terrorist cell!' On another occasion, it is said, a poor man came into the

school with a fork and spoon in his hand. Asked what he wanted, he
replied: 'It's Mlle. Weil who told me to come and eat here – she said
that, if there was enough for 350, there was enough for 351' (C, p. 75).
At the same time she continued to pursue bits of desultory manual
labour, such as helping a plumber in his shop, digging potatoes on the
nearby workers' allotments, and spending odd hours in the local paint
factory. She admired the progressive ideas of Célestin Freinet on bringing
manual labour into the classroom and even bought a small press on
which her pupils could print their compositions: but they objected
because it dirtied their hands.

Her minimalist attitude to the lycée gave Weil considerable time to
devote herself to the increasingly bitter in-fighting in the Trade Union
world – a struggle made all the more vital to her because of her
recent experience in Germany. She joined the Fédération Unitaire
d'Enseignement whose more revolutionary stance she had defended
inside the primary school teachers' union which she had joined in Le
Puy. The Fédération Unitaire d'Enseignement was affiliated to the
Communist-dominated CGTU, but the union as a whole preserved
its independence *vis-à-vis* the Communist Party, its leaders being of
revolutionary syndicalist inclination: it was in their journal, *L'Ecole
Emancipée*, that Weil published her most detailed articles on Germany.
However her own branch was dominated by Communists and Weil
entered it 'deploying the standard of the opposition'. 'Nevertheless',
she wrote, 'the atmosphere is good . . . In this region there are never
any expulsions for differences of political opinion' (P, p. 144). She was
also on good terms with the local Communist Party cell and even gave
some talks on Marx there. It was this unity within difference that Weil
was concerned to see extended to the national scene. When the
Federation was attacked by one of Thévenon's colleagues for lack of
militancy in pursuing particular claims, she responded violently in a
letter of February 1933 which summarised both her aims and her
frustration:

> This is not the moment to attack honest revolutionists, nor to confine
> oneself to 100 percent syndicalism.
> This is the moment for everyone to come to an agreement: syndicalists,
> opposition Communists – even sincere orthodox, rank-and-file Com-
> munists.
> This is the moment above all – above all for all of the young – to start
> seriously reviewing all ideas, instead of adopting 100 percent any
> programme from before the war (prewar C.G.T. or Bolshevik party),
> at the present time when *all* workers' organizations have *completely
> failed*.
> You must see that – to the degree that 'revolutionary syndicalism' is
> a dogma for you, as the 'party' is for Communists who follow the

line or belong to the opposition – I decidedly cease being with you . . .
This is not to say that I am more attracted to the Communist
movement – *on the contrary!* – but I no longer want to admit any of
those prewar ideas to the status of articles of faith, and especially since
they have *never* been seriously examined and have been disproved by
all of subsequent history. I wish that we could make a clean sweep of
all political tendencies, and that we could finally learn how to pose
problems honestly – which the militants rarely venture to do . . . I
am stifled by this revolutionary movement with its blindfolded
eyes . . . (P, p. 148)

As to her own union, she was clear that, rather than reiterating
'disgusting' slogans about class struggle and wage claims, it should
press

for the freedom to express opinions outside our professional duties;
against brainwashing on the job; against the administrative authority;
for pedagogic reforms; for a decrease of differences in salaries; and a
fight on behalf of the most exploited categories . . . We need a united
front on this basis . . . If we take any other path we can arrive only at
this string of absurdities. (P, p. 167)

And to this end she even thought of starting a union of *agrégés* to abolish
their own privileges – a project which unsurprisingly gained few
adherents.

Another aspect of politics that occupied much of Weil's attention at
this time was her work for refugees, mainly from Germany and the
Soviet Union, and the international dimension that this added to her
thinking. She persuaded her long-suffering parents to feed and lodge
many of these refugees in their Paris flat. As well as a fair assortment
of spongers and double-agents, they included eminent socialists such
as Paul Frohlich, editor of Rosa Luxemburg's works and recently released
by the Nazis, for whom Weil had once envisaged substituting herself in
prison. They also sheltered Kurt Landau and his wife, both former
Trotskyists who had quarrelled so violently with their previous comrades
that they hid in the bedroom to avoid Lev Sedov when he came to visit.
This broadening of Weil's perspective was helped by her meeting and
becoming a firm friend of Boris Souvarine, one of the founders of the
French Communist Party, from which he had been expelled in 1924 for
defending Trotsky.[16] Souvarine was the founder of the Democratic
Communist Circle, a group of thirty or so intellectuals who sustained
the short-lived but influential review *La Critique Sociale* to which Weil
contributed occasional pieces. She attended meetings of the Circle
regularly and occasionally presented a topic herself.

Meanwhile, as the academic year moved through to the annual nemesis of the *baccalauréat*, it became clear that Weil's philosophy class was not a success. Scorning standard textbooks, she used only the works of Descartes, Kant and Plato. Although she was, as usual, extremely generous with her time, both the headmistress and the rector found her teaching confused, unstructured and lacking in any pedagogical sense. And the Inspector General who visited her class in May confirmed these opinions:

> The teacher makes the mistake of speaking without looking at her pupils, she bends over her papers, and she does not pronounce her words clearly. Nevertheless, the teaching she gives seems to be substantial enough; and one is made aware of an effort to inform and of a personal reflection even when the pains she has taken do not produce a very clear or well constructed lesson. Unfortunately, her teaching is also extremely tendentious. It is a respectable point of view, no doubt – even *sympathique* in her sincerity and her conviction. But she often takes a violent or oversimplified position, and her lectures are so full of allusions to events or personalities of the present or recent past that her teaching all too often has the tone of a pamphlet or political broadside. (C, p. 80)

Weil, for her part, encouraged her pupils with the view that 'the *baccalauréat* is only a convention'. Many of them nevertheless had recourse to private tuition. All in vain: only four out of her twelve pupils passed and the authorities thought it wiser in future to amalgamate the philosophy class with that of the boys' lycée.

During the course of 1933 it became clear that Weil's political attitudes were becoming as out of place in the French Left as her philosophical teaching was in the context of the *baccalauréat*. Her German experience and her impatience with sectarian divisions were leading her to a fundamental reappraisal of her views, including her commitment to syndicalism. Indeed, she began to criticise 'the pure syndicalists who look upon the trade union ("good" unions, just as non-existent as the federal majority's "good" party!) as capable of leading the proletariat in all of its revolutionary tasks' (P, p. 163). But if she did not know yet precisely what she was for, she certainly knew what she was against and felt a strong solidarity with those who were trying to maintain a non-Communist revolutionary presence on the organised Left. This was increasingly difficult. A resolution at the local branch of the Fédération d'Enseignement Unitaire proposing to ask the Soviet Union simply for information about the imprisoned dissident socialist Victor Serge aroused as much opposition as support. Weil herself was prevented by interruptions from Stalinists from speaking at a meeting of the Action Committee against War and Fascism to which she had been nominated by her union. In August she had the same experience at her own union's annual congress. The Stalinists had brought along a Soviet delegation to bolster their cause, only to be bombarded by questions about the treatment of Serge, Trotsky, Riazanov and others. When on the last day of the congress Maria Reese, a former Communist deputy in the Reichstag, defended the policies of the Third International towards Germany, Weil took to the platform to complain about the fact that the Soviet government had closed its borders to German political refugees. She was shouted down with cries of 'viper' and might well have been bundled off the platform had her friends not protected her. On this note, it being 4.30 a.m., the president deemed it prudent to close formal proceedings.

After such a tumultuous year, Weil went off to Spain with her parents and Aimé Patri for an extended holiday. Patri was a philosophy teacher and Trotskyist sympathiser whom she had got to know in the course of her anti-Communist activities. They all spent a week in Barcelona and then she and Patri went on for three weeks in Villaneuva (where Patri had friends) and a week in Valencia. Weil attended a bullfight, which she enjoyed, went to rather *louche* night-clubs with Patri, and lived in her bathing costume – until the hotel manager told her to put on something else more seemly at mealtimes. In Barcelona she made contact with the Spanish anarchists, on whose side she would later fight in the civil war, and discovered in Valencia her ideal non-bureaucratic organisation in a dockers' union which provided its members with insurance, pensions, hospital and school, all run by the dockers themselves with the help of only one paid official. Those who knew her well said that they had never seen her so happy and relaxed.

She needed all the recuperation she could get. No sooner was she back from Spain than she attended the annual congress of the CGTU. Weil was again prevented from speaking and even from distributing tracts outside the conference hall. She made her views clear in an article on the Congress:

> The true character of the congress was fully revealed when, after the session ended Charbit and Simone Weil were brutally and physically prevented from distributing appeals in the street for solidarity with German comrades, victims of Fascist terror, who did not belong to either of the two main Internationals. Such things would be impossible in a real trade union organization. But the CGTU is an outright appendage of the Russian state apparatus . . . (P, p. 180)

In spite of all this, Weil managed still to preserve some optimism:

The small opposition in the CGTU, though persecuted and calumnied, did not lose heart. The last congress of the CGTU has brought us closer together. For the first time an agreement was reached between the militants of the Federation and the syndicalists. Let us hope that this is the initial stage toward the rallying of the revolutionary forces that have remained healthy. (Ibid.)

But these rather forced expressions of hope could not long resist the logic of her penetrating and principled analysis. Several months earlier she had explained to one of her former *agrégation* classmates that she was beginning to lose her faith even in her syndicalist comrades:

I had at first been with them, but at the moment I realize that they leave many problems unsolved. In my opinion, instead of taking such a position and becoming a partisan in this fashion, in the light of recent experiences we must pose anew and examine without prejudice the question of the organization of the proletariat. (P, p. 163)

This fresh, unprejudiced look at working-class organisation took the form of a long article in *La Révolution Prolétarienne* which both summed up her experiences of two years' activity in the syndicalist movement and laid the foundations for *Oppression and Liberty*, the *magnum opus* of this period of her life. She wrote it in sixteen hours of continuous intense outpouring which combined fire with discipline. The article was entitled 'Perspectives' to which the editors of *La Révolution Prolétarienne* added the subtitle 'Are we heading for the proletarian revolution?' Weil's reply was, to say the least, agnostic. Although convinced that capitalism had reached the limits of its development, she saw little prospect of its replacement by socialism. From 1789, through the Paris Commune to 1914, movements for working-class emancipation had ended in failure. The Soviet Union, she roundly declared, had evolved into the exact opposite of the type of government that Lenin believed would be inaugurated by the October Revolution – with the sole exception of the abolition of capitalist property: freedom of the press, the existence of parties other than the Bolshevik, a Communist party composed of active, critical members, democratic Soviets in charge of economic and political life and, above all, popular elections and control of officials – all these had gone by the board and given place to 'a permanent bureaucracy freed from responsibility, recruited by co-option and possessing, through the concentration in its hands of all economic and political power, a strength hitherto unknown in the annals of history' (OL, p. 4).

This was a new phenomenon and, as such, difficult to analyse. Trotsky's phrases about the Soviet Union still being the dictatorship of the proletariat, a 'workers' state with bureaucratic deformations', was wide of the mark:

> Descartes used to say that a clock out-of-order is not an exception to the laws governing clocks, but a different mechanism obeying its own laws; in the same way we should regard the Stalin regime, not as a workers' state out-of-order, but as a different social mechanism, whose definition is to be found in the wheels of which it is composed and which functions according to the nature of those wheels. (OL, pp. 4f)

Thus it was simplistic to talk of the Russian State as being 'transitional' – either forwards towards socialism or backwards towards capitalism, since there was no evidence that the Russian State bureaucracy was preparing the ground for any domination other than its own. A large bureaucratic caste appropriated for its personal satisfaction a vastly disproportionate part of the surplus, the residue being left for the less important problem of accumulation and development. And as for a workers' state:

> no workers' state has ever yet existed on the earth's surface, except for a few weeks in Paris in 1871, and perhaps for a few months in Russia in 1917 and 1918. On the other hand, for nearly fifteen years now, over one sixth of the globe, there has reigned a state as oppressive as any other which is neither a capitalist nor a workers' state. Certainly, Marx never foresaw anything of this kind. But not even Marx is more precious to us than the truth. (OL, p. 6)

Nor were traditional Marxist categories any more successful in coming to terms with Fascism. Drawing on her work in Germany, Weil rejected the simplistic idea that Fascism was the last resort of the bourgeoisie: the economic strength of big business was unable to control Hitler and politics in Germany bore a striking resemblance to Trotsky's characterisation of the Soviet Union: one party in power and the rest in prison. Even in the United States things were not much better: under Roosevelt's New Deal, a technocratic dictatorship was on the horizon. So, with traditional capitalism moribund and socialism nowhere in sight, Weil wished to put forward a hypothesis:

> We can say, to put it briefly, that up to the present mankind has known two principal forms of oppression, the one (slavery or serfdom) exercised in the name of armed force, the other in the name of wealth thus transformed into capital; what we have to determine is whether these are not now being succeeded by a new species of oppression, oppression exercised in the name of management. (OL, p. 9)

Whereas in early capitalism the subordination of the worker had, according to Weil, been achieved through the sale of labour power, it was now inherent in the work process. With the advance of technology, a new opposition had arisen between those of whom the machine disposed and those who disposed of the machine, between those who passively executed manoeuvres and those who directed but did not execute. And this was accompanied by a growing divorce of the owners of capital from those who directed its employment. The days of Henry Ford, when these were normally concentrated in the same hands, were over. The growth of the productive forces and the increasing drive for specialisation meant that the future was in the hands of an industrial bureaucracy, since co-ordination was now all-important:

> In almost all fields, the individual, shut in within the bounds of a limited proficiency, finds himself caught up in a whole which is beyond him, by which he must regulate all his activity, and whose functioning he is unable to understand. In such a situation, there is one function which takes on a supreme importance, namely, that which consists simply in co-ordinating; we may call it the administrative or bureaucratic function. (OL, p. 13)

What was important to grasp was that this oppressive bureaucratic function was more or less independent of capitalism. It followed that no mere expropriation of the means of production would overcome it. Nor was the American dream of an enlightened technocracy any more attractive. All powerful groups tended to increase their power and, under current circumstances, this meant preparation for war. Even the capitalist virtues of initiative and invention were being eliminated. Indeed all previous forms of social organisation, though oppressive, 'appear as forms of a free and happy existence when compared with a system that would methodically destroy all initiative, all culture, all thought' (OL, p. 13). The grim conclusion was that a form of state capitalism with a fusion of trade union, industrial and state bureaucracies was emerging – already in place in the Soviet Union, almost perfected in Germany, and well on its way in the parliamentary democracies.[17]

Under these circumstances, what hope was there for those who placed the supreme value in the individual and not the collective, and wished to give back to individuals their proper role of controlling nature, their own work process, and society itself? Although domination of nature had, over the last few centuries, outstripped all expectations, 'during the last century it came to be realised that society itself is a force of nature, as blind as the others, as dangerous for man if he does not succeed in mastering it' (OL, p. 20). In the face of this menace, the working class found itself disarmed: rationalisation and specialisation implied increasing passivity; spontaneous activity proved powerless; and organisation eventually secreted its own oppressive directorate. Moreover certain forms of working-class agitation could, and did, favour the rise of Fascism.

Despite this pessimistic catalogue, Weil did retain some hope in the capacity of trade unionists to resist. But it was a small hope. As an epigraph for her article, she had chosen the words of Sophocles's Ajax: 'I have only contempt for mortals who arm themselves with empty hopes.' And she put her main trust in lucidity: 'If we are to perish in the future battles, let us do our best to prepare ourselves to perish with a clean record of the world we shall be leaving', since 'the greatest misfortune for us would be to perish powerless either to succeed or to understand' (OL, p. 24).

Not surprisingly, such a brilliant, clear, but profoundly pessimistic assessment provoked considerable criticism. The next month, *La Révolution Prolétarienne* carried an assessment from Roger Hagnauer, one of its editors, entitled 'Not so much pessimism!', which accused her of adopting too lofty a point of view:

> Simone Weil would, at a pinch, resign herself to defeat it if she were able to identify its causes. Has this lofty intellectual resignation anything to do with our revolutionary syndicalism? . . . Will not Simone Weil's 'lucid' pessimism weaken even the most resolute? (P, p. 177)

And Trotsky himself reacted more violently: he insisted that the Soviet bureaucracy did not constitute a new class (since it did not owe its position to any new private property relations) and characterised Weil's position and person as follows:

> Having fallen into despair over the unsuccessful experiments of the dictatorship of the proletariat, Simone Weil has found solace in a new vocation: the defense of her personality against society. The hoary formula of liberalism, vivified with cheap anarchistic exaltation! And think of it – Simone Weil speaks loftily about our 'illusions'. She and those like her require many years of stubborn perseverance in order to free themselves from the most reactionary, lower-middle-class prejudices. Appropriately enough her new views have found a haven in an organ that bears the obviously ironic name, *La Révolution Prolétarienne*. This publication is ideally suited for revolutionary melancholics and political rentiers living on the dividends from their capital of recollections and pretentious philosophizers who will perhaps adhere to the revolution . . . after it has been achieved.[18]

But Weil's article also had its admirers, since its critique of the USSR and its emphasis on the individual echoed ideas current in revolutionary syndicalist circles. Monatte was said to have been very favourably impressed and Souvarine said of Weil that she was 'the only brain that the working class has produced for years' (P, p. 176).

Perspectives was published in August 1933. Although it heralded Weil's disillusion with contemporary politics of any sort, a whole year passed before she broke definitively with revolutionary syndicalism and developed the themes of her article in her major work of the period, *Oppression and Liberty*. This year she spent in the girls' lycée in Roanne, a large manufacturing town on the upper Loire, sixty miles north-west of Lyons. Her relations with the school seem to have been less tense than usual. Her colleagues remembered her as 'a fleeting, mysterious figure immersed in some great German book such as *Das Kapital*' (C, p. 95). The headmistress found it impossible to get her to give marks and assign grades; and her pupils had to clean off the inscription that they had written over their classroom door: 'No one enters here unless he [sic!] knows geometry.' But the philosophy group was a happy one:

> Our class was a small one and had a family atmosphere about it: housed apart from the main school buildings, in a little summer house almost lost in the school grounds, we made our first acquaintance with great thoughts in an atmosphere of complete independence. When the weather was good we had our lessons under the shade of a fine cedar tree, and sometimes they became a search for the solution to a problem in geometry, or a friendly conversation.[19]

And even the inspectors' reports were, for once, quite favourable.

It was at Weil's own request that she was sent to Roanne: she could revisit her old haunts and she was now no further from Saint-Etienne than she had been at Le Puy. As soon as possible she began to teach fortnightly evening classes on Marxism at the Saint-Etienne Labour Exchange. These classes were carefully prepared, with a summary distributed beforehand, and outlined a lot of what was to appear later in *Oppression and Liberty*. She often missed the last train back and spent the night dozing on the benches of the cafe opposite whose proprietor let her stay after closing time. On 22 October, Weil spoke impromptu at a meeting called to protest at the visit of the President of the Republic, Albert Lebrun, to Saint-Etienne to unveil a war memorial. According to an eye-witness account,

> The Labour Exchange had been closed by the police. The meeting took place on the pavement . . . Helped by the shoulders and hands of workers, Simone Weil hoisted herself up onto a window ledge

while plain-clothes policemen rushed through the crowd of curious passers-by. In the hubbub and turmoil of the street the demonstrators got themselves together. Drawn up in a circle, singing the *International*, arms linked to form a more solid chain underneath the windows, they managed to hold back the police. From the height of her perch, Simone Weil gratified us with a hasty exposition on the precise role of a President of the Republic. The police, freshly shaved for the official receptions, were obliged, noses in the air while they tried to break our ranks, to listen to a lecture on the 'obligations of privilege' . . .[20]

At the end of her evenings in Saint-Etienne a party would regularly adjourn to a friend's house where they would sit on piled newspapers (there being too few chairs) to smoke, drink and chat. When in the mood, Weil would sing, incredibly out of tune, student songs and recite whole pages of Greek tragedy.

In early December, 3000 miners, complete with banners and bands, marched on Saint-Etienne to protest against growing unemployment and cuts in their wages. According to one of the participants:

> At a fork in the road Simone Weil waited, surrounded by some late comrades, her face and hands slightly blue with cold. She leapt to the front rank, slid among the union militants and claimed the promised reward: the big red flag of the St. Etienne Labour Exchange. When there was a break in the trumpeting, she cried: 'So, have the miners forgotten how to sing?' and she began to march, a grave standard-bearer, well in step.[21]

But there was always a divide between Weil and her working-class acquaintances, as evidenced by an incident following the march. As the demonstration broke up, recounts the same writer:

> she was surrounded by a group of the true faithful. She was in the holiday spirit and suddenly had the idea of one of those jokes that she believed to be 'of the people'. She stopped at a street-vendor's stall and bought her friends wooden pipes in the shape of Turks' heads caricatured in violent colour. They went along with the joke and put the pipes in their mouths – then shoved them away in their pockets, a little embarrassed. She never knew that this was the kind of joke that was an affront to these men. Smoking was for them a confirmation of their virility and the pipe a sort of taboo. But they managed to hide their feelings from Simone as they hid their pipes which were never seen again. (Ibid.)

It was partly no doubt her own perception of her being an alien among the workers that prompted her decision to become a worker herself.

Another sort of gulf opened up when she finally got to meet Trotsky at the end of 1933. He had been in Paris since July, granted asylum by the French government on condition that he did not participate in any political meetings. But Trotsky was thinking belatedly of breaking with the Comintern and wished to discuss with other likely parties, and particularly the small German Socialist Workers' Party, the possibility of founding a Fourth International; and he needed a place to hold preliminary discussions. One of the Weil flats was empty and she persuaded her parents to let it be used by Trotsky for the discussions. He arrived with his wife and two armed bodyguards a day or two before the meeting, his goatee beard and moustache shaved off and his unruly hair slicked down, looking for all the world like a good Parisian bourgeois. Weil took advantage of his presence to discuss the situation in Russia where Trotsky still maintained that the October Revolution had laid the basis for a development of the productive forces that would eventually bring the workers real power. Weil objected that nothing was less likely, given the way in which the workers were oppressed by the Soviet regime. Trotsky accused her of being reactionary, of adopting a logical, juridical, idealist viewpoint, of doubting everything. The discussion became heated: her parents could hear them shouting from the next room. Weil particularly reproached Trotsky with his treatment of the Kronstadt mutineers. He retorted: 'If that's what you think, why are you putting us up? Are you the Salvation Army?' The planned meeting took place the next day and Trotsky seemed well pleased. He said to the Weils on leaving: 'You can say that the Fourth International was founded in your home' (P, p. 190).

For all his rather clichéd approach to events in Russia, Trotsky was not far wrong in saying that Weil's extreme individualism was incompatible with contemporary politics. She was beginning to feel the same thing herself. There is no mention in her letters of the Stravisky riots in Paris on 6 February, when a Fascist assault on the National Assembly was narrowly averted and she held aloof from the anti-Fascist committees of trade union leaders and intellectuals that sprang up as a result.[22] She described as 'senseless' the contemporaneous socialist rising in Vienna; and France, she felt, was rushing headlong towards Fascism or at least an extremely reactionary dictatorship. She still frequented the Saint-Etienne Labour Exchange and at the May Day demonstration was in the front rank, fist raised, singing the International. But she had finally parted company with her colleagues in *La Révolution Prolétarienne*, pouring scorn on their slogan of 'power to the unions': 'Power to the ideal trade union is similar to power to the ideal party. Our unions are real unions. They are not capable of taking power – fortunately!' (P, p. 207). Already in March she had written to Simone Petrement:

> I have decided to withdraw entirely from any kind of political activity, except for theoretical work. That does not absolutely exclude possible participation in a great spontaneous movement of the masses (in the ranks, as a soldier), but I don't want any responsibility, no matter how slight, or even indirect, because I am certain that all the blood that will be shed will be shed in vain, and that we are beaten in advance . . . (P, p. 198)

This decision to abandon politics was reiterated in a letter to one of her pupils written in the autumn of 1934: 'It is my firm decision to take no further part in *any* political or social activities, with two exceptions: anti-colonialism and the campaign against passive defence exercises' (P, p. 212). She did not, of course, keep strictly to this decision: she kept quite closely in touch with her revolutionary syndicalist friends; in early 1937, she still felt at home in the trade union movement whose syndicalist spirit she considered superior to that of contemporary Christianity; and from the Spanish Civil War to the Free French in London she was enthusiastic, on occasion, to take a very active part in politics. Nevertheless 1934 does mark a historical and political break in Weil's attitude to revolutionary syndicalism. By the time Weil got involved with it, revolutionary syndicalism was very much in decline and the unity of ethics and politics that had characterised its early years was fast breaking up: Weil conserved its attachment to the working class and an anti-authoritarian individualism, but could not find its revolutionary politics convincing.[23] During her year at Le Puy she seems to have thought that some parts at least of the trade union movement obeyed laws different from those of the rest of the political system. By 1934 she considered this to be an illusion. But she still remained strongly influenced by the ethical outlook of revolutionary syndicalism.[24] However much she scorned Marx's idea of the 'historic mission of the proletariat', she never denied its ethical mission.

Her profound pessimism about politics (though not about life: she insisted to Frohlich that it was only her historical perspective that was sad, not her world-view) had two immediate corollaries. The first was her decision, taken in June, to ask for leave from her teaching duties in order to take up factory work, an experience that was to mark the most important turning-point in her life. The second, and more immediate, was that she began the draft of *Oppression and Liberty*. This work, which started off as an article for Souvarine's moribund *Critique Sociale*, soon turned into a summation of her intellectual position, a conclusion to, and of, her syndicalist past, or, as she self-mockingly called it, a 'testament'.

4

Oppression and Liberty

'Social force is bound to be accompanied by lies. That is why all that
is highest in human life, every effort of thought, every effort of love,
has a corrosive action on the established order.' (OL, p. 145)

It was natural that Weil's testament should begin with a critique of
Marxism. Given the strength of the indigenous socialist tradition and
the influence of thinkers such as Rousseau and Proudhon, the reception
accorded to Marx in France tended to be ambivalent. And it is at least
arguable that Weil owed more to her French predecessors than she did
to Marx, complaining that, if not Marx, at least Marxism had 'seriously
debased that spirit of revolt which, in the last century, shone with so
pure a light in our country' (OL, p. 154). Indeed, she wrote,

> I do not think that the workers' movement in this country will become
> something living again until it seeks, I will not say doctrines, but a
> source of inspiration, in what Marx and Marxism have fought against
> and very foolishly despised: in Proudhon, in the workers' groups of
> 1848, in the trade union tradition, in the anarchist spirit. (OL, p. 148)

Nevertheless the massive fact of the transformation of Russia by
self-styled Marxists and the dominance of Marx's thought among
revolutionary socialists in general meant that he imposed himself
inevitably as an inescapable intellectual presence. Weil herself had been
busy lecturing on Marx at Le Puy, at Saint-Etienne, and at Auxerre. The
outlines of her lectures at Saint-Etienne in 1934 and the lessons she gave
to her philosophy class at Roanne[1] show that she had been mulling over
the themes of *Oppression and Liberty* for some time.

Marx was a good starting-point since, for Weil, no-one had produced
a better set of ideas and it was generally agreed among revolutionaries
that a firm basis for their sentiments could be found in Marx who 'gives
an admirable account of the mechanisms of capitalist oppression' (OL,
p. 40). Weil paid a tribute to the social ideals of Marx's youth which she
described as 'humane, clear, conscious, and reasoned' (OL, p. 47); but
what was new in Marx was that he saw oppression not as some
arbitrary usurpation but as caused by the material conditions of social
organisation, particularly the division of labour, and as a function of
the development of the forces of production. Echoing the famous

formula of Lukàcs in the Preface to *History and Class Consciousness*, Weil put all her emphasis on Marx's method: for in spite of the fact that the society which had given rise to these analyses was no more, Marx's doctrine was indestructible and his analyses had a value which could not disappear. But the condition of its continued life was that 'the precious tool constituted by the Marxist method should come down from generation to generation without getting rusty, each generation making use of it to define the world in which it lives' (OL, p. 125). This new (or potentially new) interpretation of history was a proof of Marx's genius and 'the Marxist view that social existence is determined by the relations between man and nature established by production remains the only sound basis for any historical investigation' (OL, p. 71).

In two earlier comments on Marx in 1932, Weil read him in a less determinist fashion. His materialism, she insisted, was not to be confused with a vulgar empiricism: indeed, 'Marx's chief claim to fame is to have rescued the study of society not simply from utopian constructions, but also, and at the same time, from empiricism' (SS, pp. 106f). And Weil compares Marx's scientific method here to that of Descartes in that both asked the question: not how does it come about that the world is known but how, in fact, do human beings know the world in such a way that their thought does not passively reflect it but exercises itself on the world both to know and to transform it (OL, p. 32). And, again in 1932, she is happy to contrast the more 'active' materialism of the early Marx with that of Engels and Lenin. Nevertheless, by 1934, it is in a sense a mechanistic materialism that Weil considers to be Marx's main contribution, in that it is the discovery of social *mechanisms* that she likes, the 'great idea' of Marx that in society, as in nature, things only happen through material transformation. This is in keeping with her own philosophical dualism whereby the physical and social worlds are seen as governed by necessity and freedom consists in contemplating the laws of this necessity. Given her preference for a static rather than a dynamic conception of history, the earlier reading of Marx from the *Theses on Feuerbach* and the *German Ideology* gives place to a finding of merit in the more determinist aspects of Marx's thought – a process which is, of course, paralleled by her growing disillusion with the syndicalist movement.

It is with the dynamic (and, to her, contradictory) aspect of Marx's thought that Weil begins to have difficulty. Indeed, given the excellence of his analysis of capitalist oppression, she writes, 'it is difficult to imagine how this mechanism could cease to function' (OL, p. 40). In Marx's view, it was precisely the development of the productive forces that would bring about the downfall of a capitalism which no longer facilitated their development, a development moreover which once released from its capitalist strait-jacket would permit the abolition of the division of labour, and drastically lessen the pressure of natural necessity and thus of social oppression. It was against this misplaced confidence in the liberating potential of productive forces that Weil devoted most of her criticism of Marx. Why, she asked, *should* the forces of production grow? Since Marx offered no explanation, his thought should be compared not, as so often, to Darwin, but to Lamarck who similarly based his whole system of biology on an inexplicable tendency of living beings to adaptation. Why, moreover, did Marx think that the forces of production *must* be more powerful historical determinants than social institutions? And why did he think that the productive forces were capable of limitless development? 'All this doctrine', she concluded, 'on which the Marxist conception of revolution is completely dependent, is absolutely lacking in any scientific character' (OL, p. 44). Marx's method must, therefore, be used to produce a profounder analysis. For a proper application of Marx's own materialist method would show that the productivity of labour was not high enough to relieve human beings of the oppression generated by contemporary working conditions – irrespective of whether the means of production were under private or public control.

More importantly, she denied that this was very likely to be the case in the future. Here she leans heavily on an article by Julius Dickmann entitled 'The True Limit of Capitalist Production', which had recently appeared in *La Critique Sociale* and of which she spoke with enthusiasm and excitement (P, p. 206). Following Dickmann, she claimed sources of natural energy were not limitless and their discovery and increasingly expensive exploitation were, at best, a matter of chance. So the sum of human effort involved in production could only be diminished by the rationalisation of labour. This, too, was a subject prone to much illusion. For the productivity of labour could only be enhanced in two ways. The first was its increasing concentration, division and co-ordination. While it was true that this had been effective in the past (viz. Adam Smith's famous example of the production of pins), these measures had reached, and indeed already gone beyond, the limit of their usefulness: industrial enterprises were now too large to be properly co-ordinated and that meant huge waste; and transport and marketing became more and more costly. The second way of enhancing productivity was the abolition of dead labour for living labour through the introduction of automated machinery. But here again, unforeseen consequences were always present, automated machinery could require more human effort rather than less, and its employment often led to over-production and waste. Weil's general conclusion was that technical progress had in fact become regressive, that businesses were refusing technical innovation on economic grounds that had nothing specifically to do with capitalism, and that Marx's idea of a higher stage of Communism as the last stage in the evolution of society was as utopian as the idea of perpetual motion.

Weil claimed that 'when, in my youth, I read *Capital* for the first time, I was immediately struck by certain gaps, certain contradictions of the first importance' (OL, p. 147). This impression of contradictoriness remained with her. The basic problem with Marx was that his materialist method contradicted his revolutionary conclusions and

> unfortunately, loath, as all strong characters are, to allow two separate men to go on living in him – the revolutionary and the scientist; averse also to that sort of hypocrisy which adherence to an ideal accompanied by action implies; insufficiently scrupulous, moreover, in regard to his own thought, he insisted on making his method into an instrument for predicting a future in conformity with his desires. (OL, p. 148)

Marx had confused historical analysis with moral judgement and had shown himself to be a complete conformist in thoroughly assimilating the superstitious belief in large-scale industrial production and in progress, with results deleterious both to science and to revolution. With the sublime confidence that the task of the revolution was simply to liberate the productive forces which themselves would create the pre-conditions for Communism, it was not surprising that Marx's disciples cared so little about workers' democracy; for they were convinced 'on the one hand, that all attempts at social action which do not consist of developing productive forces are doomed to failure, on the other hand, that all progress in productive forces causes humanity to advance along the road leading to emancipation, even if it is at the cost of a temporary oppression' (OL, p. 43). This dangerous teleology (which had its origin in Marx's materialist interpretation of Hegel's dialectic) revealed the religious dimension of Marx's thought. His talk of the 'historical mission of the proletariat' was quasi-mystical and 'to believe that our will coincides with a mysterious will which is at work in the universe and helps us to conquer is to think religiously, to believe in Providence' (OL, 44). Most ironical of all was that Marx, who saw the domination of material objects over human subjects as the very essence of capitalism, had in fact achieved the same reversal in his own theory by transferring the principle of progress from mind to matter in the shape of the productive forces. More generally, Weil continued:

> Marxism is the highest spiritual expression of bourgeois society. Through it this society attained to a consciousness of itself, in it to a negation of itself. But this negation in its turn could only be expressed in a form determined by the existing order, in a bourgeois form of

thought. So it is that each formula of Marxist doctrine lays bare the characteristics of bourgeois society, but at the same time justifies them. (OL, p. 131)

Every aspect of Marx's thought was branded with the birthmark of the bourgeois society which had brought it forth.

Weil's critique of Marx extended beyond his faith in the liberating potential of the productive forces to his whole materialist conception of history. But the basis of this critique is not always clear. In a typically over-brilliant remark she declared: 'the materialistic method – that instrument which Marx bequeathed us – is an untried instrument; no Marxist has ever really used it, beginning with Marx himself' (OL, p. 46). And she was willing to admit that the Marxist interpretation of history had given rise to some impressive particular analyses, in particular of nineteenth-century capitalism. But she insisted that Marx left certain crucial questions unanswered: granted that he had shown how the capitalist regime ended up as a barrier to production, why should this not be true of any other regime? Why should not oppression continue to be the law of history? Why had the oppressed never succeeded in liberating themselves? And how did one form of oppression change into another? The only Marxist reply available – that social oppression was explicable as a function of class struggle – was no explanation at all: it was as unsatisfactory in the social sciences as Lamarck's famous principle – that the function creates the organ – was in the biological sciences. Giraffes did not have long necks so that they could eat lofty bananas: they eat lofty bananas because they had long necks and those that were thus organically adapted would survive. This latter was the approach of Darwin and what Weil liked about it was that 'the adaptation of the organ to the function here enters into play in such a manner as to limit chance by eliminating the non-viable structures, no longer as a mysterious tendency, but as a condition of existence' (OL, p. 58). In order to become scientific, Marxism would have to accomplish a progress analogous to that of Darwin over Lamarck: in other words, 'the causes of social evolution must no longer be sought elsewhere than in the daily efforts of men considered as individuals' (OL, p. 59).

So Marxism would have to abandon its idea that there was some mysterious quality in the productive process which produced institutions compatible with it. Weil seemed to accept that Marx had made a start on this question when she stated that 'the Marxist view, according to which social existence is determined by the relations between man and nature established by production, certainly remains the only sound basis for any historical investigation' (OL, p. 71); but she immediately added: 'these relations must be considered first of all in terms of the problem of power, the means of subsistence forming simply one of the data of this problem' (OL, p. 71). Weil's main point here was that Marx had conflated two sorts of opposition that existed within capitalism: the opposition created by money between the buyers and sellers of labour-power and the opposition created by the forces of production between those who dispose of the machine and those of whom the machine disposes. This led to a confusion between exploitation, which was peculiar to capitalism, and oppression, which was not. This rejection of the mode of production as the key determinant of history, coupled with the refusal to see it as the motor of any sort of inevitable progress, led Weil to substitute psychosocial categories for (Marxist) economic ones, pointing out, for example, the difficulty all Marxist thinkers had in analysing the phenomenon of war – a topic to which she often returned (OL, pp. 151, 163).

In Weil's scheme of things the concept of exploitation (a concept she regarded as typical of the book-keeping spirit of the age) was replaced by that of oppression, the extraction of surplus value by slavery to the machine, and the transformation of property relations by the transformation of machinery and technology. She thus concentrated on the relationship of thought to action as a means of judging modes of production rather than the criterion of productivity implicit in Marx who tended, she thought, to confuse economic and moral progress. Hence her emphasis on the importance of a revolution in technology before anything social or political could be contemplated, and her demand for a critique of science itself. This is strikingly illustrated in her attitude to the labour process: while Marx considered it the essential human activity and thought that under different social relationships it could become free and creative – hunting, shooting, fishing, and reading Hegel – Weil saw work as inherently servile and, if intelligible and willingly accepted, as permitting not an embodiment, but a transcendence, of the human condition.[2]

In her critique of the Marxist interpretation of history, Weil insisted again and again on the importance of the individual. One of the things she most objected to in Marx was that the locus of the process of freedom was transferred from the individual to the species. For Weil, however, any elevation of the group above the individual was the original sin and the resulting faith in race, nation, or even class could only be catastrophic. Feuerbach had analysed the way in which humanity had alienated its own powers for imaginary divinities. And Marx's first and decisive discovery 'was to go beyond Feuerbach's rather ahistorical and abstract approach by looking for the explanation of the historical process in the co-operation of individuals, in union and struggle, and in the multiple relationships that exist between them'. Nevertheless 'Marx only managed to rise above Feuerbach's isolated "human being" by reintroducing into history, under the name of "society", the God whom Feuerbach had eliminated from it' (OL, p. 132). Although the Marx of the *Theses on Feuerbach* talked of the 'ensemble of social relations' as being the result of the historical process, his later work began to hypostatise the collectivity and make it a *condition* of individual actions, an essence which realised itself in and through the actions of individuals. *Capital* talked of the collective possession of land and means of production as the basis for individual property, but 'it is only possible to visualise a "collective possession" if one regards the collectivity as a particular substance, soaring above individuals and acting through them' (ibid.). The classical Marxist formula that social existence determines consciousness was a fine example of this dualism in Marx that was both contradictory and noxious: contradictory since, because these social conditions could only exist in human minds, social existence already *was* consciousness and could not determine it; and noxious because the positing of social existence as a factor of determination separate from our consciousness was to hypostatise it. The truth was that, if you looked closely at this 'social existence' as an element in the relationship between individuals, you saw at once that it depended on certain institutions – money for example – which were the result of conscious acts of individuals and thus determined by these acts rather than the reverse. And the idea of a collective task incumbent on the workers deprived the workers of any possibility of reacting themselves as conscious individuals against their situation.

The notion of the proletariat as a collective revolutionary agent with a revolutionary mission conveyed by History and Progress had, moreover, been undermined by history itself. The best organised proletariat in the world had already capitulated in Germany: the Russian proletariat had been duped by their own leaders; and the workers in general were in a weaker position than at any time since the death of Marx. But it was not only history that had undermined Marx: his own analyses of capitalist oppression showed that his revolutionary expectations were in fact the weakest part of his theory. Unless socialism could suddenly become universal, competition between nations and collectivities would remain and they would be forced to restrain consumption and generally oppress the workers to maximise energy and time for economic and military rivalries. Even more seriously, there were no political or legal remedies to the subordination of the worker, since this subordination lay, not in property relations, but in the structure of industrial technology itself – as Marx himself had realised in his more lucid moments: if the productive forces were so important, then socialism could only be the result of new productive forces, that is, a radically different type of machine (OL, p. 9). It was therefore vain to expect that mere technical progress would reduce in any way the subordination of the worker who would continue to be crushed both physically and morally by the division in society between those who command and those who execute.

Furthermore, with the growing specialisation and division of labour in contemporary society, science itself had become a monopoly, so accentuating the division between direction and execution. Socialism could call itself 'scientific' but science was not on the side of the workers and no science of history could predict their victory. More professional sorts of science were unintelligible to all but the initiated and even they had to subordinate their researches to results already arrived at. The outcome was that

> science, which was to have made all things clear and unveiled all mysteries, has itself become the outstanding mystery, so much so that obscurity, and indeed absurdity, appear today in a scientific theory as a mark of profundity. Science has become the most modern form of the consciousness of man who has not yet found himself or has once again lost himself, to apply Marx's telling dictum concerning religion. (OL, p. 35)

Science had succeeded to the role formerly occupied by religion and, as Marx had said of religion, the critique of science was the prerequisite of all critique.

The most fundamental conclusion was that no revolution as currently conceived would get rid of oppression by the various specialised castes of modern society. As long as the workers were, in the words of Marx, mere cogs in the machine of society, they could never aspire to become the dominant class. A profound cultural revolution would have to take precedence. What was needed was the transformation of industry, of machinery, of the work process, of the technique of administration and of war; but all these changes were slow and progressive; they were not the result of a revolution. Outside such long-term considerations the Marxist conception of revolution made no sense: 'the history of the workers' movement is thus lit up with a cruel, but singularly vivid, light. The whole of it can be summarised by remarking that the working class has never manifested strength save insofar as it has served something other than the workers' revolution' (OL, p. 55). While it was true that living standards had risen (in the countries inhabited by whites), emancipation had been made more difficult by the accompanying phenomena of Taylorism, automated machinery, increasing state power, and nationalism.

In the face of all these difficulties, Weil concluded that it was not enough to ask for a revision of Marxism. For, she wrote, 'one cannot revise something which does not exist, and there never has been such a thing as Marxism, but only a series of incompatible assertions, some of them well-founded, others not; unfortunately, the best-founded are the least palatable' (OL, p. 153). If being a revolutionary meant expecting in the near future an upheaval in society which would yield egalitarian results, she could not imagine anyone finding solid reasons for being a revolutionary. If, on the other hand, being a revolutionary meant trying to lighten the burden which crushed the majority of humanity and refusing to accept the lies which justified such oppression, then:

> it is a case of an ideal, a judgement of value, something willed, and not of an interpretation of human history and of the social mechanism. Taken in this sense, the revolutionary spirit is as old as oppression itself and will go on for as long, even longer; for if oppression should disappear, it will have to continue in order to prevent its reappearance; it is eternal; it has no need to undergo a revision, but it can become enriched, sharpened, and it must be purified of all the extraneous accretions that come to disguise and corrupt it. (OL, p. 153)

This spirit of revolt could be found in Marx's early writings but later Marxism had seriously changed the spirit which 'in the last century shone with so pure a light in our country', by adulterating and de-figuring it with 'flashy pseudo-scientific trimmings, a messianic eloquence, an unfettering of appetites' (OL, p. 154). In sum, Marx's contribution was little better than that of the nineteenth-century utopian socialists whom he so bitterly criticised: he was sensitive to injustice without properly understanding its causes.[3]

Weil never abandoned her interest in Marx. What proved to be her last substantial piece of writing was a long article on Marx written in 1943 with the title 'Is there a Marxist Doctrine?' Her answer was negative. The young Marx had elaborated a philosophy of work not far different from that of Proudhon but 'he was stopped while still young by an accident frequent in the nineteenth century; he took himself seriously' (OL, p. 169). He was not in a position to elaborate any sort of doctrine in his later work which was contradictory since 'he seized upon the two beliefs most current in his time, both of them meagre, superficial, mediocre and furthermore impossible to conceive in conjunction: the cult of science and utopian socialism' (ibid.). Marx was indeed the first (and the only) thinker to have had the double idea of taking society as the fundamental human fact and of studying its relationships of force, a kind of non-physical matter, just as a doctor studies tissues. But his own generous aspirations and a psychological need for certainty had led him into the absurd conception of matter as a machine for producing good, for while his analysis of the connection of social morality with dominant power groups and their link to the forces of production was excellent, his theory of social transformation was stupid in itself and also completely contradicted his political outlook. Hence she repeated her former criticisms of Marx's penchant for Lamarck over Darwin, his blind faith in the benefits brought by the development of the forces of production, and the lack of any evidence at all for the revolutionary potential of the working class. And her conclusion was the same:

> Marx's revolutionary materialism consists in positing, on the one hand, that everything is exclusively regulated by force, and on the other that a day will suddenly come when force will be on the side of the weak. Not that certain ones who were weak will become strong – a change that has always taken place; but that the entire mass of the weak, while continuing to be such, will have force on its side. If the absurdity of this does not immediately strike us, it is because we think that number is a force. But number is a force in the hands of him who disposes of it, not in the hands of those who go to make it up . . . and someone may knock the rider off and jump into the saddle in his place, then get knocked off in his turn; this may be repeated a hundred or a thousand times; the horse will still have to keep on running under the prick of the spur. And if the horse unseats the rider, another will quickly take his place. (OL, p. 193)

Thus there was no 'Marxist doctrine', since the contradiction between his social analysis and his revolutionary politics lay at the heart of his ideas.[4]

Weil's criticisms became harsher when she considered Marx's disciples – with the single exception of Rosa Luxemburg, for whose libertarian revolutionary ideas and personal love of life she had unstinting admiration. With Engels and with Lenin, however, it was a different matter. Weil was one of the very few thinkers in France at the time to make a distinction between the ideas of Marx and those of Engels. In particular she saw no reason to suppose any necessary link between historical materialism and dialectical materialism (P, p. 305). The fact that Marx read and approved of Engels's *Anti-Dühring* only showed that Marx had not taken the time to think enough about the question; otherwise he would have realised that his whole work was 'impregnated with a spirit incompatible with the vulgar materialism of Engels' (OL, p. 32). She quoted in this context Marx's *Theses on Feuerbach* and the *German Ideology* where, according to Marx, the proletarian revolution meant the reversal of subject and object, that is, the reversal of the subordination of the worker to the material conditions of labour and a restitution to the thinking subject of its proper role of domination over matter 'It is not surprising', she continued, 'that the Bolshevik Party whose very organisation has always rested on the subordination of the individual, and which, once in power, was to enslave the worker to the machine every bit as much as capitalism, has adopted as its doctrine the naive materialism of Engels rather than the philosophy of Marx' (OL, p. 33). For she saw a close link between the materialism of Engels and the authoritarian nature of the Bolshevik Party.

However much she appreciated the libertarian Lenin of *State and Revolution* and his economic analyses in *Imperialism*, she had nothing but contempt for his contribution to philosophy as exemplified in his *Materialism and Empirio-criticism* of 1909, which had been published in France in 1928 and received with much enthusiasm in Communist circles. Following Engels, Lenin argued that the products of the human brain were simply the products of nature – photographs, images, reflections of nature to which they therefore corresponded. But, objected Weil, the ideas of an idiot were equally 'products of nature'. Unlike Marx, who had learned from Hegel that, instead of refuting incomplete conceptions, it was better to 'conserve them and go beyond', Lenin posed a sharp dichotomy between idealism and materialism. Moreover his argument for a simplistic form of the latter was political and not philosophical:

> he does not say: such and such a conception distorts the true relationship between man and world: therefore it is reactionary; but, such and such a conception deviates from materialism, leads to idealism, furnishes religion with arguments; it is reactionary, therefore false. (OL, p. 30)

Lenin's espousal of naive materialism was thus too one-sided, too intolerant, too polemical and also destined to eliminate the subjective, active, distinctly human side of politics. This had the dual result of favouring the rise of hidebound sectarianism within the Party and also of eliminating the role of initiative and reflection among those to whom it best belonged – the workers.

Weil's critique of Marx is impressive in its sweep, its remorseless logic, and its passion, recalling the contemporary writing of Berdiaev.[5] She had a far better knowledge of Marx's writings than most contemporary critics. A fairly comprehensive (though rather bad) translation of Marx's writings began to be published by Molitor in 1925. Weil was one of the first to draw a contrast between Marx's early humanist writings and in his later more determinist studies in history and political economy: *Oppression and Liberty* was published before Molitor brought out the *Economic and Philosophical Manuscripts* of 1844, otherwise Weil might have pointed up the contrast even more. But, although she was quick to draw attention to the contradiction she saw in Marx, her own critique was not entirely of a piece. To many, her thought has seemed as functionalist as that of Marx which she so criticised on those grounds.[6] More clearly, for someone whose outlook was as determinist as her own, she sometimes conceded too much to the humanism of the young Marx. The radical mind/matter dualism that she inherited from Descartes through Alain meant that any neo-Hegelian reading of Marx was unintelligible to her. Marx was only acceptable as a determinist.

But there is, of course, much force in her general view that Marx's thought consisted in 'a series of incompatible assertions, some of them well-founded, others not' (OL, p. 153). The hollowness of hopes placed in the prospect of a genuine workers' revolution was an easy target for anyone as clear-sighted as herself – though it was perhaps less easy to adopt such a relentless perspective then than it might be now. By contrast, critiques of Marxism as a materialism which naively supposed that economic forces alone would automatically work to the betterment of society and also the claim that Marxism simply incorporated into its own perspective most of the vices of capitalism – in particular subordination of spiritual and moral values to economic materialism – were commonplaces of the time.[7] Where Weil's approach stands out is in her linking of Marx's materialist conception of history with what she saw as the myth of progress. The very breadth and incisiveness of her critique here involve her in certain over-simplifications: she glosses over the distinction between a mode of production and a technique of production, tends to adopt rather too uncritically Rousseau's view of a pre-industrial golden age, and appears (with hindsight, it is true) to be downright absurd on some of the reasons she gives for the impossibility of capitalist expansion. But she is particularly good on the typically nineteenth-century vice of extrapolation, strikingly contemporary in her warnings of the awful consequences of unchecked consumption of the world's natural energy resources, and as relevant as ever in her questioning of the link between economic progress and liberty: her criticism of Marx's 'naturalistic fallacies' whereby he deduces moral values from the natural phenomenon of productive forces applies equally to non-Marxist theories of technical progress which are just as quick to deny liberty in the name of economic growth.

If Weil was ambivalent about Marx, she was far from ambivalent about Marx's self-proclaimed disciples in the USSR. Stalinist Russia had, and has, no severer critic. And in so far as Marx placed human beings in the service of the historical progress of the forces of production, then 'whatever may be the insult inflicted on Marx's memory by the cult which the Russian oppressors of our time entertain for him, it is not altogether undeserved' (OL, p. 45). Concerning Lenin, too, she grew more critical on her return from Germany. She admired his *State and Revolution* (which she considered his most important work) but considered that it had 'established the principles of a revolution that

failed and was followed immediately by a victorious revolution, but one
that, almost from the start, was in complete contradiction with those
principles, a contradiction that has only become sharper' (P, p. 148).
Lenin had at least retained considerable liberty for writers and artists
and, in his own pronouncements, the virtue of honesty: 'Lenin, when
he retreated, said, "we are retreating". Stalin always says that he is
going forward' (P, pp. 162, 201). Whether Lenin and the Bolsheviks had
any responsibility for the degeneration of the revolution she was not
yet sure. By the end of 1933, she had made up her mind: Lenin's attitude
to philosophy was doubly linked to the growing authoritarianism in
post-revolutionary Russia: firstly, Lenin's insistence on doctrinal purity
subordinated the intellect of individual members to the Party line, and
secondly the adoption of the naive materialism of Engels rather than
the subject–object dialectic of Marx tended to view human beings as
passive rather than active, mere objects whose thoughts were no more
than reflections of existing material states of affairs (OL, pp. 31, 33).
And, on a more strictly political note:

> Lenin abandoned his democratic doctrines to establish the despotism
> of a centralised state apparatus, just like Robespierre, and was in fact
> the precursor of Stalin, as Robespierre was the precursor of Bonaparte.
> The difference is that Lenin, who had moreover prepared this
> domination of the state apparatus well in advance by forging for
> himself a strongly centralised party, deformed his own doctrines
> afterwards to adapt them to the necessities of the hour; and so he
> was not guillotined and serves as an idol for a new state religion.
> (EHP, p. 236)

If Weil's view of Lenin took some time to evolve, her negative view
of the Soviet Union was already formed by the beginning of 1932 and
got progressively harsher, culminating in the denunciation contained in
Perspectives. It cost her a lot of pain: 'It is totally against the grain that I
have been forced to admit the sad reality – particularly about Russia'
(P, p. 202). Her comments on this 'sad reality' are at first formed in the
context of the Soviet Union's foreign policy: in February 1932 she
criticised the USSR for being willing to enter into non-aggression pacts
with capitalist states. For her, this was a reformist attitude which showed
that the Soviet Union had ceased to be a proletarian state. She wrote:
'Let the hopes of all proletarians still be turned towards the USSR. But
let the sincere defenders of the working class in the capitalist countries
beware of putting the revolutionary movement in the hands of the
Russian bureaucracy' (C, p. 70). She was still willing to admit that *if*
Stalin was right and socialism could be built in the Soviet Union alone,
then the policies of the Soviet Union would be justified, but she soon

came to the view that whatever was being built in the Soviet Union, it was not socialism. Stalin's avowed admiration for American 'efficiency' showed that he had abandoned the aims of Marx for those of capitalism at its most developed, which showed that 'the Soviet Union is still a long way from possessing the basis of a working-class culture' (ibid.).

But it was her German experience and its aftermath that really focused Weil's attention on the Soviet Union. The relations of the Soviet Union with Hitler's Germany led her to the view that, at least in its foreign relations,

> the Soviet Union plays the role of a state and *not* of a representative of the proletariat . . . the oppressed proletarians still turn towards her – but in vain. The capitalists, by contrast, have stopped being frightened and horrified by the Soviet Union. No, they would like to be able 'to achieve a form of political life that was as solid in its way', in other words, to be able to bring about, without expropriation of course, a similar concentration of economic and political powers. (P, p. 165; EHP, p. 207)

This concentration of economic and political power she had already analysed at length in the long article entitled *Perspectives* published in *La Révolution Prolétarienne* in the summer of 1933. The Soviet Union, she was convinced, had already achieved the integration of the three bureaucracies of state, industry and trade unions towards which capitalist countries were moving, thus obliterating the achievements of October 1917. Lenin and Trotsky had played a role analagous to that of the large capitalist entrepreneurs in the earlier 'progressive' stage of capitalism, with results just as oppressive for the workers (P, p. 189). There were, of course, historical reasons for the degeneration of the revolution: as with the French Revolution of 1789, the Bolsheviks had had to engage in armed struggle against both internal enemies and the intervention of foreign powers. The result of five years' continuous war had been the emergence of a bureaucratic, military and police dictatorship of which the only socialist or communist component was its name. The testimony of those who had lived in the Soviet Union for years, and even the Soviet press itself (reading between the lines) yielded the inescapable conclusion that 'in no country, not even in Japan, are the working masses more miserable, more oppressed, more humiliated than in Russia' (P, p. 201). To her socialist comrades who argued that it was permissible to sacrifice the interest of the individual to that of the collective, she pointed out that capitalism too could be justified in these terms:

> the capitalist system essentially signifies the sacrifice of the workers, not to the well-being or luxury of the boss but to the growth of

enterprise, that is, the growth of the productive apparatus, the mines, machines, and factories, in short those forms of work of which one can say, and not only for Russia, that 'the community will reap the profit later on'. The only drawback of the system is that, since the worker is simply the slave of the machine, no one reaps the profits in question save the new machines; the work extorted from the worker is always used to develop the productive apparatus, and, due to competition, this process never ends. But it is precisely the same in Russia. Russia is also threatened by the competition of other countries. To defend itself, it must ceaselessly enlarge its productive apparatus . . . There is no difference . . . except that the Russian state possesses not only the means of production and exchange but also a police and an army, and by force can prevent its workers from selling their labour to another boss . . . (P, p. 184)

All states were moving towards a form of organisation that Weil, using a word recently popularised by the Nazis, called 'totalitarian' – a regime where state power saw itself as sovereign in all domains, particularly in intellectual matters: the Soviet Union was simply the state that was furthest advanced down this road.

Weil's view of the Soviet Union was both uncompromising and incisive. Its bleakness recalls Marcuse's account of capitalist society in *One-Dimensional Man*. Although the picture of Stalinist Russia that she paints is familiar to us now, it should not be forgotten that, at the time of her writing, such a clear stand was very rare on the Left, where there was much (understandable) vacillation and even bad faith on the subject of the Soviet Union. Here she was much influenced by Souvarine's pioneering biography of Stalin which he had just completed. Weil much admired the work and sent it to Alain who was one of Gallimard's readers.[8] She was also influenced by *Economie dirigée et socialisation*, by Lucien Laurat, a French Marxist and friend of Souvarine who analysed the Soviet bureaucracy as a new form of class domination which he also saw emerging in Germany and the USA.[9] This tradition was continued in the much more substantial *La Bureaucratisation du Monde* by Bruno Rizzi, first published in 1939, and the more popular versions in Djilas's *The New Class* and Burnham's *The Managerial Revolution*. Weil, for her part, considered that the Soviet experience confirmed the prescient words of Marx on the nefarious consequences of the growing division of labour.[10] But, unlike Marx, she did not attempt to trace any link between the mode of appropriation of surplus and the development of bureaucratic oppression. Her vocabulary is too fluid to produce any theory of this sort: she talks indiscriminately of a bureaucratic class and a social caste, of technocracy and of bureaucracy, and makes of technocracy a new mode of production. The result is a phenomenological account impressive in the power of its description and denunciation, but less strong on analysis and explanation. Weil tends to reduce the whole Stalinist phenomenon to that of a ruling state bureaucracy without enquiring what are the economic, sociological, political and cultural factors which allow such a dominant bureaucracy to emerge. And the obvious weakness of her approach is the inability to distinguish between Stalinism and Fascism or even (at times) Roosevelt's New Deal. The broad concepts of bureaucracy and totalitarianism are not capable of capturing the crucial differences: the Soviet bureaucracy accomplished a process of industrialisation and social homogenisation which transformed Soviet society in a durable fashion – none of which is true of the Nazi Party.

This inclination to lump together the Soviet Union, Nazi Germany and New Deal America, while neglecting differences of ideology and political constitution, had its origin in Weil's linking, in *Oppression and Liberty*, of a view of history which centred on the concept of *power* with the impact of modern technology on social relations. According to her, the struggle for power was the constant theme of human history to date. Her account of the nature and consequences of this struggle recall the theory of elites and their circulation by the Italian sociologists Mosca and Pareto, and the 'iron law of oligarchy' enunciated by Robert Michels. Primitive societies knew no oppression, being subject, instead, to the continuous and inexorable pressure of natural necessity – the search for food, clothing, and shelter. So history might appear to be the passage of humanity from subordination to nature to domination over it. In reality, however, social development had still proceeded under the force of natural necessity, only indirectly with the coming into existence of privilege:

> Certain circumstances, which correspond to stages, no doubt inevitable, in human development, give rise to forces which come between the ordinary man and his own conditions of existence, between the effort and the fruit of the effort, and which are, inherently, the monopoly of a few, owing to the fact that they cannot be shared among all; thenceforward these privileged beings, although they depend, in order to live, on the work of others, hold in their hands the fate of the very people on whom they depend, and equality is destroyed. (OL, p. 63)

In early societies, these privileged individuals would be priests, but the same function was fulfilled later by the military, by technicians, by the organisers of economic exchange, and by those in charge of social co-ordination who were the new power-brokers of modern society.

But this inequality necessitated by the growing division of labour and specialisation of knowledge did not, by itself, account for oppression. Privilege could be at least softened by the resistance of the feeble or a sense of justice among the strong. What turned privilege into a force more brutal than that of natural necessity was the concomitant struggle for power. Using a Hobbesian psychology, Weil saw all holders of power as constrained by a perpetual struggle to retain their power, both over those subordinated to them and against rival power-holders. Moreover these two aspects of struggle for power nourished each other, since success at home increased that abroad and vice versa. Therefore the idea of attaining to any stable power was vain: at the very heart of power was a contradiction which prevented it from every really existing – the only thing that really existed was the race for power, a race which enslaved the strong as well as the weak. It was this process which gave an epic grandeur to works from Homer's *Iliad*, through the historical plays of Shakespeare and Balzac's *Comédie Humaine*, to Marx's account of capitalist accumulation where consumption was seen as a 'necessary evil' as opposed to the main object of reproducing the means of production. If only, Weil continued, the commonplace complaint about the selfishness of human beings were true. The reality was, on the contrary, that people sacrificed themselves and others for things which were, and remained, only *means* to a better life:

> It is this reversal of the relationship between means and end, it is this fundamental folly that accounts for all that is senseless and bloody right through history. Human history is simply the history of the servitude which makes men – oppressors and oppressed alike – the plaything of the instruments of domination they themselves have manufactured, and thus reduces living humanity to being the chattel of inanimate chattels. (OL, p. 69)

And, since this frenzied race for power was governed by laws independent of human volition, the desires of individuals were not in a position to control it. Force, not need, was the basis of human history.[11]

Nevertheless, although power might be beyond human control, Weil did think it had its limits in the nature of things. These limits were not to be found in the development of the productive forces and consequent increase in standard of living: contrary to the views of Marx and of Trotsky, these factors alone were not enough to modify the race for power and its nefarious results. The limits were to be found, rather, firstly in instruments at the disposal of the powerful, instruments which were themselves limited; secondly, power extended only as far as control which itself depended both on the capacity of an individual and on such objective factors as transport and communication; thirdly, power always depended on the ability to produce an economic surplus as a precondition for the power struggle to take place at all; and finally, Weil pointed to a kind of Durkheimian religious cement necessary to give priests, generals, kings or capitalists the unquestionable right to command. Weil believed that the tension between the above limits on power and its inherent drive to expand involved its eventual destruction:

> It extends beyond what it is able to control; it commands over and above what it can impose; it spends in excess of its own resources. Such is the internal contradiction which every oppressive system carries within itself like a seed of death; it is made up of the opposition between the necessarily limited character of the material bases of power and the necessarily unlimited character of the race for power considered as relationship between men. (OL, p. 75)

This destruction might eventuate in a general cataclysm or, more usually, in the rise to power of new elements in society which had long been maturing their rise to dominance as, for example, the barbarians in the later Roman Empire or the French bourgeoisie before 1789.

While admitting that this neo-Machiavellian sketch of the elements necessary for a scientific study of history was woefully inadequate (it is, indeed, too functional and leaves out any strictly political factors), Weil finished her analysis of oppression with a few pessimistic remarks on the modern age. She reiterated her view that freedom from the immediate domination of nature had been exchanged for domination by society. Material progress thus achieved had been bought at the price of subordination to the commands of individuals whose power was necessary to co-ordinate increasingly complicated enterprises. But the further increase of technical progress meant that the system was beyond the co-ordination of individuals: the wheel had now come full circle 'for, in order that this may be so, cooperation has to take place on such a vast scale that the leaders find they have to deal with a mass of affairs which lie utterly beyond their capacity to control' (OL, p. 83). The apparent conclusion was a reversal of Rousseau: man is born enslaved and everywhere servitude is his appropriate condition.

Weil's analysis of power was very general. Its pessimism was reinforced by her concentration on two phenomena which she saw as both increasingly characteristic of her age and increasingly oppressive: the impact of modern technology on social relations and the spread of bureaucracy. Although her discussions of both are too stark and one-sided, they do demonstrate the sharpness of her social vision and her ability to fasten on trends which were only then beginning to be noticed and to offer comments that are still arresting half a century later. Weil's interest in the impact of machinery on the work process dated from her early days in Le Puy. Her visit to the mine at Sardou in March 1931 had made a vivid impression on her.[12] Quoting Marx, she considered capitalism to have created a new form of domination:

> capitalism is defined by the apparent fact that the worker is subjected to the capitalist; in reality, by the fact that the worker is subjected to a material capital made up of tools and raw materials, which the capitalist simply represents. The capitalist regime consists in the fact that the relationship between the worker and the means of work has been reversed; the worker, instead of dominating them, is dominated by them.[13]

But at the same time she departed from Marx's emphasis on property in that 'the oppression of the wage earners, based, to begin with, essentially on the relationship between property and exchange in the days of small work-shops, has become, with the advent of mechanisation, a mere aspect of the relationships involved in the very technique of production' (OL, p. 10). Following Saint-Simon and Proudhon, she put the emphasis on factory organisation and the machines themselves: machines were more basic than social relations and it was this subordination to inert matter that was the most characteristic aspect of capitalism. Thus Marx's great achievement lay, for Weil, in his analysis of the division of labour (OL, p. 161) and not in property relations, since 'the worker's complete subordination to the undertaking and to those who run it is founded on the factory organisation and not on the system of property' (OL, p. 41). And the consequence of this was, of course, that the preconditions for a genuine socialist revolution were much more complex and fundamental than had usually been realised.

It was thus the nature of modern technology that gave rise to the second phenomenon that gave power in contemporary society its peculiarly oppressive form – the spread of bureaucracy and the rise of the 'managerial' society. This was also a theme on which Weil had been reflecting since 1931 when she had written, in an article for *La Révolution Prolétarienne*:

> we can say, to put it briefly, that up to the present mankind has known two principle forms of oppression, the one (slavery or serfdom) exercised in the name of armed force, the other in the name of wealth thus transformed into capital; what we have to determine is whether these are not now being succeeded by a new species of oppression, oppression exercised in the name of management.[14]

By the time she wrote *Oppression and Liberty*, three years later, she had indeed determined the matter: 'The whole of our civilisation is founded on specialisation, which implies the enslavement of those who execute to those who co-ordinate; and on such a basis one can only organise and perfect oppression, not lighten it' (OL, p. 42).[15]

Around the turn of the century the introduction of industrial machinery had indeed produced skilled workers who alone could 'combine thought and action in industrial work, or who took an active and vital part in the carrying-on of the undertaking; the only ones capable of feeling themselves ready to take over one day the responsibility for the whole of economic and political life' (OL, p. 21). But progressive liberalisation and division of labour meant that the skill which remained to the average worker consisted in the execution of a smaller and smaller part of the production process. Past revolutions had depended on the gradual previous establishment of a social and economic base from which to launch their revolutionary project, as the bourgeoisie had done in feudal society: the only group whose accession to power was being prepared in capitalist and socialist societies alike was the new managerial class of technicians – evidently so in the ruling bureaucracy of the USSR, but also in the appropriately named 'Sociétés Anonymes' which had replaced individual capitalists in France.[16] It was this class which increasingly controlled both the state and industry – a new 'power elite' that C. Wright Mills later analysed in the United States.

It was not even the case that the bureaucracy could at least give society a conscious direction. Knowledge had become so complex that no-one could see the whole picture: workers had no technical knowledge; technicians and engineers neither understood the scientific foundations of their technique nor had experience of its application; scientists themselves both lacked practical knowledge and were increasingly impoverished within their own special field. Since none of these groups, let alone any individual, could aspire to any but the most partial knowledge, the function of co-ordinating all these disparate activities was more and more important. But although the indispensable bureaucracy could co-ordinate, it could not control. For the very complexity of the production process which had given rise to bureaucracy meant that, 'as a result, humanity finds itself as much the plaything of the forces of nature, in the new form that technical progress has given them, as it ever was in primitive times; we have had, are having, and will continue to have bitter experience of this' (OL, p. 83). Technology had gone beyond the control of society, whether collectively or individually.[17]

Weil's analysis of oppression past and present has the same sort of strengths and weaknesses that characterise her account of the Soviet Union. It is impressive in its broad sweep and psychosocial subtlety. It has an implacable logic and force reminiscent of Hobbes's *Leviathan*. Her pessimism about the future of capitalism stems from the economic crisis following the 1929 crash and the equation of capitalism with totalitarianism common on the French Left in the 1930s; and her neglect of the political dimension reflects the miserable irrelevance of Third Republic politicians of the time. The essential difficulty is her unexplored conflation of bureaucracy and technocracy. Nevertheless *Oppression and Liberty* is one of the very first books to probe the fact that the main institutional clustering of modern society – capitalist enterprise, production, surveillance, and control of the means of violence – are all run managerially.[18] It thus contains a wealth of ideas later explored in detail, by such writers as Marcuse on the convergence of industrial societies, or Galbraith on the new technostructure, or Wright Mills on the interlocking of military, industrial, and political elites.[19] It contains a kind of agenda for postwar discussion.

Yet Weil did not simply conclude her book with this gloomy analysis of oppression. What of the second element in her title – Liberty? She was sufficiently a disciple of Rousseau to claim that, however miserable the past and the present, 'nothing in the world can prevent human beings from feeling that they are born for liberty' (OL, p. 83). The search for a way to organise production which would not crush body and soul was, for Weil, a personal matter, a clear conception of which was necessary for her to live at peace with herself. For

> if we can manage to conceive in concrete terms the conditions of this liberating organisation, then it only remains for us to exercise, in order to move towards it, all the powers of action, small or great, at our disposal; and if, on the other hand, we realise clearly that the possibility of such a system of production is not even conceivable, we have at least gained the advantage of being able legitimately to resign ourselves to oppression and of ceasing to regard ourselves as accomplices in it because we fail to do anything effective to prevent it. (OL, p. 56)

The first step in this process was to consider the possibility of freedom.

In elaborating her theory of a free society, Weil started with a definition of liberty, considered the obstacles in the way of its realisation, sketched out, by contrast, a Utopia, and finally outlined suggestions for moving some way towards it. Her definition of liberty is severely intellectualist:

> True liberty is not defined by a relationship between desire and its satisfaction, but by a relationship between thought and action; the absolutely free man would be he whose every action proceeded from a preliminary judgement concerning the end which he set himself and the sequence of means suitable for attaining this end. (OL, p. 85)

The abstract model for this was the solution of a mathematical problem. In genuinely free human actions, the peformance of any work whatever would consist in as conscious and as methodical a combination of efforts as can be the combination of numbers by which the solution of a problem is brought about when this solution results from reflection. Man would then have his fate constantly in his own hands; at each moment he would forge the conditions of his own existence by an act of mind. (OL, p. 86)

Thus liberty consisted neither in the relation of desire to satisfaction, nor in some arbitrary existentialist choice, nor some fixed state to be defended as an essential entity; rather it was the struggle of thought against necessity, a struggle in which human beings did not merely submit to external pressure, but used their own material actions to forge an internal representation of that necessity. Of course, this was an ideal and Weil gave an extensive and detailed list of the obstacles in the way of such liberty: the play of chance; the unpredictable nature of the relationship of mind to body; the possible separation between thought and action either because the solution to a problem needed to be worked out before, or in a different sequential order to, its application – of which automated machinery would be a prime example; dependence on other human beings leading to a servitude which infringed the intellectual capacity of both oppressed and oppressors; and, finally, the dependence of individuals on the apparently arbitrary workings of the collectivity.

The ideal basis for society would therefore be:

> a form of material existence wherein only efforts exclusively directed by a clear intelligence would take place, which would imply that each worker himself had to control, without referring to any external rule, not only the adaptation of his efforts to the piece of work to be produced, but also their coordination with the efforts of all the other members of the collectivity. (OL, p. 98)

This implied that the use of any technique must involve methodical thought; that technical culture be sufficiently widespread for all to understand the problems of co-ordinating its different areas; and that, recalling Proudhon's plans for decentralised labour, collectivities be not so large as to escape the compass of the human mind, since, as she put it to her pupils in Roanne, 'it is thought that creates unity'.[20] Such a society would introduce a radical equality since

> there is but one single and identical reason for all men; they only become estranged from and impenetrable to each other when they depart from it; thus a society in which the whole of material existence had as its necessary and sufficient condition that each individual

should exercise his reason could be absolutely clearly understood by each individual mind. (OL, p. 99)

For Weil, the central image of modern society was a production line with workers producing automatically under the constant surveillance of a foreman: the image of her free collectivity is that of a handful of building workers confronted by a particular problem, each thinking of possible solutions and suggesting them to the others and then unanimously adopting the method conceived by one of them who may or may not have had any official authority over the rest.

Such a society, Weil freely admitted, was a Utopia, but it did provide a criterion for judging actually existing societies in that 'the least evil society is that in which the general run of men are most often obliged to think while acting, have the most opportunities for exercising control over collective life as a whole, and enjoy the greatest amount of independence' (OL, p. 103). It is thus her analysis of liberty that enables Weil to give the central place in her Utopia to labour as, to echo the words of Marx, 'life's prime want'.[21] Her conclusion was that 'the most fully human civilisation would be that which had manual labour as its pivot, that in which manual labour constituted the supreme value' (OL, p. 103). Here the emphasis was quite different from the religion of productivity rampant in the Soviet Union and the USA. Science would become practical rather than pure and technologies evolve not simply with a view to their productivity but also so that the labour they involved could be conscious of its own method. This method, in other words, would be in the mind of the worker rather than, as in modern technology, simply in the work itself and nothing to do with the worker.[22] Although this might seem to be a lot to ask – no less than a technical and cultural revolution – Weil finished her sketch of a free society on a positive note. There was at least a strand of contemporary civilisation which pointed in this direction for 'the idea of labour considered as a human value is doubtless the one and only spiritual conquest achieved by the human mind since the miracle of Greece' (OL, p. 106). From Descartes, whose work expressed this happy balance between mind and body, through Goethe's Faust and, above all, Tolstoy, to Proudhon and aspects of Marx and their contemporary disciples, the revolutionary syndicalists, there survived a tradition which put the dignity of productive labour at the centre of all social questions. And productive labour was the one area of life where that correspondence of thought and action which was so essential to Weil's conception of freedom could be realised.[23]

But Weil was not optimistic. *Oppression and Liberty* concluded with a section entitled 'Sketch of Contemporary Social Life', which was the bleakest of contrasts with her picture of a free society. After all, this picture was based to a great extent on the ideas of the very revolutionary syndicalism which she had just rejected. The disproportion between thinking human beings and their social world was continually increasing. Individuals remained passive under the reign of science, machinery and statistics which were co-ordinated by money and bureaucracy rather than any decision of human thought. There was a complete reversal of aims and means and control had passed from thought to things. Even old-fashioned capitalism had broken down under the pressure of excessive advertising, an overblown credit system, wild speculation, and aggressive dumping strategies, with the result that the state – the bureaucratic organisation *par excellence* – had emerged as the co-ordinating centre of the economnic and military interests which overrode all others in a society lurching through its permanent war economy towards totalitarianism which would end in general destruction. There was no prospect of salvation through revolution, for slavery never produced free-thinking individuals, but rather mental passivity:

> As always happens, mental confusion and passivity leave free scope to the imagination. On all hands one is obsessed by a representation of social life which, while differing considerably from one class to another, is always made up of mysteries, occult qualities, myths, idols and monsters; each one thinks that power resides mysteriously in one of the classes to which he has no access, because hardly anybody understands that it resides nowhere, so that the dominant feeling everywhere is that dizzy fear which is always brought about by loss of contact with reality. (OL, p. 118)

Force, as the saying went, might be unable to overcome thought; but now there was no thought to be overcome. The only solution would be the co-operation of all in the systematic decentralisation of society. But the absurd lack of realism in such a proposal was evident to all. The autodestruction of our civilisation was a problem for future generations. As for those of the present day, 'they are perhaps, of all those that have followed each other in the course of human history, the ones which will have had to shoulder the maximum of imaginary responsibilities and the minimum of real ones. Once this situation is fully realized, it leaves a marvellous freedom of mind' (OL, p. 121). Weil's conclusion was that, as far as the individual was concerned, this freedom of mind should be used to investigate what forms of science and technology might be useful for a possible future decentralised society. There was, of course, no guarantee that such researches would be in any way effective. But

> only fanatics are able to set no value on their own existence save to the extent that it serves a collective cause; to react against the subordination of the individual to the collectivity implies that one

begins by refusing to subordinate one's own destiny to the course of history. In order to resolve upon undertaking such an effort of critical analysis, all one needs is to realise that it would enable him who did so to escape the contagion of folly and collective frenzy by reaffirming on his own account, over the head of the social idol, the original pact between the mind and the universe. (OL, p. 124)

Albert Camus, who first edited *Oppression and Liberty*, said of it that 'western social and political thought has not produced anything more penetrating and more prophetic since Marx'.[24] Alain, too, thought it 'of the highest grandeur',[25] though he somewhat regretted its note of polemical pessimism. And, indeed, her firm rejection of both reform and revolution on the grounds that neither could cope with the ever more oppressive nature of modern technology means that her Utopia is in stark contrast to prevailing conceptions. Her concern in writing was that 'we will not have a method for shaking off oppression until the day when we have understood the causes of oppression as clearly as we conceive the conditions of the equilibrium of a stone' (OC, I, p. 329). It is not surprising, therefore, that her conclusions were rather lapidary and that, even in her Utopia, the central idea of work should be based on the conscious but impersonal recognition of necessity.[26] There is a tone of implacability running through *Oppression and Liberty*, a tone which springs from a combination of her extreme individualism with an equally extreme intellectualism. In the sketch of her Utopia, for example, the influence of Rousseau is evident: they both share the idea of a pact of the individual with the universe, the stark contrast of slavery and freedom, the centrality of manual labour and an educational process attuned to it. But Weil goes beyond Rousseau in extending the general will to all details of economic life. And, whereas Rousseau allows the possibility of a citizen's being 'forced to be free', all the acts in Weil's Utopia remain severely individual and are co-ordinated by the application of reason alone – unlike, again, Rousseau who allows much more place for mutual sympathy and moral aspiration as important factors in human interaction. Weil's aim, in other words, is a perfect functional harmony: and this makes it a mirror image of her analysis of oppression which is also based on a functional sociology, but one where the central metaphor is that of a machine and the most striking epithet is 'blind'. She is at pains to stress that her Utopia is directed not only towards an assessment of existing societies but also to changing them, but she has no social theory of political change since she fails to distinguish between the necessary conditions of social existence and those that are changeable, and neglects political factors such as different state forms and the impact of, for example, electoral practices. This means that her analysis of oppression is so undifferentiated as to produce what is effectively a stark contrast between Utopia and dystopia.

Weil continued to value *Oppression and Liberty* even when her interests were more focused on religion and philosophy. When she was trying to leave France in 1940, she wrote to a friend: 'In my brief-case in Paris there is a very long typewritten text . . . it dates from 1934. Nevertheless, it is very pertinent to today. I think it is worthwhile preserving it. I much regret now not having published it' (OL, p. 7). It had certainly cost her an enormous effort. She had begun writing it, as an article for Souvarine's *Critique Sociale*, around Easter 1934. It soon outgrew the dimensions of an article and, in any case, the *Critique Sociale* had ceased publication. She was still at it when the summer vacation began. She wrote to her mother in early July: 'I am at the moment like a woman in labour whose baby has got its head out and then somehow stopped . . . it is painful to extract from yourself, in one go, everything you have in your belly, and it can't be set out in detail in small bits, unfortunately' (P, I, p. 416). August she spent with her parents and brother on holiday at Chambon-sur-Lignon, near Saint-Etienne. Simone Pétrement visited her there: 'I don't remember very much about Simone from this stay, because we saw very little of her, except at meal-times . . . she remained shut up in her room, writing the "Magnum Opus"' (P, p. 210).

In September she returned to the Normandy beach at Reville and the family with whom she had spent some weeks in September 1931, before starting her teaching career at Le Puy. And it was not until November in Paris that she finally completed her long essay and got her mother to type it out. Souvarine offered to try and find a publisher, but she refused. It was while writing it that she had decided to spend some time in factory work, which she viewed as an extension of the study that had been incorporated into *Oppression and Liberty*. Her letter to the Ministry of Education requesting a year's leave from teaching stated: 'I want to prepare a philosophy thesis concerning the relationship of modern technique, the basis of large industry, to the essential aspects of our civilisation – that is, on the one hand, our social organisation and, on the other, our culture' (P, p. 205). This was indeed what she did in the next year, but her research project began on the shop floor and led to a greater change in her outlook than she could have envisaged.

5

Paris: Factory Year

'The feeling of self-respect, such as it has been built up by society, is *destroyed*. It is necessary to forge another one for oneself. Try to hold on to this other kind.' (FW, p. 225)

Given her character and the intellectual and political impasse represented by *Oppression and Liberty*, it seems almost inevitable that Weil should be drawn to some sort of manual labour. In feeling this attraction she was not, of course, alone. Short student forays into the world of the factory were being organised around this time.[1] Five years earlier George Orwell had left his upper-class background to become down and out in Paris and London, and around the same time Dorothy Day settled permanently in the slums of New York's Lower East Side; many idealists of the 1960s' New Left and China's Cultural Revolution followed the same path.[2] Already at the end of her 1933 essay, *Prospects*, Weil had written: 'The only hope of socialism resides in those who have already brought about in themselves, as far as is possible in the society of today, that union between manual and intellectual labour which characterises the society we are aiming at' (OL, p. 23). Her earliest published article had been on the nature of manual labour; and the notion of work was at the centre of her concerns until the end of her life. On graduation she had seriously entertained the possibility of becoming a factory worker; as a student she had spent weeks on end in the summer vacations harvesting wheat or digging potatoes for ten hours a day, and at Auxerre she had again worked intermittently on farms. Now she intended to devote herself to manual labour for a continuous period, and in heavy industry, an experience of which she claimed to have been dreaming for the previous ten years. Instead of bombarding workers with questions to satisfy her relentless and sometimes irritating curiosity, she would now have her own experience to guide her. To her pupils at Roanne in 1934 she had said: 'Human beings are so made that the ones who do the crushing feel nothing; it is the person crushed who feels what is happening. Unless one has placed oneself on the side of the oppressed, to feel with them, one cannot understand.'[3] And, she hoped, this understanding born of experience might help her to come to terms with some of her recently encountered dilemmas. With the pessimistic conclusion of *Oppression and Liberty* she had painted herself into something of a corner politically and hoped that direct immersion in the area of her reflection might show her a way out that a more theoretical approach had failed to reveal.

She was also increasingly dissatisfied with the more personal side of her life: surprising though it seems, she considered laziness to be her main failing, and her close involvement with the emotional difficulties of the Souvarine household led her to think that her own affective reactions were not as balanced and helpful as she would like. Souvarine's companion Colette Peignot had left him abruptly in August 1934 for the surrealist novelist Georges Bataille. This break-up of their relationship shattered Souvarine and Weil's inability (as she saw it) to help a man with whom she was closely involved emotionally further undermined her already low opinion of herself where personal relationships were concerned.[4] Although, as she herself said, she would have sold her soul for friendship, she could not find a friendship that matched her high ideals. She wrote in her notebook:

> Definitely give up the idea that X can be anything more than a shallow friend for you; he belongs, he condemns himself to belong, to the realm of shadows. You have no power to bring him out of the cave – even though you may try, but using what words? In any case, you must forbid yourself to wish it. And further, you must avoid if possible such whole-hearted attachment as you felt for S.G., and without real and fully reciprocal friendship. Those things belong to adolescence. Learn to be alone, if only to be worthy of true friendship. (FLN, p. 12)

She could only conceive of the possibility of physical love if it were devoid of desire. An encounter with an exhibitionist in the Luxembourg Gardens during her adolescence had left her with 'a revulsion and a fortunately invincible feeling of humiliation at being the object of desire' (P, p. 221). It was not, she felt, by chance that she had never been loved. She was frustrated at not being able to find a reciprocal relationship of perfect equality and without any hint of domination and hoped that the enforced and punctual discipline of factory work would enable her to become more responsible in the use of her time and in the use of her emotions.

But however much Weil may have desired factory work, there were bound to be enormous difficulties of which she herself was well aware. Her Saint-Etienne friends, led by Albertine Thévenon, were opposed to her project on the grounds that 'the proletarian condition is one of fact and not of choice, above all as far as concerns mental attitude, that is, the way of looking at life' (CO, p. 10). Moreover she was naturally clumsy, as she had abnormally slow reflexes, her health was never good, and her headaches had been getting worse. Nevertheless she was determined not to start working simply for a 'trial period': she fixed the date of her departure (August 1935) before she began and even declared that she would kill herself if she could not stick it out. Indeed she conceived of her project as a kind of death – whence, in part, her description of *Oppression and Liberty* as her 'Testament'. And to chart her new life Weil started a diary of her factory experiences, a detailed record of the jobs she was required to do, her piece-work rates and wages, and her impressions of her fellow-workers and her own states of mind. The result was, according to Hannah Arendt, 'the only book in the huge literature on the labour question which deals with the problem without prejudice and sentimentality'.[5] At the head of the diary she put the line from Homer, referring to Andromache's future enslavement, 'much against your will, under the pressure of harsh necessity',[6] highlighting the ambivalence she felt towards the whole project.

Weil started her work experience in one of the factories of the Alsthom company, recently formed from the fusion of L'Alsacienne and Thomson. The factory, which employed about 300 workers, specialised in making the electrical equipment for trams and underground railways and was situated on the south-west outskirts of Paris. The managing director of Alsthom was Auguste Detoeuf, a highly cultured and generous man of progressive views, who was particularly interested in social and industrial reforms. He was a friend of Boris Souvarine, who persuaded him to hire Weil. The understanding was that no-one in the factory would know how or why she was there. In fact, Detoeuf did inform the overseer so that he could keep an eye on her. And Weil suspected something of the sort: given the slowness of her work-rate, she would have expected to get the sack without some protection from above (SL, p. 11). She rented a bed-sitter on the top floor of a building a few hundred yards up the rue Lecourbe from the factory and resolved to live strictly on her wages, even going as far as to pay her parents (whom she visited every Sunday) an equivalent restaurant price for the meal.

Although she had originally intended to start her factory year in August, ill-health, concern with Souvarine's difficulties and, above all, the finishing of *Oppression and Liberty* meant that she did not finally begin until 4 December. To the amazement of her fellow-workers, she turned up in a white blouse – a mistake never repeated. As an unskilled novice she was put to work on various disparate jobs such as drilling, metal polishing and riveting before settling down mostly at a stamping-press turning out washers. This required a knack and manual dexterity which she found it difficult to acquire and her diary is full of calculations about meeting the rate on which earning anything above the absolute minimum wage depended. A typical entry in her diary runs:

afternoon – *stamping press*; pieces very difficult to position, at .56 per hundred (600 from 2.30 to 5.15); half an hour to re-set the machine, which was out of adjustment because I had left a piece in the tool. Tired and fed up. Feeling of having been a free being for 24 hours (on Sunday), and of having to re-adapt to slavery. Disgust at being forced to strain and exhaust myself, with the certainty of being bawled out either for being slow or for botching, for the sake of these 56 centimes . . . (FW, pp. 159f)

Conditions were indeed difficult: no breaks for tea or coffee, a time-wasting bureaucracy for which workers had to pay in docked wages, an arbitrariness in the calculation of wages which made the women dependent on the whims of the foremen, freezing washrooms, and the constant possibility of accidents. Weil saw a woman drill operator who had a clump of hair completely torn out by her machine, leaving a large bald patch on her head: she was back at work the same day, although terrified and in much pain. Above all, there was the ever-present threat of instant dissmissal.

Not surprisingly, this 'contact with reality' was in many respects not what she had expected. Although she wrote to Albertine Thévenon at the end of her first week that she was taking to her work 'like a fish to water', extreme fatigue soon deprived her of the capacity for reflection, except at weekends. The first shock of the factory deprived her of any sense of her own dignity: 'All the external reasons (which I had previously thought internal) upon which my sense of personal dignity, my self-respect, was based were radically destroyed within two or three weeks by the daily experience of brutal constraint' (SL, p. 21). She had started work in the factory with a ridiculous amount of goodwill – only to find that this was the last thing needed since the system relied not on goodwill to produce results but on mindless compulsion. Most disturbing of all was that her reaction was not one of revolt but rather of docility – the resigned docility of a beast of burden. She wrote in her diary:

The effect of exhaustion is to make me forget my real reasons for spending time in the factory, and to make it almost impossible for me to overcome the strongest temptation that this life entails: that of not thinking any more, which is the one and only way of not suffering from it . . . we are like horses who hurt themselves as soon as they pull on their bits – and we bow our heads. We even lose consciousness of the situation; we just submit. Any re-awakening of thought is then painful. (FW, p. 171)

Nevertheless Weil did not regret her decision. The combination of loud noises in the factory, although painful, gave her a profound moral joy; and above all there was the feeling that she had 'escaped from a world of abstractions, to find myself among real men – some good and some bad, but with a real goodness or badness' (SL, p. 11).

The Christmas holiday brought her little respite as she suffered from fever and headaches, but on her return she was demoted to less taxing work, placing large copper bobbins inside a furnace to be heated for varying lengths of time. Although the heat was often intolerable and she burned herself badly, Weil found the atmosphere here much better:

> Furnace. Totally different place, although right next to our shop. The foremen never go there. Relaxed and brotherly atmosphere, no more servility or pettiness. The smart young man who serves as a set-up man . . . the welder . . . the young Italian workers with the blond hair . . . my 'fiance' . . . his brother . . . the Italian woman . . . the husky fellow with the mallet . . . at last, a happy workshop. Team-work. (FW, p. 163)

Unfortunately, this happy atmosphere did not last long. She was soon back on the presses and more exhausted than ever. In mid-January, she fell ill with a serious ear infection and was off work for six weeks. She went to her parents' house to convalesce and then to Montana in Switzerland with her mother for three weeks' holiday.

During this break, Weil reflected on the state of mind that the factory had induced in her – 'that I was born to wait for, and receive, and carry out orders – that I never had done and never would do anything else' (SL, p. 22). She also took a resolution.

> I swore to myself that I would go on enduring the life until the day when I was able to pull myself together in spite of it. And I kept my word. Slowly and painfully, in and through slavery, I re-conquered the sense of my human dignity – a sense which relied, this time, upon nothing outside myself and was accompanied always by the knowledge that I possessed no right to anything, and that any moment free from humiliation and suffering should be accepted as a favour, as merely a lucky chance. (Ibid.)

But however great her resolution, two weeks more of being moved from machine to machine, trying to keep up the rate of production, and increasing headaches made her actually glad to be laid off for a week in the middle of March.

One source of comfort (but also occasionally for dismay) was the contact she had with her fellow-workers. This was particularly so when she was working at the furnace: each time she winced from the heat on her face the welder working opposite would look at her with a 'sad smile of fraternal sympathy' which did her 'untold good' (SL, p. 21).

And when, on the first evening there, she was eventually so tired that she could not perform the crucial operation of lowering the furnace damper, a coppersmith jumped up and did it for her. 'What gratitude', she wrote in her diary, 'you feel at such moments!' (FW, p. 162). A smile or the joking of her comrades in the wash-room could make her forget her fatigue. Nevertheless, although she felt that her fellow-workers were 'nice, very nice', she complained to Albertine Thévenon that, 'as for real fraternity, I have felt hardly any' (SL, p. 16). She was also struck by the atomisation of the workers and their lack of any political consciousness:

> since I have been here not *one single time* have I heard anyone talk about social problems, neither about the trade unions nor about the parties . . . I asked a worker if there really was a trade union section in the factory; all I got in reply was a shrug of his shoulders and a knowing smile . . . solidarity is largely lacking. (P, p. 235)

And this, as she remarked, was in a factory whose management had an exceptionally liberal reputation.

At the beginning of April, Weil lost her job at Alsthom. The reasons for her leaving are not clear. She may have wanted to find work for herself this time, but it rather looks from her diary as though the management wanted her out, as her productivity was well below average. She had also cut her hand badly on the pressing machines, which may have been the immediate occasion for her leaving. In any case, the enforced leisure of unemployment gave Weil time to reflect on her experiences at Alsthom, which had had a profound effect on her after the first few weeks. As she wrote to her friend Albertine, 'it is not that it has changed one or other of my ideas (on the contrary, it has confirmed many of them), but infinitely more – it has changed my whole view of things, even my very feeling about life. I shall know joy again in the future, but there is a certain lightness of heart which, it seems to me, will never again be possible' (SL, p. 15). What she found oppressive was the enforced combination of repetitive gesture and piece-work whereby 'one's attention has nothing worthy to engage it, but on the contrary is constrained to fix itself, second by second, upon the same trivial problem, with only such variants as speeding up your output from six minutes to five for 50 pieces, or something of that sort' (ibid.). All this only confirmed her already jaundiced view of mainstream Marxist approaches:

> When I think that the great Bolshevik leaders proposed to create a *free* working class and that doubtless none of them – certainly not Trotsky, and I don't think Lenin either – had ever set foot inside a

factory, so that they hadn't the faintest idea of the real conditions which make servitude or freedom for the workers – well, politics appears to me a sinister farce. (SL, p. 15)

She had expected that her work experience would arouse in her feelings of rebellion. On the contrary, she was surprised, and dismayed, to note the docility and resignation which she soon developed. The system provided no ready object for her irritation and, more immediately, any feeling of revolt or anger would be literally counter-productive and lead to a lessening of the work-rhythm and, ultimately, to starvation. The result was an abiding feeling of profound humiliation. She was a thorough intellectual – 'nothing in my past life has prepared me for this sort of effort' – and found particularly gruelling the inability to sustain 'this mental void inside me, this absence of thought indispensable to the slaves of a modern machine' (P, p. 234). For her, thought was at the core of her being, but – except, with difficulty, at weekends – thought was precisely what the imperatives of her chosen life least required.

   Nevertheless the oppressive circumstances could not prevent Weil from reflecting on the main purpose of her factory work – to get a clear idea of the organisational principles behind it. She made extensive notes on the factory hierarchy, and the origins, personalities and attitudes of her fellow-workers. But it was the machines themselves which really attracted and fascinated her, the machines about whose 'powerful beauty' she had written as a student (OC, I, p. 312). What was wrong in the factory system, she thought, stemmed from a dual mystery confronting the worker: firstly, the machine itself was a mystery for the worker who did not understand how it functioned: 'nothing is *less* instructive than a machine' (FW, p. 193). And, secondly, the manufacturing process was a mystery in that workers did not understand the contribution of their own work to the final product. The remedies that occurred to her were threefold. Firstly, there was the simple effort to make sure that there were enough stools, boxes, oil-cans and so on to make the work itself less of a burden, to regularise the arbitrary time-keeping, and to give new workers some systematic form of training. Secondly, Weil considered that the lay-out of the factory should be changed so as to give every worker a view of the whole production process and lessen the division of labour. This would also reduce the tendency implicit in Taylor's system of 'scientific management' to reduce workers as much as possible to the status of machines. Thirdly, Weil wanted to reintroduce into work the capacity for thought: 'whatever degrades the intelligence degrades the whole human being' (SL, p. 44). In her diary she reminded herself never to forget that 'in these rough beings I always found that generosity of heart and aptitude for general ideas were directly proportional to one another' (FW, p. 226). This only confirmed the view that she had expressed so forcefully during her year at Le Puy that education held the key to fundamental social change.

The time for these reflections was soon cut short by the necessity of looking for another job. Now she was on her own with no tame managing director to open the door for her; and, with the unemployment rate approaching 20 per cent, finding work was no easy matter. For two days she tramped around the western suburbs of Paris without success. On the third day, she queued up with two metal fitters:

> all morning, extraordinarily free and easy conversation among the three of us, on a plane above the miseries of existence that are the dominant preoccupation of slaves, especially the women. After Alsthom, what a relief! Total comradeship. For the first time in my life, really. No barrier at all, either in the difference of class (since that has been removed) or in the difference of sex. Miraculous. (FW, pp. 199f)

She soon found a job at the factory of J-J. Carnaud et Forges de Basse-Indre at Boulogne-Billancourt, not far from where she was living. She had heard the Forges de Basse-Indre spoken of as a sympathetic little establishment and was at first grateful that it had deigned to employ her. But disillusion followed swiftly. Queueing up to wait for doors to open, she was struck by the dejected look of the women waiting and learned that most of them were only there as a last resort, the factory being notorious for its frantic pace, numerous accidents and ruthless sackings. These opinions were borne out by the fact that the workers were kept waiting, even in days of pouring rain, outside an open door which they could only enter when the bell summoning them to work was finally rung. This memory of an unprotesting herd of women waiting in the rain before an open door remained firmly implanted in Weil's mind and she returned to it frequently in her later writings (FW, p. 202; CO, pp. 163, 281).

As she wrote to Souvarine, the Carnaud factory proved to be 'a fairly large establishment and, above all, a foul, a very foul establishment. And in that foul establishment there is one particularly loathsome workshop: it is mine' (SL, p. 17). She was put at a press stamping out metal pieces in a suffocating atmosphere made worse by the odours of paints and varnishes. She only managed to do four hundred pieces an hour and was told by the foreman: 'If you don't do 800, I won't keep you. If you do 800 in the 2 hrs. that are left, I will *perhaps consent* to keep you. There are some who do 1,200' (FW, p. 201). Seething with rage, she managed to get up to 600 and was told that they would probably consent to keep her on, but that she would have to work faster. In her diary she recorded her impressions of the day:

> In spite of my fatigue, I am so in need of fresh air that I go on foot as far as the Seine; there I sit on the bank, on a stone, gloomy, exhausted, my heart gripped by impotent rage, feeling drained of all my vital substance; I wonder if, in the event that I were condemned to live this life, I would be able to cross the Seine every day without some day throwing myself in.[7]

The next day, however, was easier. The foreman took her off the machine (although she got a bawling-out for not standing immediately to attention when told to stop work) and soon she found herself in a 'quiet little corner' with workers who took things much easier: 'I should never have believed that there could be such differences between two corners of the same place' (SL, p. 19). Nevertheless her impressions of the Carnaud factory confirmed those of Alsthom. She was struck again by the separation of the sexes and the contempt of the men for the women. And, as at Alsthom, there was no protest or reaction from the workers. 'In this kind of life', she wrote, 'those who suffer aren't able to complain. They would be misunderstood by others, perhaps laughed at by those who are not suffering, thought of a tiresome by those who, suffering themselves, have quite enough suffering of their own. Everywhere the same callousness' (FW, p. 203). Anyone with their heart in the right place, she thought, would have to weep tears of blood to find themselves swept into such a vortex. But she did not feel tempted to give up, even when at the limit of her endurance. She explained to Souvarine in words that foreshadow her later mystical approach: 'Because I don't feel the suffering as mine, I feel it as the workers' suffering; and whether I personally suffer it or not seems to me a detail of almost no importance. Thus the desire to know and understand easily prevails' (SL, p. 18). The work at Basse-Indre was probably the hardest she had to cope with: her diary for the four weeks she spent there is blank. On 7 May she was abruptly dismissed. She asked for an explanation but was told she had no right to one. The next week she spent in a state of dismal prostration reinforced by continual headaches.

For a second time Weil went looking for work. She also knew it was to be the last time: on 31 May she applied to the Ministry of Education for a post as teacher of philosophy for the next academic year, requesting that she be placed in a town near Paris. But meanwhile she was finding it impossible to get employment. For three weeks she traipsed daily from factory to factory, casting her net ever wider, chatting with her fellow unemployed and recording their conversations in her diary. During the third week she decided to spend only F3·50 a day, including transportation. 'Hard', she wrote in her diary, 'to walk like this when you are not eating . . . hunger becomes a permanent feeling. Is this feeling more painful than working and eating, or less so? Unresolved question . . . Yes, more painful, on the whole' (FW, p. 205). On 5 June she finally found a job at Renault. She had been there at least twice before but this time decided to embellish her appearance. She had become aware that employers looked over their potential recruits like horses and had heard that, particularly at Renault, the man in charge of hiring went for the prettier women. She persuaded Simone Pétrement to help her put on some lipstick and rose-coloured make-up on her cheeks. According to Pétrement, '. . . she was transformed. One saw how she could have looked if she had taken the slightest trouble to fix herself up' (P, p. 240). She was hired immediately.

However depressing the long search for work had been, she found the actual prospect of it even more distressing:

> Terrible emotional state, the day I was hired, and the next day setting out to confront the unknown; in the Metro early in the morning (I arrive at 6.45), extremely apprehensive, to the point of being physically ill. I see people are looking at me; I must be very pale. If ever I have known fear, it is today. I imagine a shop with presses, a ten-hour day, brutal foremen, cut fingers, heat, headaches . . . The woman who used to work on presses whom I talked with in the hiring office didn't help to raise my spirits. When I arrive at Shop 21, I feel my will grow weak. (FW, p. 205)

Fortunately, she was not put on presses but was assigned to a 2.30–10.00 p.m. shift running a milling machine. For the first two weeks, she was less tired than she had expected, but then the extreme fatigue returned: 'Going to the shop is extremely painful; each step an effort (morally; returning, it's a physical effort). Am in that half dazed state in which I am the victim destined for any harsh blow' (FW, p. 207). The harsh blow did indeed come, in that she milled the end of her thumb and had to visit the infirmary. There was a return of the feeling that she had so often experienced at Alsthom of just sticking it out one day at a time. She began to return for the night more frequently to her parents' house. Her original contract had been for a month's trial period and she felt that she would not be able to hold on beyond its end. Then there was the continual and inexorable pressure to keep up the pace of production, aggravated by competition among the workers for the few available boxes in which to put the finished pieces; also the dependency on the unreliable set-up men to repair the machines which constantly needed attention.

But she *was* kept on for a second month and things improved slightly in spite of her suffering from eczema and an abscess in her hand which had been lacerated by metal shavings. There was one disastrous incident when she broke a tooth in her saw while day-dreaming about Trotsky's youth and his choice between Populism and Marxism: but she scored an exhilarating victory when she finally managed to set up and centre her machine on her own. She also experienced occasional feelings of joy and even euphoria. But even during her last days the feelings of distress did not desert her: 'Monday, in a bad way. Going to work infinitely more painful than I would have thought. The days seem an eternity to me . . . prostration, bitterness and stupefying work, disgust. Fear also, all time of the cutter coming loose' (FW, p. 223). And the impression of slavery never left her. This feeling deepened during the two months at Renault. One morning, when getting on the bus, she asked herself:

> how is it that I, a slave, can get on this bus and ride in it for my twelve sous just like anyone else? What an extraordinary favour! If someone brutally ordered me to get off, telling me that such comfortable forms of transportation are not for me, that I have to go on foot, I think that would seem completely natural to me. Slavery has made me entirely lose the feeling of having any rights. It appears to me to be a favour when I have a few moments in which I have nothing to bear in the way of human brutality. These moments are like smiles from heaven, a gift of chance. Let's hope that I will stay in this state of mind, which is so reasonable. (FW, p. 211)

Whereas at Alsthom she had rebelled at least on Sundays, her time at Renault led her to develop a more stoical attitude.

This time of trial came to an end in August. Weil had decided long beforehand to leave at the end of July but she worked on well into August: her Works Certificate says that she stopped on 22 August, though she may well have left as early as the ninth. Soon afterwards she went with her parents on a month's cruise around Spain and Portugal – 'Only the sea can wash away from me all this accumulated exhaustion' (P, p. 248). It was here that she had the first of what she later called her 'contacts with Catholicism that really counted' (WG, p. 19). While in Portugal she set off alone to walk to the little seaside village of Povoa do Varzim on the feast of Our Lady of the Seven Sorrows.

> It was evening and there was a full moon. The wives of the fishermen were going in procession to make a tour of all the ships, carrying candles and singing what must certainly be very ancient hymns of a

heart-rending sadness. Nothing can give any idea of it. I have never heard anything so poignant unless it were the song of the boatman on the Volga. There the conviction was suddenly borne in upon me that Christianity is pre-eminently the religion of slaves, that slaves cannot help belonging to it, and I among others. (WG, p. 20)

In her later years she was to elaborate this into a profound religious metaphysic. For the moment, however, she mentioned it to no-one and returned at the end of September to resume life as a philosophy teacher.

Weil was anxious to take stock of her years' factory work and to come to some conclusions. 'What have I gained from this experience?' was the question she put to herself at the end of her diary. Her immediate anwer was that she had had a 'direct contact with life' which had given her 'the feeling that I do not possess any right whatever of any kind'. And this feeling in turn had enabled her to acquire 'the ability to be morally self-sufficient, to live in this state of constant latent humiliation without feeling humiliated in my own eyes' (FW, p. 225). Indeed the dialectic of humiliation and self-respect is the central theme of her diary. Later, she summed up the two main lessons that she had learned from her experience as, firstly, 'the bitterest and most unexpected, that oppression, beyond a certain degree of intensity, does not engender revolt but, on the contrary, an almost irresistible tendency to the most complete submission'; and, secondly, that 'humanity is divided into two categories – the people who count for something and the people who count for nothing' (SL, p. 35). It was not, she insisted, that she was unaware of the necessity for discipline and obedience in any type of organised manual labour. But she felt that the kind of obedience that she had been required to practise was directly humiliating for several reasons: the repetitive nature of the work meant that her attention was limited to a few seconds at a time and she had no control over future time; the dependency on the orders of the foremen induced a state of almost constant apprehension; the factory discipline relied on the sordid motives of money and fear. 'I have sometimes thought', she wrote, 'it would be better to be subdued to that sort of obedience by external compulsion, such as the whip, rather than have to subdue oneself to it by repressing all that is best in oneself' (SL, p. 56). The self-hatred induced by these forms of obedience led to a kind of despair which concealed a rage below its surface, a rage which was liable to break out in domestic or social violence. The fact that the humiliation of workers was more important to them than their suffering also had ominous lessons for contemporary politics. Hitler had understood better than most forms of Marxist materialism how to offer only too attractive remedies to the humiliated: not the alleviation of their suffering but a pride based on the appeal of force.

Weil had also learned important things about herself. Whereas in *Oppression and Liberty* she had confidently affirmed that 'nothing on earth can stop man from feeling himself born for liberty. Never, whatever may happen, can he accept servitude; for he is a thinking creature' (OL, p. 83), she now realised that 'an obviously inexorable and invincible form of oppression does not engender revolt as an immediate reaction, but submission' (FW, p. 226). After the first few weeks of factory work she realised that to preserve her freedom and dignity in any form would be a terrible struggle:

> It means a daily struggle with oneself, a perpetual self-mutilation and sense of humiliation, and prolonged and exhausting moral suffering: for all the time one must be abasing oneself to satisfy the demands of industrial production and then reacting, so as not to lose one's self-respect, and so on indefinitely. (SL, pp. 38f)

She had succeeded in her resolution to forge for herself an inner self-respect. But the effect on her psyche was profound and it left an indelible mark:

> After my year in the factory . . . I was, as it were, in pieces, body and soul. The contact with affliction had killed my youth . . . What I went through there marked me in so lasting a manner that still today when any human being, whoever he may be and in whatever circumstances, speaks to me without brutality, I cannot help having the impression that there must be a mistake and that unfortunately the mistake will in all probability disappear. There I received the mark of slavery . . . (WG, p. 33)

But she never regretted her factory experience: it enabled her to test herself, to experience in the most direct manner possible things that she had previously been able only to imagine. The result was that she was 'morally hardened' (SL, p. 20). When she attended a meeting of the *Révolution Prolétarienne* group towards the end of her time at Renault, her old friend Louzon did not recognise her. 'You look tougher', he said (FW, p. 212). At the same time, her personality softened somewhat. Her friends were relieved to find that, while she could be as intransigent as ever, the former stridency and intolerance were gone.

But Weil felt that what she had learned at Alsthom, Carnaud and Renault was not only personal. It is true that her immediate impressions were, in good part, highly relative. She entered factory work at the worst time of the Depression and as a member of the most oppressed group: unskilled female workers. In poor health, naturally maladroit, and with her extreme sensitivity in contact with others, she undoubtedly suffered more than most of her fellow-workers. And, after all, she was only there for a period. But, she insisted, she had had advantages to counter-balance her sensitivity and physical weakness. She had also systematically eliminated anything that could remind her that her experience was only a sort of experiment. Most importantly, her impressions were confirmed by those of her fellow-workers. For anyone who had spent the time in the factory that she had, these impressions were incontestable, for she had seen her own feelings echoed in the eyes, the words and the gestures of her fellow-workers (cf. CO, pp. 252f). Since, therefore, her impressions were not peculiar to her, she felt that there were general lessons to be learned from her experience and she was at pains to try to use it to suggest plans for a reform of the factory system. These suggestions were presented in a fragmentary form in her diary, in subsequent letters when she reflected on her experience, and in later articles. She also sketched out, in a long letter to Alain, a research programme for adapting physics and mathematics to the needs of the work-place.

Weil had formulated the problem of work in industrial society at the end of her diary: 'Objective conditions that allow men to be (1) nice guys and (2) productive' (FW, p. 225). A factory, she thought, should be 'a place where one makes a hard and painful, but nevertheless joyful, contact with real life' (SL, p. 20), with relationships of 'complete co-operation' (SL, p. 41) as the ideal. As steps towards this she suggested that workers could be given the opportunity to acquire a knowledge of the whole production process, and thus appreciate their part in the whole rather than, as at present, expanding their energies in a sort of void. A knowledge of the necessity of their work would make it less painful. Regular tours of the factory in works time and the encouragement of visits by families would enhance the feeling of a collective task in which the role of each individual was fully appreciated. Automation, also, presented great opportunities. Weil considered some predictions of the lessening of the working day to be ridiculously exaggerated and 'to make people a mass of idlers who are slaves two hours a day is not desirable even if it were possible'.[8] Nevertheless the advance of technology could remove the repetition from much work and leave the worker free for more thought-demanding tasks. In addition, autonomy at the individual and workshop level should be encouraged so that workers could talk in the same proprietorial way about their work-place as a cook did about 'my kitchen'. The result of this would be that workers would be able to envisage what they would be doing over the next week or two and even plan the order of execution. They would thus gain some control over their time-table, both in the short and in the long term, rather than have their attention confined to each atomised instant.[9]

Nationalisation did not form part of Weil's proposals. It was in the factories themselves that solutions were to be found. And here her principal concern was to fight the growing influence of Taylorism. The first industrial revolution had consisted in the scientific management of matter; the second, whose apostle was Taylor, consisted in the scientific management of human beings. Mindlessness on the part of the workers was the order of the day: the lack of any visible *product* meant that the worker has the impression of being a bit like a child whose mother, to keep it quiet, gives it beads to string with a promise of sweets as a reward (CO, p. 113). Talk of 'rationalisation' masked a system in which workers were trained like dogs, used like electricity, and valued much less than their machines. Taylor himself was no more than a *petit-bourgeois* foreman whose main aim had been to give the bosses the means of controlling the rhythm of work, a system carried even further by Henry Ford and chain production. It was significant that the triumph of Taylor was in part due to the exigencies of war, his methods being much more suitable for producing weapons and luxury goods than such necessities as food. Continually, Weil warned workers against being bamboozled by 'experts', the best remedy against which was to acquire some scientific knowledge for themselves.

Almost all of Weil's suggestions about increased autonomy and responsibility for workers as individuals or groups have been echoed in more recent studies by sociologists of work. And her points about Taylorised mass production often pandering to the most futile desires and resulting in massive de-skilling are well taken. Indeed they are even more relevant today when, even within areas of professional employment, control over the work process is diminishing.[10] But she wished to go further by placing the whole concept of work in a wider context so that it became one of the centres of her world-view. 'Bourgeois society' she wrote 'is infected by a monomania; the monomania of accounting. For it, the only thing that has value is what can be counted in francs and centimes. It never hesitates to sacrifice human life to numbers which look well on paper, a national budget or industrial accounting figures' (CO, pp. 216f).

But the problem went even deeper than questions of exploitation. It lay in the nature of modern technology itself. The advance of this technology meant that the optimistic master/slave dialectic of Hegel no longer operated: whereas before slavery lay in the circumstances, which could be character-building, now it lay in the work itself. A stoic attitude to suffering and privation was no longer possible to the modern worker who, given the rapidity and mechanical nature of movements required, could only find stimulation in fear and the need for money. Any viable solution must include the involvement of the intellect in the work process, the authority of human beings over things and not over other human beings, with machines dealing with anything that did not involve the translation of thought into action. The real enemy was thus the division of labour whereby one person made the parts and another thought how to put them together. 'Work', as she claimed, 'should tend, to the full extent that it is materially possible, to be an education. And what would one think of a class in which there were radically different exercises for the good pupils and the bad?' (SL, p. 34). Of course there were natural inequalities; but 'social organisation can be called good morally speaking, insofar as it tends to lessen them (by levelling up, and not down, of course), and bad insofar as it tends to accentuate them, and odious if it creates water-tight compartments' (ibid.). The current alienation of workers stemmed from the way in which this division of labour was systematically embodied in the structure of the factory where the link between mystery and domination paralleled that in society:

> Cooperation, understanding, mutual appreciation in work are the monopoly of higher spheres. At the level of the worker, the relation-ships established between the different jobs, the different functions, are relationships between things and not between human beings. The parts circulate with their labels, the indication of their name, their shape, and their material; you could almost believe that it is they who are the people, and the workers who are the interchangeable parts. (CO, p. 247)

Weil insisted that she was not (like William Morris, for example) looking backwards to a golden age, and referred to the 'sterile contrast between the factory worker and the artisan'.[11] She was not opposed to factories and modern production as such; but she did wish to see the same union between worker and machine as Conrad described between skilled sailor and boat. While admitting that it was 'rather vague', she sketched out her vision as follows:

> I imagine a de-centralised economy where our industrial prisons would be replaced by workshops scattered all over the place. In these workshops there would be extremely flexible automated machinery which would be able to satisfy to a large extent the industrial needs of the region. The workers would be very highly qualified and spend most of their time in supervision. The distance between worker and engineer would tend to disappear in that both jobs could perhaps be done by the same person.[12]

In all her suggestions for reform Weil had in mind the distinction between work and labour later elaborated by Hannah Arendt:[12] she wished above all to restore to the worker the possibility of intellectual activity that modern machinery had taken away.

Many would claim that the technological advances of the last 50 years have made Weil's proposals for industrial reform no less relevant today. The fact that working conditions have improved considerably in advanced capitalist countries does little to meet her requirements. For Weil was no superficial reformer: she wished 'to change the nature of the stimulants of work, to diminish or abolish the causes of disgust, to transform the relationship of each worker to the functioning of the factory, the relation of the worker to the machine, and the way time passes in work' (CO, p. 253). The advent of Taylor and Ford had led to the de-skilling and atomisation of workers. But Weil hoped that increases in automation might mean that the impact of the industrial revolution would prove only an unfortunate interlude between the artisan labour of the past and the more decentralised and autonomous labour of the future. At the same time, however, she saw great dangers in automation. It threatened to produce individuals whose abundant free time would be devoted to indulging their aggressive instincts; to foster a consumer-led increase in production based on artificial needs and all sorts of superfluity; and, above all, to result in the removal of thought from individuals and its crystallisation in impersonal processes whose blind domination would oppress modern human beings just as harshly as the forces of nature oppressed primitive peoples. Nevertheless Weil maintained not only that automation could, and did, relieve people of painful tasks but also that it *could*, given sufficient imagination and will, afford the technical basis for the kind of smaller, decentralised, highly participatory work units that she envisaged.[14] It has to be recognised, however, that the way in which automation has been exploited to date has not been along these lines, and that Weil's ambivalence has been more than justified.[15]

Weil's factory experience consummated her farewell to revolutionary politics. One important lesson she had learned at Alsthom was that the kind of inexorable oppression exercised by the factory produced submission rather than revolt. She had, therefore, very sadly become convinced that 'the capacity of the French working class not only for revolution but for any action at all is almost nil. I think it is only the bourgeois who could have any illusion in this matter' (SL, p. 35). She still longed with all her heart for 'the most radical possible transformation of the present regime in the direction of a greater equality in the relations of power' (SL, p. 40), but did not think that a revolution, as currently understood, could bring this about. She explained that

this consideration, however, does not put me *against* the parties described as revolutionary. Because every significant political group nowadays tends equally towards accentuating oppression and getting all the instruments of power into the hands of the state; some of them call this process working-class revolution, some call it fascism, and some call it the organisation of national defence. Whatever the slogan, two factors always predominate: one of them is the subordination and dependence which are implied in modern forms of technique and economic organisation; and the other is war. All those who favour the increase of 'rationalisation', on the one hand, and preparation for war, on the other, are the same in my eyes; and they include everybody. (SL, p. 40)

Her previous talk of class struggle and direct action was replaced by the notion of class collaboration and the tactic of the lesser evil. While not abandoning her ideas for a fundamental restructuring of society, her immediate views on working-class politics became decidedly reformist. The concept of revolution kept a certain validity for her as an ideal, but her hope was that

> those who despise reforms as cowardly and ineffective will come to see that it is more important to change things than words; while those who hate reforms as utopian and dangerous will realise that they believe in an illusory fatalism, and that the fears, the exhaustion and the despair are perhaps not as indispensable to social order as they imagine. (CO, p. 233)

The abandonment of any revolutionary perspective did not lead Weil to be any less active. After sailing round Spain with her parents, she took up the teaching post she had requested while still working at Renault. But instead of one of the industrial towns near Paris, for which she had specifically asked, she was assigned to the lycée at Bourges, a quiet provincial town 160 miles south of Paris. Accompanied once again by her mother, she found lodgings with Alice Angrand, a teacher of English at one of the town's other schools, before moving after a term into a tiny attic room of her own. She liked Bourges better than the other provincial towns in which she had taught and her relations with the school authorities were relatively good. She taught philosophy, with Greek as a subsidiary subject. In her lessons she used more classical and contemporary novels than philosophical texts and drew a lot on her factory experience for examples, concentrating more on psychology and ethics than on metaphysics. Her tone, too, was less one of indignation than of muted pity. Her pupils were less receptive to her ideas than in previous years but at least respected her genuineness. The inspector was fairly critical:

the general appearance of Mlle. Weil is none too distinguished and by all present accounts shows a lack of grooming. This young teacher fulfills her obligations satisfactorily: the results would be better were the pupils to take part more fully in the class-work and if the lectures were presented more clearly and in a less monotonous tone of voice. In the town, Mlle. Weil's attitude has provoked astonishment. (C, p. 117)

The results of the *baccalauréat*, at least, were satisfactory: nine out of her twelve pupils passed.

The headmistress complained that Weil neglected her administrative duties and spent little time with her colleagues. In fact, she was much more occupied in trying to renew her contacts with the working class. These efforts were not particularly fruitful. 'She lunched', it is reported, 'in October at the "fixed-price" restaurant where she could talk to the waitresses: they told her that they earned 300 francs per month and lacked nothing; they were uninterested in her arguments about the hardships of the worker. Often she invited workers to share her lunch, but none of them shared her ideas or even understood them' (C, p. 122). Weil was also keen to get to know the life of farm-workers at first hand. On one occasion, when out for a walk in the country, she asked a peasant to let her drive his plough: he was furious when she overturned it immediately. More extended – but no more successful – was her contact with the Belleville family, parents of a pupil of Mme. Coulomb, one of her colleagues, who had a small-holding at Caron de Gron to the east of Bourges. Having obtained their agreement for her to come and work on an occasional basis, she arrived unannounced (so as not, she said, to disturb the routine of the house) early one March morning and immediately began to lift beetroots, prepare cows' fodder, heap up manure, and even to try to milk the cows. And always questions, questions about their life-style, how they managed, their returns, their desires. Weil wanted to live with the family and proposed to pay them rent. But when she made it clear that she would wish to go out at any time of the day or night and mingle with the peasants, they refused: 'Anyone who knew the country would know that that was not possible: after she left, life would have been impossible for us' (C, p. 128). A little later, even the daily visits became too much. Mme. Belleville came to see Coulomb at Bourges and, after much beating about the bush, declared that she could not have Mlle. Weil any more: she never washed her hands before milking the cows; she never changed her clothes; and, worst of all, her constant lectures about the troubles of the world were giving them a nervous breakdown. Later she wrote:

my husband and I used to say: the poor young girl, so much study has driven her out of her wits; and we were sorry for her; while really it was we who were out of our depth. But what could we do? All the intellectuals we knew put barriers between themselves and the peasants. Simone Weil threw down these barriers and put herself at our level. (Ibid.)

But it was to the factory that Weil still really felt drawn. She was worried that her abrupt change of life-style might in some way corrupt her and tried to maintain much of her previous year's way of life. Although her year of industrial labour had left an 'indelible bitterness' in her heart, she kept alive the prospect of resuming factory work. Alice Angrand's cousin owned a factory nearby which made wood-working machinery and Weil obtained permission to spend an afternoon visiting it. The father of one of her own pupils owned a factory at Rosières. It employed nearly a thousand workers, was situated in open countryside, and run on paternalist welfare lines with housing, health services and schooling provided by the management. Weil struck up an acquaintance with the technical director of the factory, Monsieur Bernard, and canvassed with him the possibility of her being taken on as a shop-floor worker, wishing, as she put it, 'to collaborate, from below, in the same business, with the man who directs it' (SL, p. 32). Bernard had introduced innovations inspired by a recent visit to America, including the publication of an in-house newspaper entitled *Entre Nous* (Between Ourselves). Weil asked if she might write an article for it. She entitled her piece 'An Appeal to the Workers at Rosières'. It was addressed to her 'Dear unknown friends who are toiling in the Rosières workshops', and invited them to send her, for inclusion in the paper and under guarantee of complete anonymity, their feelings about their work, grievances, suggestions for improvement and so on. Such public self-expression for the workers would, she hoped, raise their morale and also make the management better informed.

Not surprisingly, Bernard rejected her article, accusing her of stirring up a spirit of class antagonism, and also gave her to understand that there was no prospect of her being employed in the factory. Weil defended herself:

I have absolutely no desire to stir up a spirit of revolt – not so much because I am interested in preserving order as because I am concerned for the moral interests of the oppressed. I know too well that those who are in the toils of too harsh a necessity, if they rebel at one moment, will fall on their knees the moment after. The only way to preserve one's dignity under inevitable physical and moral sufferings is to accept them, to the precise extent that they are inevitable. But acceptance and submission are two very different things. (SL, p. 41)

The kind of self-expression she wished to encourage among the workers would, by affording it an outlet, soften their bitterness; in any case, it would be a small step in helping them retain or recover their sense of dignity. Bernard did not acknowledge the validity of her approach but they remained in close touch for the next six months. Weil admitted that the factory had become an obsession to her: she visited it several times and even revived the project of going to work there. In her long letters to Bernard she described at length her own experience and feeling at Alsthom and at Renault and tried to make him understand the position of the workers – those who counted for nothing – and his own power: more of a god than of a man. She was well aware that Bernard might find her remarks distressing. She did not want needlessly to disturb his happiness since 'happiness in my eyes is something precious and worthy of respect. I do not want to spread around me to no purpose the indelible bitterness with which my experience has left me' (SL, p. 43). Her efforts, she insisted, were merely to get the workers to count for something in the factory by encouraging them, to begin with, to hold up their heads. The social welfare schemes of the company were no help in this regard: 'Everything you do for the workers is done gratuitously, from generosity; so they are perpetually obliged to you. Whereas everything they do is done from necessity or for gain' (SL, p. 42). The key to the recovery of dignity was intellectual stimulation – the only thing to build on was the very feeling and experience of serfdom. 'What confirms me in this opinion', she wrote 'is that there are in general only two types of workmen who educate themselves on their own initiative: those who want promotion, and rebels' (SL, p. 36).

Having failed to convince Bernard of her point of view Weil suggested that she try her hand at making the masterpieces of Greek poetry accessible to the mass of the people. Surely Sophocles could not be regarded as subversive? The great poetry of Greece 'would be a hundred times closer to the people, if they could know it, than French literature both classical and modern' (SL, p. 49). She chose to begin with an account of *Antigone* which was published in *Entre Nous* under the pseudonym of Cleanthes, a Greek stoic philosopher who earned his living as a water-carrier. Weil had finished another piece on *Electra* and was contemplating a series on the creation of modern science by the Greeks – 'a marvellous story and not known even to cultivated people' (SL, p. 50) – when mass strikes broke out early in June. Weil wrote to Bernard expressing her 'feelings of unspeakable joy and relief' (SL, p. 52) that the workers had for once made their employers give way. As she had feared, Bernard responded in a short and frosty letter which precluded any further contact between them.

The wave of strikes so welcomed by Weil started in the weeks following the electoral victory in early May of the Popular Front which, under the leadership of Léon Blum, had been formed two years earlier by the main parties of the Left as a response to the growing menace of Fascism inside France. The strikes were in anticipation of the social and economic reforms that it was hoped the Blum government would introduce, and took the novel form of an occupation of the factories. Weil had defined her attitude to such an event more than two years earlier when she wrote that her decision to withdraw entirely from any kind of political activity 'does not absolutely exclude possible participation in a great spontaneous movement of the masses (in the ranks, as a soldier)' (P, p. 198). She had been reticent about the formation of the Popular Front: she felt it increased the possibility of war, mistrusted the participation of the Communists, and thought that its programme of nationalisations would merely aggravate state control. Nevertheless her participation in the general euphoria of the time was instinctive and enthusiastic.

As soon as her teaching duties were over, she was off to Paris, in spite of the imminent arrival of the annual inspection. The academy inspector exclaimed to the headmistress: 'I can't account for what I've just seen: the Inspector General is here and I've just seen Mlle. Weil taking the train to Paris!' (P, ii, p. 86). But she was more interested in her former fellow-workers than in the Inspector General. She immediately visited several factories and described in an article published a few days later in *Révolution Prolétarienne* the 'pure joy' that a visit to Renault afforded her:

> What joy to go into a factory with the smiling authorisation of the worker who guards the door. What a joy to see there so many smiles and to hear so many words of fraternal welcome. How much one feels among comrades in those workshops where, when I worked there, each person felt so alone at his machine! What a joy to walk freely through the workshops . . . to talk, to eat a snack. What a joy to hear, instead of the merciless racket of the machines, music, songs, and laughter. (P, p. 265)

The whole article is a vivid evocation of the spirit of fete or holiday outing reminiscent of certain aspects of May 1968, and the exact opposite of the feelings recounted in her factory diary. And, in addition to the feelings of joy, there was the impression that the workers had recovered their dignity: 'after always yielding, submitting to everything, swallowing everything in silence for months and years – now it's about at last being able to hold up your head. To stand upright. To take your turn in speaking out. To feel yourself, for some days at least, a human being' (CO, p. 169).

But however unbounded her joy at the outbreak of the strikes, Weil was too clear-sighted to be confident of the outcome. The strike was based on despair and therefore could not be reasonable. She had informed Bernard before the strikes began: 'When the victims of social oppression do in fact rebel, they have my sympathy, though unmixed with any hope; when a movement of revolt achieves some partial success, I am glad' (SL, p. 41). And to the same correspondent she wrote: 'I never at any time had any illusion about the possible results of the strikes; I did nothing to promote or prolong them' (SL, p. 54). For the habit of submission acquired over long years would not disappear in a few days. She noticed that the militants were in charge of negotiating terms with the employers and that the ordinary workers were not consulted. More generally, her experience and thinking over the last two years had led her to conclude that the working class was simply not prepared to assume the responsibilities correlative to its potential force, and that a revolution was impossible.

Although Weil felt that the strike movement was unlikely to result in profound social transformation, she nevertheless saw a possibility of introducing important reforms in working conditions. Already, in her *Révolution Prolétarienne* article, she had suggested that the account books of the companies be made open to the workers; that wage differentials should be abolished, or at least diminished; and that the oppressive character of the piece-work system be mitigated by a guaranteed minimum wage; but she could still see no solution to the ultimate sanction of the employer – the sack. By the time her article was published the Matignon agreements which provided for a considerable increase in wages and the full recognition of trade union rights had already been signed between the CGT and the representatives of the employers. Nevertheless labour unrest continued to be widespread well into the following year and Weil continued to follow events closely. In December 1936, she persuaded Belin, deputy general secretary of the CGT, to send her to investigate the industrial unrest in the north. In her report she criticised the indiscipline of some workers, the lack of quality control, and the tendency of some workers' delegates to go beyond the mandate given them by the union by deciding themselves who should work and when. For the moment, at least, Weil saw the 'lesser evil' to consist in realising that both workers and employers shared a common interest in stabilising the progress achieved in the Matignon agreements.

In a further document submitted to Belin she stressed the balance to be struck between workers' rights and the needs of production. What the union should aim for immediately, she felt, was to ensure that the workers could 'bring into play the faculties that no normal human being can allow to be stifled without suffering and self-degradation: initiative, inventiveness, choice of the most effective procedures, responsibility, and understanding of the work to be accomplished and the methods to be used' (CO, p. 209). For this degree of work-enrichment to be achieved, an equilibrium between union and management had to be established. This would involve very strong limitations on the power to sack workers with a strict appeals procedure, a measure of workers' control by involving union representatives in financial decisions, a right of the workers to further training, and the abolition of piece-work.

But these projects were not to be realised. In a letter to Belin, Weil wrote that she saw no lasting gain in

> the fact that they have loosened the vice of social constraint, that they have gained a little well-being, free time, and liberty. Certainly this is very fine, and I rejoice every day in the thought that they no longer suffer in the factories as they suffered the year when I lived this existence. But nothing has been changed in the structure of the social machinery, and when the enthusiasm of June has died away the vice will no doubt be tightened at least as harshly as before . . . (P, p. 295)

For all her initial enthusiasm, the experience of the ineffectiveness of the Popular Front only confirmed the conclusions of her factory year and marked the definitive end of her revolutionary hopes. In fact they had already been laid to rest in the major themes of *Oppression and Liberty*. But now her ideas had the solid underpinning of bitter experience.

But Weil did not abandon, along with her revolutionary hopes, all interest in labour questions. On the contrary, they remained with her for the rest of her life. She stayed in contact with Detoeuf and participated in the *Nouveaux Cahiers* group of reformist employers, intellectuals and trade unionists who met regularly in Paris to discuss social questions. As late as 1941, she was using her factory journal to write articles outlining reforms in the organisation of labour. For all that her later thought took on a profoundly religious dimension strongly influenced by Greek philosophy, she continued to think that the contempt of the Greeks for manual labour was a striking gap in their conception of the world. For manual labour gave the worker direct contact with time and space, with the material reality of the world. This experience of the constraints of natural necessity afforded an opportunity for the exercise of the discipline and obedience which were the foundation of any genuine spiritual life.[16] Her last major work returned to the question of how to achieve autonomy in the work-place and ended with the words: 'It is not difficult to define the place that physical labour should occupy in a well-ordered social life. It should be its spiritual core' (NR, p. 288). On a more personal level, the factory work and her continual reflections on it led to the replacement of the term 'oppression' by that of 'affliction' (*malheur*), a concept which involves a combination of physical pain, spiritual distress and social degradation, and which had its experiential roots in her factory year and which is such a pivotal idea in her later writings. Undoubtedly, too, her factory year was a necessary pre-condition for the various conversion experiences that she was to undergo in the late 1930s.

6

Paris: The Drift to War

'Present society can only heap misfortunes and disappointments on those who refuse to adapt to oppression and lies. We don't live in one of those periods when rebels are stimulated and supported by large currents of opinion. The rebel is morally and materially alone.' (P, p. 201)

In addition to her conversion to a form of Christian belief, the last three years of the decade also saw Weil occupied with the drift towards war in Europe, and moving from an ardent pacifism to a strongly anti-pacifist stance.

Already during her year at Bourges in 1935/6, Weil had entertained the possibility of giving up teaching. She continued to be passionately interested in the relationship between technology and the work-place. In addition to her connection with Bernard and the Rosières factory, she took part in the meetings of the Association of Young Factory Owners founded by Auguste Detoeuf (to whose factory she was thinking of returning) and also the meetings of the Union of Socialist Technicians. In Bourges she attended the local committee of the anti-Fascist intellectuals and maintained contact with the local branch of the CGT. She was insatiable in her curiosity about the manufacturing process and alienated more than one engineer by her incessant questioning. She was particularly interested in how the sciences could be taught by means of analogy and how to avoid abandoning the role of co-ordination of ideas to signs, particularly mathematics, which remained unintelligible to most people. 'The proper function of the mind', she wrote, 'is to coordinate. Whenever the mind abdicates this function, there is servitude.' Thus she concluded that 'the transformation of science, the transformation of work, and the transformation of social organisation, are three aspects of one and the same problem' (P, II, p. 78). Weil devoted so much time herself to the study of mathematics while at Bourges that her pupils thought that she was preparing a PhD in the subject. But at the same time as wishing to undertake this immense research programme, Weil felt that her resources of physical strength had declined:

For some years now I have seen my capacity for work diminish progressively due to a bad physical condition. Today it is as it were nil, to the point that I have resolved to take a year's rest at the end of the school year. If I manage to build up the physical resources that would permit me to work and live with the intensity I require, I hope that I will regain a little of all the time I have so deplorably lost. (P, pp. 259f)

She felt convinced that she had inside her head 'the germs of great things' (P, p. 261), but she was all the more led to a state of despair by the way in which her physical state and particularly her headaches (which occasionally made her feel literally suicidal) prevented her from working. She had decided once and for all not to depend on her parents: 'One's family is a precious thing, provided it is kept at a little distance; if not, it can stifle you' (P, p. 261). One solution that she envisaged was applying for a Rockefeller grant and going to America with her brother to pursue her researches.

But, as far as the next year at least was concerned, events dictated otherwise. In July 1936, the Spanish Civil War began. In February 1936, Spain, too, had elected a Popular Front majority. But on 17 July Franciso Franco and his fellow-generals launched an insurrection against their government from military bases in Spanish North Africa and invaded Spain in order to bring down the Republican government. Weil had no hesitation in deciding to go and fight. She had visited Asturias and Galicia the summer before with her parents and had formed a very favourable impression of the Catalonian anarchists, though not of their leaders, when visiting Barcelona with Aimé Patri. She saw the anarchist movement there as

> the natural expression of the Spanish people's greatness and of its flaws, of its worthiest aspirations and of its unworthiest . . . an extraordinary mixture, to which anybody at all was admitted and in which, consequently, one found immorality, cynicism, fanaticism and cruelty, but also love and fraternal spirit and, above all, that concern for honour which is so beautiful in the humiliated. (SL, pp. 105f)

Thus her resolution to go and fight was a personal one: she approved of the Blum government's decision, arrived at under strong pressure from Great Britain, not to intervene on the Republican side, as she had approved of the French inaction in the previous March when the Germans had reoccupied the demilitarised Rhineland in violation of the Versailles Treaty and the Locarno Pact. At the time of the reoccupation of the Rhineland, Alain had asked the question, 'Are the men who speak of dignity and honour as being more precious than life disposed to be the first to risk their lives? And if not, what should we think of them?' In her answer, Weil maintained that 'dignity' and 'honour' were dangerous words, particularly when used in a national context:

contemporary wars in which slaves were asked to die for a dignity that had never been granted them constituted the main wheel in the mechanism of social oppression. And, as for honour:

> the free decision to risk one's life is the very soul of honour; honour is not involved where some men make decisions without taking any risks, and others die in order to carry out their decisions. And if war cannot be a means of safeguarding anyone's honour, we must also conclude from that fact that no peace is dishonourable, whatever its terms may be. (FW, p. 253)

In Spain, as in the Rhineland, the main aim should be to prevent local conflicts turning into a general European war. But the risk of her own life was another matter. As she wrote later to Bernanos:

> I do not love war; but what has always seemed to me most horrible in war is the position of those in the rear. When I realised that, try as I would, I could not prevent myself from participating morally in that war – in other words, from hoping all day and every day for the victory of one side and the defeat of the other – I decided that, for me, Paris was the rear and I took the train to Barcelona, with the intention of enlisting. (SL, p. 106)

To her, as to Malraux, Saint-Exupéry, Nizan, Orwell and so many others, Spain presented a challenge that she could not refuse.

Weil arrived at the Spanish frontier town of Port-Bou on 8 August. Several of the houses had been destroyed by bombs, the railway bridge had been precariously shored up, and People's Commissars sporting official armbands had taken over from the former immigration authorities in dealing with the hundreds of people waiting to get through to Barcelona. Charles Dreyfus, a French journalist in the queue, remembered Weil:

> I see, holding in her hand a small square of crumpled paper, a young woman with a Basque beret on her rather frizzy hair which hung over her spectacles perched on an aquiline nose. Her lips were finely chiseled, she wore no make-up, and her chin was forceful. Over a light grey shirt she carried a tourist bag stuffed to the brim; round her waist she had a short dark grey skirt with knee-length socks protecting her thin legs and climbing shoes on her feet. Her voice was soft and high-pitched and her eyes shone with intelligence. She left us quickly. The crumpled paper that she presented timidly but with a proud certainty had opened up for her the path she wished to follow.[1]

Dreyfus and his companions caught up with Weil later and invited her to join them in a drink while waiting for the train: 'I don't drink alcohol, I'm an anarchist', she replied curtly and went on to demonstrate with strict logic the justice of the Republican cause.

As soon as she got to Barcelona, Weil began a journal that she kept intermittently throughout her short stay in Spain. The city, she wrote, had not changed 'except in a small matter: power is in the hands of the people. This is now one of those extraordinary periods, which up to the present have never lasted, when those who have always obeyed take charge. That is not without its inconveniences, to be sure, when you give kids of seventeen years old loaded guns in the middle of an unarmed population . . .' (EHP, p. 209). She wrote almost daily to her parents who, thinking she might need their help, had armed themselves with letters of recommendation from the Paris railwaymen's union and followed her down to Perpignan. Her letters spoke of the lack of danger, of her desire, as a journalist, to study the recently inaugurated socialist production methods, and of her return to France in a week or so. In reality, she had far different ideas in mind. She began by seeking out Julian Gorkin, one of the leaders of the Trotskyist POUM (Partido Obrero de Unificacion Marxista) who had heard of Weil from Souvarine and others while he was in exile in Paris. Souvarine's brother-in-law and founder of the POUM, Joaquin Maurin, had been in nationalist Galicia when the war broke out and there was much speculation as to whether and how he had managed to survive. Weil suggested to Gorkin that she be commissioned to go behind the Francist lines to find out whether Maurin was still alive. Gorkin thought such a plan would involve a quite useless sacrifice and maintained his refusal in spite of a stormy argument.

Having failed to get her way with Gorkin, Weil was determined to expose herself by enlisting in the ranks of the anarchist militia. Like Orwell, who had himself arrived at the Aragon front as a journalist, Weil felt that joining the militia was 'the only conceivable thing to do'.[2] She left Barcelona with a party of journalists and managed to get to the front at Pina on the river Ebro, the furthest point reached by the Catalan drive westwards into Aragon. This invasion was spearheaded by the legendary warrior of the revolution, Buenaventura Durruti, whose column, six thousand strong, remained poised for an attack on Saragossa, whose string of lights, as George Orwell put it, twinkled tantalisingly before them at night 'like the lighted port-holes of a ship'.[3] Having got to the Front as a journalist, Weil managed to get herself accepted by a small commando group of foreigners who operated alongside the Spaniards as the embryo of what were later to become the International Brigades. She listened to Durruti addressing the peasants and noted the lack of enthusiasm for their proposed liberation. She was also present in a car taking a priest to his execution. Although she had not actually decided to prevent the killing, if necessary by interposing her own body, she spent the journey thinking about what life would be like for her if she failed to intervene. In the event, a 'lucky accident' meant that the opportunity did not arise (cf. EHP, p. 221). On Monday 17 August, just as she was writing a letter to Souvarine, saying that she had not seen a shot fired in anger, some enemy planes came over, but only released one ineffective bomb. The same day the group crossed the Ebro to burn three enemy corpses, although they knew that Fascist troops were in the vicinity. Weil was so evidently short-sighted and clumsy (her comrades kept well out of the line of fire at target practice) that the leader of the group refused to take her until she made a scene. After dealing with the corpses, some of the group decided to reconnoitre a nearby house. Weil wrote in her journal:

> We go through the brush. Heat, a little anxiety. I think it's idiotic. Suddenly I realise that we are on a mission (against the house). Now I *do* get nervous (I don't know how useful all this is, and I know that if you are captured, you're shot). We divide into two groups. The chief, Riedel, and three Germans belly-crawl up to the house. We, behind in the ditches (afterwards the chief bawls us out: we should have gone all the way to the house). We wait. We hear someone talking . . . exhausting tension. Then we see our pals coming back without hiding; we join them and go quietly back across the river. This mistaken manoeuvre could have cost them their lives . . . This expedition is the first and *only* time that I was frightened during my stay at Pina. (EHP, p. 212)

In the middle of the following night another crossing of the Ebro was made, this time to sabotage a railway line and perhaps establish a bridgehead. Weil was ordered to join a young German who had been appointed the expedition's cook: 'From time to time, the young German lets out a sigh. He is frightened, visibly. Not me. But how everything, around me, seems intensely to exist!' (EHP, p. 214). But, apart from considerable aerial bombardment, the day passed off without incident. In spite of her eagerness to see action, Weil could not bring herself to be enthusiastic about the expedition, particularly given the gulf which separated the local peasants, with their humble, submissive and timid attitude, from the confident, off-hand and condescending militiamen.

The next morning her comrades' worst fears about Weil's physical disabilities were fulfilled. They had dug a deep hole to conceal the flames of the kitchen fire from enemy view. Weil did not see the large pot of boiling oil which had been placed on the fire at ground level and stepped right into it. Her foot was protected by her shoe but the whole of the bottom half of her left leg was badly burned. She was taken back across the river to Pina, but returned the same evening with the men bringing the rations. Her friends insisted, however, that she return to Pina. Here she was so disgusted with the treatment she got at what passed for a hospital (the head doctor was a barber) that she set off with her haversack, limping back along the road to Barcelona. An army colonel and a Swiss trade unionist gave her lifts and she arrived in Barcelona the following day.

Her parents, meanwhile, had crossed the frontier and arrived in Barcelona. They found the greatest difficulty in getting accommodation and could not get any news of their daughter except that she had gone off to the Front. They spent a week waiting half the night on the Ramblas opposite the POUM offices to meet the convoys returning under cover of dark from the Aragon Front. In the end, she turned up, cool and smiling, as they were having lunch in a cafe. Her father took one look at her leg and got her into the military hospital which had been installed in the Hotel Terramar at Sitges, a seaside resort a few miles down the coast. The hospital authorities were unsympathetic to anarchists and Weil was left untended for days with an unremarked fever. Finally, her father insisted on removing her from the hospital: she departed on a stretcher, but laughing at the furious doctor who pursued her, belated thermometer in hand. She was taken to the boarding house where her parents were staying and spent the next three weeks convalescing. She used the time to make notes on the rather unsatisfactory methods of co-operative production being introduced in Barcelona and on the executions carried out by the anarchists. On 25 September she returned to France with her parents. Her accident had saved her life. Shortly after her departure, the international group she had been with was cut to pieces at Perdiguera; all the women died.

The burns on her leg were slow to heal and Weil renewed her request for sick leave at the beginning of each of the three terms in the academic year of 1936/7. Indeed, apart from a term's teaching at the end of 1937, she was on constant leave until the outbreak of war. It was a period rich in reflection which marked a turning-point in her political thought.

In the Autumn of 1936, Weil was a fervent supporter of the Republican cause in Spain. She attended pro-Republican meetings in Paris, wearing the red and black scarf of the Spanish anarchists and the militia uniform that she had brought back with her, and defended the social achievements of the Catalonian anarchists. But, although she had been set on returning to Spain, she was clear-sighted enough to appreciate what was going on there and her enthusiasm for personal participation began to wane. She did not question the good faith of her anarchist comrades in Catalonia but 'there also we see forms of compulsion and instances of inhumanity that are directly contrary to the libertarian and humanitarian ideal of the anarchists. The necessities and the atmosphere of civil war are sweeping away the aspirations that we are seeking to defend by means of civil war' (FW, p. 256). She was now active in the broadly-based Committee of Anti-Fascist Intellectuals founded by Alain in 1934 and spoke out in favour of sending technical assistance and raw materials to Spain; however she resolutely supported Blum's policy of non-intervention, which was under strong attack from the Communists, particularly after the Stalin–Laval pact of 1935, in which the Soviet Union had given its support for French rearmament. 'For some comrades', she wrote, 'it is no longer a matter of turning international war into civil war, but civil war into international war' (ibid.). For her, opposition to Fascism was an opposition to all forms of authoritarianism and any recourse to war was a selling-out to the logic of military prestige and power inherent in fascism itself. The conclusion was unequivocal:

> One must choose between prestige and peace. And whether one claims to believe in the fatherland, democracy, or revolution, the policy of prestige means war. And if the misfortune of the time decrees that civil war today must become a way like any other, and must almost inevitably be tied to international war, we can draw only one conclusion: we must avoid civil war. (FW, p. 258)

This being the case, Weil detected an ambivalence in the foreign policy of the French government. If a doctrine of mutual assistance and collective security were reasonable, then the situation in Spain where a military caste had attacked the workers armed only with rifles and grenades would provide the best example of when France should intervene. But France had proclaimed neutrality, for fear of setting all Europe ablaze. In that case one should be consistent: 'I defy anyone, including Léon Blum, to explain why the reasons that deter us from intervening in Spain would be less compelling if it were a question of Czechoslovakia's being invaded by the Germans' (FW, p. 262). The reference to Czechoslovakia was prophetic: Weil was to remain faithful to this point of view up to, and including, the Munich crisis.

Weil had been interested in colonial questions since her tears of shame during her student days when she first learned about the murderous treatment of coolies in Indo-China. In January 1937, the rumour that German troops were about to embark in Spanish Morocco moved Weil to write two historical articles in an ironical tone which showed how underhand and reprehensible were the means by which France had acquired its major part of Morocco. When seventeen striking miners were shot in Tunisia two months later, she castigated the Popular Front government, but even more the French people, for their indifference to suffering in the colonies. Her conclusion was harsh: 'A European war can serve as a signal for the great revenge of the colonial peoples, which will punish our unconcern, our indifference, and our cruelty . . . it is not a joyful prospect, but it would offer a certain satisfaction of the need for imminent justice.'[4]

Weil was not solely preoccupied with foreign affairs. Her view that the French government should adopt a more pacific attitude was partly the result of her conviction that at least relative disarmament was a precondition for any worthwhile improvement in the condition of the working class. Two years previously, in 1934, she had declared that, apart from anti-colonialism and passive defence exercises, she would withdraw from social and political activity. Nevertheless she was as concerned as ever about the state of French society under the Popular Front. She persuaded René Belin, the deputy general secretary of the CGT, to commission her to produce a report on trade union activities in the north-east of France, in which she tried to balance workers' rights against the interests of productivity.[5] She continued to attend trade union congresses, and made her views clear in the anarchist trade union journal *Le Libertaire*. She considered that continual agitation in factories could prejudice what the workers had achieved in June 1936. There was, too, a link here with foreign affairs since 'the Communist Party is interested in maintaining a permanent effervescence in the factories, so as to have a means of blackmailing the government on the question of foreign policy' (P, p. 283). The most aggressive employers also had an interest in disorder as it would drive all those who were not consciously revolutionary towards Fascism. The only solution was 'an energetic, prudent, methodical, coordinated trade union action, with a well-defined objective: workers control' (ibid.). Weil was concerned that the employers might succeed in reimposing the vicious and arbitrary power over the workers that they had enjoyed before the victory of the Popular Front. But she was also worried about the Communist predominance in the newly united trade union movement. Even capitalism, she wrote to Belin, was preferable to a totalitarian state on the Soviet model.

In February 1937, she attended the congress of Paris trade unions. Some of her old friends from the *Révolution Prolétarienne* were there and she published her reflections in their journal. The Communist influence was evident, she wrote, 'not so much because of the debates but because at certain times one rediscovered an atmosphere, so familiar to some of us, that smacks both of a political rally and a religious ceremony' (P, pp. 287f). The mass ritual, with its clenched fists, the singing of the Internationale, the whole art of stage-managing imported from Moscow was only too familiar. The show trials had recently opened in Moscow and Weil and her friends had managed to get congratulatory references to the 'liquidation of the vanguard of Fascism in the USSR' removed from the official record. But the next day saw a reversal:

Impossible to describe the brutality, the baseness with which the Russian delegate expressed himself, for many long minutes, concerning the last batch of Russian leaders who have been shot. The claque worked efficiently. Our people kept silent . . . they were dispersed throughout the hall; they had not established contact; they were paralysed by rage or disgust. This apology for the death sentences was saluted by the 'Internationale' sung standing up. (P, p. 289)

She herself had got into the habit of sitting ostentatiously on the floor whenever the Internationale was sung. From now on, she feared, a Communist-dominated CGT would become the principal factor making for chauvinism and war.

This disillusion with the way in which the CGT was moving prompted Weil to wonder whether a counter-balance to the Communist influence might not be found in the adhesion to the CGT of the Christian Trade Union movement. In March 1937, she wrote a long letter about this to Emanuel Mounier, founder of the Personalist movement and editor of the leftish Catholic review *Esprit*. Competition between trade unions, she wrote, could only harm the workers' cause; and the traditions of the two unions were not incompatible.

For my part, I am personally not a Catholic; but I consider the Christian idea, which has its roots in Greek thought and in the course of the centuries has nourished all of our European civilisation, as something that one cannot renounce without becoming degraded: this does not prevent me from feeling at home in the CGT. Our trade unionism does not preach hate; it was not hatred that inspired its precursors, its founders, and its pioneers. (P, p. 290)

She wished that Catholics would insist on upholding the purity of their principles as much in matters of social justice as in other areas. Since society was bound to involve both class struggle and class collaboration there was no necessary clash between the two trade union traditions. And an influx of genuine Christianity might help modify the self-righteous judgemental attitude of the CGT demagogues. But Weil's ecumenical attitude was ahead of its time and only found a partial realisation under the more dramatic pressures of the Resistance.

During this period Weil regularly attended the meetings of academics, civil servants and industrialists organised by Auguste Detoeuf to discuss questions of the day on a non-partisan basis. The group met every Monday evening in the Café de Flore, a favourite location in which they had been preceded by the Action Française and were to be succeeded by the existentialists. People as varied as Souvarine, de Rougement and Maritain were regular participants and out of the group issued, in April

1937, a fortnightly journal entitled *Nouveaux Cahiers*. It was in the first issues of this journal that Weil published a long and brilliant essay which summed up her political stance at this time. The title of the essay, 'Let us Not Begin Again the Trojan War', was inspired by a recent play of Jean Giraudoux, *The Trojan War Will Not Take Place*, whose pessimistic pacifism Weil had much admired. Her enforced leisure had also given her the opportunity of doing a lot of reading in Greco-Roman history and she had composed several short articles for Belin's trade union paper *Syndicats*, drawing lessons for modern problems.[6] The sub-title of the *Nouveaux Cahiers* essay was 'The Power of Words' and its general thesis was that the destruction wrought by war was in inverse proportion to the official pretexts for fighting it. The worst conflicts were those which had no definable objective. The ten-year-long Trojan War was fought for a person about whom the participants (except perhaps for Paris) cared little or nothing – indeed in Euripides's version Helen was not even in Troy at the time. In more modern times wars were fought in the name of words beginning with capital letters, abstract entities which corresponded to no clear idea in the minds of those under their sway and whose analysis would show them to be much more relative, and therefore less dangerous.

Weil's first example of a concept that needed demystification was that of national interest and, in particular, the idea that antagonism between capitalists was the prime cause of war. For her, Anatole France's view that 'you think you are dying for your country but in fact you are dying for a few industrialists' was, alas, too optimistic. Increasingly the economic interests of capitalists overstepped national boundaries and, in any case, what was really meant by the national interest of a country was not what gave life to its citizens but what gave it the means to make war. If countries were divided by a real opposition of interest, a compromise would be possible. But

> when economic and political interests have no meaning apart from war, how can they be peacefully reconciled? It is the very concept of the nation that needs to be suppressed – or rather, the manner in which the word is used. For the word national and the expressions of which it forms part are empty of all meaning; their only content is millions of corpses, and orphans and disabled men, and tears and despair. (SE, p. 159)

Another example of this absurd, but murderous, thinking was the opposition between Fascism and communism. No two nations had a structure as similar as Germany and Russia. The anti-Fascist position was that anything was better than Fascism – anything, including Fascism, so long as it was called communism. And the anti-communist position was that anything was better than communism – including communism itself, so long as it was labelled Fascism. Even the phantom of Helen had a substantial reality compared to such non-existent distinctions.

Even the opposition between democracy and dictatorship, although a real opposition, lost a lot of its force if these words were taken not as representing some discrete entity but as criteria for measuring the characteristics of a given social structure. It would then be clear that democracy was not more inherent in France than dictatorship was in Germany and that both were the result of determinate situation open to analysis and change. But the current climate of opinion was opposed to such analysis. If anyone were to suggest an armistice in the Spanish Civil War, the suggestion would be greeted with derision on both sides:

> each of them has unconsciously lost sight of his ideal and replaced it by an entity without substance. For each the victory of what he still calls his idea can no longer mean anything except the extermination of the enemy; and each of them will scorn any suggestion of peace, replying to it with the same knock-out argument as Minerva in Homer and Poincaré in 1917: 'the dead do not wish it'. (SE, p. 162)

In all human conflict, Weil claimed, the only legitimate and serious one was class struggle. But it was a struggle of the oppressed against their oppression and not a war; it could result in a compromise and a new balance of forces, as in June 1936 in France.

In the final section of her essay, Weil tried to establish the relationship of these empty abstractions with real life. Clearly every abstraction was connected with a social group aiming at power. At the centre of power was the illusion of prestige without which power would become even less stable than it was. Priam and Hector could not have returned Helen to the Greeks without giving the impression of weakness which would have invited attack from the Greeks or even their own subjects. The result was that

> the essential contradiction in human society is that every social *status quo* rests upon an equilibrium of forces or pressures, similar to the equilibrium of fluids; but between one prestige and another there can be no equilibrium. Prestige has no bounds and its satisfaction always involves the infringement of someone else's prestige or dignity. And prestige is inseparable from power. This seems to be an impasse from which humanity can only escape by some miracle. (SE, pp. 169f)

The real problems of contemporary politics were obscured by a swarm of vacuous entities or abstractions and 'to sweep away these entities from every department of political and social life is an urgently necessary measure of public hygiene' (ibid.). Above all it was necessary to seek international peace without opposing the legitimate claims of the under-privileged: 'What is required is discrimination between the imaginary and the real, so as to diminish the risks of war, without interfering with the struggle between forces which, according to Heraclitus, is the condition of life itself' (SE, p. 171). Weil's conclusion was in keeping with the pacifist, internationalist feelings of many at the time and this essay attracted more attention than anything else published by Weil during her lifetime.

By the time her essay was published Weil was in Switzerland en route for Italy. She took advantage of her lack of teaching commitments to visit a clinic in Switzerland which promised some treatment for her headaches; and she continued on to Italy which she had long wanted to visit, mainly for its artistic treasures but also to see Italian Fascism at first hand. She spent six weeks at the La Moubra clinic, which catered mainly for tubercular patients and was situated in Montana in the Valais, the town where she had gone to recuperate after her factory year. She was not confident of the value of this treatment and she wrote to her parents suggesting her father come and take a look himself. They both came and stayed a fortnight. Her father took her to Zurich to consult a well-known opthalmologist and they took advantage of this to spend Easter at the nearby Abbey of Einsiedeln to listen to the Gregorian chant. Her father found it monotonous; she could (and did) listen to it for hours. Although the treatment at the clinic proved ineffective, Weil spent a happy time there. She was particularly friendly with Jean Posternak, a medical student with whom she had a lively correspondence during the subsequent year and whose records of Bach's 'Brandenburg' Concertos she greatly appreciated.

The eight weeks Weil spent on her own in Italy were among the happiest of her life. She stopped first at Pallanza beside Lake Maggiore, crossed the lake to spend a night at Stresa and went on to Milan. To her parents she wrote of her enthusiasm for the piazzas of the city and their cafes. She went to see Verdi's *Aida* and Donizetti's *Elixir of Love* at the Scala. She liked the Donizetti more than the Verdi but preferred to both of them a charming little puppet theatre on the Piazza Beccaria. But it was the paintings that claimed most of her attention. She was particularly struck by Mantegna's *Dead Christ*, a tour de force of technical perspective, in the Brera gallery and she would have liked to spend her whole life in front of Leonardo's *Last Supper*. She wrote to Posternak about its composition:

There is a point on the hair on the right side of Christ's head toward which all the perspective lines of the roof converge and also, approximately, the lines formed by the Apostles' hands on each side of him. But this convergence (which is discreetly emphasised by the arc above the window, of whose circle the same point is the centre) exists only in the two-dimensional space which it evokes. Thus there is a double composition; and the eye is led back from everywhere towards the face of Christ, by a secret, unperceived influence which helps to make his serenity appear supernatural. (SL, pp. 75f)

She considered that the secret of Leonardo's composition was contained in his Pythagorean conception of life. She also spent hours in the working-class districts of Milan and read the same servitude in their eyes that was only too familiar from her own factory days in Paris.

After Milan she visited Bologna, Ferrara and Ravenna, where she admired the young peasants in the market-place: 'When Providence places beautiful people among beautiful things, it is a superabundance of grace. Every day, in this country, one notes in certain men of the people a nobility and a simplicity of manner and attitude that compel admiration' (SL, p. 77). Then on to Florence where she felt so much at home that she was sure she had lived there in a previous life. Although she did not like the Cathedral, at least from the outside, she spent hours in the Medici Chapel looking at Michelangelo's *Dawn* and *Night*. For her they represented 'the awakening and sleep of a slave for whom life is too bitter. *Dawn* has vividly evoked my own awakenings, when I was a worker and lived on the rue Lecourbe' (P, p. 302). She overcame her dislike of museums to the extent of seeing the Titians and Botticellis in the Uffizi and the *Concert* of Giorgione, by far her favourite of all the Florentine paintings. She left Florence for Rome in time to hear the liturgy of Pentecost. She spent all of the Sunday at St Peter's: 'The music, the voices, the words of the liturgy, the architecture, the crowd, some kneeling – there you have the comprehensive art that Wagner was seeking' (SL, p. 80). Day after day she wandered, still limping, around the sights, finishing up with a midnight tour of the Coliseum by moonlight.

Wherever she went, Weil entered easily into conversation with strangers she met and was particularly interested to learn about people's perceptions of Fascism. She had, for example, two long conversations with a Fascist student whose address Posternak had given her. She was grateful, she wrote to Posternak, since she had long wanted to have a frank discussion with

one of those characters full of repressed ardour and lofty, unavowed ambitions. He thinks that my normal and legitimate place in society is at the bottom of a salt mine. I quite agree with him on that. A mine would seem less stifling to me than this atmosphere, this obsessive nationalism, this worship of force in its most brutal form – namely, collectivity . . . this camouflaged deification of death. (SL, pp. 84f)

But she did not let her interest in current political issues stop her indefatigable pursuit of art. In the Vatican museums she was fascinated by Leonardo's painting of Saint Jerome, in contrast to Raphael's frescos, which she admired, but which did not detain her. In the Sistine Chapel she lay down flat to get a better view of the ceiling but only succeeded in annoying the keeper. The only thing more beautiful than Michelangelo were the Greek statues: she was, she wrote to her parents, 'drunk' with them and returned again and again to enjoy them.

From Rome she moved north to Assisi. Except for what had been put up in honour of Saint Francis, she found everything there marvellously Franciscan. 'When I saw Perugia and Assisi', she wrote to her parents, 'all the rest of Italy was wiped out for me. Never would I have dreamed of such a countryside, so splendid a race of men, and such moving Chapels' (P, pp. 306f). It was here that she had, as she was to write later, the second of the three contacts with Catholicism that really counted:

In 1937 I had two marvellous days at Assisi. There, alone in the little Twelfth Century Romanesque chapel of Santa Maria degli Angeli, an incomparable marvel of purity where St. Francis often used to pray, something stronger than I was compelled me for the first time in my life to go down on my knees. (WG, p. 20)

As with her experience in Portugal, she mentioned this to no-one at the time. She returned to Florence in time for the May music festival and spent another two weeks there re-visiting her favourite sights. She went to the *Marriage of Figaro* and to Monteverdi's *Coronation of Poppaea*. She climbed up to Fiesole and read Dante, Petrarch, Machiavelli and Galileo. She bought the latter's collected works and 'spent some luminous hours one afternoon perusing his extraordinary original insights about uniformly accelerated motion. That is as aesthetically pleasing as anything, especially when one reads it here' (SL, p. 83). On 16 June she returned to Paris.

Although her trip to Switzerland and Italy did little to improve her health, it did mark an important stage in her spiritual development. The contact with the art of Italy, and particularly her visit to Assisi, brought her nearer to Christianity. It also marked a shift in her aesthetic sensibility. Previously she had considered Michelangelo and Beethoven as the supreme examples of artistic genius. Now she found them too forceful, too expressive of their own emotions. Musically, she began to prefer the purer, less personal form of Bach and, particularly, Monteverdi. In painting, this was paralleled by a preference for Giorgine and, even more, Giotto. But above all, Greek statuary made a lasting impression on her. Her later writings are full of references to Greek statues whose impersonal embodiment of balance and proportion was, for her, the counterpart of the Platonism that was to be central to her religious philosophy.[7]

On her return from Italy, Weil began to try her own hand at sculpture and poetry. She was haunted, she wrote to Posternak, by the idea of

> a statue of Justice: a naked woman, standing, her knees a little bent from fatigue (sometimes I see her kneeling, with chained feet, but that would not be so sculptural), her hands chained behind her back, leaning – with a serene face in spite of all – towards scales (sculpted in higher relief in front of her) with unequal arms, which hold two equal weights at unequal levels. (SL, p. 91)

And she did tentatively execute some small models in limestone. She went to see Giraudoux's *Electra* and wrote a long letter to the author outlining a superior plot in which the catastrophic effect of a clash between individual virtue and social evil would have been clearer. She also began again to write poetry and sent a *Prometheus* to Paul Valéry who admired its composition, though he also found it a little too didactic. Nor did she neglect the sciences: she studied de Broglie's theories and had nothing but admiration for his wave version of Planck's quantum theory and its confirmation in experiments showing that electrons could form diffraction patterns. But she could not accept the idea that the wave concept was primary in explaining the structure of matter. For her, there was nothing shocking in the contradiction between the wave and the particulate nature of matter and energy, since both were simply analogies. Nor did she think that Heisenberg's indeterminacy principle in any way invalidated the determinism of the natural world, since 'determinism has never been anything more than a directing principle in science and will always remain so' (SS, p. 119). She added that science seemed to be entering a crisis that was liable to be made all the more serious (and possibly fatal) by the rise of the totalitarian state and the general obeisance being made to purely political values.

These reflections were made against the background of a pessimistic assessment of the political situation. In general she felt that France was declining to a second-rank power – a transition extremely difficult for a country that had always believed itself both the terror and the darling of the world. 'This transition', she wrote to Posternak, 'brings with it an incredible degree of lying, of false news, of demagogy, of boasting mixed with panic (awful mixture!), of disarray, and finally an intolerable moral atmosphere' (SL, p. 94). The Popular Front of 1936 had offered some hope; but scarcely had she returned to France when the Popular Front government fell. Although Blum continued to be Vice-President, in Weil's view the Popular Front, although continuing in name, was in reality dead. In an unpublished article, entitled 'Reflections on a Corpse', Weil delivered her post-mortem. She insisted on the paramount role of imagination in politics: 'Imagination is always the fabric of social life and the dynamic of history' (SE, p. 150). Blum had failed to build on the possibilities unleashed by the Popular Front victory a year earlier. Intelligent and sincere though he was, he had not managed to appreciate that 'the material of the political art is the double perspective, ever shifting between the real conditions of social equilibrium and the movements of collective imagination' (SE, p. 152). Machiavelli was a better teacher here than Marx, and one of Machiavelli's maxims was that anyone acceding to power should take harsh measures immediately since 'the fundamental principle of power and any political activity is that there should never be any appearance of weakness. A force makes itself not only feared but also at the same time a little loved even by those whom it disgusts with violence . . . this force whose empire extends into people's minds is in large part imaginary' (EHP, pp. 406f).

These considerations were equally valid for economics. Contrary to popular opinion, economies seldom collapsed; but an unsound economic condition could undermine the prestige of power so important for securing popular obedience. However this bitter truth had been neglected by Blum, who had succumbed to the common failings of social democracy: excellent intentions but lacking the touch of cynicism essential for perspicacity, and hampered by a doctrine which included the dogma of progress and an unshakeable faith in history and in the masses. Her conclusion was even more pessimistic than that of her teacher, Alain:

> The social order, though necessary, is essentially evil, whatever it may be. You cannot reproach those whom it crushes for undermining it as much as they can . . . neither can you reproach those who organise it for defending it, or make them out to be forming a conspiracy against the general welfare. The struggles between fellow citizens do not spring from a lack of understanding or goodwill; they belong to the nature of things, and cannot be appeased, but can only be smothered by coercion. For anyone who loves liberty, it is not desirable that they should disappear, but only that they should remain short of a certain limit of violence. (OL, p. 146)

Meanwhile Weil had started teaching again. She had been appointed to teach philosophy and Greek at the lycée of Saint-Quentin, a large industrial town seventy miles north of Paris. It was a post that she had coveted since her days at Le Puy. Instead of taking her pupils through the ordinary philosophical texts, she made them read the novels of Balzac and Saint-Exupéry and tried to move to the abstract from the very concrete. She told her students that for the Greeks the finite was more beautiful than the infinite, that the circle was preferable to the line, and that therefore the most important ideas, from painting and sculpture to economics and politics, were those of the equilibrium of forces, of proportion, and of balance – themes that were to be pursued in her Marseilles writings. Her negative views about society were repeated in her pupils' notes: 'If it is true that society is founded only upon relations of force and if it is true that the soul is subjected to outside pressures, nothing is more injurious to man than society.' And the moral: 'For joy to be had on earth without changing the laws of necessity, it is not the great things that must be changed, but the little things, which for the soul are precisely the great things' (C, pp. 166f). The headmistress felt that Weil's methods were perhaps not sufficiently traditional for the 'average' children.

Since Saint-Quentin was within commuting distance of Paris, Weil could regularly attend the meetings of the *Nouveaux Cahiers* group where she took an active part in discussions on German racism, on industrial relations, and control of employment. She was also part of a sub-committee of the group devoted to educational reform. She was particularly opposed here to the proposal of scholarships to especially bright children to attend further education. Faithful to the principles of Alain, she saw such a system as profoundly inegalitarian, since such a creaming off would only leave the majority even more disadvantaged. But Weil felt herself alienated from French domestic politics, an alienation only increased by the growing hold of the Communist Party over the workers, and reaffirmed her resolution of three years earlier to confine her political activities to the questions of colonialism and of peace. On the first subject, she was concerned to defend the Algerian workers in France. She had had long conversations with their leader Messali Hadj and, according to Hadj, had personally persuaded Blum not to have him arrested when his organisation had been banned for stirring up anti-French feeling in Algeria. When Hadj was arrested and condemned to jail a year later for reconstituting his organisation, she got the Saint-Quentin anti-Fascist committee to pass a resolution, drafted by herself, which deplored the fact that 'North Africa remains subject to the same regime of brutality, terror, and oppression as under preceding governments', and drew attention to 'the baleful and deserved consequences that could attend despair of the indigenous masses' (P, ɪɪ, p. 176). If anyone was responsible for stirring up anti-French feeling in Algeria, it was those governmental officials who had succeeded in making the name of France odious to its inhabitants.

An additional reason for Weil's interest in colonial questions was her fear that they might lead to world war, but a more pressing threat in this direction soon presented itself. In March 1938, German troops entered Vienna and the *anschluss* with Austria was effected. She immediately joined other anti-Fascist intellectuals in signing a petition which declared that 'however distasteful it may seem, Chamberlain's policy – inasmuch as it endeavours to put a stop to the deadly armaments race – is actually the *only* one that by means of effective negotiation makes an attempt to bring about the pacification of Europe' (P. p. 326). To Posternak, she wrote that she foresaw two possibilities. The first was a war with Germany over Czechoslovakia; the second, an 'anti-democratic *coup d'état*, supported by Daladier and the army, accompanied by an explosion of violent anti-semitism (the signs are apparent every-where) and brutal measures against parties and organisations of the Left. I would prefer the latter as less murderous for the whole youth of France' (SL, pp. 94f).

A third possibility was a prolonged and irritating wait to see which of the first two would happen. Her only consolation was that all this came as no surprise to her as she had foreseen the course of events since 1932. She was willing to concede a German hegemony in Europe if it allowed the possibility of avoiding war. An attack on France did not seem inevitable. In order to deter the enemy she suggested that the political and economic decentralisation that was proposed as a defence against air attack in a lecture she attended could be carried further: an army of guerilla resistance should be envisaged in which she suggested that the strategy (since widely and successfully adopted elsewhere) should be 'not to form fronts, not to lay siege to cities; harass the enemy, break up his communications, attack him always where he least expects it, demoralise him, and stimulate the resistance by a series of small but victorious actions' (P, p. 328). Such a form of national defence, centred on the people and not on the state, could revive the true spirit of the nation. While conceding that such a plan required a civic conscience and taste for liberty currently lacking in the French people, she main-tained that one inestimable advantage of her whole attitude was that it would involve a rapid modification of France's colonial policies.

It was during this fraught political period that Weil decided to spend Easter at the famous Benedictine abbey of Solesmes by the river Sarthe in north-west France. The grimness of the political outlook was matched by Weil's worsening physical affliction. 'From 1938 until the Spring of 1940', she wrote, 'my existence seemed to be blotted out by physical pain.' At the beginning of 1938 she had to ask again to be relieved of her teaching duties, to which she was never to return. Indeed, possibly later in the year, 'a time came when I thought my soul menaced, through exhaustion and an aggravation of the pain, by such a hideous and total breakdown that I spent several weeks of anguished uncertainty whether death was not my imperative duty – although it seemed to me appalling that my life should end in horror' (SL, p. 140). Two years earlier she had been in exactly the same state of mind. The ten days she spent at Solesmes from Palm Sunday to Easter Saturday marked an important turning-point in her spiritual development. Although she had gone there primarily for aesthetic reasons (Solesmes was well known for the excellence of its plain chant and as a centre of liturgical renewal), her stay there involved the third and most decisive of her contacts with Catholicism.

Unlike her mother, who accompanied her, Weil attended all the services, sitting towards the back on the left side. She later wrote:

> I was suffering from splitting headaches; each sound hurt me like a blow; by an extreme effort of concentration I was able to rise above this wretched flesh, to leave it to suffer by itself, heaped up in a corner, and to find a pure and perfect joy in the unimaginable beauty of the chanting and the words. This experience enabled me by analogy to get a better understanding of the possibility of loving divine love in the midst of affliction. It goes without saying that in the course of these services the thought of the passion of Christ entered into my being once and for all. (WG, p. 20)

This was not, however, a conversion that came from nowhere, like that of Paul on the road to Damascus. Although Weil had professed herself an atheist in her youth, her attitude had rather been the sympathetic agnosticism of Alain, who had already discerned a mystical tendency in his pupil (cf. P, i ,p. 30). Like Simone de Beauvoir, she had seen the idea of equality as central to Catholicism and her attraction to the Christian idea of God as powerless had been reinforced by her factory year. Indeed later she claimed that 'I was born, I grew up and I always remained within the Christian inspiration', by which she meant simply that 'with regard to the problems of this world and this life I shared the Christian conception in an explicit and rigorous manner, with the most specific notions it involves' (WG, p. 16). Her open letter to the Rosières workers embodied, she protested to Bernard, 'purely and simply the Christian spirit' (SL, p. 23). This attitude, coupled with the long periods of meditation to which she had been given since her student days, and the recent strong impressions of Italy and particularly Assisi, prepared the ground for something new: that her religious feelings, which although strong had previously been vague, were now centred on the person of Christ.

She also acquired at Solesmes the idea of the supernatural power of the sacraments, an idea which was to be of lasting (and painful) importance to her. This was brought home to her by a young Englishman, John Vernon, 'because of the truly angelic radiance with which he seemed to be clothed after going to Communion' (WG, pp. 20f). She nicknamed him 'angel boy' because he also introduced her to the metaphysical poets of whom Herbert, and particularly his poem *Love*, was to become her favourite. She also met at Solesmes and became friendly with Charles Bell, a young American then studying at Oxford. Bell was nicknamed 'Devil Boy' – Weil was reading Marlowe's *Faustus* at the time. She would read poetry with him by candlelight in his attic room. On returning to Paris she wrote him a long letter in which she expressed for the first time the concept of affliction, the combination of physical agony, humiliation and helplessness typified by Christ on the Cross, that was to become central to many of her later writings.

Thus Solesmes was only a beginning. Weil herself put the decisive point in her religious evolution several months later when what might be called her mystical experiences began. She had taken to reciting the poem *Love* as an aid to meditation. She wrote later:

> At a moment of intense physical pain, while I was making the effort to love, although believing I had no right to give any name to the love, I felt, while completely unprepared for it (I had never read the mystics), a presence more personal, more certain, and more real than that of a human being; it was inaccessible both to sense and to imagination, and it resembled the love that irradiates the tenderest smile of somebody one loves. (SL, p. 140).

It was after this moment when 'Christ himself came down and took possession of me' that 'the name of God and the name of Christ have been more and more irresistibly mingled with my thoughts'. This whole experience came as a complete surprise to her:

> In my arguments about the insolubility of the problem of God I had never foreseen the possibility of that, of a real contact, person to person, here below, between a human being and God. I had vaguely heard tell of things of this kind, but I had never believed in them. In the *Fioretti* the accounts of the apparitions rather put me off, if anything, like the miracles in the Gospel. Moreover in this sudden possession of me by Christ, neither my senses nor my imagination had any part; I only felt in the midst of my suffering the presence of a love, like that which one can read in a smile on a beloved face. I had never read any mystical works because I had never felt any call to read them. God in his mercy had prevented me from reading the

mystics, so that it should be evident to me that I had not invented this absolutely unexpected contact. (WG, pp. 21f)

A mystical experience is, by its very nature, ineffable; and its authenticity is to be judged, if at all, by the life of the person concerned. And it was indeed to trying to express, in word and in deed, the meaning of these experiences that Weil devoted the rest of her life.

Between the visit to Solesmes and the beginning of her mystical experience, Weil decided once more to visit Italy before the onset of the catastrophe that she foresaw for Europe. She left on 22 May and spent a week in Florence revisiting her favourite places. Her visit was spoilt to some extent by the over-zealous attentions of some English ladies in the boarding house that Charles Bell had recommended to her. She was glad to get away for a few days to Fiesole and read Dante. Thence she went on to Padua where she became 'drunk, completely drunk' on the frescoes of Giotto. At the end of the first week of June she joined her parents in Venice, the city that inspired the play, *Venice Saved*, that she wrote two years later. On a visit to Ascolo, a small village in the foothills of the Dolomites, Weil discovered the traces of a fresco that had been painted over and which she was convinced was a tenth-century work. She was keen to get the original uncovered and restored, but when this was eventually done, after her death, the fresco turned out to be from a good three centuries later. Also at Ascolo, Weil was threatened with prison for calling a Fascist cinema attendant a liar; and in Verona she and her mother remained deliberately seated during the playing of a Fascist hymn preceding a performance of Verdi's *Nabucco*, and were forcibly raised to their feet by an indignant audience. Leaving Italy, they spent six weeks in the Tyrol and Switzerland and returned to Paris on 14 August. The next month saw the culmination of the crisis over the Sudetenland and the signing of the Munich agreement.

Before leaving for Italy, Weil had published an article entitled 'Europe at war over Czechoslovakia?', in which she maintained her pacifist position and expressed with forceful logic what most people at the time were thinking. The Czechoslovakian question could be considered, she said, from four points of view. From the point of view of rights, the Sudeten Germans had a certain right to self-determination. If it was exercised and they became a part of Germany then, because the geographic, economic and ethnographic maps of Europe did not co-incide, the probable result would be that Czechoslovakia would become a German satellite. But it might still be able to preserve its culture, its language, and its national characteristics. Since the Nazi ideology was simply racist and its only universal content was anti-Communism and anti-semitism, 'the Czechs can ban the Communist Party and exclude Jews from all relatively important positions without losing anything of their national life. In short, injustice for injustice – since there must be some form of injustice in any case – let us choose the one that has the least risk of leading to war' (FW, p. 265). Secondly, the balance of power would then shift towards Germany. But 'if one country must dominate the centre of Europe, it is in the nature of things that it will be Germany'. Moreover

> in the long run hegemony always weakens the country that has achieved it. But until now, both the acquisition of hegemony and the weakening that follows from it have always, if I am not mistaken, been brought about by wars. If this time the same process could take place without war, wouldn't that be real progress? (FW, p. 266)

Thirdly, treaty obligations had never been considered as overriding in international relations. But, fourthly and most importantly, the essential question was whether the chances for peace would be improved if France and Britain guaranteed the territorial integrity of Czechoslovakia. Weil saw only two choices:

> either France and England declare that they will go to war to maintain Czechoslovakia's integrity, or they openly agree to a transformation of the Czechoslovakian state that would satisfy the main German aims. Apart from these two choices, there can only be terrible humiliations, or war, or probably both. It's obvious to me that the second choice is infinitely preferable. (FW, p. 268)

Finally Weil asserted, no doubt rightly, that public opinion both in France and in Britain would not support a war on behalf of Czechoslovakia.

Although Weil herself came bitterly to regret her attitude at this time, it certainly seemed to follow both from her previous views and from the pacifist attitudes of a large part of the non-Communist Left. From her days at Henri IV and the Ecole Normale she, in common with many of her fellow pupils, had had an abhorrence of flag-waving patriotism. This antipathy was not diminished by her turn to Catholicism, which she, unlike so many traditional Catholics, refused to link with nationalism. Like most intellectuals of her generation, she had believed that resistance to Fascism and resistance to war went hand in hand. When there then appeared to be a dilemma between keeping the peace and stopping Hitler's ambitions for a *Grossdeutschland*, she chose the former. She was never a pacifist in the narrow sense of the word, as shown by her unbounded admiration for T. E. Lawrence, who was her model of a soldier saint.[8] She was aware of the possible necessity of dirtying one's hands and faced up to it with her usual lucidity:

participation, even from a distance, in the play of forces which control the movement of history is not possible without contaminating oneself or incurring certain defeat. Nor is it possible, without great lack of conscientiousness, to take refuge in indifference or in an ivory tower. Thus there remains the formula of the 'lesser evil', so discredited by the use which the social-democrats have made of it, as the only one applicable, provided it be applied with the coldest lucidity. (OL, p. 146)

Thus she always viewed war as in the larger context of the sufferings and oppression that it would entail for the mass of the people. But when war eventually came and some of her former pacifist colleagues (together with most of those on the Right) were willing to join Vichy in compromising with Hitler, Weil was not among them.

Meanwhile, as Europe hung precariously on the verge of war, Weil felt in her own person the profound disarray and humiliation inflicted by the Munich agreements which she had nevertheless supported. She feared the danger of a strong reaction in which 'all other ideas – whether of preserving and increasing the leisure, well-being, and liberty of the people at the expense of privilege, or of preserving privileges and the pride that goes with them – vanish in the face of the desire to aggrandise the nation' (FW, p. 274). The present situation was intolerable and the only rational course 'consists in keeping alive in one's mind, in addition to the present, a past and a future that bear no resemblance to it' (FW, p. 277). The only ray of hope that the Munich agreements offered was on the colonial question. In an essay published at the end of 1938, Weil again rehearsed the injustices and humiliations involved in the colonial enterprise on which her views were always both just and prescient. Nevertheless she did not believe that the solution consisted in armed revolt, since

the achievement and maintenance of independence in such conditions, the necessity of assuring a defence both against the previous colonial power and against other predators would necessitate such a moral tension, such an intensive mortgaging of all material resources that the population would risk getting neither well-being nor liberty. (EHP, p. 353)

Rather, she suggested, a progressive emancipation would be in everyone's interest. Such a reformist strategy might not appeal to revolutionaries and it might also come too late, but at least it might preclude the three disasters that would follow an armed uprising: frenzied nationalism, excessive industrialisation combined with mass poverty, and exacerbated militarism with state power controlling the whole of social life.

Weil sought relief from the depressing political situation in extensive reading. She delved widely into Greco-Roman and medieval history, read a lot of poetry and researched the more esoteric religious texts – the Egyptian *Book of the Dead*, works on Assyrian religion and on Manichaeism. She argued with Malraux about the Soviet Union, tried to persuade Gide to re-edit the works of Théophile and got to know the son of the last Turkish Sultan. This latter, who also happened to be brother-in-law of King Zog of Albania, had taken up temporary residence in the ground-floor flat in the rue Auguste Comte. Weil had long conversations with him and planned a trip to Albania. She was also friendly with a young civil servant, Pierre Dantu, and discussed at length with him problems of technology and mathematics. She persuaded him to take her to a brothel, disguised in her blue factory overalls and a beret. The visit was not a success: Weil's disguise was soon penetrated and the couple were almost lynched.[9]

One final time before the outbreak of war Weil returned to comment on the political situation in a long unpublished article. In March, Hitler's troops had occupied Prague; in April, Mussolini had invaded Albania and Britain had introduced conscription; in May, Germany and Italy had concluded a military alliance. For Weil this meant that the pacifism of previous years was no longer an option. For while 'both war and the domination of civilian life by the military are evils as great as enslavement by foreigners' it was equally true that 'an enslaved country may be subjected to a military regime and compelled to participate in its conqueror's wars' (SE, p. 178). In an era of unlimited or total war such as the present, any peace was likely to be as catastrophic as the war which preceded it. Since security could only be achieved by universal domination, the objective of the democratic powers could only be the annihilation of Germany, which implies 'either that some other country will acquire "universal domination" – which will be no less of an evil in its hands – or, more probably, since there seems to be no country of sufficient calibre for the role, the total ruin of Europe, which will thereafter no doubt become, in its turn, a colonial territory' (SE, p. 180). In an era of total war, negotiation simply became a phase of the war itself, designed above all to preserve that prestige which was the essence of power.

For Weil the key to the current situation did not lie in speculating about the psychology of Hitler. He was no maniac obsessed with delusions of grandeur: 'The appetite for power, even for universal power, is only insane when there is no possibility of indulging it; a man who sees the possibility opening before him and does not try to grasp it, even at the risk of destroying himself and his country, is either a saint or a mediocrity' (SE, p. 184). Nevertheless, in the long term, totalitarian regimes such as Hitler's were subject to fundamental weaknesses. The examples of imperial Rome and the Soviet Union showed that the constant purging of the top echelons of society undermined the continuous and reliable team-work demanded by action on a grand scale. Also, when the only incentives remaining were fear or ambition for power, weaknesses in the technical field would soon become apparent. Most important was the strain on the human material: 'The real stumbling-block of totalitarian regimes is not the spiritual need of men for freedom of thought; it is men's inability to stand the physical and nervous strain of a permanent state of excitement, except during a few years of their youth' (SE, p. 189). Enthusiasm was a machine which wore out and in the end produced the combination of docility and rancour characteristic of slaves.

Any sensible policy for the present time, therefore, should be to try to hold out as long as the German system was in its phase of expansion. An intuitive tactic of standing firm or giving way according to circumstance might yet circumvent the choice between enslavement and war. But Weil was now clear that her previous pacifism was no longer applicable: 'Only ten years ago France had the power to behave with generosity in Europe; even three years ago she could still at least have behaved with moderation; today she is able to do neither because she is not strong enough' (SE, p. 192). But France's attitude could not remain purely defensive, since such a stance would be bad for morale and unlikely to succeed. Only an appeal for genuine liberty could galvanise the people of France and further afield. But for that a new atmosphere was necessary: 'It is not enough that France should be regarded as a country which enjoys the remains of a freedom acquired long ago. If she is still to count in the world – and if she does not intend to, she may as well perish – she must be seen by her own citizens and by all men as an ever-flowing source of liberty' (SE, p. 194). Weil's conclusion did not go as far as to state, as she did later, that her former pacifist stance was mistaken – only that it was no longer applicable. But her words do parallel the tone of disillusion that followed her anarcho-syndicalist activities in the early years of the decade. In *Oppression and Liberty* she had said farewell to many of the expectations that had inspired her commitment to the workers' movement. Now she had, regretfully, to admit that her aims in international relations had proved equally elusive.[10]

During May 1939, Weil fell ill with pleurisy and only recovered slowly. Her doctors suggested a convalescence in the mountains of Switzerland. On her way there with her parents she spent a fortnight in Geneva. The treasures of the Prado had been sent there to escape the ravages of the civil war and were on exhibition. She spent long hours contemplating

1. (*left*) Selma Weil.

2. (*right*) Bernard Weil.

3. Aged two, with her brother André.

4. Aged six, with her father in Mayenne.

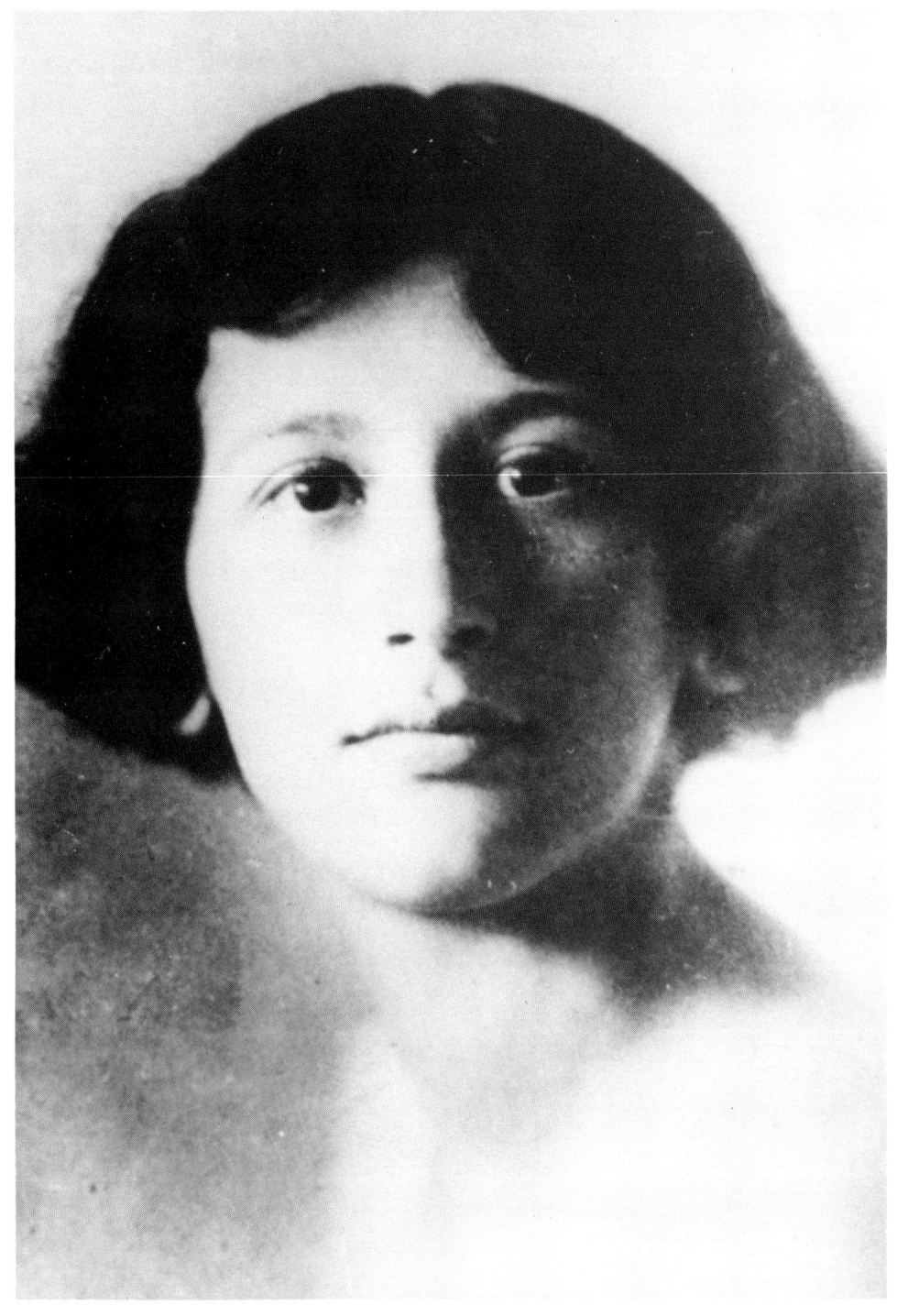

5. Aged thirteen, studio portrait taken during a visit to Baden-Baden.

6. Aged thirteen, with her brother at Knokke-le-Zoute in Belgium.

7. Surrounded by her pupils in the courtyard of the Lycée in Le Puy, Spring 1932.

8. (*left*) In the family flat in Paris, probably 1933.

9. (*right*) A cartoon by one of her Roanne pupils, during 1933–4. The light-bulb represents a platonic sun labelled 'good' with 'truth' descending on the heads of her pupils. Simone Weil is saying: 'I am convinced that we will soon be having a dictatorship.'

10. (*above*) Simone Weil with her pupils at Roanne in the school gardens. Anne Reynaud, who later published her notes of Simone Weil's lessons, is kneeling in front.

11. (*below*) The philosophy class at Roanne in the school gardens.

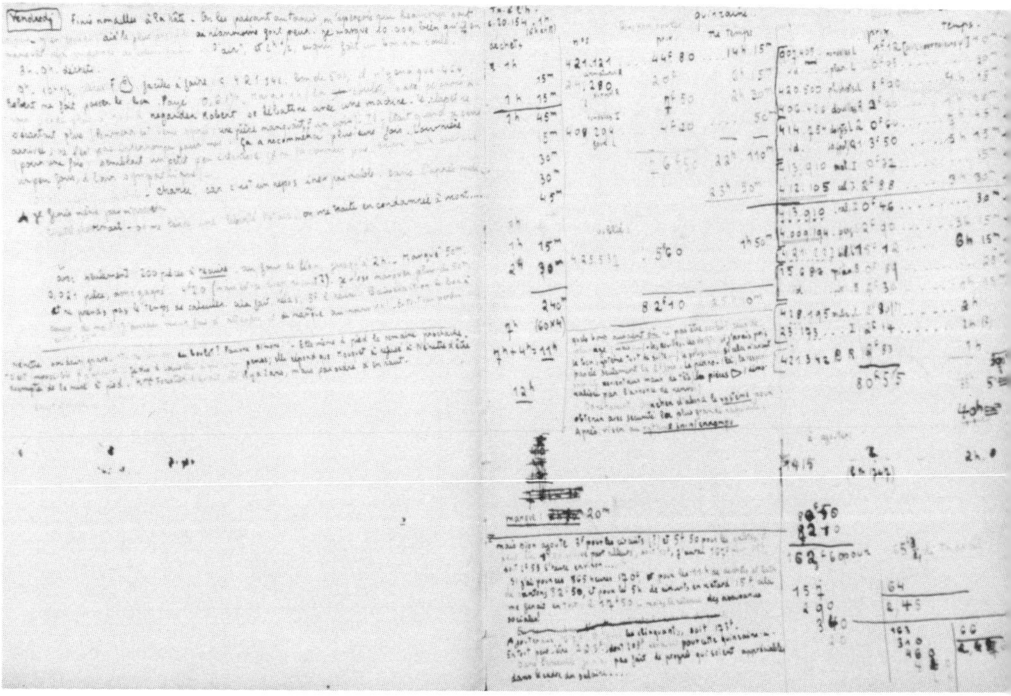

12. (*above*) A page from Simone Weil's *Factory Journal* showing her calculations of piece-rate earnings towards the end of her time at Alsthom.

13. (*below*) Simone Weil's fellow-workers at Alsthom. Photo taken during the sit-in strikes of June 1936.

. In the uniform of the anarchist militia, taken in Spain after her return from the Front in 1936.

Love

—

Love bade me welcome; yet my soul drew back,
    Guilty with dust and sin.
But quick-eyed Love, observing me grow slack
    From my first entrance in
Drew nearer to me, sweetly questioning
    If I lack'd anything

A guest, I answer'd, worthy to be here.
    Love said, You shall be he.
I, the unkind, ungrateful? Ah, my deare,
    I cannot look on thee.
Love took my hand and smiling did reply:
    Who made the eyes but I?

Truth, Lord; but I have marr'd them; let my shame
    Go where it doth deserve.
And know you not, says Love, who bore the blame?
    My deare, then let me serve.
You must sit down, says Love, and taste my meat.
    So I did sit and eat.

George Herbert.
1633.

15. The Poem 'Love' by George Herbert copied into her notebook by Simone Weil. It was while reciting this poem, and the 'Our Father', that she had several of her mystical experiences beginning in November 1938.

Parfois il se taisait, tirait d'un placard un pain, et nous le partagions. Ce pain avait vraiment le goût du pain. Je n'ai jamais plus retrouvé ce goût.

Il me versait et se versait du vin qui avait le goût du soleil et de la terre où était bâtie cette cité.

— Parfois nous nous étendions sur le plancher de la mansarde, et la douceur du sommeil descendait sur moi. Puis je me réveillais et je buvais la lumière du soleil.

Il m'avait promis un enseignement, mais il ne m'enseigna rien. Nous causions de toutes sortes de choses, à bâtons rompus, comme de vieux amis.

Un jour il me dit : "Maintenant va-t'en." Je tombai à genoux, j'embrassai ses jambes, je le suppliai de ne pas me chasser. Mais il me jeta dans l'escalier. Je le descendis sans rien savoir, le cœur comme en morceaux. Je marchai dans les rues. Puis je m'aperçus que je ne savais pas du tout où se trouvait cette maison.

Je n'ai jamais essayé de la retrouver. Je comprenais qu'il était venu me chercher par erreur. Ma place n'est pas dans cette mansarde. Elle est n'importe où, dans un cachot de prison, dans un de ces salons bourgeois pleins de bibelots et de peluche rouge, dans une salle d'attente de gare, n'importe où, mais non dans cette mansarde.

Je ne peux pas m'empêcher quelquefois, avec crainte et remords, de me répéter une partie de ce qu'il m'a dit. Comment savoir si je me rappelle exactement ? Il n'est pas là pour me le dire. Je sais bien qu'il ne m'aime pas. Comment pourrait-il m'aimer ?

16. A page from the 'Prologue' to her notebooks, written in Marseilles in the Spring of 1942.

17. Simone Weil with Lanza del Vasto, Marseilles, 1942.

18. Simone Weil in Marseilles, 1942.

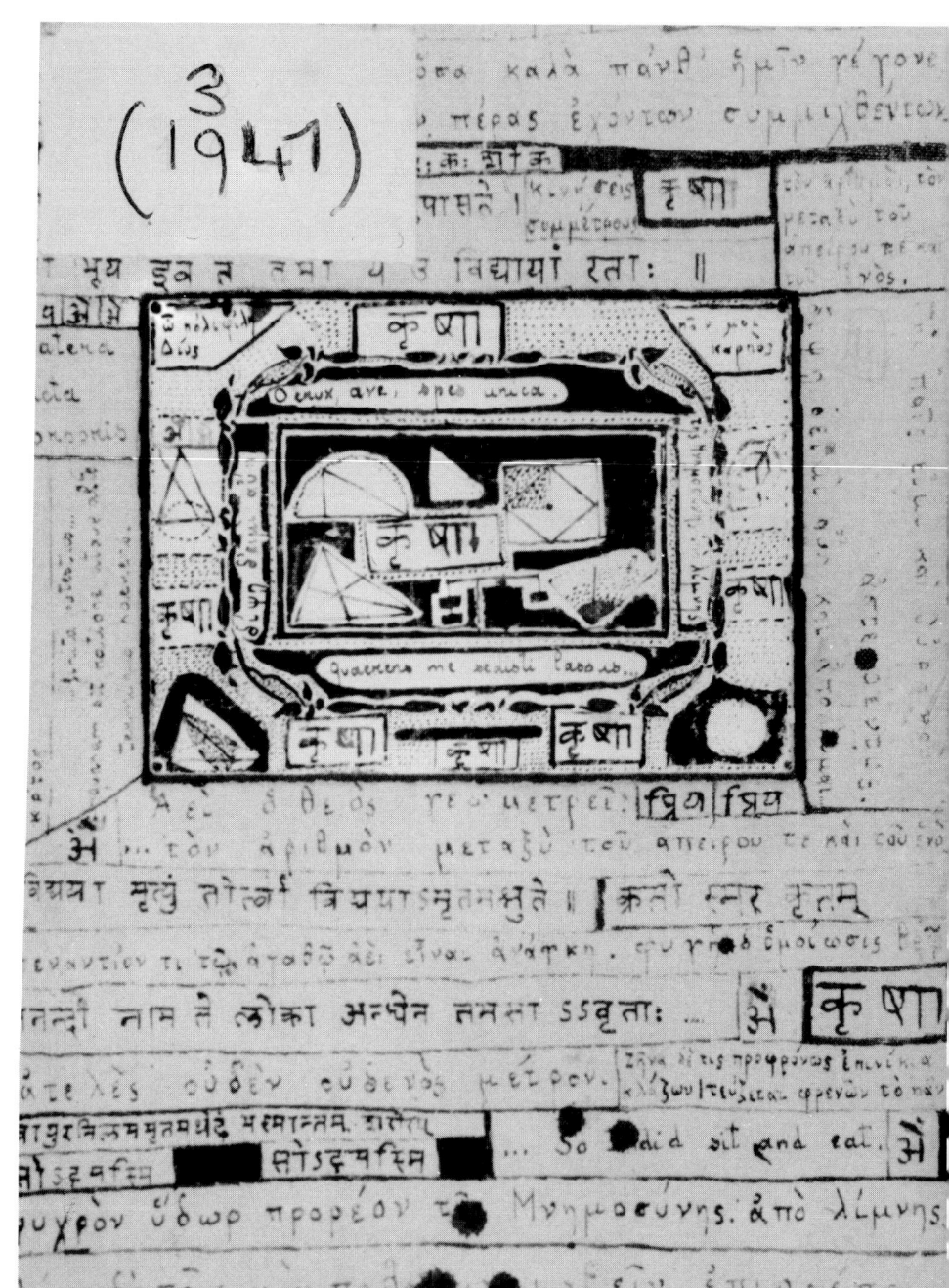

19. The cover of one of Simone Weil's notebooks, dating from 1941. The quotations are in Greek and Sanskrit.

20. (*left*) Passport photo taken in New York, October 1942.

21. (*below*) Simone Weil's Resistance pass dated two weeks before she entered the Middlesex Hospital.

FRANCE COMBATTANTE

LAISSEZ - PASSER

No. *1663*   Nom *lle Weil*

Prenoms *Simone*

Grade ou Profession *Redactrice*

Bureau ou Service *C. N. I*

Londres le *30 Mars 1945*

Le Chef du Service de Sécurité

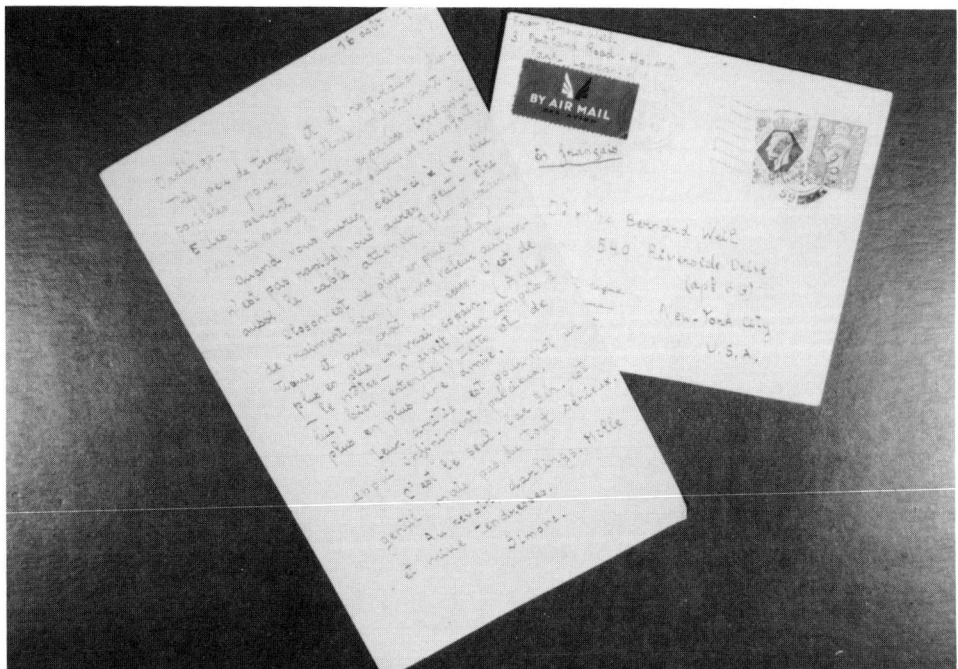

22. Last letter to her parents written from the Middlesex Hospital a week before her death. Note that she still gives her Portland Road address.

23. Simone Weil's grave in the New Cemetery in Ashford, Kent.

the paintings of Velasquez. From Switzerland they went to Peira-Cava in the hills above Nice, intending to spend the winter there, but on the outbreak of war returned to Paris.

7

Paris: War and History

'Something of the social labelled divine: an intoxicating mixture which carries within it every sort of licence. Devil disguised.' (GG, p. 145)

The war was to dictate the geographical context of the rest of Weil's life. Uprooted from Paris and the family flat which had been a focal point for her during the previous decade, she was to become an exile in the south of France, in New York, and finally in London. But the first nine months of the war – the 'phoney' part – did not have any dramatic impact on the Weil household. German troops smashed through Poland, Russia invaded Finland, but on the Western Front all remained quiet.

Weil used this time to do a lot of historical reading and illuminate the present discontent by reconsidering what were commonly listed in the France of her time as the three main sources of western European civilisation – Rome, Greece and Israel. Her preference for Greece over Rome and Israel sets the vital historical background for all her later religious speculation. But, like all Weil's writing, these historical studies had a strongly contemporary relevance: she was continuing to attend the meetings of the *Nouveaux Cahiers* group where the causes of the war were much debated. Some maintained that the main cause was the inherently aggressive nature of the German people and that the aim should be the destruction of Germany as a nation. Weil maintained, on the contrary, that nations did not possess unchanging characteristics and that the cause of the war was much more in the characteristics of the modern state which produced tendencies towards universal domination and that, therefore, the creation of an international order of a decentralised, federal nature that would prevent not only Germany, but other nations also, from aiming at universal domination was much to be desired.

This position was argued forcefully in a long article entitled 'Reflections on the Origins of Hitlerism' destined for publication in the *Nouveaux Cahiers*. In fact, its central section dealt exclusively with Rome and the parallels with Hitlerian Germany were only occasionally drawn. Her bitter hostility to the Romans and all their works is central to Weil's vision of history and politics. This hostility was acquired early. Even before she could read, pictures of the Romans led the tiny Simone to exclaim: 'Is it true that Romans exist? I am afraid of the Romans!' (P, I, p. 8). The French Romantic movement, Chateaubriand, Michelet had strongly criticised the Romans and it was common in left-wing circles in the 1930s to express a preference for Greece over Rome, in whose historical wake Maurras and the *Action Française,* by contrast, saw themselves firmly situated. Nevertheless admiration for Roman statecraft, law and literature as the foundations of European civilisation was widespread and it was this that Weil contested.

She chose as the period to illustrate her thesis not the corrupt Empire nor the civil war leading up to it but the founding of the Roman *Imperium* under the Republic of the second and third centuries BC. She returned to the original sources in Polybius and Appian to show that, contrary to the fanciful Nazi mythology, it was the Romans rather than the Teutons who most resembled the Germany of Hitler: indeed, 'the analogy between the systems of Hitler and of ancient Rome is so striking that one might believe that Hitler alone, after two thousand years, has understood directly how to copy the Romans' (SE, p. 101). Weil outlined her main thesis as follows:

> The Romans conquered the world because they were serious, disciplined, and organised; because their outlook and methods were consistently and continuously maintained; because they were convinced of being a superior race, born to command. And also because they successfully employed the most ruthless, premeditated, calculated, systematic cruelty, combining or alternating it with cold-hearted perfidy and hypocritical propaganda. With unswerving resolution, they always sacrificed everything to considerations of prestige; they were always inflexible in danger and impervious to pity or any human feeling. They knew how to undermine by terror the very souls of their adversaries, or how to lull them with hopes before enslaving them by force of arms; and, finally, they were so skilful in the policy of the Big Lie that they have imposed it even on posterity, and we still believe it today. Can anyone fail to recognise this character? (SE, p. 102)

As examples of Rome's systematic treachery and cruelty Weil chose the premeditated massacre in 210 BC of the inhabitants of Carthegena, a Carthaginian colony in Spain; the total destruction of Carthage itself in 146 BC contrary to formal guarantees; the similar fate of Numantia in Spain a decade later; and finally Julius Caesar's own account of his killing 40 000 Gauls, including children, on capturing the city of Bourges, and his wiping out of a German tribe of some half-million during his campaigns on the Rhine: 'If anyone resembles Hitler in his barbarity, premeditated perfidy, and skill of provocation, it is certainly Caesar' (SE, p. 100).

What Weil found even more repulsive than the brutality of the Romans was the pride they took in maintaining their prestige, their sense of mission, their conception of their bloody march to universal domination as an almost sacred duty: 'The Romans enjoyed that tough, unshakeable, impenetrable collective self-satisfaction which makes it possible to commit crimes with a perfectly untroubled conscience' (SE, p. 116). They made a desert – and called it peace. This prestige, moreover, could only be maintained by a huge propaganda drive which engulfed even such fine poets as Virgil. The Romans built good roads and bridges, but these did not make up a civilisation. In their sickening delight in gladiatorial contests, their persistent cruelty to slaves, and their rapacious attitude to their subjects, they were better at destroying other people's civilisations than at creating their own. Under the Empire, their politics became totalitarian: literature (with a few exceptions such as Juvenal) was in the service of the State, religion was largely the worship of their own nation, and their only contribution to science was the murder of Archimedes.

The severity of Weil's judgement on Rome springs from her view that the Roman system was based entirely on force which corrupted all that it touched. But her arguments for the view that the Roman conquests were 'the greatest catastrophe of history' (EHP, p. 298) are nevertheless questionable. Her teacher at Henri IV had complained that Weil considered herself 'above' history; and there is certainly an impression that here history is being interpreted according to a very ahistorical scheme of values. The facts she reports are indeed taken from reliable sources, but she is very selective, and tends to underemphasise similar cruelties perpetrated by the conquered. And some of her opinions, such as that pre-Roman Gaul enjoyed a superior civilisation, seem rather fanciful. But she does have a strong point in saying that, 'according to the nature of things, documents originate among the powerful ones, the conquerers. History, therefore, is nothing but a combination of the depositions made by assassins with respect to their victims and themselves' (NR, p. 215). She is also successful in combating the racist interpretation of German history current at the time. And her conclusion (referring to themes elaborated in *Oppression and Liberty*) that Hitler's rise to power had as its pre-condition the modern nation state is well taken:

Every new development for the last three centuries has brought us closer to a state of affairs in which absolutely nothing would be recognized in the whole world as possessing a claim to obedience except the authority of the State. The majority of people in Europe obey nothing else. Family authority is weak with the young and non-existent with the rest; local and regional authorities, in most countries, possess only such power as is delegated to them by the central authority. In the sphere of production, obedience is not offered to the managers, it is sold for money; so the managers' authority has no basis in tradition nor in any sort of tacit mutual agreement, but solely in a bargain without any trace of dignity and without guarantees unless enforced by the State. Even in the domain of intellect the State has become, thanks to the diplomas it confers, almost the only source of effective authority. (SE, p. 136)

By contrast to this worship of collective power, Weil suggested that 'there are two types of de-centralised organisation about which history gives us fairly full information: the small city and the feudal society. Neither of them offers a guarantee against tyranny or war, but each of them does more than the centralisation of Roman and modern times to stimulate and favour the better forms of life' (SE, p. 140). In the event, only the part dealing with the foreign policy of Rome was published in the *Nouveaux Cahiers*: the rest was suppressed by the censorship authorities, no doubt owing to the parallels she drew between the centralising and warlike tendencies of Hitler and those of Louis XIV and Napoleon.

A central theme of the article comparing Hitler and Rome was the role of force in history. The coming of the war prompted Weil to elaborate on this theme, this time with the focus on Greece and in a very different tone. She had already taught the *Iliad* to her pupils at Saint-Quentin two years earlier. Now she elaborated these ideas in a strikingly original essay, subtitled 'Poem of Force', which is one of her finest. In Weil's view, 'the true hero, the true subject, the centre of the *Iliad*, is force' (MILES, p. 183). Force was that which turned anyone subjected to it into a thing, whether by simple killing or by petrifying the living. With the aid of her own beautifully crafted translations, Weil showed how Homer believed all to be subject to its power:

> Force is as pitiless to the man who possesses it, or thinks he does, as it is to its victims; the second it crushes, the first it intoxicates. The truth is, nobody really possesses it. The human race is not divided up, in the *Iliad*, into conquered persons, slaves, suppliants, on the one hand, and conquerors and chiefs on the other. In this poem there is not a single man who does not at one time or another have to bow his neck to force. (MILES, p. 191)

What particularly impressed Weil about the *Iliad* – in contrast to current attitudes generated by the war with Germany – was firstly how Homer refused to veil the miseries of war with conceptions of glory or patriotism, and secondly how he distributed his sympathy even-handedly between the victors and the vanquished. Homer reflected her own feelings on the war, her distrust of triumphalism, her disillusion with both sides.

But however unvarnished and impartial the account of the battles, the subjugation of all the combatants in the Trojan War to the empire of force would be monotonous and desolate were it not relieved by occasional luminous moments: Hector before Troy in the last moments of his life tries to face up to his destiny without any help from gods or humans; love in its many forms makes brief but continuous appearances, culminating in the friendship that arises between the mortal enemies Priam and Achilles. But these moments only served to highlight the incredible bitterness that permeated the *Iliad*.

> It is in this that the *Iliad* is absolutely unique, in this bitterness that proceeds from tenderness and that spreads over the whole human race, impartial as sunlight. Never does the tone lose its colouring of bitterness; yet never does the bitterness degenerate into lamentation. Justice and love, which have hardly any place in this study of extremes and of unjust acts of violence, nevertheless bathe the work in their light without ever becoming noticeable themselves, except as a kind of accent. Nothing precious is scorned, whether or not death is its destiny; everyone's unhappiness is laid bare without dissimulation or disdain; no man is set above or below the condition common to all men; whatever is destroyed is regretted. Victors and vanquished are brought equally near us; under the same head, both are seen as counterparts of the poet, and the listener as well. If there is any difference, it is that the enemy's misfortunes are possibly more sharply felt. (MILES, p. 208)

For Weil, the heart of this epic was the retribution which attended the abuse of force with geometrical rigour. This idea of Nemesis for overstepping a limit had been lost in the West where 'conceptions of limit, measure, equilibrium, which ought to determine the conduct of life, are restricted to a servile function in the vocabulary of technology. We are only geometricians of matter; the Greeks were, first of all, geometricians in the apprenticeship to virtue' (MILES, p. 195).

The *Iliad*, however, did have one (and only one) worthy successor: 'The Gospels are the last marvellous expression of the Greek genius, as the *Iliad* is the first: here the Greek spirit reveals itself not only in the injunction given mankind to seek, above all other goods, "the kingdom and justice of our Heavenly Father", but also in the fact that human suffering is laid bare, and we see it in a being who is at once divine and human' (MILES, p. 212). The sense of human misery was the precondition for justice and love, since 'he who does not realise to what extent shifting fortune and necessity hold in subjection every human spirit, cannot regard as fellow-creatures nor love as he loves himself those whom chance separated from him by an abyss' (MILES, p. 212). Very soon, however, this message began to be lost, as when Christian martyrs welcomed suffering and death with joy – as though grace could do more for a human being than it did for Christ.

Weil's conclusion that 'nothing the peoples of Europe have produced is worth the first known poem that appeared among them' (MILES, p. 214) is certainly striking. It is doubtful whether Homer's heroes do have quite all the attributes that Weil gives them, but her whole interpretation illustrates her ability to cast her own original perspective on subjects that had hitherto seemed thoroughly familiar. It fits the mood of hopelessness and all-pervasive dehumanisation engendered by an era of total war, and recalls her bleak analysis of power six years earlier in *Oppression and Liberty*. The close link she tries to establish between Greek thought and Christianity is, of course, a large and controversial subject to which she devoted much of her later writing.

Given Weil's low opinion of the contribution of the Romans to western civilisation, it is not surprising to find them cited as one of the reasons for the eclipse of the Greek/Christian spirit praised at the end of the *Iliad* article. But there was, for her, a further and equally nefarious influence, that of Judaism. 'It was a second misfortune', she wrote, 'that Christianity's place of origin bequeathed to it a heritage of texts which often express a cruelty, a will to domination, an inhuman contempt for conquered or potentially conquered enemies, and a respect for force, which are extraordinarily congenial with the Roman spirit' (SE, p. 133). Thus, 'throughout twenty centuries of Christianity, the Romans and the Hebrews have been admired, read, imitated, both in deed and word; their masterpieces have yielded an appropriate quotation every time anybody had a crime he wanted to justify' (MILES, pp. 213f), and the twin influences of Rome and Israel prevented authentic Christianity emerging, except in underground and heretical forms.

Weil read the Old Testament as much more of an outsider than anyone would who had been brought up in the Christian tradition, and her judgement on it is indeed severe. Abraham began by prostituting his wife and adopted a God who allowed human sacrifice and all sorts of turpitude. Isaac preferred Jacob to Esau simply because he fed him better. Jacob was nothing but a crook and his sons were criminals, including Joseph whose behaviour towards the Egyptians was appalling. Israel, like Rome, was a rootless artificial city made up of refugees and incapable of civilisation or spirituality. Thus 'everything is of a polluted and atrocious character, as if designedly so, beginning with Abraham inclusive, right down through all his descendants (except in the case of some of the prophets – Daniel, Isaiah; any others ????) – as though to indicate perfectly clearly: Beware! that way lies evil' (NB, II, p. 568).

Weil used the story of Noah's sons Shem, Ham and Japheth to construct a counter-mythology of Mediterranean civilisation to that prevailing in the Judaeo-Christian tradition. In Weil's version, it was not Ham (and thus his descendants the Canaanites) who was cursed for discovering his father naked and drunk. This was a version put about by the Israelites when they had murdered the Canaanites. In reality, 'every civilisation bordering the Mediterranean immediately before the time of recorded history can be traced back to Ham' (WG, p. 158). The truly civilising peoples were thus the Phoenicians, Philistines, Sumerians, Hittites and Egyptians. It was the Semitic descendants of Shem and the Indo-European descendants of Japheth who were subject to the curse. But those of them who assimilated the spirituality of those they conquered redeemed themselves: the Celts, the Greeks, and the Babylonians. Others – Romans, Assyrians and pre-exilic Israelites – remained obstinate and deaf to any real spirituality.

Weil was not universally condemnatory of the Old Testament and its ethos. Although she read the whole of it carefully, her annotations show that she was chiefly interested in the Pentateuch and the first Prophets: she seemed to be much less interested from Isaiah onwards. Her opinion that 'the Hebrews, having rejected the Egyptian revelation, got the God they deserved – a carnal and collective God who never spoke to anyone's soul, up to the time of the exile' (NB, II, p. 570) was modified when it came to the post-exilic writings. She made an exception for Isaiah, Job, the Song of Songs, Daniel, some of the psalms and some of the Wisdom literature, because the exile had exposed the Israelites to the ideas of the Chaldees and also severely modified the social character of their religion:

> Through the monopoly of the Temple the Hebrew priests tried to make religion a purely social thing. It was Israel, not this or that individual Israelite, who had dealings with God. This is why it was only through exile, which completely destroyed the people, that they were able to find God, the God of the solitary soul, the Father who is in secret. Daniel prayed alone in his room. The cult had become a secret one. Hence the tone of the book of Isaiah and some of the psalms, etc. (FLN, p. 259)

But Weil took back the force of the exception she made in her condemnation of the Old Testament canon by claiming that the bits of which she approved were due to foreign influences on Israel. Her overall judgement was clear:

> I have never been able to understand how it is possible for a reasonable mind to regard the Jehovah of the Bible and the Father who is invoked

in the Gospel as one and the same being. The influence of the Old Testament and of the Roman Empire, whose tradition was continued by the Papacy, are to my mind the two essential sources of the corruption of Christianity. (SL, pp. 129f)

She found it impossible to accept the credal assertion that the Spirit had spoken through the Prophets. It was her refusal of Israel, every bit as much as her refusal of Rome, that was crucial in her refusal to join the Church.

In terms of historical scholarship,[1] many of Weil's views of the Old Testament seem far-fetched, as in her denial of Israelite origin to many of the bits of the Old Testament that she admired: 'Job was a Mesopotamian, not a Jew' and 'the first part of Genesis, before the genealogy of Abraham, can only be a transposition of Egyptian material, more or less well understood and adapted' (WG, p. 164; FLN, p. 251). This was because 'Israel learned the most essential truth about God (namely, that God is good before being powerful) from foreign traditional sources, Chaldean, Persian or Greek, and thanks to the exile' (LP, p. 14). Although she is right to detect Mesopotamian influences on the book of Job, the idea that the first chapters of Genesis were of Egyptian origin is pure fantasy, as is her explanation of the rapid conquest of Canaan by Joshua:

> At the very time when Moses judged, whether by divine inspiration or not, that the Hebrews had wandered long enough in the desert and could enter Palestine, the country was emptied of its warriors by the Trojan War, the men of Troy having called even fairly distant peoples to their assistance. The country, left undefended, fell an easy prey to the Hebrews who, under Joshua, needed few miracles to enable them to massacre the population without difficulty. But one day the warriors returned from Troy. Then the conquests were halted. At the beginning of the Book of Judges we even find the Hebrews much less advanced than at the end of the Book of Joshua; moreover we see them battling with populations which they were said to have utterly exterminated under Joshua. (WG, pp. 168f)

Historico-critical methods of analysis were far enough advanced at that time to have prevented Weil from making such statements – had she cared to look at the history of Israel from this point of view. But her approach was radically different. When her brother André contested some historical interpretation, objecting, 'That's not based on anything', she replied: 'It's based on what is beautiful, and if it's beautiful, it must be true' (SWNYL, p. 29). As her friend Perrin wrote:

Her supra-intellectual tendency is complicated by another that could be called subjectivist. Simone Weil had an inclination to judge everything by her interior feelings; she transposed onto what she was reading what she felt inside herself. If her soul was profoundly moved by some phrase in a book, particularly in the sacred writings of Egypt, of Greece, of ancient India, it did not occur to her to look for its meaning in relation to the time, to the media, or to the people concerned. She did not simply read. As she said herself, she consumed books and nourished herself therefrom.[2]

Her reading of the Old Testament, however selective and biased, was not arbitrary: it was strongly coherent with the religious views that she was developing.

The reasons for her negative reading of the Old Testament lie mainly in her conception of God. In spite of the presence in the Old Testament of numerous mediators such as angels, prophets, priests, Weil considered the God of Israel to be one who acted in history without the benefit of any mediation. But

> there cannot be any contact as from one person to another between man and God except through the person of the Mediator. Apart from him, the only way in which God can be present to man is in a collective, a national way. Israel, at the same time, and at one stroke, chose the national God and rejected the Mediator. It is possible that Israel may from time to time have sought after a genuine monotheism. But it always fell back upon, and could not do otherwise than fall back upon, the tribal god. (NB, II, p. 581)

According to Weil, human life and human institutions could have no immediate contact with the absolute. Pre-exilic Israel's conception of God was too monotheistic: 'When God is conceived only as One and not as Two (whence Three), that obliges one when one represents him to oneself as creator to confound the necessary with the good – as in the case of Israel, Islam . . .' (NB, II, p. 379). Thus the Hebrews attributed to God everything which was 'extra natural, devilish things just as much as divine things and that because they conceived of God under the attribute of power and not under the attribute of good' (PSO, p. 55). Moreover, the God of Israel was highly personal, whereas for Weil 'truth and beauty dwell on the level of the impersonal and the anonymous. This is the realm of the sacred' (SE, p. 13). Israel's God was also present and active in creation and subsequent history; whereas for Weil God was strikingly absent from history. Her conception of God was negative, supernatural and spiritual; that of Israel, by contrast, was positive, of a God only too busily involved with the natural and the secular. She differed, therefore, from the account given in Genesis of the creation of the world and the origin of evil. For her, 'on God's part creation is not an act of self-expansion but of restraint and renunciation. God and all his creatures are less than God alone. God accepted this diminution. He emptied a part of His being from Himself' (WG, p. 87). Thus she could not say, as does the author of Genesis, that creation is good: it is simply subject to the laws of necessity and characterised by the absence of God who alone is good. Thus, also, her view that original sin did not follow creation but was co-terminus with it; time itself was part of the created order and a derogation from the eternity of the absolute.

Although some of this religious metaphysics is obscure, the main reason for Weil's rejection of Israel is clear: she considered that 'they only considered God under the attribute of power and not under the attribute of good . . . to know the divinity only as power and not as good, is an idolatry and it does not matter whether there be one God or many. It is only because the good is unique that it is necessary to recognise only one God' (PSO, pp. 55, 48). The Old Testament was full of condemnations of idolatry: but Israel was itself idolatrous, not only in its deification of power but also in its conception of Providence and itself as the Chosen People. This gave divine sanction to the social idol which she had so savagely criticised in *Oppression and Liberty* (cf. OL, pp. 56ff). The idea of providence in the Old Testament was as idolatrous as Marx's conception of history and the proletariat. Both were simply mistaken, since the world just did not work like that. The Old Testament views of Providence and the Chosen People were bound to be exclusive and sectarian and contrary to Weil's view of the continuity of traditions and the universality of the religious spirit. She could not abide the separateness of Israel, any more than she could that of the Catholic Church. The history of battles, massacres and near genocide were no different from the general run of things: what Weil found totally unacceptable to the point of blasphemy was that these things should be attributed to the activity of God in the world.

The picture of the God of the Old Testament was, of course, partial – and Weil occasionally admitted this.[3] Some of it probably came from her father who had reacted strongly against the very strict orthodoxy of his upbringing. And her strong individualism was in stark contrast to the idea of a collective destiny which is so strong in Judaism. More importantly, Alain was severely critical of 'this God of the Bible who is always massacring' and many of Weil's statements are echoes of her previous teacher's views of Israel as a religion of power.[4] Bernanos's *Grands cimetières sous la lune*, which Weil admired very much, contained similar sentiments.[5] But whatever their provenance, Weil undoubtedly carried these views to their extreme in her brutal and uncharacteristic reading of the Old Testament.[6] A latter-day follower of Marcion, the Second Century heretic who wished to exclude the Old Testament from the Christian canon, she showed against the Old Testament the same selective intransigence with which she reproached Israel. It was one of the several paradoxes of her life that, of Jewish origin herself, it should be her refusal of the Old Testament that kept her out of the Catholic Church.

At the same time as she was articulating these negative views of Rome and Israel, Weil was developing, as a counterpoint to them, an enthusiasm for the lost civilisation of the Languedoc, which she saw as the cradle of those western humanist values currently being threatened by Hitler. This civilisation flourished in the south of France during the twelfth century AD as Europe began to emerge out of the Dark Ages. It was a rich civilisation: its capital Toulouse was the third city of western Europe after Rome and Venice. Languedoc had, as its name implied, a distinct language known as Oc. It also had a distinct literature, that of the Troubadours, and a distinct political organisation, a mixture of monarchy and democracy which borrowed a lot from antiquity and was not unlike some of the Italian city states emerging at the same time. Most striking of all, the Languedoc of that time was the centre of the Catharist heresy. Catharism was a different religion to Christianity from which, nevertheless, it had borrowed some elements: it believed in reincarnation, thought that the world was created by the devil, and held that the body was an obstacle to spiritual perfection. The civilisation of the Languedoc perished in half a century of bitter wars when the forces of the Pope and of the Kings of France under Simon de Montfort combined in a series of crusades to wipe out the Albigensians – as the Cathars were known in the Languedoc.

Weil felt that the twelfth-century Languedoc embodied the kind of virtues which were so cruelly lacking in Rome and Israel. During the following year in Marseilles, Weil wrote two articles entitled 'The Agony of a Civilisation' and 'In What Does the Occitanian Inspiration Consist?', in which she expressed her admiration for the civilisation of the Languedoc. And just as her discussion of the *Iliad* had the contemporary defeat of France as its backcloth, so Weil saw the defeat of the Albigensians as contributing to the troubles of her own time. The forcible annexation of the Languedoc, the end of a Renaissance which held a far greater promise than the one that occurred three centuries later, had marked the beginning of the emergence of the centralised French nation state of Richelieu and all its attendant evils. It was the triumph of the spirit of Rome and Israel over Greece and held inescapable lessons for the immediate future. For what attracted Weil to the Languedoc of the eleventh and twelfth centuries was that it had its roots in the pre-Roman world:

Twenty-two centuries ago the Roman arms killed Greece and their
domination brought sterility to the Mediterranean basin . . . but
once in the course of the last twenty-two centuries there arose a
Mediterranean civilisation which would perhaps with time have
attained a degree of spiritual freedom and creativity as high as that of
Ancient Greece – if it had not been killed. (SE, pp. 37f)

The religious centre of this civilisation – Catharism – drew its inspiration
from sources as wide apart as Platonic thought and the wisdom of the
Druids. As well as by their representing 'the last living expression in
Europe of pre-Roman antiquity', Weil was attracted to the Cathars by
'their opinion about the Old Testament . . . that the worship of power
caused the Hebrews to lose the idea of Good and Evil' (SL, pp. 129f).
Like the heroes of the *Iliad*, the inhabitants of the Languedoc understood
the real meaning of force, which was 'to recognise that it was almost
absolutely supreme in this world, and yet to reject it with loathing and
contempt' (SE, p. 48). The counterpart of this rejection of force was their
conception of love, which was

> simply a patient attention towards the loved person and an appeal
> for that person's consent. The word *Merci* by which the Troubadours
> designated this consent is very close to the notion of Grace. Such a
> love, in its plenitude, is the love of God through the person loved. In
> this land, as in Greece, human love was one of the bridges between
> man and God. (SE, p. 50)[7]

These high ideals were sustained by a decentralised public life which,
like Greece, was based on small city states. There was a remarkable
cohesion between the different orders of society united by an informed
obedience and the object of their strong patriotism, which they defined
not as territory but as their common language – the *Langue d'oc*. This
social ethos was due in large part to the 'miracle' of Catharism in that
'around Toulouse in the twelfth century the highest thought dwelt
within a whole human environment and not only in the minds of a
certain number of individuals' (SL, p. 130). Catharism was one of the
least dogmatic of religions and enabled them to live in harmony with
the orthodox Catholics. The same spirit of harmony was to be found in
their art: in the Romanesque Church which – unlike the taint of power
and pride displayed in the thrust of Gothic spires and arches – 'is
suspended like a balance around its point of equilibrium, a point which
is real although there is nothing to show where it is'; and in the
Gregorian chant which 'rises slowly until, at the moment when it seems
to be gaining assurance, the ascending movement is broken off and

goes down; the ascending movement is always conditioned by the descending. The source of all this art is Grace' (SE, p. 50).

Weil realised that she was painting a somewhat idealised picture: 'In the Toulouse of the early years of the thirteenth century social life was polluted no doubt, as it is always and everywhere' (SE, p. 52). But at least the inspiration, she continued,

> composed solely of civic spirit and obedience, was pure. Among those who attacked it victoriously, inspiration itself was polluted . . . The Gothic Middle Ages, which began after the destruction of Languedoc, were an essay in totalitarian spirituality. The profane as such had no rights any more. This lack of proportion is neither comely nor just; spirituality is necessarily degraded by becoming totalitarian. This is not what Christian civilisation is. Christian civilisation is the Romanesque civilisation, which disappeared prematurely by assassination. (SE, p. 48)

This totalitarian spirituality had produced its opposite in the sixteenth-century Renaissance whose secular humanism continued some of the spirit of the Languedoc but without any supernatural light, and developed like a plant deprived of chlorophyll. In her own day, Weil thought this humanism was under attack from two sides:

> There are those who look for [its] opposite in the adoration of a force, of the collective, of the social beast; others seek it in a return to the Gothic Middle Ages. The former is possible and even easy, but it is evil; the latter, too, is not desirable, and moreover it is entirely chimerical, since it is impossible for us to undo the fact that we have been brought up in an environment almost exclusively composed of profane values. Salvation would be to go to the place of purity where the opposites are one. (SE, p. 53)

She realised, of course, that there was no direct road to such a place and concluded:

> What has been killed can never revive; but its equivalent can be called into being, by a reverence kept alive through the ages, when circumstances are favourable again. Nothing is more cruel to the past than the commonplace which asserts that spiritual values cannot be destroyed by force; on the strength of this belief, civilisations that have been destroyed by force of arms are denied the name of civilisation; and there is no risk of our being refuted by the dead. In this way we kill once again something that has perished, and ally ourselves with the cruelty of the sword. Piety enjoins reverent

attention to the traces, however scarce, of destroyed civilisations, and an attempt to conceive what their spirit was. The spirit of the civilisation of the *langue d'oc* in the twelfth century corresponds, so far as we can discern it, to aspirations which have never died and which we must not allow to die, even though we cannot hope to fulfil them. (SE, p. 43)

In her last work, *The Need for Roots*, Weil was to sketch out in some detail what this inspiration might mean for postwar France.

It was not only history that engaged Weil's attention during the first year of the war. At the same time as casting her critical eye over the intellectual and spiritual antecedents of Europe's plight, and its possible remedies, she was also engaged in trying to do something more immediate. She longed to have some active part in the war and expose herself to the same dangers as the combatants. To this end she elaborated two projects which could give her this active role. The first concerned Czechoslovakia, where the Germans had brutally suppressed a revolt of students in Prague. Weil worked out a plan to parachute troops and arms into Czechoslovakia to ferment a revolt among the population and rescue those in prison. She tried to interest the authorities in the project, insisting that she herself would be one of the participants. Every day for weeks she anxiously scanned the newspapers to see whether her idea had been adopted, but without result. Her second and marginally less impractical idea was to form small groups of specially selected nurses who would come to the aid of the wounded and dying in the Front Line. Many soldiers died, she argued, for want of immediate attention, and the nursing skills required to save them would be elementary. But there was another point to her proposal:

One must remember the essential role played in the present war by moral factors . . . Hitler has never lost sight of the essential need to strike everybody's imagination – his own people's, his enemies', and the innumerable spectators' . . . For this purpose one of his most effective instruments has been such special bodies as the SS, and the groups of parachutists who were the first to land in Crete, and others as well. These groups consist of men selected for special tasks who are prepared not only for risking their lives but for death . . . We cannot copy these methods of Hitler's. First, because we fight in a different spirit and with different motives; and also because, when it is a question of striking the imagination, copies never succeed. Only the new is striking. But if we neither can nor ought to copy these methods, we do need to have their equivalents. This need is perhaps a vital one. (SL, pp. 148f)

It would, she thought, be difficult but not impossible to find women who possessed both the cold resolution and the tenderness to fulfil such a role. They would in any case not be numerous (ten would do to start with) and Weil intended to be one of them. In fact, her project was much more suited to the conditions of the First World War than those of the Second. Nevertheless she got her ideas to the attention of the Army Commission of the Senate and claimed to be well on the way to success before being overtaken by events. But the implementation of the project remained almost an obsession with her until the end of her life.

The one way in which the outbreak of war did affect Weil most directly was the imprisonment of her brother André on a charge of desertion. In April 1939, he had been sent, with his wife Eveline whom he had married two years earlier, on a scientific mission to Scandinavia. When war broke out he sent Eveline back to France but stayed in Finland, as he had decided to take no part in the war and continue with his mathematical researches. When Russia attacked Finland, however, he was arrested as a spy and almost executed. Instead, he was deported to Sweden and, since he had asked to be repatriated, sent on to Britain and thence to France. He arrived at Le Havre at the beginning of February, was immediately arrested and spent three weeks in prison before being moved to Rouen where he spent two months awaiting trial. All this time, his sister was distraught with anxiety, blaming herself for having encouraged his pacifist tendencies. Together with her parents she visited him in prison as frequently as possible and above all tried to take his mind off present troubles by writing him long letters about mathematics. This rekindled her interest in the significance of science which was to preoccupy her henceforth and form one of the important bases of her *Notebooks*.

Weil's main point in her letters to her brother was that the sort of mathematics he was pursuing seemed to her to be too abstract and removed from concrete problems. At the back of her mind was the idea that she had so often expressed in the early 1930s: that contemporary science and mathematics were becoming increasingly distant from the problems of real life, the preserve of an intellectual elite, and devoted to solving questions about means without any regard to ends.[8] 'Present-day mathematics', she wrote to her brother, 'considered either as science or as art, seems to me to be singularly far from the world. Could not an effort of reflection and criticism bring it closer? . . . It is one of the goals to which I would have loved to devote my entire life; but, alas, I have several goals' (P, p. 368). To this end, she nevertheless pursued extensive researches into the history of mathematics. She did not much like the Babylonians, who were too devoted to abstract exercises concerning numbers and too keen on algebra, and the Egyptians were too concerned with the direct solution of straight-forwardly empirical problems. The Greeks, on the other hand, managed to apply a rational method to concrete problems and the study of nature. Unlike the Babylonians, they 'attached no value to a method of reasoning for its own sake, they valued it insofar as it enabled concrete problems to be studied efficiently' (SL, p. 117). And, unlike the Egyptians,

> this was not because they were avid for technical applications but because their sole aim was to conceive more and more clearly an identity of structure between the human mind and the universe. Purity of soul was their one concern: to 'imitate God' was the secret of it; the imitation of God was assisted by the study of mathematics, insofar as one conceived the universe to be subject to mathematical laws, which made the geometer an imitator of the supreme law-giver. (SL, p. 117)

Far from the discovery of incommensurability (of the diagonal of a square, say, to the sum of its size) being the disaster for Greek thought that some historians had claimed, it enabled them to evolve the conception of geometry as a science of proportion by which to approach these problems. She was thus, she told her brother, totally opposed to Nietzsche's account of the Dionysian and Apollonian elements in the Greeks:

> If, by the sense of disproportion between thought and the world, you mean the sense of being an exile in the world, then I agree; the Greeks experienced intensely the feeling that the soul is in exile. It was from them that this feeling passed into Christianity. Such a feeling does not involve anguish, however, but only bitterness. Moreover, if the Stoics – as I am convinced – invented nothing, but only reproduced in their language the thought of Orphism, Pythagoras, Socrates, Plato, etc., one can then say that this place of the soul's exile is precisely its fatherland, if only it knew how to recognise it . . . More than any other people, the Greeks possessed the feeling of necessity. It is a bitter feeling, but it precludes anguish. (SL, p. 125)

This was the same theme that she had elaborated in her essay on the *Iliad*. These letters to her imprisoned brother show once again Weil's penchant for speculative reconstruction of history and also her strong attachment to the past: 'If only I had a machine to travel through time, I would not turn towards the future but towards the past. And I would not even stop among the Greeks; I would at least go all the way back to the epoch of the Aegean-Cretans. But this very thought has the effect on me that a mirage has upon a man lost in a desert. It makes me thirsty' (P, p. 371). This feeling of nostalgia is one running through all of Weil's writings.

André Weil's case came up for trial in early May and he was sentenced to five years' imprisonment, which was suspended while, at his own request, he was sent to the Front. His sister meanwhile continued to make every effort to get sent there herself. Instead the Front came rapidly to her. On 10 May, a week after her brother's trial, the Germans unleashed their blitzkrieg. Holland and Belgium were rapidly overrun. By 20 May, Guderian's Panzer Divisions had reached the Channel, all but capturing the entire British Expeditionary Force. The defence of France had collapsed and the Weils could observe from their flat the floods of refugees leaving Paris for the south. Her parents wished to join them, but Weil insisted on staying, hoping that Paris would be defended against the Germans as it had been in 1870. But by 13 June the Germans were at the gates. The Weil family were out shopping together when they saw the notices declaring Paris an open city. This finally convinced her to leave and all three went, just as they were, without returning to the flat, to the Gare de Lyon, where they managed to scramble on the last train to the south. They went as far as Nevers, hoping that the Front would stabilise itself on the Loire. But the Germans arrived the same night. After several days they learned of the Armistice and the establishment of a non-occupied zone. They decided to go there on foot, buying baskets in order to look like peasants. After walking for miles, they eventually got a lift to Vichy. They arrived just as Pétain was installing his government there.

Weil spent two months in Vichy with her parents. Her mood was one of anger – against herself for her former pacifism, against the French government for abandoning its powers and the war, and against several of her former friends such as Rèné Château, for drawing collaborationist conclusions from their pacifism.[9] During the trek from Nevers, a sore had developed on her leg and it refused to heal. She spent most of the time in her sleeping-bag, working away at a play entitled *Venice Saved* which she had begun in Paris a few months earlier. The play expressed in dramatic form the themes of the opposition between the forces of society and the individual, of the identity of the beautiful and the real, and the value of redemptive suffering that she was to struggle to express for the rest of her life. She took her plot from the Abbé de Saint-Réal's account of the conspiracy of the Spanish Empire against the city of Venice in 1618. Spain stands here for the collectivity, the social beast which inevitably expands – the Roman Empire in the past and Hitler's Germany in the present.[10] The conspirators suborned by the Spanish ambassador inside Venice are a bunch of uprooted exiles and mercenaries who wish, in their turn, to uproot and destroy the civilisation of Venice's city-state. In the play, Jaffier, the leader of the invasion party, is suddenly struck by the beauty of Venice, realises all will be lost if the city is destroyed and betrays the conspiracy of the Council of Ten in return for a promise (later abjured) to spare the lives of his fellow-conspirators. Jaffier is a sort of Christ-like anti-hero who is granted a moment of supernatural intuition when the innocence, vulnerability and beauty of Venice, indeed its sheer *existence*, impress themselves so vividly upon him that he is capable of a self-sacrificial gesture which frustrates the otherwise implacable laws of social force. In contemplating the beauty of Venice, Jaffier is enabled to leave the dreams and illusions imposed by his social role and get in touch with reality: for a moment, he possesses the purity which stops evil, but at the price of his own destruction and that of his companions. The parallel with Weil's own project for front-line nurses is evident.[11]

Venice Saved was never finished, though she continued working at it until the last weeks of her life. Weil's main desire was, and continued to be, to get to England and join those who were continuing the war. To this end she sent in to the Minister of Education, Georges Ripert, an official request for a teaching post 'abroad or in the Colonies'. Anticipating the lack of any positive response, she moved, with her parents, to Toulouse, where they stayed two weeks. She obviously hoped to get out through North Africa. In Vichy she had met Guindy, a fellow-student at Henri IV and the Ecole Normale Supérieure, whose current job as a civil servant in the Treasury enabled him to travel between Vichy and Paris. She wrote to him from Toulouse asking him to go to the flat in the rue Auguste Comte and get the manuscript of *Oppression and Liberty* for safe keeping. She added: 'Although one cannot foresee what the future will bring, I feel that I have lost all wish to return. And it's not just because of the circumstances. I have always thought that one day I would leave like this. You can write in care of Poste Restante in Casablanca' (P, p. 383). The obvious route to North Africa was through Marseilles and it was there that she arrived with her parents in the first half of September, en route, as she thought, to North Africa, America and England. But nothing endures like the temporary. It was to be twenty long months before she could even start that journey.

8

Marseilles: Life

'The handshake of a friend on meeting again after a long absence. I do not even notice whether it gives pleasure or pain to my sense of touch: like the blind man who feels the objects directly at the end of his stick, I feel the presence of my friend directly. It is the same with life's circumstances, whatever they may be, and God.' (GaG, p. 21)

Marseilles in the late 1940s was the turbulent centre for refugees of all sorts and many who were trying to get out of France. The Weil family put up in a small pension on the sea front for a month while they tried to get exit visas to Morocco or Portugal. When this failed, they paid a lot of money for visas to Siam, on the assurance that once they had left France they were not obliged to go to Siam and could go anywhere they wanted. Once the money had changed hands, however, it appeared that the visas were only valid on Siamese boats – which did not exist. So they settled down for a long wait and rented a small flat on the rue des Catalans just by the old port. It was on the seventh floor of a relatively new block and had splendid views of the beach and the sea. Things began to improve when they managed, just before the closing of the frontier with German-occupied France, to get their maid Adèle to send from Paris several trunks of their belongings, including Weil's manuscripts and most of her books. André Weil also managed to get to Marseilles by boat from England. He moved almost immediately to Clermont Ferrand where the University of Strasbourg, to which he belonged, had been relocated, and within a few weeks had got a visa for the United States. On his arrival in New York, Weil wrote to him that their parents were keen to get to America. As for herself,

my attitude has not changed. I don't wish to stay in America for a whole pile of reasons . . . the fact of being far from Europe would make me suffer to the point of losing all moral equilibrium. Being in France, the stories about, for instance, famine in France don't upset me; even if a real famine occurred, I would undergo it like the others and my imagination would not be unduly affected by it; but in America, even though theoretically I know very well the exaggerations that newspapers are capable of, reading articles on this subject would upset me enormously. Whether it be simply from an instinct of self-preservation or not, I must above all avoid going over there to live. (P, pp. 396f)

The one exception to this was if her going to America could help her to realise her project of front-line nurses, a subject on which she pressed her brother to send her precise information.

Meanwhile Weil's request three months earlier to be reappointed to a teaching post had been overtaken by the 'Statute on Jews' brought into force by the Vichy government which prohibited the employment of Jews in schools. Weil responded to the Minister of Education with an ironical letter which barely concealed her anger at being defined by anything but her own intellectual commitments:

> I do not know the definition of the word Jew; this subject has never been part of my programme of studies. True, the text says whoever has had three Jewish grandparents is to be considered a Jew; but this clarification only puts the difficulty back for two generations. Does this word designate a religion? I have never entered a Synagogue and I have never witnessed a Jewish religious ceremony . . . Does this word designate a race? I have no reason to suppose that I have any sort of tie, either through my father or my mother, with the people who lived in Palestine 2,000 years ago . . . For the rest, one can conceive of the inheritance of a race, but it is difficult to conceive of the inheritance of a religion. As for myself, who do not practise any religion and have never done so, I have not inherited anything of the Jewish religion . . . If there is a religious tradition that I regard as my patrimony, it is the Catholic tradition. The Christian, French, Hellenic tradition is mine; the Hebrew tradition is foreign to me; no text of a law can change that for me. If nonetheless the law demands that I regard the term 'Jew', whose meaning I do not know, as an epithet applicable to my person, I am disposed to submit to it as to any other law. But then I want to be officially informed, since I do not possess any criterion susceptible of resolving this point. (P, pp. 391f)

This letter, too, received no reply.[1]

Within days of arriving in Marseilles, Weil, typically, had got in touch with the poorest section of its society – the immigrant Indo-Chinese workers. The government had drafted them into France in their thousands at the outbreak of war to help in the production of munitions. Now they had flowed to Marseilles and were being interned in the large Baumettes prison which, being still under construction, had no heating or light. As a long-standing critic of French colonial policy, Weil was appalled. One of the inmates told her that he had signed on to see France but had seen nothing – on the contrary, 'I live in darkness and am dreadfully bored', words which Weil herself 'repeated in a voice dark with emotion'.[2] The winter of 1940–1 was one of the coldest within living memory in Marseilles and the Indo-Chinese workers were issued with brooms and told to go and sweep up the snow. 'There was nothing more pitiable', she said 'than these poor people, standing there in the middle of the snow, in their torn, ragged clothes with not the faintest idea of what they were supposed to do!' (P, p. 387). She gave most of her food coupons to the Indo-Chinese. She also wrote several letters to an old class-mate of hers in the Vichy government, describing conditions in the prison and suggesting that the governor was corruptly putting the free labour of the Indo-Chinese at the disposal of building contractors. This time she had more success: the governor was dismissed and conditions improved.

Weil was also concerned about the camps where foreigners, mostly anti-Fascist refugees from neighbouring countries, had been hurriedly interned. Nicholas Lazarévitch, a Belgian friend from the days of *La Révolution Prolétarienne*, had told her from his own experience about the terrible conditions there. Not getting satisfaction this time from her contacts in the government she wrote to Admiral Leahy, United States Ambassador to Vichy:

> You know, of course, all the facts about the bad treatment of aliens in France, the concentration camps, etc. – facts which I, as a Frenchwoman, can scarcely bear to think upon for very shame. In spite of all official promises, these shameful things are still going on. I even happen to know that in the Camp du Vernet there has been lately an aggravation. For the sake of these unhappy people, for the sake, also, of the French men and women to whom honour is dearer than food, I think America should refuse to give any help until these cruel treatments have really ceased. (P, II, pp. 307f)

Lazarévitch had also mentioned to her a Spanish anarchist named Antonio Atares who was an inmate of the Camp du Vernet whom he much admired. Since Antonio knew no-one outside the camp and never got a letter or a parcel, Weil entered into a correspondence with him (which she kept up even from New York), sending him books and money, and tried continuously to get him released.

Very soon after arriving in Marseilles, Weil made contact with the *Cahiers du Sud*, which after the fall of Paris had become the most important review in France. Although a provincial review, it aimed to be universal and considered Paris to be just another province. Since its foundation by Marcel Pagnol it had gone through a surrealist phase and still printed a lot of poetry.[3] Its small offices on the top floor of a building overlooking the Old Port were the focal point of intellectual life in Marseilles. The Director of *Cahiers du Sud*, Jean Ballard, refused Weil's poems, judging them too traditional, but was enthusiastic about her essay on the *Iliad* which appeared in the December 1940 issue of the

Cahiers. Given the anti-Semitic climate, it appeared over the anagram-matic pseudonym, Emile Novis. Weil became a regular, even daily, visitor to the attic offices near the Old Port. The poet Jean Tortel, one of the regular collaborators of the *Cahiers du Sud*, has left the following rather overwritten description of her at this time:

> A kind of body-less bird, withdrawn inside itself, in a large black cloak down to her ankles that she would never take off, still, silent, at the end of an old settee where she would sit alone – a settee overloaded with books and magazines – alien yet attentive, both observant and distant. Letting us talk, she was often deeply plunged in some book, reading in the midst of conversations from which she seemed absent. She was a presence, someone who was simply there, unusual and perhaps incomprehensible. A stranger amongst us, redoubtable (and a little feared). Extremely ugly at first sight, a thin and worn face under her large black beret, straight hair, an absent body, with only heavy black shoes to be seen beneath the cloak, she would look (whenever she did look) through her spectacles, her eyes very much to the fore as also her head and her bust, centring on the thing she watched with her invasive short-sightedness, with an intensity and also a kind of questioning eagerness that I have never encountered elsewhere. . . . She did not let us go. The eagerness in Simone Weil's eyes was unbearable. In her presence, all 'lies' were out of the question. But I also sometimes felt the need simply to escape from her denuding, tearing and torn eyes which would swallow up and leave helpless the person she was looking at, transported against their will into the depths of Being. Yet this eagerness was balanced, and somehow contradicted, (as well as multiplied), by the imploring expression of her mouth, her large humid lips seemed to be endlessly making a request which was both smiling and desperate. . . . She spoke with a calm, soft voice, slowly, revealing her slightly decayed teeth. It was as though she wanted to encircle and keep her interlocutor with her – as though, I sometimes thought, she was trying to wrap him up. But she spoke to very few people. She was there. Thus in the attic of the *Cahiers* where on certain evenings people crowded in, she was both the essential distance and the essential presence. (P, II, pp. 293f)

What attracted Weil to the *Cahiers* was the openness of its editorial policy which placed it at variance with Vichy (it was frequently in trouble with the censors) and the spirit of friendship and intellectual enquiry that animated its contributors.

The atmosphere of the *Cahiers* was also instrumental in encouraging Weil to put the composition of her *Notebooks* on a more regular basis.

She had already been making lengthy notes on science and culture before arriving in Marseilles. In the first of her *Notebooks* proper she recopied a passage (NB, pp. 6f) on science from her already extensive jottings and the regular 'system' of composition was under way. She used the yellow-covered exercise books of the Ecole Normale. The eleven notebooks eventually published were evidently written with a view to incorporation in the books she hoped to write. They are often elliptical and allusive but show the impressive effort of reflection on the most diverse subjects in which many of her articles had their origin.

Weil was particularly enthusiastic about a special number then being planned on the civilisation of the Languedoc. She immediately wrote the article on 'The Agony of a Civilisation' (see pp. 154ff above) which was much appreciated by Ballard. He lent her a small book on Catharism by the historian Déodat Roché. She wrote to him immediately:

> Never has the revival of this kind of thought been so necessary as today. We are living at a time when most people feel, confusedly but keenly, that what was called Enlightenment in the Eighteenth Century, including the sciences, provides an insufficient spiritual diet; but this feeling is now leading humanity into the darkest paths. There is an urgent need to refer back to those great epochs which favour the kind of spiritual life of which all that is most precious in science and art is no more than a somewhat imperfect reflection. (SL, p. 131)

For the rest of her life she was to remain inspired by the distant history of the land where she now found herself.

Weil contributed other more occasional pieces to the *Cahiers du Sud*. At the end of March she attended a meeting of the Jeunesse Ouvrière Chrétienne (Young Christian Workers) in Marseilles and was favourably impressed. What particularly struck her was that the JOC (as it was known) was so unlike the other youth movements of the day with their slogans, their collectivism, their obsession with power. Her comments connected her factory experience with her developing religious views:

> It is the pure spirit of the worker, without any adulteration, that is expressed in the J.O.C. Politics do not enter into it, nor religion itself except in a translated form. These young people have felt that, over and above the economic system and the employers, it is matter itself which weighs them down and oppresses them every day – matter that they handle hour after hour, under order, despite fatigue . . . They are more subject to matter than others, but, from the moment they achieve self-awareness, they feel this subjection more keenly than others and that is an immense superiority. . . . Among them, Christianity has its authentic accent, the one which gave the slaves a

supernatural liberty. In the hard and brutal life of a factory, the spirit always appears as what it really is, something supernatural, a miracle, a grace. (P, II, pp. 315f)

She also took issue, in a letter to the *Cahiers du Sud*, with an article published in the *Cahiers* which criticised the view, popular with the Vichy authorities, that France's intellectuals bore a large part of the responsibility for the 1940 defeat. Weil agreed with this view, though she thought it too narrowly expressed:

> The essential characteristic of the first half of the twentieth century is the growing weakness, and almost the disappearance, of the idea of value. This is one of those rare phenomena which seem, as far as one can tell, to be really new in human history . . . It has appeared in many domains outside literature, and even in all of them. In industry, the substitution of quantity for quality; among the workers, the discrediting of skilled workmanship; among students, the substitution of diplomas for culture as the aim of education. Even in science there is no longer any criterion of value since classical science was discarded. But above all it was the writers who were the guardians of the treasure that has been lost; and some of them now take pride in having lost it. (SNL, p. 167)

Dadaism and Surrealism might be extreme examples of this tendency, but with very few exceptions most writers had contributed to the elevation of words such as spontaneity, sincerity, gratuitousness, enrichment over others such as virtue, nobility, honour, honesty, generosity – words which had either become impossible to use or acquired bastard meanings. Bergson's influential ideas about creative evolution made no reference to considerations of value. The same was true of Proust:

> In a general way the literature of the twentieth century is essentially psychological; and psychology consists in describing states of the soul by displaying them all on the same plane without any discrimination of the value, as though good and evil were external to them, as though the effort towards the good could be absent at any moment from the thought of any man. (SNL, p. 168)

The task of literature was to express the human condition and this had essentially to do with the opposition between good and evil. Of course

> it is true that there is a certain kind of morality which is even more alien to good and evil than amorality is. Those who are now blaming the eminent writers are worth infinitely less than they, and the 'moral

revival' which certain people wish to impose would be much worse than the condition it is meant to cure. If our present suffering ever leads to a revival, this will not be brought about through slogans but in silence and moral loneliness, through pain, misery, and terror, in the profoundest depths of each man's spirit. (SNL, p. 169)

Her views on literature, therefore, were nothing if not categorical.

As a professional philosopher, Weil also attended the meetings of the Marseilles Society for the Study of Philosophy run by an industrialist and part-time philosopher called Gaston Berger. She wrote an article for the *Cahiers du Sud* on the work of the Society which reflected her own breadth of interest. Marcel Brion, in a lecture on painting and philosophy in China, had drawn what she felt was too strong a contrast between East and West:

> If we could but realise it, we would recognise that there is in Oriental thought that which is most intimate to every one of us. Every Taoist saying awakens a resonance in us, and the Taoist texts evoke by turns Heraclitus, Protagoras, Plato, the Cynics, the Stoics, Christianity, and Jean-Jacques Rousseau. Not that Taoist thought is not original, profound, and new for a European, but like everything truly great, it is both new and familiar; we remember, as Plato used to say, having known it on the other side of the sky. (FW, pp. 283f)

Another lecture, this time on Hippocratic medicine, gave her the opportunity to observe that all the activities of the Greeks,

> have at their centre the idea of balance that goes with proportion, the soul of geometry. With this idea of balance, which we have lost, the Greeks created science, our science. Imbalance was inconceivable to them except as something that comes after equilibrium, in relation to it, as a breaking of the equilibrium; illness for example as a disturbance of health. (FW, p. 286)

She also commented on Gaston Berger's public defence of his doctoral thesis which she had gone to Aix to hear. Berger's subject was the conditions of knowledge and Weil approved of his method, which was 'not to ask himself whether an idea or an assertion he has encountered is true, but to ask what it means' (FW, p. 287). This was the method that Socrates had used, followed by philosophers such as Descartes and Kant, as opposed to the system-builders such as Aristotle and Hegel.

In the Marseilles of that time philosophy was apt to overlap with politics. Although Weil got involved in serious resistance work only a year later, she did briefly join a group with which Jean Tortel had put her in touch. She was under the impression that they might help her to get to England. However the group was soon betrayed by an informer and early one morning the police called at the Weil flat:

> They showed Simone the application she had filled out and questioned her. They showed her some photographs: did she know any of these people? She recognised one of the faces, but told the policeman that she didn't know a single one. They asked her who had put her in touch with this organisation; she said that it was someone with whom she had struck up a conversation while waiting for a bus and that she didn't know him in any other way. They asked her for a description of this unknown person; she gave them a made-up, very vague description. With a touch of humour, one of the policemen summed it up: 'In short, no particular distinguishing marks'. They then wanted to search her room, which was full of manuscripts. (P, p. 408)

Shortly after she was asked to go to the police station. Fearing she might be arrested, she packed a suitcase. Her parents went along with her and kept vigil in a cafe across the road. She was interrogated by a military examining magistrate.

> He asked her abruptly, without beating around the bush, 'What are your feelings in regard to England?' Simone burst into laughter and declared, 'My feelings in regard to England are feelings of the greatest sympathy'. A trifle disconcerted by the fact that she didn't hide these feelings and that he could not surprise her, he said to her, 'I can understand that before you may have had sympathy for England, but after Mers el-Kebir . . .' She replied that she had not changed and tried to show him that England should be supported. They discussed this for some time. He then said, 'You are carrying on pro-English propaganda'. She denied this. 'You see,' he said, 'though knowing what a risk you are taking, you still tell me your pro-English feelings, so wouldn't you try to get other people to share these feelings in a more ordinary situation?' 'If someone asks me what my feelings are,' she replied 'I don't hide them; but I don't tell them to someone who doesn't expressly question me about them'. He asked her about the application, in which she had spoken of her plan for a group of front-line nurses. He said of this plan: 'That's a very good tactical idea. Did you attend Staff College?' 'No more', she said, 'than a lot of people who are concerned about the war'. (P, p. 409)

She had to go to the police station on two further occasions and duly packed her suitcase. But she would not give them any information, in spite of threats:

At last an irritated policeman said to her, 'You are a little bitch. You know that I could have you thrown into jail together with a bunch of whores'. She replied, 'I have always wanted to know that environment and I can't see any better way than going to prison to find out about it'. Another policeman said to the first, 'I told you that we can't get anything out of her'. They tried to play on her emotions by showing her her parents, who were waiting for her across the street: 'Doesn't that mean anything to you, seeing your poor parents waiting for you?' In the end they let her go. (P, p. 410)

In spite of her resumption of Resistance work six months later, the police were not to bother her again.

During her time in Marseilles, Weil established a wide circle of friends. After meeting him quite by chance in the street she saw a lot of Camille Marcoux, her old comrade with whom she had given lessons to the railway workers in the rue Falguières in 1929. She also spent a lot of time with René and Vera Daumal.[5] René Daumal was a friend of Jean Ballard and Weil had known him at Henri IV. He had been a Surrealist but then had turned towards a serious study of Oriental thought. He helped Weil to learn Sanskrit, which left an indelible impression on her; as she wrote later: 'The memory of both of you and that of the months of mingled happiness and sorrow which have composed this year are for me no longer separable from the form of these Sanskrit characters. I hope never to stop loving these characters, which are sacred and which perhaps have never served as the vehicle of anything base' (P, p. 422). The Daumals introduced her to Lanza del Vasto, a poet, philosopher, and larger-than-life disciple of Gandhi: his plans to found a community along the lines of the Master made Weil very enthusiastic.[6] Through the *Cahiers du Sud* she also got to know Gide's son-in-law, Jean Lambert. He would come up to her flat after his morning swim and they would talk about the Greek conception of beauty and Weil read him her poems in her monotonous voice with the cries from the beach below as a background chorus.[7] She also spent time with Gilbert Kahn, a fervent disciple of Alain, who was to do so much later to make her writings known. Finally she acquired close friends in Pierre and Hélène Honnorat. Pierre was a mathematician and had been at the Ecole Normale Supérieure with André Weil; his sister Hélène taught at the girls' lycée in Marseilles. She was a fervent Catholic and it was through her that Weil was introduced to the Catholic community in Marseilles and in particular to Joseph-Marie Perrin with whom she was to form one of the closest relationships of her life.

Perrin was a thirty-four-year-old Dominican, extremely thin, soft-voiced, already three-quarters blind, whose home was the Dominican House in the rue Edmond Rostand in the east of Marseilles. Most of the priests there had strong social commitments: one of Perrin's closest friends, Loew, had foreshadowed the worker-priests' movement by becoming a docker. Perrin himself spent a lot of time helping refugees, and Hélène Honnorat thought he might be able to find Weil some work as a farm labourer. Since the possibility of her getting to England seemed, at least for the moment, fairly remote, Weil was looking for opportunities to work on the land, a desire which she had had for a long time. When she first tried to get in touch with him, Perrin was away in the Sahara preaching a retreat to the recently demobilised Little Brothers of Charles de Foucauld, but they finally met in the Dominican House on 10 June 1941. Weil talked of her desire to become what she called a 'farm servant'. Perrin immediately wrote to his friend Gustave Thibon who, together with his wife Yvette and father, lived on their small family farm of eight hectares in the village of Saint-Marcel d'Ardèche, about a hundred miles north of Marseilles. They had become friends four or five years earlier and been particularly close during the spring of the previous year, when Thibon had lived in the Dominican House during his short period of mobilisation. Thibon was a self-taught philosopher who had already published some of his writings. He held deep-rooted Catholic beliefs and Perrin hoped that he would provide a stimulating intellectual companion for Weil. He also expressed his hope that Yvette Thibon would be able to make sure that Weil looked after herself more adequately. (When Weil later learned of this aspect, she was extremely annoyed.) After some initial hesitation, Thibon agreed to take her into his own house and she eventually left for Saint-Marcel on 7 August.

While all this was being arranged, Weil continued to visit the Dominican House regularly. Perrin wrote: 'She used to come to see me as often as it was possible for both of us to fit it in . . . With her extreme consideration for others, she used to wait quietly in the passage, letting two or perhaps three people pass before her. After they had gone we talked for whatever moments remained' (PT, p. 35). Perrin and Weil were immediately attracted to each other. Perrin's impression was that 'her love of Christ seemed to be enough for her, and the extremely superficial idea she had of the Church and Catholics was not of a nature to suggest the slightest question in her mind' (ibid.). He raised the possibility of her being baptised, which she had not previously consi-dered. She immediately had difficulties. Baptism seemed to her to imply an exclusive attachment to Christianity and a rejection thereby of the truth she had found in other great religious traditions. In this connection, she was keen on trying to get a clear answer to the question of whether there could be salvation outside the Church.[8] It was a question she discussed while scrambling over the cliffs round Marseilles with Louis Bercher, an old friend from the *Révolution Prolétarienne* days, who was then a ship's doctor and, although not a believer himself, had a sister who was a Benedictine nun. Bercher wrote to Perrin later:

> Simone suffered because you could not, on occasion, step outside the visible Church and become a Minister of the complete Church. She confided this to me at least twice, with visible suffering (her voice became hoarser), and, of course, without naming you. 'Yet they still have got something missing!' she said, 'To convince someone of their conception, they imagine that the other person has already acquired precisely this conception'. (P, p. 418)

More importantly for her, there was the problem of Israel. In his first letter to her, Perrin had expressed his 'love for Israel' – he was one of the main promoters of Jewish–Christian dialogue in Marseilles – and thought to find a sympathetic response in her.[9] He soon realised how wide of the mark he had been: 'Israel was the very citadel of all her oppositions, the nub of all her resistance.'

One of Perrin's colleagues, Raymond-Leopold Bruckberger, has left a slightly different impression of Weil at this time:

> She hung around the Dominicans as a moth around a lamp, burning herself less than she burned others . . . It was on the Dominicans that she concentrated all her quarrels with Catholicism, it was them that she ceaselessly reproached with having allowed the fundamental revelation to be degraded; she was not far from treating them as starvers of the public, hoarders of the bread of truth in time of famine. Her conversation was all dialectic, irony, attacking the front or the flank, disdaining all explanations, all rejoinders, all apologetics, all of which seemed to her derisory. Were we or were we not the Order who had the vocation of reconciling the intellect with revelation? How far had we got with this reconciliation? . . . Faced with this constant battling aggression I was reduced to asking myself whether my imbecility had not made me into a traitor.[10]

Bruckberger would, he continued, have thought her a 'pain in the neck' to be avoided at all costs were it not for two other factors. Firstly, however bitterly she criticised the Church, when it came to the central tenets of Christianity, such as the Trinity, the Incarnation, the Crucifixion and Resurrection of Christ, she accepted these mysteries as self-evident and her attitude was one of docile reverence. Secondly, the impression of intellectual arrogance was profoundly modified by Weil's devotion to the Eucharist. Bruckberger recounts how one day he left her in the Church after a typically fruitless argument: 'I went to do some shopping in the town and, on returning, went into the Church: two hours after I had left her she was still there in the same position, nailed to the spot by a prodigious attention, exposed, offered to the irradiation of the Invisible Presence, as a woman wanting a tan will let the sun turn her golden' (ibid.).

The Dominicans of the rue Edmond Rostand were given a rest in early August when Weil moved up to the Thibon household in Saint-Marcel d'Ardèche. Thibon's original proposal was that she spend a few weeks in his house in order to get some idea of the different kinds of agricultural work while she was waiting to become a real farm-hand for a large landowner in the vicinity, whose agreement he had got to employ Weil for a year as from October. Weil accepted with enthusiasm, remarking ironically that she was thereby being an obedient citizen, since the Vichy government, at the same time as it deprived Jews of the right to exercise professions, suggested that they go and work on the land. But she insisted to Thibon that no concessions be made to her, since 'I want my time and the current of my thoughts, insofar as they depend on my body, to be subjected to the same necessities as those that weigh upon no matter what farm-hand' (PT, pp. 114f). To her friend Simone Pétrement she drew a parallel with her decision to work in a factory six years previously:

> I feel that there are things that I can do, but I don't yet see clearly enough which ones (although I see several, indeed too many); but I feel that this must come first. I also felt this way about the factory, and I was right. If I were so weak as to retreat before the harshness of the life that awaits me, I know that I could then never do anything else. (P, p. 433)

Remembering her factory experience, she expected that exhaustion would prevent her from using her intellect. Whereas at Alsthom this had caused her great distress, now her anticipations were slightly different: on the one hand, 'I regard physical work as a purification – but a purification in the order of suffering and humiliation. One can also find in it, in its very depths, instants of profound nourishing joy that cannot be equalled elsewhere' (P, p. 423). On the other hand, she wished to explore precisely that part of her mind that was not subject to physical pressure, since 'if there is something irreducible, it is that which has an infinite value. I am going to see whether this is so' (ibid.). If, as she thought,[11] her manual labour was a pre-condition for the marvellous writings of the next, and last, eighteen months of her life, then her hopes were more than fulfilled.

Thibon met Weil in Avignon and they went up to Saint-Marcel by train. His first impression was not favourable: 'This first contact aroused feelings in me which, though certainly quite different from antipathy, were nonetheless painful. I had the impression of being face to face with an individual who was radically foreign to all my ways of feeling and thinking, and . . . that, for me, represents the meaning and savour of life' (PT, p. 116). She refused the bedroom that had been prepared for her and wanted to sleep outdoors. But eventually she compromised on a small half-ruined two-up–two-down house belonging to Thibon's parents-in-law half a mile or so away and a hundred yards from the banks of the Rhône. She called it her 'fairy-tale house'. With her sleeping-bag on a pine-needle bed in one room and her work-table in another she was extremely happy: 'admirable landscape, delicious air, rest, leisure, solitude, fresh fruits and vegetables, spring water, wood fires – nothing but sensual pleasures and nothing to produce nightmares, far from it' (P, p. 426). It was for her in many ways the ideal life, combining solitude, manual labour and intermittent agreeable companionship.

She enjoyed the time she spent in the Thibon household. She would often share meals with them but kept very strictly to the rationing then in force. Some days she would go to the Mass with the Thibons in the rather ugly nineteenth-century church in the middle of the village. She worked energetically on the land where 'her clumsiness was only equalled by her goodwill – the latter ending by triumphing over the former' (PT, p. 124). In the evenings she would sit on a bench outside with Thibon and help him improve his Greek. They read Plato's *Phaedo* together and he paid tribute to her gifts as a teacher. And there were discussions, interminable discussions. Weil and Thibon disagreed about politics, where Thibon was relatively sympathetic to Vichy, and about a lot of philosophy, where Thibon's speciality was an interest in German romanticism not calculated to appeal to Weil. 'She went on arguing', recalled Thibon, 'ad infinitum in an inexorably monotonous voice, and I emerged from these endless discussions literally worn out' (GG, p. viii). As the night wore on it was always Thibon who insisted that they break it up and go to bed. But however inflexible Weil was in her opinions, she was never touchy about being contradicted. And Thibon, who had himself written on mysticism, was drawn by this side of her personality. The farm had a magnificent view over the Rhône Valley towards the Mont Ventoux and Thibon described how, on the day of her arrival he left her for a few minutes and then

> returned to find her sitting on a tree-trunk in front of the house, lost in contemplation of the valley of the Rhône. Then I saw her gaze gradually emerge from the vision in order to come back to ordinary sight; the intensity and purity of that gaze was such that one felt that she was contemplating interior depths at the same time as the magnificent perspective that opened at her feet, and that the beauty

of her soul corresponded with the tender majesty of the landscape. (PT, p. 116)

And this impression was confirmed when he got to know her better:

I have witnessed too much of the daily unfolding of her existence to be left with the slightest doubt as to the authenticity of her spiritual vocation; her faith and detachment were expressed in her actions, sometimes with a disconcerting disregard for the practical, but always with absolute generosity . . . her asceticism might seem exaggerated in our day of half-measures; nevertheless, it was free from any emotional excess. (GG, p. ix)

For Thibon, Weil was someone who was more agreeable the better you knew her: your second impressions of her were infinitely better than the first. She had two very different sides to her. She could be difficult in that she 'could not bear the course of events or the kindness of her friends changing by one inch the positions of the stakes with which her own will had marked the path of her immolation' (PT, p. 119). As Thibon so percipiently remarked, 'the way she mounted guard around her void still paid witness to a terrible preoccupation with herself . . . her *ego*, as it were, was like a word that she may perhaps have succeeded in *obliterating*, but that was still *underlined*' (ibid.). But although she was solitary and liked meditation, she admired the kindness of his wife, the rugged reflections of his father, and could be a delightful companion, full of jokes about herself and others: 'She knew how to joke without bad taste and could be ironical without unkindness. Her extraordinary learning, so deeply assimilated that it can hardly be distinguished from the expression of her inner life, gave her conversation an unforgettable charm' (P, p. 428). All in all the months in Saint-Marcel were one of the happiest times of her life.

Indeed, life in the Ardèche was so attractive that she suggested to her parents that, if they did not manage to get to the United States, they should settle with her somewhere in the surrounding countryside. She would read, write and give some lessons; her father could practise his medicine; and they would all grow vegetables together. Her parents came to visit her for a week in early September. They stayed in the village's small hotel where one of the peasant women told Selma Weil the latest gossip – how Monsieur Thibon had installed a mistress in his own house – and a mad and ugly one at that! Although Thibon did not get on very well with Selma Weil, whom he found too inquisitive and domineering, he took a great liking to the doctor and his fund of vaguely anti-Semitic jokes.

The time had come for her to leave Saint-Marcel. She was anxious to participate in the grape harvest and Thibon had found her an employer in the village of Saint-Julien du Peyrolas a few miles away. Before going to Saint-Julien she accompanied her parents for ten days to Le Poet in the French Alps. Simone Pétrement came and spent a couple of days with her friend, whom she found changed: 'What struck me most of all at this meeting was a gentleness and serenity that I had never known in her to this extent. She could still become indignant, but so much less than before. With a more tender, wiser goodness, she had become a person whose company was, more than ever, extremely charming' (P, p. 435). They talked incessantly: of science and whether Einstein's views did not contain a fundamental contradiction, of philosophy and the validity of Hegel's dialectic, of folklore and the collection of texts from different philosophical and religious traditions that Weil wished to publish under the title 'Wisdom from all Ages and All Countries', of the *Upanishads* that she was continuing to study in the original, of whether it was possible for human beings to live solely on sunlight and certain mineral substances, and of the project for a team of front-line nurses that Weil always kept at the forefront of her mind, the possible realisation of which would, as she wrote to her brother, govern her decision as to whether to leave for America or not. They also found time to help the villagers in their potato harvest.

During her stay at Le Poet she read the works of Saint John of the Cross in Spanish which Thibon had lent to her. She also began to pray for the first time in her life. Hitherto she had been too afraid of the influence of autosuggestion that, she felt, accompanied prayer. But while doing Greek with Thibon she had been through the Our Father word for word and they had promised each other that they would learn it by heart. Weil did so and was so overwhelmed by the 'infinite sweetness of this Greek text' that she could not stop herself repeating it over and over again for several days. The effect was to deepen her mystical experience:

> At times the very first words tear my thoughts from my body and transport it to a place outside space where there is neither perspective nor point of view. The infinity of the ordinary expanses of perception is replaced by an infinity to the second and sometimes the third degree. At the same time, filling every part of this infinity of infinity, there is silence, a silence which is not an absence of sound but which is the object of a positive sensation, more positive than that of sound. Noises, if there are any, only reach me after crossing this silence. Sometimes, also, during this recitation or at other moments, Christ is present with me in person, but His presence is infinitely more real, more moving, more clear than on that first occasion when He took possession of me. (WG, p. 24)

She made a practice of reciting the Our Father every morning with what she called 'absolutely pure attention'.

After the ten days at Le Poet, Weil spent a month working on the grape harvest in the vineyards of André Rieu near the village of Saint-Julien du Peyrolas. Rieu was a neighbour of Thibon's and it was on Thibon's recommendation that she was given the job. She got board and lodging in the Rieu household, but put in eight hours a day with the other seasonal workers. She found it hard to keep up: 'Sometimes I am crushed by fatigue, but I find it a kind of purification. Right at the very bottom of my exhaustion I encounter joys that nothing else will give me' (P, p. 441). When she was too tired to stand, she would continue to pick the grapes lying down. She confessed to Thibon that one day she wondered whether she had not died and, without noticing, fallen into Hell, which consisted of an eternal grape harvest.

In the farm Weil refused to have a room of her own and slept in the dining-room, which soon became a mess of her papers. During the night time she read and wrote. In the mornings she went milking, in the evenings she washed the dishes, peeled the vegetables and helped the children with their homework. The first Sunday she asked for a missal and went to Mass. 'The other Sundays', wrote Rieu, 'she spent her time walking in the more deserted part of the countryside. In the evening, after dinner, when night had fallen, she would put on her cape and go to sit on the bench in the garden and stayed there for a long time looking at the stars (or so we thought) and smoking a cigarette' (P, p. 443). They found Weil mysterious and enigmatic but could not help admiring her iron will and her boundless charity.

Life as a farm-hand pleased Weil. She liked the feeling that intellectual activity was now a free option rather than her profession and she liked, too, the poverty and simplicity: 'Since my adolescence I dreamed of the marriage of St. Francis with poverty, but I felt that, as for myself I must not go to the trouble of marrying it, since one day it would come to take me by force and it would be better so' (P, p. 435). Just before the end of the grape harvest she wrote another sharply ironical letter in the same vein to Xavier Vallat, the Commissioner for Jewish Affairs. She noted that the government had not given her the severance pay due on being deprived of her teaching post, but remarked that this gave her at least a lively feeling of satisfaction at having no part in the country's financial difficulties. She pointed out once again that she did not consider herself to be Jewish and continued:

> I consider the Statute concerning the Jews in a general way as being unjust and absurd, for how can one believe that a university graduate in mathematics could harm children who study geometry by the mere fact that three of his grandparents attended a Synagogue? But, in my

particular case, I would like to express the sincere gratitude I feel toward the government for having removed me from the social category of intellectuals and given me the land and, with it, all of nature. For only those possess nature and the land who have been penetrated by it through the daily suffering of their limbs broken by fatigue. The days, months, seasons, the celestial vault . . . belong to those who must cross the space of time that each day separates the rising from the setting of the sun by going painfully from fatigue to fatigue. These people . . . live through each day, they do not dream it. (P, p. 443f)

This letter received no reply.

In spite of the fatigue, Weil was enthusiastic about her work on the land and anticipated continuing for a whole year. However the market gardener at Maillane, with whom Thibon had arranged a job for her, refused at the last minute to take her, claiming that he could not afford board and lodging for outsiders and would therefore only take people from his own village. So, after spending a few days with the Thibons, she rejoined her parents in Marseilles at the end of October. It was to be six months before her departure for the United States. This period of waiting, she said, encouraged her 'natural laziness'. In fact these six months were, intellectually, among the most fruitful of her life. She wrote a second article on the Cathars for the *Cahiers du Sud*, entitled 'In what does the Occitanian Inspiration Consist?', in which she expressed her admiration for the civilisation of the Languedoc (see pp. 154ff above). She also wrote, for the same journal, two review articles on science. The first dealt with a many-handed book celebrating the arrival of the new science that was displacing the Newtonian conception of the world. Weil was particularly struck by de Broglie's article on the contribution of the new science to philosophy. She disagreed strongly with his idea that recent science had helped to make additional progress in philosophy:

Philosophy does not progress or evolve; and philosophers are uncomfortable today, for they must either betray their vocation or be out of fashion. The fashion today is to progress, to evolve. It is indeed something even more compulsive than a fashion. If the great public were aware that philosophy is not susceptible to progress, there would no doubt be resentment at its getting any public funds. To find a place in the budget for the eternal is not in the spirit of our age. So the majority of philosophers keep quiet about that eternity which is their privilege. (SNL, p. 70)

This theme was taken up in the second article prompted by a recent book by Planck. Science, she claimed, was the preserve of a small, exclusive and highly specialised minority – a 'village' – and as subject to the vagaries of fashion as other bodies of people. The present fashion for quantum theory would lead, she felt, to a weakening of the idea of truth to which nineteenth-century science had still been strongly attached. And once truth had gone, utility inevitably took its place:

> That is where we are today. Everything is oriented towards utility, which nobody thinks of defining; public opinion reigns supreme, in the village of scientists as in the great nations. It is as though we had returned to the age of Protagoras and the Sophists, the age where the art of persuasion – whose modern equivalent is advertising slogans, publicity, propaganda meetings, the press, the cinema, and radio – took the place of thought and controlled the fate of cities and accomplished *coups d'état*. So the ninth book of Plato's *Republic* reads like a description of contemporary events. Only today it is not the fate of Greece but of the entire world that is at stake and we have no Socrates or Plato or Eudoxus, no Pythagorean tradition, and no teaching of the Mysteries. We have the Christian tradition, but it can do nothing for us unless it comes alive in us again. (SNL, p. 64)

In an age, she concluded, in which force of arms was putting everything else in question, the prestige of contemporary science should not be exempt.

During her last months in Marseilles, Weil was also very active in the Resistance, which was then still fairly disorganised and embryonic. The Dominican House was strongly anti-Vichy and gave a lot of clandestine help to refugees. The *Cahiers du Témoignage Chrétien*, virulently opposed to contemporary Fascism in general and racism in particular,[12] started publication in December 1941, and Perrin put Weil in touch with Malou David, a young teacher who had found herself responsible for distributing the periodical, which appeared every two months or so. The two young women met almost every day, Weil acting as David's letter-box and contact with those above her in the Resistance chain. As such, wrote David, 'Simone did not merely help "some" Jews in difficulty, or merely distribute "some" periodicals, she was the very basis of the organisation and distribution of the *Cahiers du Témoignage Chrétien* in Marseilles'.[13] Weil's totally uncompromising attitude fascinated Malou David who thought the key to her personality was the way in which she resonated with all the sufferings of the world. Weil insisted that, if David were arrested, she should attribute all the responsibility to Weil and thus remain free to carry on her Resistance work. Weil continued to work with David until the day of her departure for the United States and built up a network of contacts which she bequeathed to her companion.

The question of whether to become a Catholic was at the forefront of Weil's mind during this period and she interviewed several priests in a rather inconclusive effort to find what exactly were the dogmas to which she would be obliged to subscribe. But it was to Perrin that she returned again and again to converse in the bare parlour of the Dominican House. Weil was reading a lot of Saint John of the Cross while keeping up her study of the Baghavad Gita and venturing into Zen Buddhism. But it was still the Greeks who held her attention and she formed the project of writing a book with Perrin, commenting on non-Christian texts on the love of God. As part of this enterprise, Perrin organised meetings in the long low crypt of the Dominican House, where Weil would read and comment on Greek texts to a small circle.

On finishing her work as a farm labourer, Weil had written to Perrin thanking him for 'opening up the earth' to her. He replied by asking when he would be able to open up Heaven. Their conversations on this subject were evidently slightly at cross-purposes. Perrin treated Weil as though she were virtually a Catholic and someone who might be expected to join the Church in the near future. Weil, on the other hand, felt that she could not be too blunt with him as she did not want to hurt him. 'When I talked to Father Perrin, I was paralysed by pity', she later confided to her friend Simone Deitz, 'I could not tell him everything. He could not see' (C, p. 269). Weil could not abide the sight of tears, and as Perrin dried his permanently irritated eyes on his white robes he seemed to her almost to be weeping. Had he had access to the writings she gave him on her departure from Marseilles he would have seen that she was perhaps further from the Church than he thought.

So in January she wrote him two long letters on the subject, 'to bring our conversations about my case to a conclusion'. In the first letter, she talked of her feelings of inadequacy for the Sacraments (shades of Jansenism) and her impression that it simply was not God's will that she should enter the Church. More specifically, she could not help wondering whether 'in these days when so large a proportion of humanity is sunk in materialism, God does not want there to be some men and women who have given themselves to him and to Christ and who yet remain outside the Church' (WG, p. 4). Whatever intellectual reservations she might have, this was perhaps her gut feeling: 'When I think of the act by which I should enter the Church as something concrete which might happen quite soon, nothing gives me more pain than the idea of separating myself from the immense and unfortunate multitude of unbelievers' (ibid.). It was also the Church as a social institution that she found an unavoidable stumbling-block, as she made clear in the profession of faith with which she concluded her letter:

> I love God, Christ and the Catholic Faith as much as it is possible for
> so miserably inadequate a creature to love them. I love the Saints

through their writings, and what is told of their lives – apart from some whom it is impossible for me to love fully or to consider as Saints. I love the six or seven Catholics of genuine spirituality whom chance has led me to meet in the course of my life. I love the Catholic liturgy, hymns, architecture, rites and ceremonies. But I have not the slightest love for the Church in the strict sense of the word, apart from its relation to all these things that I do love. (WG, p. 6)

In the second letter she elaborated on her distrust of the Church as a social structure. This distrust, she claimed rather disingenuously, was not motivated by a sense of individualism: on the contrary she feared being swept away by its collectivist attitudes and the triumphalism that had been responsible for the Crusades and the Inquisition. In the end it was a question of obedience: 'If I had my eternal salvation placed in front of me on this table, and if I only had to stretch out my hand to take it, I would not put out my hand so long as I had not received the order to do so' (WG, pp. 11f). However valid many of Weil's reasons were for resisting Perrin's blandishments, the general impression is that she is looking round for reasons to justify a position anchored in a deeper level of her personality. God certainly had not given her any order and, given the purity of intention and intellectual commitment that she required of herself for such a step, it was unlikely to be forthcoming.

By the end of March 1942, it was clear to Weil that she would very shortly be able to leave for the United States. She determined to spend Easter at the Benedictine Abbey of En Calcat. The Abbey was twenty miles north-west of Carcassonne and she stopped there for three days on the way. She was particularly anxious to meet Joe Bousquet, a poet and writer who had been severely crippled at Verdun in 1918. Bousquet was a frequent contributor to the *Cahiers du Sud*, whose leading figures often made 'the pilgrimage to Carcassonne' and its editor Ballard accompanied Weil on her visit. Although their train did not arrive until the early hours of the morning, Weil and Bousquet talked until daybreak. It was an immediate meeting of minds. Although Bousquet found Weil too ascetic and too uncompromising in her attitude towards evil, he admired the way in which she was, as he put it, 'at home with thoughts that deprived me of my rest'.[14] A man of no particular religion but with a strong emotional attachment to the Cathars, Bousquet was impressed by the purity of Weil's spirituality. She wrote to him after their meeting:

It is granted to very few minds to discover that things and people exist. Since my childhood I have desired only to receive the complete revelation of this before I die. I think that you are engaged in the same discovery. For this reason, I think that since I came into this part of the country, I have not met anyone whose destiny is not much inferior to yours.[15]

(The one exception, she went on to say, was Perrin.) On a more mundane level, Weil agreed to get Bousquet from Marseilles a supply of opium which he regularly smoked to relieve his pain. The main reason for Weil's attachment to Bousquet was that his war wounds put Bousquet in a special position, since 'fortunate are those in whom the affliction which enters their flesh is the same one that afflicts the world itself in their time. They have the opportunity and the function of knowing the truth of the world's affliction and contemplating its reality. And that is the redemptive function itself' (SL, p. 137). Bousquet's disabilities also impressed Weil in quite another way: as a former officer who had had direct experience of what it was like to be seriously wounded at the Front, she was anxious to have his comments on, and endorsement of, her front-line nurses project to take with her to America. And eventually, after some prompting from her, he did indeed give it his support.

Weil met Bousquet at least once more and stayed in Carcassonne for three days in the house of Suzette and Louis Roubaud who had both been fellow-students at the Ecole Normale. On each day she went to see Canon Fernand Vidal, to whom she was introduced by Hélène Honnorat, to make yet more enquiries about the possibility of baptism and the content of Catholic doctrine. She rehearsed her views about the Old Testament and Jahveh as God of Battles. 'I found in her', noted Vidal, 'not in her heart which I found very open to charity (in the evangelical sense of love) but in her spirit, something crude, rigid, and intransigent – the same quality for which she reproached the Jewish people' (P, p. 457). She believed, she said, in the divinity of Christ, but held that there had been incarnations of the Word prior to Jesus – as in Melchisidech, Osiris, Krishna. Vidal did not think that it was lack of humility that kept Weil out of the Church. It was rather that she had only recently come into contact with Catholicism and 'she was not accustomed to our categories' (ibid.). At any rate, it was clear to him that she was not ready for baptism and he told her so. Surprised and disappointed she confided to Hélène Honnorat: 'as our conversation proceeded, I saw myself getting further and further away from baptism' (P, p. 458). At the Abbey of En Calcat she attended all the Easter services and discussed her problems with one of the monks, Dom Clément Jacob, from whom she got an even blunter response. She actually submitted to him a list of questions asking whether it was possible to become a Catholic while rejecting the Christian conception of history, adhering to the doctrines of Marcion, believing that there were incarnations of the Word prior to Christ, that God could not have ordered the massacres described in the Old Testament, and thus that Israel could not have known the true God, and finally thinking it probable that true knowledge of God was as widespread in antiquity and contemporary India as in Christendom (cf. PSO, pp. 69ff). Jacob was irritated by what he saw as her insistence and her arrogance and told her outright that her opinions were heretical. Although she got on much better with one of the Benedictine nuns, her visit to Carcassonne and En Calcat marked a turning-point. Previously, she had imagined, in spite of her objections, that she was getting nearer to the Church. Now, sadly disappointed, she saw the possibility of baptism becoming increasingly distant.

Back in Marseilles, she was now certain that her departure was imminent. Although she was concerned that her parents should be in a safe place and that they would not leave without her, her main object in leaving was to expose herself to the dangers of the war, particularly in connection with her nurses project. For her this was 'the thought which guides me, and which has been in my mind for years, so that I dare not dismiss it although there is little chance of carrying it out' (WG, p. 13). Her worst fear, amply fulfilled by later events, was that the situation in Marseilles would get worse once she had left and that she would prove to have exchanged danger for security rather than the other way round. In any event, she spent her last months in Marseilles in a veritable orgy of writing, distilling in limpid, beautifully written essays the random thoughts with which she had been filling her notebooks.

Perrin had recently been appointed Superior of the Dominican House in Montpellier and came into frequent contact with the students at the university there. In order to encourage him in his work, Weil wrote him a short essay entitled 'Reflections on the Right Use of School Studies with a View to the Love of God'. 'Although people seem to be unaware of it today', she wrote, 'the development of the faculty of attention forms the real object and almost the sole interest of studies' (WG, p. 51). Attention had very little to do with will-power: it was above all a negative effort, since 'our thought should be empty, waiting, not seeking anything, but ready to receive in its naked truth the object which is to penetrate it' (WG, p. 56). Those who had begun to acquire this faculty of attention would also be able properly to love their fellow human beings. For 'the capacity to give one's attention to a sufferer is a very rare and difficult thing; it is almost a miracle; it *is* a miracle. Nearly all those who think they have this capacity do not possess it. Warmth of heart, impulsiveness, pity are not enough' (WG, p. 58). Thus academic work, approached in the right manner, was a training for contact both with God and fellow human beings.

Four further essays, found later among her papers, were reflections on her experience as a worker. The two entitled 'Some Reflections on the Love of God' and 'Some Thoughts on the Love of God' (which are, in effect, two parts of a single essay) established the basis of her approach. They continued the theme of attention which alone could diminish the evil in the world. To remain motionless waiting on God was the most effective of all actions, despite all appearances. Pascal's words 'You would not seek me if you had not already found me' expressed too activist an approach:

> It is not for man to seek, or even to believe in, God. He has only to refuse His love to everything which is not God. This refusal does not pre-suppose any belief. It is enough to recognise, what is obvious to any mind, that all the goods of this world, past, present or future, real or imaginary, are finite and limited and radically incapable of satisfying the desire which burns perpetually within us for an infinite and perfect good. All men know this, and more than once in their lives they recognise it for a moment, but then they immediately begin deceiving themselves again so as not to know it any longer, because they feel that if they knew it they could not go on living. And their feeling is true, for that knowledge kills. But it inflicts a death which leads to a resurrection. (SNL, p. 158)

This resurrection and the transformation of the evil in us could only be accomplished through contact with pure objects. The Lord's Prayer and Christ in the Blessed Sacrament were, for Weil, such objects.

But she was also concerned that this process should be able to occur in the places where everyday life was lived, and especially in places of work. Her essay, 'Christianity and Life in the Fields' dealt with this topic. Instead of the present largely formal and boring Sunday Masses that she had experienced in the Ardèche, she produced detailed suggestions for linking Christ's parables with the experiences of farm workers. Her desire was that daily life itself should become a metaphor of divine significance, since 'Christianity will not impregnate society unless each social category has its specific, unique and inimitable link with Christ' (PSO, p. 31).[16] The same theme was continued in 'The Primary Condition for Non-servile Labour', an article that Weil intended for the Dominican review *Economie et Humanisme*. Here Weil returned to themes that she had pursued during and immediately after her factory work of 1934/5. She repeated her views on the monotony and pointlessness of much modern work which left a void which could be filled neither by the bourgeois desire for money nor by the dream of revolution: it was revolution, more than religion, which was the opium of the people. The only thing that could illuminate this void was the light of eternity, that is beauty:

Human nature will accept the yearning of the soul, not for what might exist or what will exist, but for what actually does exist, in one case alone. That is, in the case of beauty . . . Since working people are obliged to direct all their desire towards what they already possess, beauty is made for them and they are made for beauty. Poetry is a luxury for other social classes, but working people need poetry as they need bread. (C, p. 254)

It was from this perspective that she now continued to praise Marx's views on the division of labour and to oppose the Taylorised system of production, both of which destroyed the workers' capacity for attention. If, as she believed, the human vocation was to get to the pure joy that lay beyond suffering, then workers were better placed to achieve this in the most real manner. But only if technology and the economy were organised in function of work rather than the other way around.

Finally, the two essays she gave to Perrin on her departure from Marseilles – 'The Love of God and Affliction' and 'Forms of the Implicit Love of God' – were of a general nature. The former, in particular, is Weil at her most poignant and most beautiful.[17] Affliction was, for her, something very different from suffering. More than her constant headaches, it was her factory year that had made her aware of affliction: 'As I worked in the factory, indistinguishable to all eyes, including my own, from the anonymous mass, the affliction of others entered into my flesh and my soul' (WG, p. 19). Thus 'affliction is an uprooting of life, a more or less attenuated equivalent of death, made irresistably present to the soul by the attack or immediate apprehension of physical pain' (SNL, p. 171), and accompanied by the expectation (or fear) of social degradation. Affliction induced a feeling of horror in which there was nothing to love and God seemed totally absent. More insidiously, affliction induced self-contempt and even complicity in the awful situation. Christ suffered affliction in his abandonment by God on the Cross. This consideration led Weil to the heart of the mystery.

As for us men, our misery gives us the infinitely precious privilege of sharing in this distance placed between the Son and his Father. This distance is only separation, however, for those who love. For those who love, separation, although painful, is a good, because it is love. Even the distress of the abandoned Christ is a good. There cannot be a greater good for us on earth than to share in it. God can never be perfectly present to us here below on account of our flesh. But he can be almost perfectly absent from us in extreme affliction. For us, on earth, this is the only possibility of perfection. That is why the Cross is our only hope. (SNL, p. 177)

The only path to this realisation was to appreciate the beauty inherent in the order of the world, an order of natural necessity. The apprenticeship to obedience would involve both joy and suffering – joy in that the beauty of the world penetrated our soul, and suffering in that it penetrated our body.[18] We could not take any step towards God: it was God who crossed the universe and came to us. All we could do was to consent to His coming. If the soul did consent, then

> the love within it is divine, uncreated, for it is the love of God for God which is passing through it. God alone is capable of loving God. We can only consent to give up our own feelings so as to allow free passage in our soul for this love. That is the meaning of denying oneself. We were created solely in order to give this consent. (SNL, p. 181)

This return journey of love to God was only possible through affliction:

> The man whose soul remains oriented towards God while a nail is driven through it finds himself nailed to the very centre of the universe; the true centre, which is not in the middle, which is not in space and time, which is God. In a dimension which is not spatial and which is not time, a totally other dimension, the nail has pierced through the whole of creation, through the dense screen which separates the soul from God. (SNL, p. 183)

This true centre of the universe, Weil concluded, the intersection between Creation and Creator, was the intersection of the two branches of the Cross.

In the second half of her article, Weil turned to the more practical consequences of her doctrine. Affliction, being against nature and necessarily suffered unwillingly, was not something that could be desired. The *possibility* of affliction was something to be loved: affliction was truly at the centre of Christianity and the Cross of Christ was the only source of light bright enough to illuminate it:

> God is joy, and Creation is affliction; but it is an affliction radiant with the light of joy. Affliction contains the truth about our condition. They alone will see God who prefer to recognise the truth and die, instead of living a long and happy existence in a state of illusion. One must want to go towards reality; then, when one thinks one has found a corpse, one meets an angel who says: 'He is risen'. (SNL, p. 194)

After various suggestions as to how Christianity could enter and permeate profane life, Weil concluded by insisting that there was no answer in this world to questions about the purpose of affliction, just as there was no answer to the question as to why something was beautiful. The experience of joy and of affliction were, for Weil, closely linked:

> The man who has known pure joy, if only for a moment, and who has therefore tasted the flavour of the world's beauty, for it is the same thing, is the only man for whom affliction is something devastating. At the same time, he is the only man who has not deserved this punishment. But, after all, for him it is no punishment; it is God Himself holding his hand and pressing it rather hard. For, if he remains constant, what he will discover buried deep under the sound of his own lamentations is the pearl of the silence of God. (SNL, p. 198)

The final essay that Weil gave to Perrin was entitled 'Forms of the Implicit Love of God'. Here Weil discussed four types of love: love of neighbour, love of the beauty of the world, love of religious practices, and love of friendship. These loves were said to be implicit because of their indirect participation in God's goodness. The first section explicated the notion of charity through that of justice. Justice could only exist between equals. To treat as equals those who were weaker was, thought Weil, a supernatural attitude and 'the most Christian of virtues' (WG, p. 86). The corollary of this was that punishment could only cease being a cruel farce if it operated within a shared religious context. The second section continued the same theme, applying it to the order of the world:

> To empty ourselves of our false divinity, to deny ourselves, to give up being the centre of the world in imagination, to discern that all points in the world are equally centres and that the true centre is outside the world, this is to consent to the rule of mechanical necessity in matter and of free choice at the centre of each soul. Such consent is love. The face of this love which is turned towards thinking persons is the love of our neighbour; the face turned towards matter is love of the order of the world, or love of the beauty of the world which is the same thing. (WG, p. 99)

Weil deplored the fact that the sense of the world's beauty, so vivid in passages of the Old and New Testament, in Saint Francis and Saint John of the Cross, had faded from Christianity after the early Middle Ages. Science, physical labour, sexual love, all had the beauty of the world as their object and essentially expressed a longing for the Incarnation. Attachment to the beauty of the world was also a clue to the impersonality of God who was 'the Divine model of a person who

passes beyond the self by renunciation' (WG, p. 114). This in turn led
to the thought that it was 'because the renunciation of the personality
makes man a reflection of God that it is so frightful to reduce men to
the condition of inert matter by plunging them into affliction' (ibid.).
Therefore it was imperative that we preserve the independence of each
and every human being, since 'he who is perfectly obedient sets an
infinite price upon the faculty of free choice in all men' (WG, p. 115). In
the third section on religious practices, Weil again insisted on the
importance of impersonality. At the centre of the Catholic religion was
a small piece of matter: this was 'the great scandal and yet the most
wonderful virtue of this religion' (WG, p. 130). Thus religion was not
something social, nor a system of morality, nor a striving after goodness.
Religious practice was simply attention animated by desire; it was God
who sought human beings, rather than the other way round.

Finally, Weil counterbalanced the emphasis on impersonality in the
first three sections with a discussion of friendship. If it was reciprocal
and not possessive then, 'a pure friendship is an image of that original
and perfect friendship which belongs to the Trinity and which is the
very essence of God. It is impossible for two human beings to be one
while scrupulously respecting the distance which separates them, unless
God is present in each of them. The point at which parallels meet is
infinity' (WG, p. 37). All these indirect loves – of our neighbour, of the
world, of our friends, of religious practice itself – were, for Weil, only
indirect, implicit, preparatory forms of the love of God:

> After God has come in person, not only to visit the soul as he does
> for a long time beforehand, but to possess it and to transport its centre
> near to his very heart, it is otherwise. The chicken has cracked its
> shell, it is outside the egg of the world. These first loves continue,
> they are more intense than before, but they are different. He who has
> passed through this adventure has a deeper love than ever for those
> who suffer affliction and for those who help him in his own, for his
> friends, for religious practices and for the beauty of the world. But
> his love in all of these forms has become a movement of God himself,
> a ray merged in the light of God. That at least is what we may
> suppose. (WG, p. 138)

The writings that Weil gave to Perrin on her departure represent a
kind of testament, similar to her *Oppression and Liberty* prior to her
'departure' into the factory. Indeed the idea of departure held a constant
fascination for Weil. A journey into the untried and untested involved
an open-endedness and a vulnerability. It was the foreshadowing of the
great journey at the end of life. She marked her departure from Marseilles
with three long letters addressed to those to whom she felt closest and

who had given her the friendship that she felt was 'an incomparable, immeasurable boon, and a source of life – not metaphorically but literally' (SL, p. 141). To Bousquet she wrote: 'I am convinced that affliction on the one hand, and on the other hand joy, when it is a complete and pure commitment to perfect beauty, are the only two keys which give entry to the realm of purity, where one can breathe: the home of the real' (ibid.). He had asked her for an account of her mystical experiences and she responded with a brief spiritual autobiography culminating in the time at Solesmes when she had felt 'a presence more personal, more certain, and more real than that of a human being, inaccessible both to the sense and to the imagination' (SL, p. 140). Previously, she said, she had never spoken of this to anyone. With her letter she sent copies of T. E. Lawrence, Swinburne, the poem of the Holy Grail, and – 'jewel of jewels' – the Gospels in Greek. Thibon she saw for the last time towards the end of April 1942, in Marseilles. They talked almost all night. For him it was an unforgettable experience:

I had the impression of being in the presence of an absolutely transparent soul that was ready to be re-absorbed into original light. I can still hear Simone Weil's voice in the deserted streets of Marseilles as she took me back to my hotel in the early hours of the morning; she was speaking of the Gospel; her mouth uttered thoughts as a tree gives its fruit. (PT, pp. 131f).

The next morning she saw him off at the railway station. She handed him, absent-mindedly and carelessly, a package of a dozen large notebooks that were later to become so famous. A few days before embarkation she wrote to him:

Soon there will be distance between us. Let us love this distance, which is thoroughly woven with friendship, since those who do not love each other are not separated. Meeting and separation are the human images of the absolute union between the Father and the Son in the Trinity and of the inconceivable rapture between the Father and the Son at the moment of the words 'My God, why hast Thou abandoned me?'. That is why for us human beings, here below, separation is more fitting. For we have the good fortune to have been thrown by our birthright at the foot of the Cross.[19]

To Perrin she wrote an extremely long letter containing an extended version of the spiritual autobiography that she had sent to Bousquet. This account was intended as a background to her conclusion that God did not want her in the Church and probably never would 'except perhaps at the moment of death' (WG, p. 26). She ended her letter:

Goodbye, I wish you all possible good things except the Cross; for I do not love my neighbour as myself, you particularly, as you have noticed . . . This wish is not due only to the frailty of human friendship. For, with no matter what human being, taken individually, I always find reasons for concluding that sorrow and misfortune do not suit him; either because he seems too mediocre for anything so great, or, on the contrary, too precious to be destroyed. One cannot fail more seriously in the second of the two essential Commandments. And as to the first, I fail to observe that in a still more horrible manner, for every time that I think of the Crucifixion of Christ, I commit the sin of envy. (WG, pp. 32f)

With the letter she enclosed various additions to their joint work on Greek texts.

Weil left Marseilles with her parents on 14 May on board the *Maréchal Lyautey*, bound for Morocco. The night before she had spent with Hélène and Pierre Honnorat who accompanied her to the boat. When they said, 'Au revoir in this world or the next', she replied firmly (as she had done to Thibon): 'No. In the next world, there will be no meeting again.' To her friend Hélène, she remarked smilingly that at least if they were torpedoed the sea would make a good baptismal font.

9

Marseilles: Thought

'We are a part which has to imitate the whole.' (GG, p. 127)

It was in Marseilles that Weil worked out the definitive outlines of her thought, particularly in the areas of religion and metaphysics. Her thinking was tentative and open-ended, enquiring, probing, and therefore the very opposite of systematic. This makes it impossible to summarise easily. Nevertheless the main outlines are clear.

An obvious question to start with is: was Weil a Christian? She certainly considered herself to be a Christian; and the more interesting question is thus what sort of a Christian she was. She claimed to have been a Christian in a broad sense and implicitly all her life, in spite of her lack of any religious upbringing. In her *Notebooks* she wrote that 'if we love God, even though we think he doesn't exist, he will make his existence manifest' (NB, p. 583). This is what happened at Solesmes, after which 'the name of God and the name of Christ have been more and more irresistibly mingled with my thoughts' (SL, p. 140). To Perrin she roundly declared: 'I love God, Christ and the Catholic faith as much as it is possible for so miserably inadequate a creature to love them' (WG, p. 6), and added to the list for good measure, and no doubt thinking of Solesmes, 'the Catholic liturgy, hymns, architecture, rites and ceremonies' (ibid.). A year later she wrote to Maritain, that, if anyone asked her whether she was a Catholic, she felt it would be lying to say 'No'.

Nevertheless it is obvious that Weil's understanding of Christianity is peculiar. This is partly because her religious attitudes arose more or less directly from her practical experiences. Hers was a mind that fastened on contemporary history, the people she met, the books she came across, and nourished its thought therefrom. And it was in the context of this rather haphazard approach that her Christianity took its shape. There were of course, also, the more abiding influences of Alain and of Greek thought which preceded her more specific adherence to Christianity and which coloured her whole view. But however unorthodox Weil's approach, there is no doubt that her religion was Christocentric: her attitude to Christ is one of reverence and awe. And it is on the Crucifixion of Christ that she concentrates her attention, since 'there is not, there cannot be, any human activity in whatever sphere, of which Christ's Cross is not the supreme and secret truth' (SNL, pp. 195f). What marked the importance of Christianity was the role of Christ as mediator. The Incarnation and Crucifixion of Christ lay at the very centre of her thought. For it was Christ's Cross alone that could make some sense of affliction. Christ was no heroic martyr – Weil had little sympathy for martyrs in general, who she considered too active in seeking their own destruction. Rather Christ was the meeting-point of the divine and the human by being obedient to the laws pertaining to both of them, revealing both the nature of God and the fundamental reality of human nature. God renounced himself in creating the world which was essentially both good and evil and, being pure good, could only come down to earth to become incarnate by undergoing the extremest form of suffering. As for human beings, 'we needs must have a just man to imitate so that the imitation of God does not simply remain an empty phrase; but it is also necessary, so that we may be carried beyond the boundaries of the will, that we should not be able to desire to imitate him. One cannot desire the Cross' (NB, p. 415). For the Cross was the supreme form of affliction and affliction was, by definition, something which could not be desired.

If Weil felt the Cross to be the centre of Christianity, she was less enthusiastic about the Resurrection: 'Hitler could die and return to life again fifty times, but I should still not look upon him as the Son of God. And if the Gospel omitted all mention of Christ's Resurrection, faith would be easier for me. The Cross by itself suffices me' (LP, p. 55). The ideas of personal salvation and eternal life were also alien to Weil. This was because she stressed the impersonality of God, who was 'an impersonal person who loves not as I love but as an emerald is green' (FLN, p. 129). It followed that 'it is impossible to go beyond a certain point on the path of perfection if one only thinks of God as personal. To go further it is necessary – by force of desire – to make oneself resemble an impersonal perfection' (ibid.). The link between the impersonal side of God and the Incarnation was to be found in the doctrine of the Trinity:

> Before all things, God loves himself. This love, this friendship of God, is the Trinity. Between the terms united by this relation of divine love there is more than nearness; there is infinite nearness or identity. But through the Creation, the Incarnation, and the Passion, there is also infinite distance. The interposed density of all space and all time sets infinite distance between God and God. (SNL, p. 176)

The Trinity and the Cross represented for Weil the two poles, the two essential truths of Christianity.

Weil's attitude to dogma as a whole was tentative: rather than saying that what was not Christian was not true, she preferred to say that what was true was Christian. Whoever read the Gospels and did not realise that they came from God evidently had no discernment for holy things (cf. FLN, p. 80). But 'it is a question only of discernment for a divine inspiration, not for the particular nature of this inspiration. As for the common identity linking together the Word and this Man, there is nothing to show that the affirmation of such a link is a condition of salvation, and such a thing would be absurd' (NB, p. 246). Miracles in the ordinary accepted sense of the word she considered to be 'meaningless' (FLN, p. 80): they were merely natural phenomena which happened to people in particular states such as sainthood, hysteria or asceticism. The Sacraments she regarded as material souvenirs and, just as genuine lovers were keen on exchanging souvenirs, so it was doubtful whether there could be any genuine religion that was not sacramental (cf. NB, p. 335). This 'materialist' side to Weil's view of religion led her to sympathise with the orthodox Catholic doctrine on the real presence of Christ in the Eucharist, a sympathy which had been evident even in her early school essays (cf. OC, I, p. 92f). She wrote:

The virtue of the dogma of the real presence lies in its very absurdity. Except for the infinitely touching symbolism of food, there is nothing in a morsel of bread which can be associated with our thought of God. Thus the conventional character of the Divine Presence is evident. Christ can only be present in such an object by convention. For this very reason he can be perfectly present in it. God can only be present in secret here below. His presence in the Eucharist is truly secret since no part of our thought can reach the secret. Thus it is total. (WG, p. 121)

Thus, although the Eucharist was a 'convention', it was a convention ratified by God, whose conventions were creative of truth and thus finally more real than any form of matter.[1]

But however strongly Weil might feel herself attached to the Trinity and the Real Presence, there were two aspects of the dogmas of the Church that she found objectionable. Firstly, these dogmas were intended to be *mysteries*, but 'in the Church, considered as a social organism, the mysteries inevitably degenerate into beliefs'. Dogmas were not something to be affirmed, but to be regarded with attention, respect, and love. Secondly, the maintenance of dogma was used to exclude people from the Church. Although it was necessary, at least at certain times, that 'the Church should preserve the Christian dogma in its integrity, like a diamond, with incorruptible strictness' (SE, p. 52), this did not entail condemnation of others, still less their persecution. It was the use of this *anathema sit* by the Church that Weil considered unacceptable.

Indeed the whole conception of the Church as institutionalised tradition she found very difficult. By claiming to instantiate transcendence in itself the Church had become a social idol. Christ had refused the temptation of the devil who offered him the kingdoms of this world; but his Bride, the Church, had succumbed to the temptation. Born of the historical conjuncture of Israel and Rome, the Church had allowed the emergence of a religious faith which had little room for authentic personal relationship to the transcendent: the Church was seen as the truth of God rather than God as the truth of the Church. This degeneration of the Christian message into the radically inauthentic doctrines and practices of a social organism set in early: it was connected with the notion of progress and the idea that the path of history was also the unfolding of God's providence: 'Primitive Christianity concocted the poison represented by the notion of progress through the idea of a divine system of education preparing men so as to make them fit to receive Christ's message. This fitted in with the hopes of a universal conversion of the nations and the end of the world, regarded as both being imminent' (NB, p. 615).

Weil drew here several parallels between the development of Christianity and that of the Communist movement with its expectation of imminent revolution (cf. NB, pp. 350f). The victory of Christianity could be explained partly by the immense dynamic provided by its eschatological beliefs which enabled it to conquer the Great Beast of Rome. But it also led Christianity to forget 'the immense distance which separates the necessary from the good' and itself to succumb to the spirit of the institutions it had vanquished. The Church which sprang up on the ruins of the Roman Empire was the social organism which turned mysteries into beliefs. Thus Weil left no room for the Messianic tendencies so powerful in Christianity and a sociopolitical theology of liberation is as foreign to her as the urgings of a Bultmann for demythologisation and the creation of a true community. Her Christianity was both older and less contingent. But it is equally clear that what she believed was indeed a version of Christianity. However much her anarchist past and radical individualism might affect her view of the history of the Church, she adhered to the central tenets of Christianity, such as the Incarnation and the Trinity. Having come comparatively late in life to these doctrines, she expressed them in the language of concepts that had become hers. It should also be remembered that her criticisms were addressed to those she thought of as fellow-Christians: her opposition to some aspects of Christianity (sometimes violent) were those of someone who considered herself an insider. Ten years earlier her strongest criticism of socialism was reserved for other socialists; now it was as a Catholic by right that she attacked those attitudes in the Church that she considered to be preventing her from becoming a Catholic in fact: *fidelia vulnera amantis*.

The portrait of Weil as a (sort of) Catholic Christian has been challenged by those who think her religious opinions are more appropriately described as Gnostic.[2] Gnosticism was a system (or systems) of speculation with origins in oriental (Babylonian, Iranian, Egyptian) rather than Greek thought, which became widespread in the first two centuries AD. Although the beliefs of the various Gnostic sects were many, varied and sometimes extremely weird, their central tenets can be reduced to three: firstly, that the whole of the created world is fundamentally and irredeemably evil and is thus not the work of God, but of some fallen angel or demiurge who had rebelled against God; secondly, that, nevertheless, there was hidden deep inside every human being some spark of the divine essence; thirdly, that there was available a salvific knowledge or *gnosis* which could be attained through various rites or practices and which yielded direct and absolute contact with God. These tenets (particularly the first and the third) were at variance with mainstream Christianity and Gnosticism was fiercely contested by the early apologists of the Church such as Irenaeus and Tertullian and eventually condemned as heretical. It was given a fresh impetus by the teaching of Mani, a third-century Iranian, whose followers, known as Manichees, were among the chief opponents of Saint Augustine, who had once been a Manichee himself. Gnostic beliefs survived the Dark Ages and resurfaced in the early Middle Ages among such communities as the Bogomils in Hungary and the Cathars of the Languedoc.

Because of the complexity of the Gnostic phenomenon there is no simple answer to the question of how far Weil shared their beliefs. She was certainly very enthusiastic about the Cathars. One of the centres of her intellectual life in Marseilles was the *Cahiers du Sud* which was then preparing its special issue on 'The genius of Oc' to which she contributed two beautiful articles expressing this enthusiasm. To Déodat Roché, a historian of Catharism, and one of the instigators of the special number, she wrote that, although she knew little about the Cathars, she had long been attracted to them because of their rejection of the Old Testament and her impression that 'Catharism was the last living expression of pre-Roman antiquity'. She saw Plato as summing up in magisterial fashion these ancient traditions of the eastern Mediterranean, and 'it is from this thought that Christianity issued; but only the Gnostics, Manichaeans, and Cathars seem to have kept really faithful to it' (SL, p. 130). Weil was undoubtedly attracted by the way the Cathars stressed the gulf between God and the world and their emphasis on purity (the meaning of the Greek word from which 'Cathar' was derived); and she was keen to study their writings in the original texts. But it is doubtful whether she pursued this study very far[3] – indeed her specific knowledge of gnosticism seems to have been sparse.[4] Her enthusiasm was largely due to her profound sympathy for the vanquished civilisation of the Languedoc and the values of measured obedience, tolerance, and non-violence that it embodied. And the very fact that Catharism was a past phenomenon meant, as she herself admitted (NB, p. 350), that it was impossible in the twentieth century to be one of its adherents.

As for the wider phenomenon of gnosticism, Weil was undoubtedly attracted by some of its formulations. She, too, insisted that God was absent from the world, that the world of God, the real world, was at an infinite distance from the world we inhabit. She, too, saw our world as governed by a blind necessity which imprisoned and destroyed its inhabitants. And she, too, talked of a point in the human soul, distinct from both body and psyche, which was itself divine and capable of eventual union with God. But, however attractive to Weil was the lost civilisation of the Languedoc, however striking she found certain gnostic formulations, and however much her intellectualism in matters of faith has gnostic echoes, her thought remained fundamentally at variance with central gnostic tenets. For the Gnostics, the main purpose in acquiring the secret knowledge or gnosis was that it enabled its possessors to escape from the world. For Weil, on the other hand, the world was not something to be fled but something to be experienced in all its plenitude, however painful that might be, since

> one must tenderly love the harshness of that necessity which is like a coin with two faces, the one turned towards us being domination and the one turned towards God, obedience. We must embrace it closely even if it offers its roughest surface and the roughness cuts into us. Any lover is glad to clasp tightly some object belonging to an absent loved one, even to the point where it cuts into the flesh. We know that this universe is an object belonging to God. (SNL, p. 186).

Therefore 'all sins are an attempt to escape from time' (FLN, p. 102) and the root of evil was an exercise of the imagination as an escape from reality.

Again, for the Gnostics, the world was so irredeemably evil that it could not possibly be the creation of God. But for Weil the world, however subject to the blind mechanisms of necessity, offered all sorts of bridges to God. Work, art, science were all worldly activities which found their ultimate meaning as investigations of the incarnation of God in the world. Weil's writings are full of marvellous passages on the beauty of the physical world (cf. for example, WG, pp. 97ff). Finally, and most decisively, the gnostics denied the human reality of Jesus who, in so far as he was a messenger of God, could not have become truly incarnate. For Weil, on the other hand, the humanity of Jesus and the reality of the Cross are at the very heart of her meditations. She who was so opposed to all forms of anathema was in favour of it in one case only: those who denied the reality of the Incarnation.

Although, therefore, it would be misleading not to call Weil a Christian, the way in which she expressed her Christianity was indeed unusual. This is partly because she was a mystic. Her experiences at Solesmes, in the Ardèche, and above all in the encounter with the bewitching stranger recounted in what was intended as a preface to her *Notebooks*[5] – all these were clearly mystical experiences. And her description of affliction and the attendant absence of God recalls the 'dark night of the soul' of Saint John of the Cross to whom Weil made frequent reference. But mystical experiences are essentially impossible to put into words; and the effort to do so has led most Christian mystics, however closely attached they may have been to the Church, to be attacked for lack of orthodoxy. And Weil is no exception. Nevertheless the main reason for the alien nature of some of her interpretations of Christianity is that she was by training a philosopher and the structure of her religious thought is primarily a philosophical structure and not a religious one. Weil had been in dialogue with the great philosophers of the West (often as refracted through the teaching of Alain) for fifteen years before she started to think seriously about Christianity. Thus when she did so think, she expressed herself in categories largely unfamiliar to those brought up in a Christian milieu. Moreover these categories are often apparently contradictory: Weil purposely used contradiction as a method for transcending a particular and limited perspective, for (as she put it) 'emerging from a point of view' (NB, p. 46). Nevertheless this metaphysical background, revolving around the concepts of necessity, God, creation, evil and freedom is essential for an understanding of her religious outlook.[6]

From her earliest years the idea that the world was governed by necessity had great force for Weil. And throughout the *Notebooks* she constantly reminded herself of Plato's injunction 'not to confuse the necessary with the good'. Nevertheless necessity for Weil presented itself under two aspects which are difficult to reconcile. On the one hand, she talked of the 'pitiless necessity of matter' (FLN, p. 103), an apparently arbitrary combination of blind forces – whence her irritation with the idea that the world could contain any sort of Providence: 'the world is necessity and not purpose . . . whenever we look for final causes in this world it refuses them' (SNL, p. 197). This was because

> God wants everything that takes place *to a like degree*, not certain things as means and certain other things as ends. Similarly, He wants *to a like degree* the whole and the parts, each portion, each slice that can be cut out of continuous reality. This can only be represented to the human intelligence in the following terms: He wants necessity to exist. (NB, p. 266)

On the other hand, Weil sometimes referred to necessity as the law-like network of relationships that underlay and knitted together the material world whose author in some sense was God: 'in order that Good may pass into existence, Good must be able to be the cause of what is already entirely caused by Necessity' (NB, p. 99). The way in which matter was formed and ordered gave some clue to the nature of the Good. Thus she could go as far as to say that 'Necessity, insofar as it is absolutely other than the Good, is the Good itself' (GG, p. 99), which amounted to deifying necessity. If we contemplated the world of things with sufficient detachment and attention, we would begin to know and love God.

One reason for this apparent contradiction was that, although Weil was clear about the absence of God from the world of necessity, at the same time she was fascinated by mathematics and in particular by the vision of God as the Eternal Geometer.[7] Her *Notebooks* are full of attempts to describe analogies between mathematics and theology. In the spirit of Descartes she saw the foundation of the world as mathematical connections 'harder than any diamond' (NR, p. 275). The problem of the discovery of incommensurables in early Greek mathematics (which she had discussed with her brother in 1940) provided her with means of dealing with real contradictions. Eudoxus had worked out how incommensurable lines could be brought into a common ratio by considering their *relative* magnitude, thus yielding a real number system that would encompass both natural and irrational numbers. Similarly, Weil thought, 'since it is possible in this way to equalise the notions in the case of two completely different pairs of magnitudes, one could hope to be able also to apply the notion of ratio to psychological and spiritual matters' (C, p. 162). Thus it was this enthusiasm for geometry that led Weil to view one form of necessity (mathematical) with approval while seeing necessity in its mechanical form as something opposed to the Good. The higher unity into which incommensurables could be mediated avoided the strict Manichaean dichotomy of good and evil to which Weil's thought would otherwise be subject. Geometry also provided her with some of her main symbols, which she was able to invest with a startling degree of reality. An example was a balance whose fulcrum was a point without any magnitude or force which nevertheless governed the forces on either side of it by imposing a necessary relationship on them. And Weil sometimes described the intersection of the Cross of Christ as this kind of a balance or world-axis.

This contadictory approach was present in her concept of God. Necessity as a principle of order in the world presented one face of God: it was an image by which the intelligence could grasp the indifference and impartiality of God. This led Weil to describe God as ultimately impersonal rather than personal – the God who 'maketh His sun to rise on the evil and on the good, and sendeth rain on the just and on the unjust'. But Weil at the same time described necessity as 'the veil of God' (NB, p. 266) because God was manifested by the universe but also hidden: 'God turns Himself into *necessity*. Two sides to necessity: the side exercised and the side endured. Sun and Cross' (NB, p. 190). The other face of God was that of love. It was under this aspect that God was a hidden God, absent from the world 'except in the existence of those in this world in whom His love is alive' (FLN, p. 103). Thus to affirm both the existence and the non-existence of God, equally true, presented Weil with no problem:

> I am absolutely certain that there is a God, in the sense that I am absolutely certain that my love is not illusory. I am absolutely certain that there is not a God, in the sense that I am absolutely certain that there is nothing real which bears a resemblance to what I am able to conceive when I pronounce that name, since I am unable to conceive God. But that thing, which I am unable to conceive, is not an illusion. This impossibility is more immediately present to me than is the feeling of my own personal existence. (NB, p. 127)

Atheism could, therefore, be purificatory since religion, in so far as it was a source of consolation, was a hindrance to true faith.

This dual face of God as present necessity and absent love led to the problem of creation which lies at the centre of Weil's metaphysics. For her, creation was itself a contradiction: 'It is contradictory that God, who is infinite, who is all, to whom nothing is lacking, should do something that is outside Himself, that is not Himself, while at the same time proceeding from Himself' (NB, p. 386). (Pantheism simply suppressed one term of the contradiction.) Creation was an abdication of the omnipotence of God who was only all-powerful in that He had willed His abdication. This abdication on the part of God was a renunciation, a sacrifice. Creation represented a tearing asunder of God from God. Whereas traditionally creation was thought of as being 'outside' God, for Weil the world was what separated the two parts (or persons) of God. It was between the two pincers of God as Power and God as Love. But it was not being as such that was an obstacle between the two pincers of God. For necessity, as we have seen, could be conceived of as a mirror of God. It was human autonomy that constituted not a mirror but a screen between God and God.

This again resulted in a contradiction, which together with its solution, Weil expressed with her customary logic: 'If one believes that God has created in order to be loved, and that He cannot create anything which is God, and further that He cannot be loved by anything which is not

God, then he is brought up against a contradiction. The contradiction contains in itself Necessity' (NB, pp. 330f). This was the process that Weil referred to as 'de-creation'. De-creation was 'the transcendent completion of creation; annihilation in God which confers the fullness of being upon the creature so annihilated, a fullness which is denied it so long as it goes on existing' (C, p. 471). It was this approach that lay behind her antipathy to concepts such as that of the person, of imagination, of individual perspective – all of which seemed to her to enhance the distinctiveness of the individual over against God. For Weil, the vocation of human beings was to be nothing so that God might be all in all. The whole of Weil's religious philosophy revolves around this vision of a God who suffers because God is separated from God by human autonomy and the corollary that the human vocation is to remove this obstacle by association with the Cross of Christ, which removes the distance and unites God with God.

Although Weil occasionally spoke as though the whole of existence were evil, she normally spoke of creation as being essentially both good and evil, and identified the source of this evil in the autonomous will, the ego:

> In relation to God, we are like a thief who has burgled the house of a kindly householder and been allowed to keep some of the gold. From the point of view of the lawful owner this gold is a gift; from the point of view of the burglar it is a theft . . . it is the same with our existence. We have stolen a little of God's being to make it ours. (FLN, p. 269)

Thus the process of de-creation was also the destruction of evil: 'Evil is the distance between the creature and God. To abolish evil means to de-create but that is something which God is only able to do with our cooperation. Destruction is the opposite extreme of de-creation' (NB, p. 342). Evil was thus, for Weil, not, as in some facile views, merely an absence of good, nor a mere appearance when compared to a more fundamental level of reality. Evil was part of the very fabric of the universe. Nor, at least in its extremest form – afflication – could it be seen as at least instrumentally good: 'I must not love my suffering because it is useful, but because it *is*' (NB, p. 434). Nevertheless, although suffering could not be useful, it could be redemptive: to feel simultaneously the reality of evil and the absence of God was to bring the presence of God into the evil, to purify it, and to remove it as an obstacle to the re-unifying of God with God. This was what happened at the Crucifixion when Christ concentrated all the evils of creation upon Himself. Thus Weil is able to arrive at the paradox that the existence of evil reveals the goodness of God: 'Pure goodness is not anywhere to be found (in this world). Either God is not almighty or he is not absolutely good, or else he does not command everywhere where he has the power to do so. Thus the existence of evil here below, far from disproving the reality of God, is the very thing that reveals him in his Truth' (WG, p. 87). God is both supreme and impotent. Weil projected into the very heart of God the suffering of the world of which she was so acutely conscious.

Weil's views on the nature of creation and the reality of evil are stark and grim. However they are counterbalanced by her theory of intermediaries for which she used the Greek word *metaxu*, which means 'between'. The *metaxus* were links with God, bridges towards the transcendent. The most evident of these *metaxus* was beauty, since 'thanks to God's wisdom, who has printed on this world the mark of the good, in the form of beauty, one can love the Good through the things of this world' (FLN, p. 139). Mathematics was another example: its practice demanded concentration and the kind of self-renunciation wherein lay, finally, our only good (cf. NB, p. 193). Although neither intrinsically good nor evil, these *metaxus* could, given the right attention, become a mirror and a magnet, reflecting the nature of God and attracting the soul towards it. Thus they were forms of the implicit love of God and are detailed in her essay of that title.[8] Indeed Weil's whole social programme can be seen as a *metaxu*, since the concept forms the link between the practical and the mystical sides of her thought.

Aided by these *metaxus*, the role of the individual was to renounce being something and thus to imitate God who in creation had renounced being everything. This involved a kind of non-active action which, because it pursued no particular end, could reconcile the necessary and the good. Human beings were inevitably subject to necessity. As intelligent beings we could consent to this necessity or be coerced by it – that was the only choice open to us. Thus for Weil obedience was the supreme virtue, but obedience which was not the result of will-power but of attention to the right relationship of things:

> If we suspend the filling-up activity of the imagination and fix our attention on the relationship of things, a necessity becomes apparent which we cannot help obeying. Until then we have not any notion of necessity and we have no notion of obedience. After that we cannot be proud of what we do, even though we may accomplish marvels. (GG, p. 43)

This attitude involved becoming attuned to the universe as though it was our second body and thus consenting to become a sort of conductor through which the love of God could pass.

If Weil's religious conceptions can only be understood in the context of their metaphysical background, it is also true that an understanding

202 *Simone Weil: Utopian Pessimist*

of her metaphysics requires some appreciation of how imbued she was with Greek philosophy and particularly with Plato. In the words of one of her best commentators, 'no thinker of this century has been more influenced by Plato than Simone Weil and almost all the fundamental questions of Christian Platonism are discussed in her work which is the only example in our century of mystical speculation which is both Platonist and Christian.[9] In Weil's opinion, the Greeks were pre-eminent in creating those bridges to God that she considered so important: 'The whole of Greek civilisation is a search for bridges to relate human misery with the divine perfection. Their art, which is incomparable, their poetry, their philosophy, their science (geometry, astronomy, mechanics, physics, biology) which they invented, were nothing but bridges. They invented (?) the idea of *mediation*' (SNL, p. 90).

Whereas Weil came to Christianity comparatively late in her short life, her interest in Greek philosophy had begun early. Plato was the main philosopher that Alain discussed in his class during Weil's first year at Henri IV; and she originally intended to make substantial allusions to Plato in her diploma dissertation (cf. OC, I, p. 344). Her enthusiasm for Plato was evident even in her political writings of the 1930s (cf. OC, II, p. 354; OL, p. 273); and he became for her the best example of a 'true philsopher' who was 'unsurpassable' (PSO, p. 66)., At the same time, Weil came to see Plato and the Greeks as summing up the end of a long tradition which had, prior to the emergence of Greek civilisation, flourished in the Eastern Mediterranean among such peoples as the Phoenicians, the Sumerians, the Hittites, and particularly the Egyptians: it was in Egypt that Pythagorean thought, which so influenced Plato, had its origin.

It was out of this rich matrix of Mediterranean spirituality that Christianity eventually emerged with a gospel which was 'the last marvellous expression of the Greek genius' (MILES, p. 212). Rome destroyed all spiritual life in Greece as in all the other countries she subdued. Only under the shield of Israel's determined resistance to the Romans did a little of the Greek spirit survive. Thus

> after three barren centuries, amid the burning thirst of so many peoples, there sprang up the fount of perfect purity. The idea of mediation achieved full realisation, the perfect bridge was seen, divine wisdom became visible, as Plato had hoped, to mortal eyes. In this way the Greek vocation was perfected by becoming the Christian vocation. (SE, p. 46)

The unity of Greek and Christian thought had been sundered by the Renaissance, a state of affairs that could only be remedied 'by recognising in Greek thought the whole of the Christian faith' (NB, p. 465). It was to an intensive study of this problem that Weil devoted most of her time in the winter of 1941/2, assembling many of the relevant texts with a view to publishing, with Perrin, a book on the subject.[10]

This Greek revelation, which found its perfection in Christianity, consisted in 'the revelation of human misery, of God's transcendence, and of the infinite distance between God and men' (SE, p. 46). In Greek philosophy, myth and tragedy Weil found those prophecies of the Gospels that a more orthodox Christianity had been accustomed to see in the Old Testament. One of her favourite examples was the figure of Prometheus, the benefactor of humanity who willingly suffered the anger of Zeus. The story of Prometheus was 'like the refraction into Eternity of the Passion of Christ' and Prometheus himself could be seen as 'the Lamb slain from the foundation of the world' (IC, p. 70). Another example was the sufferings of the perfectly just individual as described in Plato's *Republic*, which 'expounds the idea of Divine Incarnation more clearly than any other Greek text'. Both Prometheus and the perfectly just individual were anticipations of Christ just as much as the suffering servant of Isaiah.

Weil saw in Greek tragedy in general the theme of the persecution of justice. Just as with the *Prometheus* of Aeschylus, so in the *Antigone* and *Electra* of Sophocles the theme was one of injustice and rebellion followed by suffering and a lonely cry for wrongs to be righted. Greek tragedy was a lesson in which the order of the world impressed itself implacably on the human soul:

> Man must submit to what he does not wish, he must find himself subject to necessity. Misfortunes leave wounds which bleed drop by drop even in sleep; thus little by little they train man by force and dispose him to wisdom in spite of himself. Man must learn to think of himself as a limited and dependent being; and only suffering teaches him this. (SG, p. 44)

And Weil drew parallels with the Gospels and the 'dark night' of Saint John of the Cross. Her view of Greek thought was thus strikingly at odds with that of Nietzsche, with whose style of sweeping and imperious judgement she nevertheless has so much in common. She did not share Nietzsche's pessimistic, catastrophic interpretation of Greece (nor, incidentally, the romantic nostalgia of Hegel). She wrote:

> The Greeks had no taste for affliction, disaster, disequilibrium. Whereas there are so many modern people (and notably Nietzsche, I believe) in whom sadness is connected with a loss of the very instinct for happiness; they feel a need to annihilate themselves. In my opinion, there is no anguish in the Greeks. That is what makes them

dear to me. In struggling against anguish one never produces serenity; the struggle against anguish only produces new forms of anguish. But the Greeks possessed grace from the beginning. (SL, p. 123)

Whereas, for Nietzsche, Dionysus represented the pagan God *par excellence*, desperate and intoxicated, for Weil he was, like Prometheus, a forerunner of Christ. Where Weil and Nietzsche did agree was in the connection between Plato and Christianity. But whereas, for Nietzsche, Plato was part of the anaemic decadence of Greece of which Christianity was simply a vulgarisation which heralded the disastrous triumph of the weak, for Weil Plato embodied all that was most valuable in Greek spiritual achievement.[11]

Weil was particularly concerned to uncover the sources of Platonic thought in such thinkers as Heraclitus, Pythagoras and the speculations of Greek science in general. In Heraclitus, who lived in Ephesus from around 535 BC to 475 BC, Weil admired the emphasis on the contradictory nature of reality as we observe it.[12] One of the reasons that make her own *Notebooks* so difficult to understand is that she is often recording there the contradictory nature of her own observations. It was a mistake to try to resolve these contradictions on the same level as they occurred: 'The bad union of opposites (bad because fallacious) is that which is achieved on the same plane as the opposites. The veritable union takes place on the plane above, Mathematics' (NB, p. 601). There were 'few more completely false ideas' than that history was some sort of directed continuity, since this idea 'seeks harmony in Becoming, in what is the exact opposite of the eternal. It is a bad union of opposites' (NB, p. 616). The irreducible contradictions in reality were due to the perspective of the individual and could only be resolved at a level where the personal had been eliminated.

The stress on the irreducible contradictoriness of existence and the consequent recourse to a supernatural reason which could be illuminated by a study of number was, according to Weil, a fundamental doctrine of Pythagoreanism. Pythagorus was born on the island of Samos around 580 BC but spent the latter part of his life in southern Italy where he founded an influential school. Weil saw Pythagoreanism as tremendously important, in that it permeated the whole of Greek philosophy in general and was the source, in particular, of the spiritual element in Plato. She devoted a large part of her study of the precursors of Christianity to elaborating on the Pythagorean doctrines; and it is in this context that she presents her most systematic discussion of the philosophical bases of Christian theology (cf. IC, pp. 151ff). She has to admit, however, that Pythagorean thought was 'the great mystery of Greek civilization' in that 'today we can only appreciate something of the basic Pythagorean doctrine by exercising a kind of intuition and such an intuition can only be exercised from the inside; that is to say only if one has truly drawn spiritual life from the texts studied' (IC, p. 153).

The result is that Weil is more certain about the essence of Pythagorean thought than anyone else has managed to be. One of the few surviving doctrines of the Pythagoreans is that 'all is number'. Weil interpreted this as saying that all created things were number, or plurality, as against God who was symbolised by one which was itself not number. Nevertheless numbers could be brought into some kind of unity through proportion. The methods of achieving this – use of squares and of geometry – partook, therefore, of the Divine. This is obscure, but what Weil took the Pythagoreans to be conveying was the virtue of proportion, harmony and the notion of equilibrium; and that these ideas could be best appreciated through a study of the foundations of mathematics and geometry. An example she mentioned in her *Notebooks* was the comparison between equilibrium as the proportional mean between weight and weightlessness and justice as the proportional mean between supernatural freedom and force (NB, p. 508). Or more specifically: 'If one takes harmony in the sense of geometric mean, if one conceives that the only mediation between God and man is a Being at once God and Man, one passes directly from this Pythagorean equation to the marvellous precepts of the Gospel of St. John' (IC, p. 170). Thus the Cross of Christ could be seen as the point of equilibrium between God and the world of matter since, although reduced to matter through affliction, Christ continued to exercise the spiritual and, in a sense, divine faculties of consent and love.

One reason why Weil was so enthusiastic about the Pythagoreans was that she shared with them the conviction that mathematics was one of the most important bridges leading to God. What she called the fundamental doctrine of Pythagoreanism, of Platonism, and of early Christianity, and described in her *Notebooks* as 'the most important truth' was that there were two different kinds of reason: 'What is contradictory for natural reason is not so for supernatural reason, but the latter can only use the language of the former. Nevertheless, the logic of supernatural reason is more rigorous than that of natural reason. Mathematics offers us an image of this hierarchy' (FLN, p. 108). Mathematics enjoyed a clarity and rigour of demonstration which meant that it was 'an intermediary between the whole natural part of man and the infinitely small portion of himself which does not belong to this world' and thus could be 'at the intersection of the two worlds' (IC, p. 182). Thus for the Greeks 'the imitation of God was assisted by the study of mathematics, in so far as one conceived the universe to be subject to mathematical laws, which made the geometer an imitator of the supreme law-giver' (SL, pp. 117f).

This religious centre of Greek mathematics lay, for Weil, in the way in which geometry aided the discovery of a proportional mean between otherwise unassimilable numbers. Here she quoted Plato: '. . . what is ridiculously called land-measuring and is really the assimilation to one another of numbers not naturally similar, an assimilation made manifest by the destiny of plane figures. It is clear to anyone who is able to understand it that this marvel is not of human but of divine origin' (SNL, p. 142). Through their investigations of the properties of right-angled triangles, the Greeks had discovered the miracle of a proportional mean, that is, a value b such that $a:b$ equals $b:c$ where c was a whole number and thus not capable of being directly related to a. Geometry thus revealed a science of real numbers and irrational square roots which was capable of rigorous abstract demonstration but at the same time was incomprehensible to the imagination.

This idea of mathematical proportion that was a rational construct rather than a matter of observation fascinated Weil as much as it had fascinated the Greeks. It made it possible to see the universe as similar to a work of art and to find regularity in diversity. The Pythagorean formula about everything being number should be understood, she thought, as meaning that there obtained relations between all things that were analogous to the relations between numbers. Weil returned, for illustration, to her favourite example of Lagneau's cube: we never see all its sides and angles simultaneously, but we know 'that the cubic form is what determines the variations of the apparent form' (IC, p. 179). Weil agreed with the Pythagoreans about the purifying nature of these considerations:

> Mathematics alone makes us feel the limits of our intelligence. For we can always suppose in the case of an experiment that it is inexplicable because we don't happen to have all the data. In mathematics we have all the data, brought together in the full light of demonstration, and yet we don't understand. We always come back to the contemplation of our human wretchedness. What force is in relation to our will, the impenetrable opacity of mathematics is in relation to our intelligence. This forces us to direct the gaze of our intuition still further afield. The universe of signs is transparent, and yet remains infinitely hard to penetrate. (NB, p. 511)

She herself used these ideas of mathematical proportion in an extended and beautiful discussion of the nature of the Trinity (cf. pp. 108ff). The study of mathematics led to an appreciation of the order of the world and thus to its beauty. Just as originally religion had given rise to mathematics, so mathematics should, according to Weil, give rise to religion.

It was this conception of the importance of mathematics that lay at the centre of Weil's nostalgia for Greek science. It was her dream 'to restore to science as a whole, for mathematics as well as for psychology and sociology, the sense of its origin and veritable destiny as a bridge leading toward God – not by diminishing, but by increasing precision in demonstration, verification and supposition' (NB, p. 441). By 'science' here she meant not the physics of Democritus and Aristotle but the more speculative science of such thinkers as Pythagoras or Eudoxus. With these thinkers, Greek science had put harmony and proportion at the centre of its researches. Its basis was piety and not pride. A return to such an attitude could overcome the quarrel between science and religion which had been fostered by the narrowing of scientific vision and, more importantly, by the introduction into Christianity of the ridiculous notion of Providence as being a personal and particular intervention of God for particular ends (cf. NR, pp. 269f). It was the genius of Greek science to have found a bridge or mediation between the nothingness of human beings subject to the laws of implacable necessity and the transcendent plenitude of God.

For many of her ideas on Greek mathematics and science Weil relied on the pre-Socratics, whose work only survives in fragments, and so her interpretation was bound to be highly speculative. But she saw their work as continued in the corpus of Plato whose voluminous writings were a continual source of inspiration to her. Whereas she considered Aristotle to be the first philosopher 'in the modern sense' (SNL, p. 89), Plato, under the influence of Orphism, the Eleusinian mysteries and Pythagoras, was 'a mystic, the inheritor of a mystical tradition which permeated the whole of Greece' (ibid.). Thus 'Plato's wisdom is not a philosophy, a research for God by means of human reason. That research was carried out as well as it can be done by Aristotle. But the wisdom of Plato is nothing other than an orientation of the soul towards grace' (SNL, p. 99). In her interpretation, Plato's essential idea was that the invisible was much more real than the visible. To take once again the example of the cube: the cube as seen was not the same as the cube as thought, since it was the idea of the cube which enabled the mind to order the appearances correctly. What actually existed as seen by the observer lacked the plenitude of truth and reality and 'the veritable cube – which is never seen – is an example of that absence which is sovereign presence' (NB, p. 484). 'The universe is providentially constituted in such a manner that knowledge of the concrete is dependent on knowledge of the abstract. The universe thus guides the soul from abstraction to abstraction to that supreme reality which is pure Good.'[13] This transcendent reality was the equivalent of God. Unlike most commentators, Weil read Plato as a monotheist. It was one of her most fundamental convictions that all desire was desire for the good – a view which Plato certainly shared – and that this good was God. She was particularly keen on his *Timaeus*, where the world is depicted as a work of art with God as both its model and its author. Weil went further when she identified Plato's God with the Christian God and found the idea of the Trinity in Plato's triads of knower, known and knowledge in the *Republic*, of lover, beloved and love in the *Phaedrus*, and of artist, work and inspiration in the *Timaeus*.

Weil was a true follower of the Platonic tradition in identifying the supreme reality with the Good. This implied a twin assent of the soul towards God by using two different bridges or *metaxus*, one of the intellect and the other of love. In discussing the first, Weil referred continuously to Plato's allegory of the Cave where prisoners sit chained facing a wall on which are thrown shadows from various objects being manipulated behind the prisoners' backs. Since the shadows are the only things that can be seen the prisoners take them for reality. On being freed from the chains, the prisoner 'walks through the Cave. He perceives nothing, and he is in fact in semi-darkness: and in any case it would serve no purpose if he stopped to examine his surroundings. He has to continue walking, no matter how painfully and although he is ignorant of where he is going' (SNL, p. 110). On getting out of the Cave, however, the prisoner finds the pain is even sharper, because of the brilliant light, but he is in safety: 'No further efforts of will are needed; one has only to remain in a state of attention and contemplate something whose dazzle is almost unbearable' (ibid.).

This is a conversion in the literal sense – a 'turning towards' the light. It is important to note that the shadows in the Cave are not *un*real: it is the ability to perceive their relative and contradictory reality that represents for Plato and Weil the beginning of enlightenment. 'For wherever there is the appearance of contradiction there is a correlation of contraries, that is to say there is relation. Whenever the intelligence is brought up against a contradiction, it is obliged to conceive a relation which transforms the contradiction into a correlation, and as a result the soul is drawn upwards' (SNL, p. 113). The royal road to this emancipation was, of course, mathematics. Thus Plato's theory of ideas implied a kind of religious asceticism. Those still in the Cave were idolatrous in that they took the relative for the absolute. Weil insisted that the myth of the Cave was only comprehensible when taken in conjunction with the other great myth of the *Republic*, that of the Great Beast in which Plato imagined someone learning how to approach and handle some powerful animal by studying its humours and desires, systematising this knowledge into a doctrine and calling what pleased the Beast good and what annoyed it bad, thus thoroughly confusing the difference between the necessary and the good. Such teachers and those who followed them (which for Weil was roughly the whole of contemporary society, though she singled out Marxism as a particularly good example) were still in the Cave and victims of all its illusions.

The other bridge to God which Weil found in Plato was that provided by beauty. In true Platonic fashion she linked the intelligible with notions of beauty, love and good. The way of beauty, represented by Dionysus, the god of mystery, was described in Plato's *Phaedrus* as 'a way of salvation which is not in the slightest degree intellectual; it involves nothing resembling study or science or philosophy, but is salvation through feeling alone – a feeling which, at the beginning, is purely human' (SNL, pp. 117f). God has put beauty in the world as a trap for us just as Proserpine was tempted to eat the pomegranate seed and be drawn forever into Hades. In a splendid passage Weil linked beauty with the appreciation of necessity:

> It is the beauty of the world which permits us to contemplate and to love necessity. Without beauty this would not be possible . . .
>
> And pure joy is nothing but the feeling of beauty . . . And beauty touches us all the more keenly where necessity appears in a most manifest manner, for example in the folds that gravity has impressed upon the mountains, on the waves of the sea, or on the course of the stars. In pure mathematics also, necessity is resplendent in beauty . . .
>
> This cluster of marvels is perfected by the presence, in the necessary connections which compose the universal order, of divine verities symbolically expressed. Herein is the marvel of marvels, and as it were, the secret signature of the artist . . . (IC, pp. 190f)

This conception of the role of beauty was closely connected with that of love, since 'it is the beauty of the world which permits us to contemplate and love necessity' (IC, p. 190). It was impossible to love necessity as such because the object of love could only be a person and not matter. Thus when we contemplated and consented to necessity it was because the universe appeared to us like a souvenir or a work of art. We would not know who the artist was but

> when love, from which the consent to necessity proceeds, exists in us, we possess experimental proof that there is an answer. For it is not out of love for other men that we consent to necessity . . . It is for the love of something which is not a human person, and who is yet something like a person . . . Whatever the belief professed with regard to religious matters, including atheism, wherever there is a completely authentic and unconditional consent to necessity, there is the plenitude of the love of God; and nowhere else. This consent constitutes participation in the Cross of Christ. (IC, pp. 183f)

Weil did not share the interpretation of Platonic love as egocentric, possessive and self-divinising.[14] For her, Platonic Eros and Christian Agape were one and the same. As she wrote in her *Notebooks* in capital letters: 'There is not and there cannot be any other relation of man to God except love. What is not love is not a relation to God' (SNL, 104). It was in love that the two assents of the soul to God, by intellect and by beauty, were finally united.

Following Plato's marvellous account of the linking of intellect, beauty and love, Weil saw Greek thought as the product of a civilisation in decline – particularly with the advent of Rome. But she did see one last flowering of the Greek spirit (apart, of course, from early Christianity) in Stoicism, which was itself 'almost exclusively love of the beauty of the world' (WG, p. 99). By Stoicism Weil did not understand what she thought of as its degenerate Roman form which depended on will-power and a stiff insensibility in the face of suffering: in its Greek form the Stoics had simply continued the ideas of Pythagoras and Plato in their teaching that 'this world is the fatherland of the soul and it must recognise its fatherland even in the place of its exile' (SS, p. 242). Before her experience at Solesmes, as she wrote to Joe Bousquet,

> my only faith had been the Stoic *amor fati* as Marcus Aurelius understood it, and I had always faithfully practised it – to love the universe as one's city, one's native country, the beloved fatherland of every soul; to cherish it for its beauty, in the total integrity of the order and necessity which are its substance, and all the events that occur in it. (SL, p. 140)

Although she had previously on occasion opposed Stoicism to Christianity (cf. OC, I, pp. 300ff), she now saw it as 'infinitely close' (WG, p. 99) to primitive Christianity and especially to the writings of Saint John who in his description of Christ as Logos had encompassed the whole Stoic doctrine of *amor fati*:

> *Fatum* is necessity, necessity is the *logos*, and *logos* is the real name of what we most ardently love. The love which St. John bore for Him who was his friend and his Lord when he was leaning on His bosom during the Last Supper, is the same love which we should bear toward the mathematical progression of causes and effects which, from time to time, make of us a sort of formless jelly. (IC, p. 184)

Her conclusion was that 'Christianity will not be incarnated so long as there is not joined to it the Stoics' idea of filial piety for the city of the world, for the country of here below which is the universe. When, as the result of some misapprehension, very difficult to understand today,

Christianity cut itself off from Stoicism, it condemned itself to an abstract and separate existence' (WG, p. 111). Both Stoicism and Christianity had as their centre the ideas of humility, obedience and love.

In her reading of Greek thought in general Weil is as selective and idiosyncratic as in many of her historical essays. Her interpretation of the pre-Socratic thinkers is necessarily highly speculative, since so few of their writings survive. With Plato, however, she is equally speculative: most contemporary theologians emphasise the difference between Plato's philisophico-religious conceptions and those of Christianity, whose Judaic roots are becoming ever clearer; and most contemporary philosophers are keen to portray Plato as an incipient rationalist emerging out of a mist of religious myth. Weil, by contrast, sees Plato as the inheritor of a long tradition of religious speculation and an authentic precursor of Christianity. She achieves this by being very selective in the attention she pays to Plato's writings. She only looks at nine of his dialogues, concentrating on those of his middle period. This means that she has no interest in Socrates, whose personality and ideas were to the fore in Plato's early work, nor in the Parmenidean side of Plato's thought, which is evident in his late work and has affinities with Aristotle whom Weil so decisively rejected. Even in the dialogues she *does* consider, Weil is quite happy to abstract from the dialogue form (thus attributing to Plato himself ideas that may well not have been his) and even at points to force the translation. This is partly because she believed Plato's dialogues to be works of vulgarisation intended for the public at large and thus not containing the profounder aspects of his doctrine (cf. SNL, pp. 91f). But perhaps it is rather beside the point to ask whether she is right about Plato. Her *Notebooks* show us a Plato who is just as much a disciple of Weil as Weil is of Plato. However speculative is her interpretation of his works, it serves her admirably as a framework for her own religious and philosophical doctrine. This Platonic framework does, however, mean that she emphasises transcendence at the expense of empirical reality. The aspiration towards unity and metaphysical monism tends to reduce the terrestrial world almost to non-existence. The contingent and the historical have no place in this scheme of things: the historicity of the Christian religion and in particular of the Incarnation seem to be eclipsed.

If Weil's interpretation of Christianity was fundamentally affected by her attachment to the Platonic side of Greek philosophy, the same is true of her interest in non-Christian religions, the religions of ancient Egypt, Buddhism and, particularly, Hinduism. Her view of religion was fundamentally egalitarian, but not syncretist. She believed that 'it is impossible that the whole truth should not be present at every time and every place, available for anyone who desires it. "Whoever asks for bread". Truth is bread . . . whatever has not been available at all times and places to whoever desires the truth is itself something other than truth' (FLN, pp. 302f). She was therefore against missionary activity and believed it was better to stay in the religious tradition in which one was rooted. But no tradition being complete, and her own (as she saw it) severely deformed, there was everything to be gained by a study of other religions which she saw as complementary to her conception of Christianity, which 'should contain all vocations without exception since it is Catholic by right' (WG, p. 26).

In the spring and summer of 1942 she paid a lot of attention to ancient Egypt and even tried to learn its hieroglyphic script. Each people of antiquity had had its special vocation: that of Egypt was 'immortality, salvation of the just soul after death by assimilation with a suffering God dead and resurrected, and charity towards one's neighbour' (SNL, p. 89). Even before her studies in Marseilles Weil had been impressed by the moral philosophy enunciated around 2000 BC in the Egyptian *Book of the Dead*: 'I have not made anyone weep. I have not made anyone afraid. I have not adopted a haughty tone. I have not lent a deaf ear to just and true words' (NB, p. 369). Such statements had the same purity for her as that of a Gregorian chant or of Monteverdi. For the Egyptians knew 'the true religion, the religion of love, in which God is a sacrificial victim as well as being an all powerful ruler' (LP, p. 43). Following Herodotus, she believed that all genuine religion in the Eastern Mediterranean had its origin in Egypt.

Foremost among those indebted to Egypt were the Greeks themselves and, in particular, Pythagoras, through his supposed master Pherekydes. She declared roundly:

> All the religious thought of the Hellenes came to them from the Pelasgians who had received it almost entirely from Egypt through the Phoenicians. A magnificent passage in Ezekiel[15] further confirms Herodotus, for there Tyre is likened to the Cherub who guards the tree of life in Eden, and Egypt to the tree of life itself – that tree of life with which Christ compared the Kingdom of Heaven and which had for fruit his very body hanging on the Cross. (WG, p. 160)

This view was connected with her idiosyncratic reading of the story of Noah. According to the account in *Genesis*, his younger son Ham found him drunk and naked. Ham alerted his two brothers Shem and Japheth who covered their father and retreated without looking at his nudity. On awaking Noah cursed Ham's descendants and condemned them to servitude because their father had seen him naked. In Weil's interpretation, the nudity of Noah represented something like the naked truth, the genuine religion whose followers were indeed condemned to servitude by the powers of this world. Ham's descendants (as opposed to those of Shem and Japheth) were the guardians of the 'authentic tradition' which the Egyptians transmitted to the Greeks and, to a certain extent, to the Jews, in that Moses had been educated in Egypt.

It was in the Egyptian cult of Osiris that Weil saw the most evident anticipation of Christianity. After her mystical experience at Solesmes she had come to feel that Osiris was 'in a certain sense Christ Himself' (WG, p. 22). In the myth (which had affinities with the *Book of the Dead*), Osiris, who was originally a King of Egypt responsible for dramatic improvements in agriculture, was shut up in a wooden chest by his brother Seth and killed by molten lead poured over him. The chest was eventually found in Phoenicia by his wife and sister Isis and carefully hidden. But Seth found it and cut the body into fourteen pieces which he scattered all over the world. These pieces were collected and reassembled by Isis, who buried them in Upper Egypt. When Horus, son of Osiris and Isis, grew up, he avenged his father by killing Seth. Osiris was the only God to be worshipped throughout ancient Egypt and regarded as the source of life. Weil identified him with Dionysus and Prometheus: Osiris was the image of the perfectly just person suffering on behalf of others. Thus, for Weil, 'if Osiris is not a man having lived on earth while remaining God, in the same way as Christ, then at any rate the story of Osiris is a prophecy infinitely clearer, more complete and closer to the truth than everything which goes by that name in the Old Testament' (LP, p. 19), and she was perfectly ready to refer to him as the Incarnate Word (cf. NB, p. 470); and, once again, Saint John's Gospel was her New Testament reference.

The religion of Ancient Egypt was, for Weil, an apparent polytheism concealing a latent monotheism. She held the same view of Hinduism, the religious tradition with which, outside Christianity, she felt the closest affinity. Reading the Hindu scriptures reminded her of her beloved Greeks: 'The Greek and Hindu traditions represent one and the same thing' (NB, p. 502). In the Parisian student world of the 1920s there had been an interest in things oriental, focusing on translations of Tagore and abetted by Lawrence's *Seven Pillars of Wisdom*. More to the point, André Weil had learned Sanskrit while a student at the Ecole Normale and read the *Bhagavad Gita* in the original. Weil read it also in the spring of 1940 and was immediately captivated: the following year in Marseilles she, too, learnt Sanskrit from her friends Vera and René Daumal, both serious Indianists, and read the Upanishads in the original; her *Notebooks* bear witness to the excellence of her Devanagari script.

Weil found two central ideas in her reading of the Upanishads. The first was the concept of *Atman* which she described as 'exactly, identically' (C, p. 502) the same as Plato's idea of the Good: the principle governing the world with which the human soul should try to identify itself to the point of self-extinction. From the point of view of the individual, the fundamental problem was the duality of attachment and renunciation. From her reading of the Chhandogya Upanishad in particular she got the idea that if you go inside yourself in a state of perfectly pure meditation, the distinction between desire and object will disappear. It was mistaken, in other words, to go searching for God who was to be found inside the human soul (cf. FLN, p. 261). This interiority of God was, again, a central Upanishad idea: 'God is not what is manifested by the word, but that by which the word is manifested; God is that by which everything is manifested and which is not manifested by anything' (FLN, p. 151). The second main idea that Weil found in the Upanishads was that of *Dharma* – a principle of autonomous and impersonal order which governed the world and turned it into the shadow of God.

> After having passed by the way of absolute good, one again comes up against the illusory and partial forms of good, but disposed in an hierarchical order which makes it so that one only allows oneself to seek for a certain particular good within the limits imposed by the concern for a certain other particular good. This order is transcendent in relation to the various forms of good, and a reflection of the absolute good. This order constitutes *Dharma*. (NB, p. 551)

And once again Weil found a parallel in Greek philosophy, since the notion of *Dharma* was precisely that of equilibrium.

Weil's favourite passage from the Upanishads was that in the Mundaka Upanishad: 'Two birds, united always and known by the same name, closely cling to the same tree. One of them eats the sweet fruit; the other looks on without eating.'[16] And her interpretation of this: 'Man's great affliction, which begins with infancy and accompanies him till death, is that looking and eating are two different operations. Eternal beatitude . . . is a state where to look is to eat. That which we look at here below is not real, it is a mere setting. That which we eat is destroyed, is no longer real' (NB, p. 637). Almost inevitably, we preferred eating: but salvation was only to be found in looking.

This dialectic of attachment and renunciation that fascinated Weil in the Upanishads found a more particular application in perhaps the best loved of all Hindu scriptures, the *Bhagavad Gita*, references to which abound in Weil's *Notebooks*. The *Bhagavad Gita* tells how the King Arjuna is overcome by doubt and pity before an important battle in which thousands of people, including some of his friends and relations, are bound to lose their lives. The major part of the poem consists in the reply given to Arjuna by his charioteer, who is the god Krishna incarnate. Arjuna is told that he can escape the harm to his soul that the performance of evil actions (killing in battle) might bring, provided that he performs these actions without any thoughts of personal gain:

> The man who sees worklessness in work itself, and work in work-lessness, is wise among his fellows, integrated, performing every work. When all a man's enterprises are free from desire for fruit and motive, his works burned up in wisdom's fire, then wise men call him learned. When he has cast off all attachment to the fruits of works, ever content and on none dependent, though he embarks on work himself, in fact he does no work at all.[17]

If Arjuna divests himself of his possessive self-interested ego then he can be both a warrior *and* a follower of *yoga*. An additional point of the *Bhagavad Gita* is that Arjuna does not really have a choice. According to the Hindu principle of *Kharma*, individuals, in previous incarnations and in the course of a single life, construct their own natures and destinies. Previous actions set the pattern and habit which determine the present ones. Thus the *Kharma* which constrains the individual is bound up with *Dharma* as the necessary order of the universe as a whole. Weil drew the following lessons from Arjuna's dilemma:

> Note that the *Dharma*, since it depends on caste, therefore on birth, therefore on previous incarnation, depends on an antecedent choice. It is not that one has not the choice, but that, if one situates oneself at a given moment in time, one no longer has the choice; it is useless to dream of doing something else; but it is a good thing to rise above what one is doing at the time. By that means one chooses, for later on, something better. Arjuna's moment of pity – it belongs to the order of dreams. His display of weakness before proceeding to kill is comparable to the display of weakness at approaching death. *At a given moment* one is not free to do anything whatever. And one must accept this internal necessity; accept what one is, at a given moment, as a fact, even one's shame. (NB, p. 56)

Again, Weil found a parallel in a Greek conception, that of Nemesis: 'Nemesis, at once the outward image of and (by that very fact) the remedy for *Kharma*. Whoever has killed will kill. Whoever has killed shall be killed. Both are true. The latter is a remedy for the former. Mobile image of the balance' (NB, p. 64). Weil was particularly struck with the *Gita*'s concept of non-active action. She translated the following words of Krishna in the margin of her copy: 'I am the doer, the agent, – this know – and yet I am the Changeless One who does not do or act. Works can never affect Me. I have no yearning for their fruits.'[18] Thus all hope of reward should be given up and duty done with complete indifference, resulting in an absence of any desire. The meaning of the *Gita* was that 'the pure and simple accomplishment of prescribed actions and neither more nor less, in other words obedience, is the same thing for the soul as immobility is for the body' (FLN, p. 336). Action was indeed to be for the good of society and its members, but it was action stripped of the ego. The dilemma of Arjuna spoke particularly to Weil's own personality and the problems posed by contemporary events. She first studied the *Bhagavad Gita* at the time of the outbreak of the War. Arjuna's questions were her own and Krishna's response united the militant activist, the metaphysical and the mystic in a way that perfectly suited her own temperament.

Obviously Weil was not equally enthusiastic about other aspects of Hindu religious thought.[19] Most evident is her lack of interest in reincarnation and the possible effects of action on rebirth, in spite of the presence of such ideas in Plato's *Republic*. Neither did she take up the idea that the soul is a part of the divine essence and thus not really something created. And she was of course not attracted by the more social or collective side of the concept of *Dharma*. Nevertheless the affinities between Weil's outlook and the Hindu tradition are striking. As outlined above, she found rich material for reflection in the stress on individual action and the doctrine of non-attachment. She was also attracted by the Hindu emphasis on the *im*personal nature of the divine, by the idea of several incarnations rather than the unique Incarnation of Christianity and, finally, by the lack of a historical dimension in Hindu thought and the preference for the idea of balance over that of progress.

Weil was also interested in Buddhism, though she came to it later than to Hinduism and knew it less well. Her references were to the Mahayana version of Buddhism (which is also closer to Hindu conceptions) rather than to the more negative and mystical Theravada tradition: the concept of *Nirvana* did not hold her attention. She was particularly interested in Tibetan Buddhism and copied long passages from Alexandra David-Neel's *Mystics and Magicians of Tibet*. Her most frequent reference is to the Tibetan sage Milarepa, in whose teachings she saw parallels with Arjuna's non-active action. It was recounted of Milarepa that he began to sing when his only remaining possession, a bowl, was broken: 'He had lost everything, renounced everything, but had not yet felt with his whole being that his bowl itself was liable to destruction' (NB, p. 233). Religion, too, was a transitory phenomenon and Milarepa only attained to spiritual progress when he recognised that it was an illusion. Weil was also interested in the Zen Buddhism of Japan as recorded in Susuki's *Essays in Zen Buddhism*, whose object she felt to be (echoing Plato): 'To discover how much the essence of existence differs from that of the intelligible' (NB, p. 446). The aim was 'to perceive *purely*, without any admixture of reverie' (NB, p. 406). This was obviously akin to her own idea of attention as described in *The Love of God and Affliction*. She was particularly struck by the Zen *Koan* which was typically some sort of logical absurdity such as the sound of one hand clapping. To solve such riddles, she wrote, 'means to understand that there is nothing to be solved, that existence possesses no significance for the discursive faculties, and that the latter must not be allowed to wander outside their role as mere exploratory instrument of the intelligence with a view to making contact with brute reality' (NB, p. 446). Zen Buddhism provided her with examples of what she had been seeking all her life: thought without an object.

One of the facets of Tibetan Buddhism that interested Weil was its penchant for basing its teaching on tales incorporating magic and folklore. Weil herself was constantly on the look-out for legends and myths, the older the better. Her writings abound with references to folk-tales from the most diverse traditions: African, Chinese, Australian, Gypsy, Welsh, American Indian, Albanian – all these (and more) were grist to her interpretative mill, and complemented her study of religion. Although these references are particularly frequent in her last *Notebooks*, her interest in folklore was life-long: her earliest preserved writing is a fairy tale entitled 'The Fire Sylphs' that she wrote at the age of ten. And this penchant for folklore was reinforced by the teaching of Alain, for whom popular myths were the highly significant matrix of all subsequent thought. Plato, too, made use of myths to illustrate philosophical truths, particularly in the *Symposium* and the *Republic*. Weil was not interested in the sociological or anthropological dimension to myth investigated by Malinowski and Durkheim; she was nearer to writers such as Frazer, Eliade and even Lévi-Strauss in that she was interested in discovering the common structure to myths and legends from widely different times and places. Unlike them, however, she was interested in interpreting these common themes in a highly spiritual manner. For example, she found the theme of a God who entered the human condition and was put to death for the subsequent benefit of humanity to be common to stories about Odin, Prometheus, Dionysus and Osiris, all of whom she saw as images of Christ. A good example of Weil's approach is the interpretation of one of her favourite myths – the Celtic story of the Duke of Norroway. She told it as follows:

> A king has three daughters. One night they talk about marriage –
> One of them wants a king – The second wants a prince – The third
> (the most beautiful) 'I would be content with the Red Bull o'
> Norroway' –
> Next day, the Red Bull comes to find her. She is hidden by her
> parents, but they are compelled to hand her over. The Princess and

the Bull journey through many lands. One day she sees a pin in his hide. She pulls it out. A handsome prince appears and falls at her feet and thanks her. Then he immediately disappears. She searches for him.

Half dead with thirst and hunger, she meets an old woman who gives her three nuts which she must not crack 'till her heart was like to break, and over again to break'.

She comes to a land where everyone is talking about the 'Duke O'Norroway's' wedding, which is to take place that very day – she sees him – her heart was now like to break – she cracks the nut – finds inside it 'a wee wife carding'. Offers it to the betrothed in exchange for one night with the Duke – sings:

'Far hae I sought ye, near am I
    brought to ye –
Dear Duke O'Norroway, will ye no
    turn and speak to me?'

The Duke's servant, who has heard the singing and lamenting, advises him not to drink a sleeping potion – the Duke recognises the voice of the Princess and tells her he has been in the power of an enchantress. They get married. (FLN, p. 167)

Weil interpreted this story as an illustration of the search of God for humanity: the Princess is the impoverished God who seeks the human soul (the Prince) even when, at its first contact, it has fled. The myth of Persephone and of Orestes and Electra had the same meaning. This meaning was also a Christian one: 'In mythology and folklore there are a great many parables similar to those in the Gospel; they only need to be picked out' (FLN, p. 268). Myths, for Weil, were yet another bridge between the natural and the supernatural, a half-way house between the language of philosophy and the purely spiritual.

In spite of her sensitivity to religion and myth in their most diverse forms, Weil was not a syncretist. Her aim was not to construct some sort of universal religion out of diverse parts. Rather, 'each religion is alone true, that is to say, that at the moment we are thinking of it we must bring as much attention to bear on it as if there were nothing else; in the same way, each landscape, each picture, each poem, etc. is alone beautiful. A "synthesis" of religions implies a lower quality of attention' (NB, p. 228). The religion to which she paid most attention was the Christian religion. Since it had been her road to religious truth and she believed that the truth was available to all who genuinely searched, then it must also be available in non-Christian religious traditions. Thus 'if the anguished waiting for a Saviour led to a mistaken identification of the person known as Buddha with this saviour, and if he is invoked today as a perfect, divine man and redeemer, then this invocation is as efficacious as those addressed to Christ' (FLN, p. 121). These traditions were by no means identical in that, for example, the *Bhagavad Gita* and the Gospels 'complete each other' (NB, p. 25). Therefore 'we should conceive the identity of the various traditions, not by reconciling them through what they have in common, but by grasping the essence of what is specific in each. For this essence is one and the same' (NB, p. 502). Weil always held firmly together two fundamental views which were inevitably in tension. On the one hand, 'I believe that the mysteries of the Catholic religion are an inexhaustible source of truths concerning the human condition. (In addition to which, they are for me an object of love)' (NB, p. 190). On the other hand, 'nothing prevents me from believing the same thing with regard to other mysteries, or from believing that some of these truths have been directly revealed elsewhere' (ibid.). The tension between diversity and unity was not reconcilable on a logical or philosophical level but only on terms peculiar to religion, which meant ultimately in mystical terms. This mystical side of her thought became more marked as she moved to New York and to London.

10

New York: Waiting

'Two prisoners whose cells adjoin communicate with each other by knocking on the wall. The wall is the thing which separates them but is also their means of communication. It is the same with us and God. Every separation is a link.' (GG, p. 132)

The route to New York was circuitous. The *Maréchal Lyautey* took six days to get to Casablanca via Oran. Most of the nine hundred passengers, including the Weils, were put in a camp at Ain-Seba on the outskirts of Casablanca where they had to wait more than two weeks for their passage to New York. After the last feverish days and nights of activity in Marseilles, Weil rested and wrote. She did not take kindly to the majority of her fellow refugees, mostly Jews, and the conditions at Ain-Seba were harsh. Life in the camp was agreeable enough: 'I feel fine here as I have found one or two sympathetic people and have flowers around me and a deep blue sky above' (P, ɪɪ, p. 417). She was also surprised and delighted at the *Hassidim* ritual of the orthodox Jews who said their prayers in the vegetable garden (cf. C, p. 274). Although she had previously expressed a strong interest in Muslim culture and the effects of colonialism on the Moroccan people, she only left the camp once. She was anxious to finish her long commentary on the Pythagorean texts.[1] To this end she commandeered one of the eighteen chairs in the camp and got her parents to occupy it for her when she had to leave it. The other refugees took her to be some sort of exceptionally dedicated journalist.

Before leaving Casablanca, Weil finished her commentary and sent it off to Perrin. With it she enclosed a final long letter. She expressed her gratitude for Perrin's friendship, which was unique in that it had never been a source of hurt to her. But her main point was the influence of her study of Greek and Oriental thought on her view of the Church. 'In theory', she wrote to Perrin, 'you fully admit the possibility of implicit faith. In practice also you have a breadth of mind and an intellectual honesty which are very exceptional. Yet they still seem to me very insufficient' (WG, p. 42). This insufficiency came from his attaching himself to the Church as to an earthly country, whereas 'we have to be catholic, that is to say, not bound by so much as a thread to any created thing, unless it be to creation in its totality' (WG, p. 44). What was needed was a totally new form of saintliness, since 'the world needs

220

saints who have genius, just as a plague-stricken town needs doctors'
and 'where there is a need there is also an obligation' (WG, p. 46). Weil
did not see herself as such a saint: 'it is a great sorrow for me to fear
that the thoughts which have come down into me should be condemned
to death through the contagion of my inadequacy and wretchedness'
(WG, p. 47). Nevertheless she concluded with the hope that Perrin
might be able to be a better populariser of her thought than she herself
could ever be.

Eventually Weil left for America with her parents on 7 June on board
the *Serpa Pinto*, a Portuguese boat which took a month to get to New
York via Bermuda. She insisted on travelling fourth class, but ended up
sleeping on deck. She spent a lot of time continuing her *Notebooks* and
did not mix with the other passengers. The only people she had much
time for were a Classics teacher who had views about the early spread
of Christianity to Rome, a young mental defective, and a young man
called Jacques Kaplan who remembered her as follows:

> She was very pleasant, very protective, very sarcastic. What especially
> struck me was the astonishing contrast between her and normal
> people – or, rather, ordinary people. She couldn't bear the cabin-class
> passengers, because they openly enjoyed comforts that those in the
> steerage were deprived of. She took an interest in me because being
> a 'scout', I volunteered to take charge of the refugee children in the
> hold. (C, p. 275)

The *Serpa Pinto* docked in New York at the end of the first week in
July. The Weils stayed a few days in a hotel and then moved to an
apartment block in the Upper West Side of Manhattan at 549 Riverside
Drive, not far from Columbia University. The apartment was on the
fifth floor and had a good view of the Hudson river and New Jersey on
the far side and of the George Washington Bridge to the north. But
however interesting and attractive New York City might be, Weil had
only one thought in mind – to get to London and to take an active part
in the war. Almost as soon as she arrived, André, who was teaching at
Haverford College in Pennsylvania, made it clear to her that getting to
England would be much more difficult than she had imagined. She
wrote to the influential philosopher, Jacques Maritain, about her project
for front-line nurses, enclosing letters from Perrin and Jacob, and
Bousquet's endorsement: she even thought that he might get her an
interview with Roosevelt. She also wrote to Admiral Leahy, who had
recently returned from France, and to the future Gaullist Minister
Jacques Soustelle in London whom she had known slightly at the Ecole
Normale. She placed most faith (rightly) in Maurice Schumann who was
working with the Free French in London and to whom she wrote two

letters at the end of July. She reminded Schumann of the times when
they had sat side by side at Henri IV listening to Alain's lectures, and
appealed to him as a comrade to help her get to London. She enclosed
a detailed version of her 'Plan for an Organisation of Front-Line Nurses'.
The organisation would be highly mobile and

> should in principle be always at the points of greatest danger, to give
> 'first aid' during battles. It could start as an experiment with a small
> nucleus of ten, or even less; and it could come into operation at the
> shortest possible notice, because hardly any preparation is required.
> An elementary knowledge of nursing would suffice, because nothing
> can be done under fire except dressings, tourniquets, and perhaps
> injections. (SL, p. 146)

Weil emphasised the practicability of her proposal with references to
the *Bulletin of the American College of Surgeons* on the effects of shock and
recent progress in plasma injections. But it was the effect on morale that
she was concerned to stress most:

> a courage not inflamed by the impulse to kill, but capable of
> supporting, at the point of greatest danger, the prolonged spectacle
> of wounds and agony, is certainly of a rarer quality than that of the
> young S.S. fanatics. A small group of women exercising day after day
> a courage of this kind would be a spectacle so new, so significant,
> and charged with such obvious meaning, that it would strike the
> imagination more than any of Hitler's conceptions have done. What
> is now necessary is to strike harder than he. This corps of women
> would undoubtedly offer one way of doing so. (SL, p. 151)

In a second letter, entrusted to Captain Pierre Mendès-France, a friend
of the Weil family and later Prime Minister in the Fourth Republic, she
asked to be sent over to France to liaise with the Resistance. She claimed
that 'a woman is as suitable for this type of mission as a man, even
more so provided she has a sufficient amount of resolution, sang-froid,
and a spirit of sacrifice' (SL, p. 154) and said that she herself was ready
for any kind of sacrifice, including certain death, provided that the
objective was sufficiently important. She concluded, 'I beg you, get me
over to London. Don't leave me to die of chagrin here. I appeal to you
as a comrade' (SL, p. 155).

But things moved slowly. Passages across the North Atlantic were
few and much in demand; she needed authorisation from the Americans,
the British and the Free French. Maritain was away and when he did
eventually reply, although he was kind and encouraging, could only
suggest that she talked to the philosopher Alexandre Koyré, who could

recommend her to some of de Gaulle's collaborators in London. Soon Weil began to think that it was a grave mistake ever to have left France. She was particularly distressed on reading a report in the *New York Times* about a spontaneous demonstration in Marseilles on Bastille Day: thousands had taken part and two women had been killed and several people injured by gunfire. As July turned into August and August into September, Weil became more and more depressed. Her headaches returned and she would sometimes spend whole days on the floor in her sleeping-bag. Life had become for her 'morally impossible' (EL, p. 221). If things did not improve, she said to her mother, she would go to the South and work with the blacks (cf. P, p. 477).

Although too depressed to write much (her *Notebooks* at this period contain little but bibliographical references), she did make one important new friendship. While waiting one day at the French Consulate, she met Simone Deitz, a young French woman whom she had known slightly in Marseilles and who was also trying to get to England. Weil asked her point-blank, 'Would you like to be my friend?' and thereafter the two became virtually inseparable. It was a friendship of contraries. Deitz was expansive and exuberant; Weil was remembered by a secretary at the Chancellery of the Free French as

> very thin, very withdrawn, very reserved. She remained distant through a sort of pride as though she wanted to exorcise ill-fortune by an apparent lack of interest. Her companion spoke for both of them. She herself, dressed with her usual indifference, stayed separate, resting her foot against the wall, knee bent, like some old sea-dog. Her hair unkempt, glasses on her nose, cigarette in her mouth, she hid, under the mask of an expressionless face, the urge to get away that was eating her up. Whether by desire for anonymity, or her need for mystery, or her affectation of indifference, she prevented people from sympathising with her but not from noticing her presence. (SWNYL, p. 35)

The two Simones went regularly to Harlem to follow a course in first-aid, thinking it might help them with their applications for a passage to Britain. Weil failed her first attempt at the practical, owing to nerves. She also formed a poor opinion of the American educational system when she found herself confronted in the written exam with questions such as 'Is iodine a disinfectant or a plant?'. Anxious about her friend's health, Deitz would invite her to a meal in her house where her father would provoke Weil into an argument by declaring the superiority of Judaism over Christianity, while sliding more food surreptitiously onto her plate.

Ever the teacher, Weil initiated her friend into the mysteries of ancient Greek. Much of the long conversations between the two Simones centred on religion. Deitz had converted to Catholicism and Weil was as absorbed as ever by the reasons which prevented her from doing likewise. Weil objected, understandably, to Saint Augustine's view that unbaptised infants went to Hell; less convincingly, she felt that this view was *de rigueur* for any consistent Catholic. Nor could she accept the doctrine of the Communion of Saints: she herself was far too reprobate to be included, even eventually, in such a company.

Despite these disagreements, Weil went to Mass almost daily at the Franciscan Church of Corpus Christi at 121st Street, five minutes' walk away across Broadway. The Church was light and airy, with a panelled wood interior painted white and Weil particularly appreciated the fact that the dialogue of the mass was in English – Latin being a legacy of the Roman imperialism so foreign to the original message of Christianity. On Sundays she went further afield, to a small synogogue of Ethiopian Jews and to a Baptist Church in Harlem on 125th Street. She began to go regularly to the Baptist Church and wrote enthusiastically to her friend Bercher:

> Every Sunday I go to a Baptist Church in Harlem. I am the only white person in the Church. After a service of one or two hours, when the atmosphere is established, the religious fervour of the Minister and the congregation explodes into dances much like the Charleston, exclamations, cries and the singing of spirituals. That's really worth seeing. A true and moving expression of faith, it seems to me. (P, p. 478)

Once she was accompanied by her friend Simone Deitz, who nevertheless remained mistrustful of that type of religious enthusiasm. Harlem became Weil's favourite area in New York: she would wander round its streets in the evenings and spend hours watching the children at play.

On 15 September, her sister-in-law Eveline gave birth to a baby girl, who was named Sylvie. Weil had already expressed her view that the forthcoming child should be baptised and she wrote at length to her brother:

> I would not hesitate for a second if I had a child to have it baptised by a priest. There would be only one reason to hesitate; if the child might regret it later on. Sylvie would not have the shadow of a reason to regret having been baptised by a priest unless she later turned towards a fanatical Judaism, which isn't very probable. If she turns to atheism, Buddhism, Catharism, Hinduism, or Taoism, what would

it matter to her that she had been baptised? If she turns to Christianity, Catholic or Protestant, which is indeed her right, she will be very happy about it. If her fiancee is a Jew, an atheist, Buddhist, etc., her baptism will not be an inconvenience; she will not be responsible for it. If a more or less anti-semitic piece of legislation grants advantages to baptised half-Jews it will be agreeable for her, probably, to enjoy these advantages without having done anything cowardly. In summation, I believe that if she is not baptised, in twenty years she may be discontented with you. (P, p. 481)

Her advice was followed.

The question of her own baptism continued to preoccupy her. On the recommendation of Perrin, she went several times to see Dietrich von Hildebrand, Professor of Philosophy at Fordham University, and she spent a whole afternoon in a frank exchange of views with Fr Oestreicher. The topic of conversation with both was the same: the superiority of Greek philosophy and poetry over the Old Testament as a precursor of Christianity. Her views did not gain acceptance and her appetite for incessant argument was no more welcome in New York City than it had been in Marseilles. She herself had a wry appreciation of the situation. To her parents, who had gone to visit André and Eveline in Haverford, she wrote:

> I have seen the Jesuit to whom the nun from the convent in Brooklyn sent me. After an hour of theological discussion, he explained to me that to his great regret he travelled too often to be able to have repeated meetings with me, and that another Jesuit there, whom he named, would deal with me. That reminded me of 'It's noon, time to go to lunch'.[2] I wonder whether this other fellow will pass me on to a third, and so on, until none of them is left. I feel sorry for them. (P, p. 479)

What really bothered Weil was the lack of precision over what the doctrines of the Catholic Church actually were. Her acute philosophical mind had to know exactly to what baptism would be committing her. But there was no clear agreement about what was, and what was not, *de fide*: 'Even in the minds of priests, Catholicism doesn't have fixed frontiers. It is at once rigid and imprecise. There are things of "strict faith", but it is impossible to know which they are' (ibid.). To her irritation, different priests apparently well instructed in theology gave different answers to her questions.

During this period Weil's sense of isolation and frustration increased. She was pleased to meet her old friend Boris Souvarine again but she felt cut off from her previous life. A letter from Thibon in early September was the first she received from France. No letters came from Perrin and she concluded (quite unjustly)[3] that 'Father Perrin, after having gotten to know the prose sent from Casablanca, has arrived at Father O's conclusion as to my spiritual affiliation (the Devil via Marcion) and that the absence of letters is explained in this way' (P, p. 480). In reply to Thibon she wrote that 'the mere recollection of the streets of Marseilles and of my little house by the Rhône pierces my heart' (ibid.). She was continuously anxious about her friends in France and felt that she had deserted them and her country in their hour of affliction; and although 'one should manage to welcome joys and sorrows with exactly the same gratitude, it is not possible when the sorrow is mixed with remorse'.[4] Things took a distinct turn for the better, however, in mid-September when she received a letter from Maurice Schumann in London, encouraging her to think that a post would be found for her with the Free French there in the near future.

With the prospect of being able to get to London, Weil's spirits revived. She replied enthusiastically to Schumann, asking to be found some kind of dangerous employment: 'The suffering all over the world obsesses and overwhelms me to the point of annihilating my faculties and the only way I can revive them and release myself from the obsesssion is by getting for myself a large share of danger and hardship. That is a necessary condition before I can exert my capacity for work' (SL, p. 156). With the return of this capacity for work, Weil also found a suitable partner for her continuing dialogue about her relationship to the Church. This was Edouard Couturier, a Dominican to whom she had been recommended by Maritain. Her problem, as she explained to Schumann, was that she adhered totally to the mysteries of the Christian faith but was kept outside the Church by 'certain philosophical difficulties' (SL, p. 155) which she felt to be irreducible. Nevertheless she found Couturier intelligent and broad-minded and even suggested to her brother that Couturier give Eveline's ten-year-old son Alain religious instruction.

To further her dialogue with him she prepared a list of questions, a longer version of the list that had had so little success with Clément Jacob the previous Easter at En Calcat. Instead of asking what was the content of the Catholic faith, she began from the other end and composed a list of potential heresies. She expanded them to thirty-five in the next few weeks before her eventual departure for London; they were subsequently published under the title *Letter to a Priest*. Weil outlined her dilemma as follows:

> When I read the catechism of the Council of Trent, it seems as though I had nothing in common with the religion there set forth. When I read the New Testament, the mystics, the Liturgy, when I watch the

celebration of the Mass, I feel with a sort of conviction that this faith is mine or, to be more precise, would be mine without the distance placed between it and me by my imperfection. (LP, p. 9)

Once again, she insisted on clarity and precision. There was to be no room for any beating about the bush:

I ask you to give me a definite answer – leaving out such expressions as 'I think that', etc., – regarding the compatibility or incompatibility of each of these opinions with membership of the Church. If there is any incompatibility, I should like you to say straight out: I would refuse baptism (or absolution) to anybody claiming to hold the opinions expressed under the headings numbered so-and-so, so-and-so, and so-and-so. I do not ask for a quick answer. There is no hurry. All I ask for is a categorical answer. (LP, p. 10)

She prefaced the list by saying that she had been thinking about these questions for years with all the love and attention of which she was capable. During this time the bonds which attached her to the Catholic faith had grown stronger and ever more deeply rooted in her heart and her intelligence. But, at the same time, the thoughts that separated her from the Church had also gained in force and clarity. Her summary of these points contained two main themes and two long postscripts. The first theme began with the familiar idea that 'if we take a moment in history anterior to Christ and sufficiently remote from him – for example, five centuries before his time – and we set aside what follows afterwards, at that moment Israel has less of a share in God and in Divine Truth than several of the surrounding peoples (India, Egypt, Greece, China)' (LP, p. 12f). It followed that the content of Christianity had existed before Christ: after all, the advent of Christ had not changed human conduct to any noticeable extent. Weil then went on to her favourite contrast between Israel and Greece. The problem of the contemporary world sprang from the abandonment of the unity of the sacred and the profane so evident in Greek thought: 'Europe has been spiritually uprooted, cut off from that antiquity in which all the elements of our civilisation have their origin; and she has gone about uprooting the other continents from the sixteenth century onwards' (LP, p. 31). The missionary activity of the Church, particularly since the condemnation of the Jesuit policy in China in the seventeenth century, was very largely misplaced and did not pay sufficient attention to the fact that other religions contained explicitly truths which were only implicit in Christianity. A change of religion was as dangerous as a change of language would be for a writer: it could be a success, but was equally likely to prove disastrous. Since it abandoned the legacy of Greece, 'Christianity was responsible for bringing this notion of progress, previously un-known, into the world; and this notion, become the bane of the modern world, has de-Christianised it' (LP, p. 48). Eternity was not to be found in chronology.

The second theme of Weil's *Letter* concerned the notion of faith. She rejected the concept (which she associated with Aquinas) of faith as intellectual assent to a set of interlinked propositions which had to be accepted as a totality. Such a conception neglected the intimate connec-tion of faith with charity – 'it is not those who say unto me "Lord, Lord" – and implied a totalitarianism at least as stifling as that of Hitler. In Weil's opinion, the traditional Catholic view of faith was far too intellectual. It lent itself to the employment of the *anathema sit* and to all sorts of illogicalities and absurdities involved in the doctrine of salvation outside the Church. Thus the whole notion of faith needed to be thought out anew in that the dogmas of faith were not things to be affirmed but 'to be regarded from a certain distance, with attention, respect, and love' (LP, p. 48). The definitions of the Church should command a permanent and unconditional attitude of respectful attention, but not intellectual adherence: 'Intellectual adherence is never owed to anything whatsoever. For it is never in any degree a voluntary thing. Attention alone is voluntary. And it *alone* forms the subject of an obligation' (LP, p. 60).

Weil ended her letter with two long postscripts on matters that had recently been occupying her attention. The first was a miscellaneous compendium of the 'treasures' that had been lost or neglected by the Church – the doctrines contained in the Apocalypse, the meaning of the resurrection of the flesh, the indifference of God's justice, the folklore roots of the Easter liturgy, and many others. Finally, she emphasised the mysteries surrounding the origins of Christianity which made its original meaning almost impossible to recover. These two postscripts are tentative, but the rest of the letter reads like an indictment. It purposefully stresses what divided Weil from the Church, and most of her thirty-five 'opinions' are delivered with a degree of certainty which is at odds with the questioning attitude to religion that she is so much at pains to recommend. At any rate, she must have realised the incompatibility of her thoughts with membership of the Church and the letter is more of a justification of her vocation as a 'Christian outside the Church' (LP, p. 11).

The background to her *Letter* to Couturier is to be found in the *Notebooks* she wrote in New York. During the two months from mid-July to mid-September she had been too depressed to do more than collect references and note material about the Old Testament, the Church, and the concept of heresy that she would use in her *Letter*. But the prospect of departure once again spurred her creativity and she began to fill notebook after notebook. They contained, as she said, 'thoughts hastily set down, in no order or sequence' (SL, p. 159). The tone is austere and bleak. The model is Christ's cry on the Cross – a cry in the void, an eternally unanswered appeal:

> To cry like this throughout our brief and interminable, interminable and brief sojourn in this world, and then disappear into nothingness – it is enough; what more is there to ask? If God grants more, that is his affair; we shall know later on. I prefer to suppose that at the very best He grants no more than that. For that is completeness of fulfillment – if only, from now until the moment of my death, there could be no other word in my soul than this uninterrupted cry in the eternal silence. (FLN, p. 137)

Weil continued to elaborate on the metaphysical background to these ideas along the lines already set out in the Marseilles *Notebooks*. Creation was an act of abdication on God's part. God had filled us with a kind of false divinity and the purpose of our creation was that we should empty ourselves of it. We must therefore renounce our existence. It was only thus that we could truly love God, who waited patiently like a beggar for our love. Weil insisted again and again on the importance of humility, of silence, of waiting:

> God and humanity are like two lovers who have missed their rendez-vous. Each is there before the time, but each at a different place, and they wait and wait and wait. He stands motionless, nailed to the spot for the whole of time. She is distraught and impatient. But alas for her, if she gets tired and goes away. For the two places where they are waiting are at the same point in the fourth dimension . . . (FLN, p. 141)

This fourth dimension was the presence of God which lay outside time in which God had abandoned us. It was only the acceptance of time and whatever it might bring that would enable us to go to God and disappear into the Divine Presence.

Like many mystics, Weil was interested by the role of desire. Her treatment of desire and the good in the New York *Notebooks* introduced a tone of self-confident mysticism that was new in her writings. According to her, the essence of faith was that it was really impossible to desire the good and not to obtain it. The reason for this was that desire should not be attached to the things of this world, none of which were real goods. The object of desire was absolute good, which was bound to be frustrated if misdirected to objects which were, at best, only partial goods. And since, in the case of the absolute good, desire coincided with possession, 'I have no need to imagine something behind this word. On the contrary, the object of my desire must be nothing but the reality, completely unknown to me, which is behind the word' (FLN, p. 158). The ends usually proffered to humans – such as money or happiness – could not be desired unconditionally. This was only possible for the sovereign good. Moreover even the question of the existence of this good was not important. The sovereign good was 'that whose name alone, if I attach my thought to it, gives me the certainty that the things of this world are not goods' (FLN, p. 316). Our only task, one of dreadfully difficult simplicity, was to desire the good, since 'whereas all other desires are sometimes effective and sometimes not according to circumstances, this one desire is always effective. The reason is that, whereas the desire for gold is not the same thing as gold, the desire for good is itself a good' (ibid.). This was because what we called desire was, in reality, possession itself.

In discussing the relation of desire to the good, Weil stressed both the simplicity and the difficulty of the solution to the human predicament. The difficulty lay in its not being a question of will-power. What was required was a self-negation and the harder a person willed, the more they affirmed their own self. Therefore 'a strong will can obtain many things. For example, Napoleon. Many things, but not the good. Not even an atom of good' (FLN, p. 307). Make no effort, remain motionless, beseech in silence – those were the only rules. Just as the prodigal son in the parable only returned to his father when he had used up *all* his patrimony and was left without any resource whatever, so we should divest ourselves of all our voluntary energy before we could hope to return to God.

Weil's mystical beliefs did not imply an attitude of passivity towards other human beings. 'By their fruits shall ye know them' was one of her favourite sayings. It was not what someone said or did about God but what they said or did about the things of the world that showed, for her, whether that person's soul had passed through the fire of the love of God. For 'to die for God is not a proof of faith in God. To die for an unknown and repulsive convict who is a victim of injustice, that is a proof of faith in God' (FLN, p. 144). The Gospel contained a conception of human life, not a theology: it was like an electric torch whose power was judged not by looking at its bulb but by seeing how many objects it lit up. Although only spiritual things had value, only physical things had a verifiable existence and therefore the value of the former could only be verified by the illumination they shed on the latter. Her own spiritual values showed her that 'if we contemplate the Good, we see every desire, even the most horrible, as an aspiration towards good, even though erroneous' and 'to love purely is to love the hunger in a human being. Then, since all men are always hungry, one always loves all men. The hunger of a few men is partly satisfied; in them, one ought to love both their hunger and its satisfaction' (FLN, p. 284). It was only an impersonal love of this sort that could be unconditional.

These considerations help us understand the context of Weil's dreadful prayer:

> Father, in the name of Christ grant me this. That I may be unable to will any bodily movement, or even attempt at movement, like a total paralytic. That I may be incapable of receiving any sensation, like someone who is completely blind, deaf and deprived of all the senses. That I may be unable to make the slightest connection between two thoughts, even the simplest, like one of those total idiots who not only cannot count or read but have never even learned to speak. That I may be insensible to every kind of grief and joy, and incapable of any love for any being or thing, and not even for myself, like old people in the last stage of decrepitude. (FLN, pp. 243f)

She continued with a prayer that 'my faculties of hearing, sight, taste, smell and touch [may] register the perfectly accurate impress of thy creation. May this mind, in fullest lucidity, connect all ideas in perfect conformity with Thy truth'. In other words, it was her *self* that she wished to become paralytic so that God might be all in all. Her aim was to lose her personality and imitate God's own abdication by refusing the existence that had been given her and to refuse it because God alone was good. 'Our sin', she wrote, 'consists in wanting to be, and our punishment is that we believe we possess being. Expiation consists in desiring to cease to be; and salvation consists for us in perceiving that we are not' (FLN, p. 218). This salvation consisted, as Saint John said, in becoming like God through seeing God as God really was. In this assimilation to God we would no longer exist; but in this nothingness we would be more real than at any moment of our earthly life.

While composing these meditations in her *Notebooks*, Weil was preparing to take an active part, at long last, in the war effort. Her old friend Maurice Schumann had already held out the prospect of her being able to come to London in the near future. The Free French there had been expanding their activities considerably during 1942 by establishing closer contacts both with the Resistance movements inside France and with the United States which was preparing its invasion of North Africa. Schumann recommended Weil to André Philip, a pre-war socialist deputy who had been sent to London by the Resistance and appointed Commissioner for the Interior by de Gaulle in July 1942. Although Philip did not think much of Weil's plan for front-line nurses, he was willing to help her get to London and give her some work. On learning this from Schumann, she replied enthusiastically, emphasising the affinity of her religious views with those of Schumann (who was a Catholic) and asking for any useful work that involved a high degree of hardship and danger:

> If it was a job not involving a high degree of hardship and danger I could only accept it provisionally; otherwise I should be consumed by the same chagrin in London as in New York, and it would paralyse me. It is unfortunate to have that sort of character; but that is really how I am, and I can do nothing about it; it is something too essential in me to be modified. The more so because it is not, I am certain, a question of character only, but of vocation. (SL, p. 157)

Philip himself also wrote to her and she was able to see him in person when he came to New York in November on the difficult mission of persuading Roosevelt to take a more positive attitude to the Free French movement.

The interview with Philip went well and her departure date was fixed for 10 November. Before leaving she was much occupied in the kind of letter-writing that had preceded her departure from Marseilles. She finished the long letter to Couturier the day before her departure. She also wrote to the philosopher Jean Wahl whom she had known in pre-war days and just missed meeting in both Marseilles and New York. He had warned her that there were rumours among some French exiles in New York that she had pro-Vichy sympathies. Weil denied this indignantly. She continued: 'What may have given rise to such rumours is the fact that I don't much like to hear perfectly comfortable people here using words like coward and traitor about people in France who are managing as best they can in a terrible situation' (SL, p. 158). The whole nation had welcomed the Armistice of 1940 with relief and bore responsibility for it. The consequent situation had given rise to pressures that many could only resist if they were heroes. But 'most of the people here, however, who set themselves up as judges have never had an opportunity to find out if they themselves are heroes. I detest facile, unjust, and false attitudes, and especially when the pressure of public opinion seems to make them almost obligatory' (SL, p. 159). She continued by asking Wahl whether his 'existentialist' views had been modified by the events of the last few years, remarking wryly that 'the word "*Dasein*" must have a different resonance for you' since 'there is nothing like misfortune for giving the sense of existence' (ibid.). She gave Wahl a synopsis of her own ideas of the different traditions descending from the sons of Noah and the necessity of finding a modern, western, scientific expression for the truth to be found in the line of thought stretching from Pythagoras, through India and China to

Saint John of the Cross – a truth which Hitler and others were trying to abolish throughout the world.

Weil eventually left New York on the *Vaalaren*, a Swedish cargo boat, on 10 November. Simone Deitz left in the same convoy, but on a different boat. Weil said goodbye to her parents with the words: 'If I had several lives, I would devote one to you; but I have only one life and I owe it elsewhere' (SWNYL, p. 36). While Weil was on the high seas on her way to London, Rommel's position was collapsing at El Alamein and the decisive battle on the Russian front had begun at Stalingrad. The tide of war was turning. But for Weil, in London, life was about to ebb away for ever.

11

London: Politics and Death

'To uproot oneself socially and vegetatively. To exile oneself from
every earthly country. To do all that to others, from the outside, is a
substitute (*ersatz*) for decreation. It results in unreality. But by
uprooting oneself one seeks greater reality.' (GG, p. 34)

The crossing from New York to Liverpool took two weeks. There were
ten passengers on board the *Vaalaren*. Linked by a common danger,
their morale was good. Weil took the initiative in getting them together
in the evenings, telling them folk-tales and encouraging them to do the
same. She was particularly pleased when there was a clear sky and they
were able to assemble on the bridge in the moonlight. Others were not
so happy: a clear sky increased the risk of torpedoes. The *Vaalaren* docked
in Liverpool on 25 November and the passengers were transferred to
a screening centre on the outskirts of London, popularly known as the
Patriotic School. It was normal to be released after a few days, but Weil,
because of her previous pacifist and Communist connections, was kept
for about three weeks. She learned to play volley-ball, dressed up as a
ghost to amuse her fellow-inmates, and was altogether, according to
Simone Deitz, looking better than when she left New York. But three
weeks was a long time and on finally emerging she felt 'completely flat'
(SL, p. 164). In the end it was once again Maurice Schumann who came
to her rescue by obtaining her release, and on 14 December she was let
loose on London.

For the first month, Weil had a temporary billet with the Free French
women volunteers. She met Schumann and was introduced to Louis
Closon who was André Philip's deputy and had special responsibility
for relations with France. 'Schumann was as nice as possible', she wrote
to her parents, 'Closon welcomed me as though we were old friends'
(SL, p. 161). She immediately broached her plans to return to France,
but did not meet with a positive response. In Spain, in 1936, when her
project to be sent behind the Fascist lines to find Maurin was turned
down, she could nevertheless enlist surreptitiously. But there was no
such alternative open to her in London. And the recent occupation of
the Free Zone by the German army only served to sharpen her regret at
ever having left Marseilles. Neither did she make much headway with
her efforts – against her better judgement – to get her parents a passage
to England or, failing that, to North Africa which was increasingly

234

coming under Allied control. But she immediately fell in love with England:

> In one sense, both things and people here seem to me exactly as I think I expected them to be, and in another sense perhaps better. Lawrence somewhere describes England by the terms 'humour and kindness'; and one does meet with these traits continually in little incidents of daily life and in the most widely different circles. Especially *kindness* – to a much greater degree than I would have dared hope. People here do not scream at one another as they do on the Continent; nor do they where you are now, but that is because their nerves are relaxed whereas here people's nerves are strained but they control them from self-respect and from a true generosity towards others. It may be that the war has a great deal to do with all this. (SL, p. 163)

One incident that typified her impressions was when Simone Deitz's handbag was stolen in the Underground and then returned through the post with its contents intact and a note pinned to her military ID card: 'We don't steal from soldiers' (C, p. 235). She could not be happy as long as her plans for active service in France were not realised; but at least now she felt that life was no longer morally impossible for her.

In mid-January, Weil's material circumstances improved when she found congenial lodgings with a Mrs Francis, at 31 Portland Road, a three-storey terraced house in Holland Park. Mrs Francis, a kindly charwoman of spiritualist leanings, was a single parent with two boys, David aged 14 and John aged 10, her husband, a primary school teacher, having died ten years previously. Weil occupied a room on the ground floor for the first two weeks but then her landlady, who supposed from her appearance that she was very poor, suggested she move into a cheaper room on the top floor where she could cook her own meals on a small gas ring. Weil found her room 'very pretty with branches full of birds and, at night, of stars, just outside the window' (SL, p. 180). She would occasionally come down into the kitchen during air raids, but hated to have to listen to the news on the radio. Mrs Francis worried continuously about her tenant who, already tubercular, had a racking cough, refused to heat her room, and would not eat properly since (as she claimed) the French were dying of hunger. She was particularly struck by her voice which was 'ever so quiet and gentle' and her face, 'the saddest I have ever seen' (SWNYL, p. 39). Weil, for her part, found the atmosphere of the house 'pure Dickens' (SL, p. 181). She was particularly fond of the boys: she had an endless fund of stories to tell them, took John to see the Free French doctor for advice about his glandular trouble, and helped them continuously with their homework.

They would leave their exercises by her door and often she would find the younger one asleep on the landing, waiting for her return.

However congenial Portland Place might be to her and however much she might 'feel a tender love for this bomb damaged town' (SL, p. 165), Weil found the work she had been assigned increasingly unsatisfactory. Instead of active service in the Resistance she was becoming a civil servant. Every morning she would take the Central Line underground to Mayfair. The headquarters of the Free French, where de Gaulle had his offices, was in Carlton Gardens, just off the Mall – ironically, in a mansion which had once been the home of the francophobe Lord Palmerston; the interior services, under André Philip, had been hived off to Hill Street, adjacent to Berkeley Square and its nightingales. Here she was directly responsible to Louis Closon, who was at a loss as to what use to make of her:

> At our first meetings, I was put out. Philip, full of energy, a sensitive extrovert with heavy burdens, did not seem any more at ease than I when faced with this fragile creature whose dimensions did not correspond to ours however much we might try to get closer to her. Communication with Simone remained difficult. He asked me to look after her and see how and on what I could put her to work.[1]

Closon rapidly came to the conclusion that, although there was no lack of goodwill on her part, Weil simply did not fit into the mainly administrative work in Hill Street; he felt it wisest, since she was at her best on paper, to let her start at least by writing whatever she felt needed to be written.

This 'purely intellectual and entirely personal' (SL, p. 163) work consisted, in the first instance, of analysing and commenting on the various political documents that came from the Resistance Committees inside France. In the dark days of 1940 and 1941 de Gaulle and the Free French in London had had to concentrate on establishing themselves as the legitimate voice of France in opposition to the Vichy regime. In 1942, however, relations with the Resistance movements inside France had been put on a more regular basis. The fact that the Resistance was more Left-inclined and more interested in political questions, coupled with the arrival in London in the summer of 1942 of such leading socialists as Philip and Pierre Brossolette, meant that London itself became more interested in political problems.[2] In addition, the winter of 1942/3 was a difficult time for de Gaulle, whose pre-eminent position was threatened by the emergence of the conservative and megalomaniac General Giraud as Commander of the French forces in North Africa. Giraud seemed to have the support of the Americans and outranked de Gaulle, who was obliged to counter his rival by moving to the Left and conciliating the growing political interests inside the Resistance. With the prospect of final victory appearing on the distant horizon, attention began to be given to the principles on which a postwar France should be constructed. As well as prosecuting the war effort, it now became important to think about organising the peace. Ideas about a new constitution, a reformulated Declaration of Rights, the role of political parties and so on flowed into London. It was on these projects that Weil was asked to comment and to respond.

The many papers that Weil wrote in response to the material coming from France were bold and innovative. But in many respects they were no more so than the ideas on which she was commenting.[3] These ideas emanated from clandestine groups whose projects for a postwar France were not only imbued with a disgust at the semi-Fascist, authoritarian, paternalist regime of Vichy; they were also determined to turn their backs on the whole political ethos of the Third Republic and, in particular, the impotent parliamentarism and party political system that they saw as responsible for the débâcle of 1940. This disdain for the Third Republic and a desire for a completely fresh start were as strong in London as they were in France. What was distinctive about Weil's contribution was not so much her specific suggestions as the lucid and uncompromising expression of the philosophico-religious background from which she sought to justify them.

In her papers on the possible constitutional framework of postwar France, Weil shared the general search for a *tabula rasa*. In her opinion, too, June 1940 was no isolated accident. The Third Republic had long before forfeited any claim to legitimacy which was therefore 'no treasure stolen from the French nation, either by the enemy or by an internal conspiracy. The French people in its entirety, from the elites to the working masses, opened their hands and let the treasure fall to the ground without even looking to see where it went. Passers-by kicked it about'.[4] The restoration of a sense of legitimacy could not be achieved immediately. A new constitution would have to be the product of a Constituent Assembly which itself would have to emerge from something like two years of concentrated reflection and discussion. The model for this was 1789, where for a brief period the whole nation had been involved in intense, imaginative and non-partisan debate. Such a period would allow the qualities of potential delegates to the Constitutent Assembly to be known by those around them and thus avoid those elected simply being individuals who had succeeded in imposing themselves on public attention through a degrading advertising campaign. Throughout this period of reflection, however, de Gaulle would have to govern provisionally and take hard decisions in the most difficult of circumstances. Such a provisional government could only achieve the necessary legitimacy if it promulgated a fundamental Declaration of political principles and got it affirmed by plebiscite immediately on liberation. De Gaulle should then solemnly affirm his adhesion to the Declaration, agree that his conduct should be judged by a tribunal appointed by the eventual Constitutent Assembly, forswear the creation of any 'Gaullist' political organisation, and guarantee not to pursue any political career once the new constitution was in force: 'To have saved the country's honour at the moment when it fell into slavery and to save the country itself in the terrible crisis which will immediately follow liberation is infinitely finer than any political career.'[5] The novelty of such an arrangement could be the shock that France needed to bring her back to life.

Although such suggestions were not designed to appeal to de Gaulle, Weil's advocacy of a Supreme Council of Revolt met with a little more success. For any provisional government to have a chance of success, she felt it necessary that the French people should be seen, by themselves and by others, to have participated in the victory. Although France had not really been part of the war, it was vital that her deliverance come from the people as a whole. Drawing on the writings of Clausewitz and her beloved Lawrence on guerrilla war, she pointed to the importance of morale supported by deeds, not words. Sabotage of the enemy's communications was vital. A successful effort in this direction, and the mass revolt that could follow it, would need to be co-ordinated on a European scale. It could reverse the shame of June 1940, forge a European unity which would include the British, and avoid the subsequent subjugation of Europe either to American money or to Russian military power. It would need an effort of propaganda and co-ordination that only a Supreme Council of Revolt could organise. The paper in which Weil outlined these ideas, entitled 'Reflections on Revolt', was the only one that de Gaulle could be persuaded to read from beginning to end. It may have had some influence on the formation, in May 1943, of a National Council of the Resistance under the presidency of Jean Moulin to co-ordinate the Resistance effort. Contrary to Weil's intentions, however, the National Council of the Resistance was confined to France and contained representatives of the old political parties.

Although her suggestions about a postwar provisional government did not meet with de Gaulle's approval, some of Weil's more specific proposals for an eventual constitution were more in tune with the thinking in London. She wanted a firm separation of powers with an independent judiciary headed by a Supreme Court, not appointed on party political lines, with the use of referenda to settle serious disagreements between legislature, executive and judiciary. Government should be at a minimum with the conduct of society as a whole guided by the Fundamental Declaration, magistates having the power to punish anyone departing from it – employers and journalists just as much as common criminals. One of Weil's principal aims, in keeping with the anti-Parliamentary feeling then rife in London,[6] was to minimise the powers of the legislative assembly and to prevent the return of the political parties 'whose total capture of public life is what has done us so much damage' (EL, p. 89). What was important for her was not so much electoral arrangements as how power was to be limited, judged and, if necessary, punished. Following the political philosophy of Alain, she held that it was ridiculous to suppose that the whole people could govern, but they *could* set limits to the powers of those who did. Her sketch of a possible Constitution (which she admitted would take over two generations to evolve) contained the following suggestions: that a President for life be chosen by senior magistrates from among their number; that the President choose a Prime Minister for five years; that the Prime Minister could be arraigned before the Supreme Court in case of misdemeanour and in any case would have to answer before a judicial tribunal at the end of office; that a Legislative Assembly be elected every five years, and that, similarly, any members not re-elected should pass before a tribunal to have their conduct reviewed; that the judiciary should mediate serious conflicts between legislature and executive; that every twenty years there should be a national referendum on the character of public life, preceded by a period of serious reflection devoid of any sort of propaganda or campaigning; and that, if the result of the referendum was to declare public life unsatisfactory, the President should be deprived of office and a suitable punishment, including the possibility of death, inflicted.

Although Weil was conscious that, even to the radical reformers of the Resistance, such ideas might seem to be fantastic, she insisted that they were not (EL, p. 97).[7] The political system of the Third Republic had practically led to the extinction of France and it was above all necessary to prevent its return. The cancer at the heart of the Third Republic had been the sovereignty of Parliament and its manipulation by political parties; and opposition to the return of the party system was strong among Weil's colleagues in London.[8] Her longest paper for André Philip was devoted to defending a proposal for the abolition of all political parties. It strikingly echoes a paper on 'the duties of a people's deputy' written in 1929, during her first year at the Ecole Normale where, following the ideas of Alain, she condemned careerism, campaigning and any form of politics based on parties (OC, ii, pp. 51f). The paper for Philip began by pointing out how foreign to the original spirit of 1789 was the notion of a political party which emerged later with the Jacobins and led to totalitarianism. The true spirit of 1789 consisted, not in thinking that something was just because the people wanted it, but that, under certain conditions, the will of the people had more chance than any other of conforming to justice. The French republican ideal started from the idea of this General Will as contained in Rousseau's *Social Contract*. According to Weil, Rousseau started from two evident principles:

> Firstly, that reason seeks out and chooses justice and utility in a neutral manner, and that every crime has passion as its motive. Secondly, that reason is the same in all human beings whereas the passions more often than not are different. It follows that if, as far as general problems are concerned, every person reflects on their own and expresses an opinion and if then the opinions are compared one with another, it is probable that they will be the same as regards the just and reasonable part of each of them and will be different as far as injustices and errors are concerned. (EL, p. 128)

There were two pre-conditions of a just General Will. The first was the absence of collective passion whether of the whole people or of parts of them: just as water could not reflect objects if disturbed by a current, whether one or many, so the people could not reflect justice if disturbed by collective passions. Secondly, the people had to express their will on issues of public life and not on the choice of irresponsible collectivities. And it was evident that the existence of political parties vitiated these two pre-conditions.

Political parties were not only machines to promote collective passion and therefore exert collective pressure on the thought processes of their members: their one aim was their own limitless growth. Parties were an example, along with money, power, state, national glory, economic production and university diplomas, of the constant error of mistaking ends for means. An indication of this was the absence of any clear doctrine in political parties. It was difficult enough for an individual to have a doctrine: the collectivity could never produce one. A party was its own end. But this amounted to idolatry, since God alone was end and not means. And, since a political party could never have enough power, it lead straight to totalitarianism. This absence of doctrine, and its replacement by propaganda, entailed a disregard for justice and truth. Anyone who declared that, 'whenever I examine any political or social problems, I promise to forget completely the fact that I am a member of such-and-such a group and to concern myself exclusively with seeking out the public good and justice' (EL, p. 136) had better give up any idea of belonging to a party. If there was such a thing as truth, one was obliged to think only that which was true. In that case, 'you think such a thing not because you are, as it happens, French, or Catholic, or Socialist, but because the irresistible light of evidence obliges you to think this and nothing else' (EL, p. 137). Political parties had a horror of the 'personal point of view' – because these days justice and truth were regarded as merely personal matters.

Weil's polemic against political parties echoes her several polemics against the Church as a social organism. Indeed she traced the poison of the party spirit back to the Church's persecution of heretics. The demand of the Church for a total adherence to its teaching authority was paralleled in political parties, each of which was a little secular Church armed with its threat of excommunication. Candidates should not present themselves to the public with a political label but only with their own ideas: she recalled how, in the Berlin of 1933, the ordinary members of the Nazi and Communist parties were amazed to find how much they had in common on social and economic questions. If political points of view formed, they should group themselves around a review (she had in mind here the *Cahiers du Sud* in Marseilles) and not allow themselves to crystallise. The tendency to take sides for and against had spread like a disease from politics to science and art and relieved people of the obligation to think: the disease was fatal and was unlikely to be cured without the suppression of political parties.

It is partly in this context that Weil's comments on the project for a 'Basis for a Statute Regarding French Non-Christian Minorities of Foreign Origin' should be read. This project was principally concerned with Jews and Weil's attitude to it has given rise to charges of anti-Semitism.[9] While admitting that the Jewish minority had a common bond in the absence of a Christian heritage, Weil wrote that

> it is dangerous to consider these accepted premises as stable and to make them correspond to a stable *modus vivendi*. The existence of such a minority does not represent a good thing; thus the objective must be to bring about its disappearance, and any *modus vivendi* must be a transition toward this objective. In this regard, official recognition of this minority's existence would be very bad because that would crystallise it. (P, p. 509)

It is clear that Weil's recommendations for assimilation were partly prompted by her recognition of the fact that the proposals on which she was commenting emanated from a group that she rightly considered to have Fascist tendencies[10] and whose 'sole aim is to form a crystallised Jewish minority, as a readily available reserve with a view to future atrocities' (P, p. 510). At another, and deeper, level her views were based on the same opposition that she expressed towards political parties and the collective passion to which they could give rise.[11]

This fundamental opposition to the generation of partial collective passions prompted her to entitle one of her papers 'Are we Fighting for Justice?'. Justice, for her, was mutual consent: 'Human consent is sacred.

It is what human beings give to God. It is what God comes like a beggar to seek from human beings' (EL, p. 47). Thus the notion of justice 'contains all the meaning of the three words of the French motto. Liberty is the real possibility of granting consent. Human beings only have need of equality in relation to it. And the spirit of fraternity consists in wishing it for all' (EL, p. 51). It was incompatible with the predominance of money, with the hollowness of the traditional French parliamentary system, and with the modern form of patriotism. In particular such a notion of justice demanded a complete rethinking of French colonial policy, since 'the problem of finding a doctrine or faith to inspire the French people in their resistance today and in their tasks of construction tomorrow is inseparable from the colonial problem' (SE, p. 185). This was especially relevant at the present time, since 'the evil that Germany would have inflicted upon Europe if England had not stood in her way is the same evil that is inflicted by colonisation. It is the evil of uprootedness; the conquered countries would have become uprooted through the loss of their past. To lose one's past is to fall into colonial servitude' (SE, p. 199). Instead of getting little Polynesian children to recite in their school 'Our ancestors the Gauls had fair hair and blue eyes . . .', the least unsatisfactory way of proceeding would be to combine external military protection with a fostering of an indigenous sense of culture and tradition leading to independence.[12]

But, secondly, the colonial question had great importance for Europe itself, which was a sort of 'geometrical mean' between America and the East. In order to avoid the disintegration of its culture under American influence, Europe would need to rediscover the sources of its own culture in the East. The past was storehouse of all our spiritual treasure and

> if, without turning our eyes away from the future, we try to revive our contact with our own millennial past; and if we seek a stimulus for this effort in genuine friendship, founded on respect, with everything in the East that is still securely rooted, then we may succeed in saving the past from almost total obliteration, and thus also save the spiritual vocation of the human race. (SE, p. 208)

It might also help to restore to France her former spiritual radiance and gift for opening new roads for humanity.

The religious background implicit in what Weil wrote for the Resistance was developed in her paper entitled 'This War is a War of Religions'. The religious problem was posed by the intolerable burden of the opposition between good and evil in the contemporary world. The problem was open to three solutions. The first was the irreligious solution of denying the reality of the opposition between good and evil.

This led straight to ennui, madness and the draining away of any will to resist the concentration camps. The second solution, religious in the Durkheimian sense, was the adoration of the social under various divine names. Its essence was to remove some sphere from the play of good and evil. Art and science had often been such closed areas, as had the practices of Rome, Israel and the Church of the Inquisition. In contemporary society it was the nation-state, particularly the nation-state with a single party, whose members were, as such, granted immunity from sin. The third method was the mystical, which 'means passing beyond the sphere where good and evil are in opposition, and this is achieved by the union of the soul with the absolute good. Absolute good is different from the good which is the opposite and correlative of evil, although it is its pattern and its source' (SE, p. 214). Although it was impossible to hope that a whole people could accomplish this, the whole life of a people could be permeated by a religion entirely orientated towards mysticism, and 'it is only by this orientation that religion is distinguished from idolatry'' (SE, p. 215)

What was needed was a system of labour that would lead people to rediscover the beauty of the world. The basis of such a civilisation could only be spiritual poverty and it could only be accomplished by an elite who were poor not only in spirit but also in fact. A new Franciscan order would be too separate for such a task: the brothers and sisters of Charles de Foucauld were more like what Weil had in mind. Germany lived by one idolatry and Russia by another. England, it was true, 'has such continuity of history and such a living tradition that some of her roots are still nourished by a past which was bathed in the light of mysticism' (SE, p. 217) and this had enabled her to gain a brief respite in 1940. But time was short, the internal malady from which Europe was suffering would not be cured by American money and machines. This sickness could only be cured by a return to the kind of religious outlook that might inspire the mass uprising she had advocated in her paper 'Reflections on Revolt'.

The implications of this mystical approach were set out in a 'Profession of Faith' which Weil wrote as a preface to a brief statement of what she considered to be the basic human obligations. The profession, which re-cast material from her New York *Notebooks*, began uncompromisingly:

There is a reality outside the world, that is to say outside space and time, outside man's mental universe, outside any sphere whatsoever that is accessible to human faculties. Corresponding to this reality, at the centre of the human heart, is the longing for an absolute good, a longing which is always there and is never appeased by any object in this world . . . Although it is beyond the reach of any human faculties, man has the power of turning his attention and love towards it.

Nothing can ever justify the assumption that any man, whoever he may be, has been deprived of this power. It is a power which is only real in this world insofar as it is exercised. The sole condition for exercising it is consent. (SE, p. 219)

The recognition of this power was the only possible motive for universal respect towards all human beings. The expression of this respect could only be indirect and concerned

men's needs, the needs of the soul and of the body, in this world . . . Obligation is concerned with the needs in this world of the souls and bodies of human beings, whoever they may be. For each need there is a corresponding obligation; for each obligation a corresponding need. There is no other kind of obligation, so far as human affairs are concerned. (SE, pp. 221f)

The single and permanent obligation was 'to remedy, according to his responsibilities and to the extent of his power, all the privations of soul and body which are liable to destroy or damage the earthly life of any human being whatsoever' (SE, p. 222). Any state which did not recognise this obligation was not legitimate, since law was 'the totality of the permanent provisions for making this aim effective' (SE, p. 223). Weil appended a list of needs that she hoped would obtain the assent of the whole people and be guaranteed by any holder of public office. The bodily needs were for food, warmth, sleep, health, rest, exercise and fresh air. The needs of the soul, arranged in pairs to balance and complement each other, were for equality and hierarchy, obedience and liberty, truth and freedom of expression, personal and collective property, punishment and honour, security and risk. Most important of all was the need for rootedness in several natural environments. A more detailed discussion of these needs forms the opening section of what was to become Weil's major work of this period, *The Need for Roots.*

The several themes of Weil's minor writings for the Resistance were summed up in her beautiful essay 'On Human Personality'.[13] Weil began her essay by denying the idea of rights as fundamental to social organisation, and thereby putting in question the mainstream of western political thought from the founding of the United States to the Charter of the United Nations. With this rejection of rights as a starting-point, she linked an attack on the idea of the person as a proprietor of these rights. For Weil, the contemporary Faustian aspirations to self-development, satisfaction of desire and cultivation of personality were mistaken: the great achievements of humanity – the *Iliad*, Greek geometry, Gregorian chant, Romanesque architecture – were not the

product of personal desire. Truth and beauty were essentially impersonal. In mathematics, it was the varied mistakes made that reflected
the individual personalities, not the single correct answer. What was
sacred in every human being was not the contingent person but the
universal quest for truth and the belief of each individual despite all
evidence to the contrary that good rather than evil was to be expected
of fellow-creatures. The cult of the person led to social conditioning and
the subordination of the individual to the collective; and the concomitant
idea of rights depended on having the force to implement them. Weil
was not against the whole notion of human rights: but she insisted that
they could be effective in a society which had achieved a real equality
based on obligation and need. In this dense, difficult, and sometimes
seemingly contradictory distillation of her thought, Weil is showing how
the language we use is already informed by those who have power. She
moves from the highly general to her own very specific experiences: of
her year in the factories of Paris or her witnessing of the sarcastic and
arrogant attitude towards inarticulate immigrants of the only too fluent
magistrates in Marseilles. Further, the language of rights and persons
was a prison: such language could be (and was) misused; therefore it
could not be wholly good and had to be subordinate to language which
tried to convey those goods which, being supernatural, were impersonal.

The contrast between the language of rights and that of obligations
and needs formed the starting-point for *The Need for Roots*, the only book
which she ever wrote as a unit. It was written at the same time as the
various more specific papers and as an effort to establish a general
philosophico-historical framework for her thought. Given the briefness
of the time available to her, the quantity and quality of Weil's writings
at this time is extraordinary. During the four months she spend working
for the Free French she produced what amounts to about eight hundred
pages of printed material. Writing very little in her notebooks now, she
poured forth her thoughts in a series of essays and papers in an assured,
lucid and compact style. She worked continuously. Sometimes she
would stay all night in her little office in Hill Street; sometimes she
would walk back to Holland Park after the Underground had shut down
and work for another three or four hours, coughing all the time, among
the papers which were piled all around her room and which no-one
else was allowed to touch.

This intense intellectual effort was not primarily directed towards the
elaboration of a new doctrine: 'A doctrine serves no purpose in itself,
but it is indispensable to have one if only to avoid being deceived by
false doctrines' (EL, p. 151). A preliminary task was to settle accounts
with the dominant doctrines of the previous two or three centuries. It
was to exposing their grave deficiencies (as exemplified in the various
projected 'Declarations' floating around London) that *The Need for Roots*

was particularly devoted. Weil referred to it as 'a second great work' (EL, p. 237) and looked forward to her mother's typing it out just as she had done with *Oppression and Liberty*. But, although the similarities with her previous 'Testament' are evident, the emphasis on revolution and class struggle had gone: the concern for justice is the same as ten years earlier, but now it is placed in a supernatural context – 'it is only what comes from heaven that can make a real impress on the earth' (MILES, p. 86). Although much of the functional sociology of *Oppression and Liberty* is retained, *The Need for Roots* was conceived of as an attempt to influence the principles on which postwar France would be reconstructed, and is therefore more directly concerned with politics and how power should be exercised. Weil divided her work into four parts: a long list of the reciprocal duties of the individual and the state; a short sketch of the low state of morale in France in 1940; a long historical analysis of the 'uprootedness' that had led to this débâcle; and finally a proposal for a new 'rooted' form of life. Weil gave no title to her work. *Lack of Roots* would have been more appropriate, as it is to this theme that the major, and most striking, part is dedicated.

Weil's book begins with a section on the needs of the soul. She here develops the contrast between needs and rights that she had already sketched in some of her papers and in particular in her essay 'On Human Personality', which is a sort of preface to *The Need for Roots*, whose opening sentence reads: 'The notion of obligations comes before that of rights, which is subordinate and relative to the former' (NR, p. 3). She continued:

> An obligation which goes unrecognised by anybody loses none of the full force of its existence. A right which goes unrecognised by anybody is not worth very much . . . Rights are always found to be related to certain conditions. Obligations alone remain independent of conditions. They belong to a realm situated above all conditions, because it is situated above this world. (NR, pp. 3f)

Such a view ran contrary to the mainstream of western individualism by questioning the validity of basing modern democracy on the will of sovereign individuals as expressed in law or contract. While not denying the rights of individuals, Weil wished to place them in the context of a conception of justice deriving from ancient Greek and Hindu conceptions of society: throughout her discussion of needs she referred to the concepts of limit, balance and proportion that had been so central to her Marseilles *Notebooks*. In her view, the current political and social confusion of France (and the rest of the world) arose from the legacy of 1789, which had tried to turn the idea of rights, which was simply a human convention and thus dependent on particular circumstances, into an absolute principle. Since rights were only effective when there was equality of force, they could not protect the individual against the collective. Unlike obligations, rights were strictly amoral as they could be used for evil just as much as for good; and rights were bound up with the concept of person and personality that Weil found deeply unsatisfactory.[14] By contrast, the obligation which existed 'towards every human being for the sole reason that he or she *is* a human being' (NR, pp. 4f) was not based on any convention but on the common consent accorded by the universal conscience. Although the foundation of this obligation was not to be discovered in this world, the exercise of it definitely was: 'The fact that a human being possesses an eternal destiny imposes only one obligation: respect. The obligation is only performed if the respect is effectively expressed in a real, not a fictitious, way; and this can only be done through the medium of Man's earthly needs' (NR, p. 6). The question of what sort of a collectivity could best serve these earthly needs was the topic of the rest of the book.

Before embarking on this discussion, Weil offered a list of what these 'earthly needs' might be. The physical needs for food, protection against violence, housing, clothing, heating, hygiene and medical attention were easily enumerated: the parallel needs for ensuring the life of the soul were less easy to define. Weil's list was offered as a counterpoint to the various declarations of rights that were current in the Resistance movements to which she was supposed to be responding.[15] Needless to say, Weil's emphasis was very different from that of her colleagues. She stressed the limited nature of needs and arranged them in pairs to balance each other. Not surprisingly, given the state of contemporary France, she began with the need for order to lessen the confusion and incompatibility existing between obligations. Such an order had its image in the order and beauty of the natural world and in great works of art. Her first pair of needs was liberty and obedience. Liberty, the ability to choose, had to be limited by rules among those living in a community; but if the rules were sufficiently stable, general, limited in number and, above all, understood by all to be useful and necessary, then 'the liberty of men of goodwill, though limited in the sphere of action, is complete in that of conscience' (NR, p. 13). The mainspring of obedience was not fear of punishment or hope of reward but consent; and consent could only be given to rulers who were accountable. The need for equality was balanced by the need for a symbolic hierarchy such as the British monarchy. Equality 'consists in a recognition, at once public, general, effective and genuinely expressed in institutions and customs, that the same amount of respect and consideration is due to every human being because this respect is due to the human being as such and is not a matter of degree' (NR, p. 15). Unbridled equality of opportunity could make social life fluid to the point of decomposing it and, with money as the main motive of action, the poison of inequality had been introduced everywhere. A balanced society would impose burdens and risks proportionate to the power and well-being of individuals: an employer who was guilty of an offence against an employee ought to be made to suffer far more than an employee guilty of an offence against an employer. Equality would be much advanced in a society in which different human conditions were regarded as being, not more or less than one another, but simply other with miner and minister being simply regarded as two different vocations, like those of poet and mathematician.

Thus far Weil had been following the agenda of 1789, though from a very different perspective. She added two further, less obvious, pairs of needs. The first was the need for honour, where 'each of the social organisms to which a human being belongs allows him to share in a noble tradition enshrined in its past history and given public acknowledgement' (NR, p. 19). Social oppression was the enemy of such a need in that in contemporary society 'the sometimes incredible heroism displayed by miners or fishermen barely awakes an echo among miners or fishermen themselves' (ibid.). It was even worse for groups such as ex-convicts and immigrant workers who had been placed outside the social pale and totally deprived of respect. Crime alone should place anyone outside the social pale and there was a need for punishment to bring the criminal back into the chain of eternal obligations that bound society together. And there was a need for punishment to be harsher higher up the social scale. In her second pair of needs, Weil felt that the need for security against the threat of unemployment, police persecution and foreign invasion should be complemented by the need for risk which would avoid boredom, heighten courage, and enable individuals to confront their obligations. Weil also mentioned the need for both private property, particularly of homes and tools of trade, and for collective property at all levels of society.

Weil's views were at their most controversial in her discussion of the needs for freedom of opinion and for truth. She devoted as much space to these as to all the others put together. She began with a ringing declaration that 'complete, unlimited freedom of expression for every sort of opinion, without the least restriction or reserve, is an absolute need on the part of the intelligence' (NR, p. 22). This was supplemented with the bizarre suggestion that there should be a type of publication in which it would be possible to find all the arguments in favour of bad causes in which anyone could sing the praises of what they most condemned, such publications contributing a sort of preliminary tabulation of data concerning social problems. More importantly, however, Weil thought that publications destined to influence public opinion about the conduct of life should not be permitted to deny the eternal obligations towards human beings once these had been solemnly recognised by law. The entire daily and weekly press, as well as reviews and literature, should be subject to this constraint. Her reason was that she felt attempts to influence opinion to be acts and should be as subject to the law as any other type of act. People had a need for truth, the most sacred of all needs. They were to a large extent in the hands of professional writers and broadcasters. If these were convicted of intentional falsehood, they should be punished. What Weil was concerned to safeguard was the freedom of the intellect to which she felt modern techniques of propaganda and advertisement were radically hostile. Thus 'repression could be exercised against the press, radio broadcasts, or anything else of a similar kind, not only for offences against moral principles publicly recognised, but also for baseness of tone and thought, bad taste, vulgarity or a subtly corrupting moral atmosphere' (NR, p. 25). And, since freedom of opinion could be claimed only by individuals (who had opinions) and never collectives (which did not), the banning of newspapers was permitted in severe cases; individual journalists could carry on publishing their work elsewhere.

Mention of the collective led Weil on to the startling view that 'no group should be permitted by law to express an opinion' (NR, p. 26), since a group tended always to impose its opinion on its members. This, in turn, led to the familiar suggestion of the suppression of political parties. The type of party strife prevalent under the Third Republic ended in the single party, which was the worst evil of all. Organisations concerned with the defence of interests, and particularly trade unions, were different. The right to strike should be safeguarded and lock-outs punished by law. The main principle with regard to associations was that 'what has been called freedom of association has been, in fact, up to now, freedom for associations. But associations have not got to be free; they are instruments, they must be held in bondage. Only the human being is fit to be free' (NR, p. 31). Weil was aware that, especially in this area, she was confronted by the old problem of the impartiality of the judges. The only guarantee of this was that they should be intelligent, drawn from very different social circles, and recipients of a spiritual as well as a legal education.

Some of Weil's discussion of human needs may seem decidedly eccentric; but it is important to remember their historical context. Although she thought her ideas had a general application, they were conceived as a contribution to the transition from the Third to the Fourth Republic. She shared a widespread view that certain forms of literature had, just as much as corrupt parliamentarism, played a part in preparing the collapse of 1940:[16] and her views on the control of newspapers were influenced by her contempt not only for the Vichy press but also by the way in which the unbridled licence of pre-war journalism had driven innocent individuals to suicide.[17] Above all she was aware that her proposals could only be understood and implemented in a society which had realised its most pressing need – the need for roots, which was the subject of the rest of the book.

Weil began her discussion of uprootedness with a definition of what it meant to be rooted. 'A human being', she wrote, 'has roots by virtue of his real, active and natural participation in the life of a community which preserves in living shape certain particular treasures of the past and certain particular expectations for the future' (NR, p. 41). While military conquests and deportations were obviously destructive of roots, Weil pointed to two less obvious contemporary sources. The first was money, which turned desire for gain into the sole motive and had a force outweighing all other motives, since 'the effort it demands of the mind is so very much less. Nothing is *so* clear and *so* simple as a row of figures' (NR, p. 42). The second was the modern system of education which consisted of taking 'a culture very strongly directed towards and influenced by technical science, very strongly tinged with pragmatism, extremely broken up by specialisation, entirely deprived both of contact with this world and, at the same time, of any window opening onto the world beyond' (NR, p. 43) and shovelling its residue into the minds of the unfortunate individuals desirous of learning, much as you fed birds with a stick. The resulting uprootedness was the most dangerous malady to which human societies were exposed, since it was self-propagating, in that the uprooted tended to uproot others. Rome and Israel in the past, contemporary Germany and the whole European colonial enterprise were examples of this truth. In such a desperate situation, the only hope for the future had to be drawn from the past, since 'we possess no other life, no other living sap, than the treasures stored up from the past and digested, assimilated and created afresh by us' (NR, p. 49). The destruction of the past was perhaps the greatest of all crimes.

After this overview of the question, Weil turned her attention to the problem as it was found in urban industrial centres. Here she drew very much on her own experience and writings of the 1930s. The current demands of the workers – the closed shop, for example, or nationalisation – were indicators of what they were suffering rather than genuine remedies. The advent of the electronic age and of automated machinery presented opportunities for decentralised co-operative production and workers' control of the production process. But this could only be achieved, as Marx had seen, if technical research concentrated more on the needs of the workers than on those of the factory. A lack of a good apprentice system and thus of qualified workers had contributed as much as anything to the downfall of France. But the integration of the working class into society demanded much more: a reform of education and indeed of the whole contemporary idea of culture which was no more than 'an instrument manipulated by teachers for manufacturing more teachers, who, in their turn, will manufacture still more teachers' (NR, p. 65). What was needed was an effort, not of popularisation but of translation, an effort which she herself had made for the workers at Rosières. The truths of geometry could be made comprehensible through the work-place and absolutely first-class works of literature were most accessible to ordinary people since 'it is the people which has the truest, most direct experience of what this human condition is' (NR, p. 67). The unusual mingling of intellectuals with working people occasioned by the war and the Resistance afforded an opportunity not to be missed. In sum, 'the abolition of the proletarian lot, chiefly characterised by uprootedness, depends upon the creation of forms of industrial production and culture of the mind in which workmen can be, and be made to feel themselves to be, at home' (NR, p. 69). And a long-term project for achieving this would probably include the abolition of large factories and joint-stock companies and a transfer of the ownership of machines to co-operatives. Together with machinery, the state should ensure that each workman owned a house and a little land. School and further education should be closely integrated with the work process, with working hours reduced accordingly. Such a form of social existence would be neither capitalist nor socialist. It would be long and difficult to achieve but a start could at least be made on its pre-condition, the dispersal of industrial activity.[18]

Uprootedness in the towns was accompanied by uprootedness in the countryside, which was less evident because of the contempt felt by city-dwellers for the peasantry. The alienation of the French peasant from the rest of society, the depopulation of the land and the colonial attitude of city to country could only be cured by the transfer of land ownership exclusively to those who worked it, whether privately or co-operatively. Equally important was a reform of education in the countryside. Firstly, rural schools should have their own curriculum, in which a major part was occupied both by those aspects of the natural sciences particularly concerned with rural life and also by the poetry and folklore of the peasants themselves. Secondly, the old quarrel between Church and State over education should be overcome. Weil recognised that this was a difficult problem. Religion had played a dominant role, except quite recently in certain parts of Europe, in the development of human culture, thought and civilisation, and an education course that made no reference to it was absurd. It should be possible to discuss Christianity and other genuine currents of religious thought without pronouncing for or against specific dogmas. These two reforms would help establish in the countryside, as in the towns, that dignity of work which Weil felt to be so vital, since 'if we go to the heart of things, there is no true dignity without a spiritual root and consequently one of a supernatural order' (NR, p. 90). The creation of a civilisation founded upon the spiritual nature of work was the peculiar mission of our age. There were hints of it in Rousseau, Sand, Tolstoy, Proudhon, Marx and Papal Encyclicals. The welding of these together would contribute the only original thought of our age – but one which was essential to prevent the re-emergence of totalitarianism.

The central, longest, and most impressive part of *The Need for Roots* deals with the uprootedness caused by the rise of the nation as, together with money, the only bond of attachment between individuals. This was Weil's contribution to the lively debate among the London Free French as to the nature of their patriotism and how, if at all, it differed from nationalism.[19] According to her, the nation had replaced the increasingly nuclear family, professional associations, and local communities as the focus of the loyalty of its citizens. In June 1940, the nation itself had been allowed to evaporate. Now a new form of patriotism was needed. Before the advent of the modern nation-state, patriotism had indeed existed, but it had not been territorially defined. A historical analysis was therefore needed to discover how patriotism had been deformed over the centuries and how its true spirit might be rediscovered.

Weil's idiosyncratic view of French history, insightful and eccentric by turns, fits into a tradition of writing about the history of France in an attempt to discover its true identity.[20] The defeat of 1870 and the subsequent Paris Commune, the Dreyfus affair, and now, even more radically, the collapse of 1940 produced differing interpretations of the historical antecedents of these events and conflicting definitions of the 'real' France. Weil's own interpretation is based on her general scepticism of the received version of history as written by the victors. Indeed she considered the view of history as progress to be a symptom of the very illness she was discussing – uprootedness. To rediscover the spirit of true patriotism, Weil looked to the past; but it was in 'the past which is inarticulate, anonymous, which has vanished' (NR, p. 222) that it resided.

Weil found the obstacle to a genuine patriotism above all to be, firstly, the degeneration of the French monarchy into a despotism after the death of Charles V, a despotism that reached its height with Richelieu and Louis XIV and which aroused widespread, intense and continuous hatred among the people, culminating in the regicide of 1793, and, secondly, the fact that several of the lands owing obedience to the King of France regarded themselves as conquered territory and were treated as such – the Languedoc being only the most striking example. The Revolution melted all the peoples subject to the French crown into a single mass; but, instead of returning to the revolutionary tradition of d'Aubigné, Théophile de Viau and Retz, 'the influence of the Encyclopaedists, all of them uprooted intellectuals', ensured that the revolution was founded on 'the most violent break with the country's past' (NR, p. 105). The genuinely patriotic sentiments aroused in 1789 were finally extinguished with the Paris Commune of 1870. National sovereignty was seen to be a myth, the workers were treated almost as outcasts, and the Third Republic reinforced the alienation between government and people so characteristic of the previous centuries.

Weil undoubtedly exaggerated the uprooting nature of French central-isation (at least until the twentieth century), but her main theme is the rise of the state as object of patriotic feeling. It is here that she is at her most impressive, as supreme anti-nationalist and opponent of central political bonding to the State as some superior sort of entity. She had always hated the State and it was in the substitution of state for nation that she saw the long-term cause of France's present disastrous situation. Although Weil was somewhat contradictory as to when the French State actually began, she usually attributes it to Richelieu and she was insistent that the cause of the present situation of France was 'the very self-same inhuman, brutal, bureaucratic, police-ridden State bequeathed by Richelieu to Louis XIV, by Louis XIV to the Convention, by the Convention to the Empire, and by the Empire to the Third Republic' (NR, p. 122). By a horrible paradox, 'the state is a cold concern which cannot inspire love, but itself kills, suppresses everything that might be loved; so one is forced to love it, because there is nothing else' (NR, p. 109). The result was that, while there was a tendency before 1940 to talk idolatrously of 'eternal France', at the same time 'no Frenchman had the slightest qualms about robbing or cheating the State in the matter of customs, taxes, subsidies or anything else' (NR, p. 115). The development of the State had exhausted the country on which it battened and France had become the curious phenomenon of a democracy in which all public institutions were hated and despised by the entire population.

It was against this historical background that Weil worked out her own idea of patriotism, rejecting both a nationalist chauvinism and a bland pacifist universalism. She herself had a deep love for France, particularly its art and culture, but she had seen enough of some sections of the Resistance, particularly the thuggery of Colonel Passy's Bureau Central de Renseignement et d'Action, to see the danger of its becoming Fascist; for, after all, 'Fascism is always connected with a certain variety of patriotic feeling' (NR, p. 141). According to this feeling, France was something to be loved 'for her glory, her prestige, her brilliance, her conquests, her influence, her future expansion' (EL, p. 54). Such a patriotism, particularly when connected with the brutalities of colonial-ism, was difficult to distinguish from that of Hitler. This false patriotism became more insidious when given religious overtones, as in the work of Péguy. On this point, at least, Richelieu

> showed a much clearer perception when he said that the salvation of States was only brought about in this world. France is something which is temporal, terrestrial. Unless I am mistaken, it has never been suggested that Christ died to save nations. The idea of a nation being chosen by God for itself simply belongs to the old Mosaic law (NR, p. 125)

From this perspective 'Joan of Arc's popularity during the past quarter of a century was not an altogether healthy business: it was a convenient way of forgetting that there is a difference between France and God' (NR, p. 126). But it was Joan of Arc who used to say that she felt pity for the realm of France; and it was this sentiment, peculiarly appropriate under present misfortunes, that could form the basis of a new patriotism, since 'this poignantly tender feeling for some beautiful, precious, fragile and perishable object has a warmth about it which the sentiment of national grandeur altogether lacks' (NR, p. 164). Patriotism would involve a disassociation of the idea of the country from that of the State and a profound reform of the nation's institutions.

In the last part of her book Weil turned to what these reforms might be and the opportunities for a new politics offered by the present circumstances. The whole is rather nebulous and evidently unfinished, as it trails off into a long discussion of the relations of science and religion. Like her heroes, Plato and Rousseau, Weil began with the importance of education. She saw the Free French, since they possessed as yet no governmental authority over the French people, as being in an unrivalled position for educating and setting the tone for postwar France in the way that they expressed themselves and the methods of action that they adopted. Above all the relation of means to ends must constantly be borne in mind since power was to politics what a piano was to musical composition: there was a danger that any political movement would confuse the manufacture of a piano with the composition of a sonata. Government itself was a work of art and the education of a whole people could only be based on a conception of civilisation which

> must not be sought in the past, which only contains imperfect models; far less still in our dreams of the future, which are necessarily as mediocre as we ourselves are, and consequently vastly inferior to the past. The inspiration for such an education must be sought, like the method itself, among the truths eternally inscribed in the nature of things. (NR, p. 209)

In her opinion, there were four obstacles to such a civilisation: a false conception of greatness, a degradation of justice, the worship of money, and the absence of religion. The false conception of greatness viewed history as inevitable progress and tended to glorify force. Since history was written by the powerful, and the vanquished (unless they had the possibility of revenge) were forgotten, a correct appreciation of history required a very careful reading between the lines. Her own reading was sometimes highly intuitive: she was certain that the Druidic culture of Gaul was superior to that of its Roman conquerors and that the Trojans possessed a level of civilisation far higher than that of their Greek opponents. Weil was not against change, but against the worship of progress and force as such which brought dishonour on goodness by turning it into a question of fashion. On the criterion of greatness employed in most accounts of history there was no reason not to call Hitler 'great'. Culture, too, had been influenced by the false conception of greatness.[21] Rather in the spirit of Benda, she read French literature as a long *trahison des clercs*. In poetry, those who escaped her censure were Villon, Scève, d'Aubigné, Viau, Lamartine, Vigny, Nerval and Mallarmé, with most enthusiasm reserved for the first and the last. In prose, she picked out Rabelais, Montaigne, Descartes, Retz, Molière, Montesquieu and Rousseau. All of these writers had, for Weil, a saintly quality since, as Thibon, wrote, 'She links genius and sanctity and wherever she finds genius she concludes, without bothering about historical evidence, that there must be sanctity.'[22] Talent could be put to the service of any cause; but genius was one with holiness.

With such a false conception of history dominant, it was not surprising that the idea of justice – 'behaving exactly as though there were equality when one is stronger in an unequal relationship' (WG, p. 86) – was also degraded: 'where force is absolutely sovereign, justice is absolutely unreal' (NR, p. 232). Weil connected this outlook with the rise of modern science and the misguided attempts to reconcile it with a form of humanism; one such attempt was utilitarianism, which 'rests upon the supposed existence of a wonderful little piece of mechanism thanks to which force, on entering into the sphere of human relations, becomes an automatic producer of justice' (NR, p. 231). Another attempt was classical economic liberalism with its belief that, 'in order to possess this property of being an automatic producer of justice, force must take the form of money to the exclusion of all use either of arms or of political power' (ibid.). In Marxism force was equated with history, and justice was relegated to an epoch beyond class struggle. These errors were only possible in a civilisation that was vitiated by the overweening position accorded to modern science. Scientists were as subject as any other profession to the pressures of career, prestige, and fashion.[23] People were ready to question everything these days, but never science. Most scientists were interested in the successful technical application of their discoveries and not in their good or evil effects. This was another instance of false greatness: here again, the value of the product could be assessed from the motive of its creation. Since the Renaissance the very conception of science had been that of a branch of study whose object was placed beyond good and evil. Weil was not against the scientific endeavour as such: what she opposed was the false prestige given to science under the illusion that it could, of itself, ever deliver any sort of genuine meaning or truth to life.[24] Truth was an aspect of absolute goodness and only to be approached through a kind of loving attention that was quite different from a desire to acquire knowledge.

This false conception of the nature of science had been facilitated by a decline in genuine religion. From Pascal's feeble 'proofs' of what he had already determined to be the case, to Bergson's praise of religion as a kind of pink pill guaranteeing increased vitality, religion had been deprived of its role as companion and complement to scientific investigation. Stupid doctrines about miracles and divine Providence had only enhanced the opposition between religion and science. The solution was not to be found in relegating religion to a 'private' affair, since that would simply compound the difficulty. What Weil wanted to do was to rethink all aspects of society in terms of religion in its basic sense of the production of meaning by linking all aspects of life to an Absolute. But this did not mean subjecting society to some sort of religious control: the corrupting influence of Rome on Christianity had already shown what sort of noxious fruits such an approach yielded. The problem was to rediscover a sense of the sacred, not as something separate but as an atmosphere bathing the whole of society which it enlightened but did not dominate. Such a religion was entirely compatible with science, whose true definition was 'the study of the beauty of the world'. Fundamentally, the object of religion and science was identical: the unity of the established order of the universe: 'it is one and the same thing, which with respect to God is eternal Wisdom; with respect to the universe, perfect obedience; with respect to our love, beauty; with respect to our intelligence, balance of necessary relations; with respect to our flesh, brute force' (NR, p. 281). Scientific investigation, therefore, was only one form of religious contemplation.

With these remarks on religion, *The Need for Roots* ends rather inconclusively. It is important to remember that it is an unfinished work, and Weil would no doubt have wanted to improve its sometimes awkward construction. At the same time, it does represent the summation of her thought, recapitulating her favourite themes: her biting criticism of the view of history as progress; her antipathy to Rome and Israel; her admiration for the Greeks; the mistaken dominance given to science in contemporary society; her strong connection of art and literature with moral values; the centrality accorded to physical labour; her unwillingness to consider political institutions, however democratic, as the main legitimisers of the distribution of power; her awareness of the danger of all collective activity; her insistence that genuine liberty and equality could only be founded by reference to other-worldly values. Running through all these views is the idea that the main source of uprooting and destruction is the divorce of thought from action, a divorce which Weil herself had tried to overcome in theory and practice since her earliest years. Her sharpened sense of her own failure to do so was soon to be the death of her. *The Needs for Roots* returned to her passionate interest in politics of ten years earlier, but refracted through her later religious experience. Being so comprehensive, it contains, as Perrin observed, 'both the best and the worst' of her thought.[25]

It is extremely difficult to characterise the kind of politics that Weil is advocating in *The Need for Roots*. This is partly because it is stronger on the historical sources of uprooting than on its rather vague view of the future. As Mounier wrote:

> It is difficult to imagine any text that is apparently less political. But there is none which leads us in a more pressing manner to reflect on what is and what is not *political*, to ask ourselves whether there is not some permanent blackmail on this subject on the part of those who have the inclination and interest to preserve a certain sort of politics as being the only serious one.[26]

Weil's book is at one remove from contemporary politics: it is a sort of prolegomenon to political life. As Eliot wrote in his Introduction to the English translation: 'This is one of those books which ought to be studied by the young before their leisure has been lost and their capacity for thought destroyed in the life of the hustings and the legislative assembly; books the effect of which, we can only hope, will become apparent in the attitude of mind of another generation' (NR, p. xii).

But, despite the book's prefatory nature, some commentators have seen Weil's ideas as modelled largely on the Vichy regime and even as verging on Fascism.[27] Leaving aside the question of how Fascist Vichy really was,[28] Weil made it quite clear that, while she did not reject some of the slogans of Vichy, she wished, unlike Vichy, to make them into a reality (cf. NR, p. 158). And it was rather to the inspirational potential of the Free French in London that she looked to achieve this.[29] Nor did Weil have much in common with those who wished to restore the imagined idyllic life of the Middle Ages and the traditional approach to history of the French Right. If she went back anywhere, it was to the Greeks. She did not share Barrès's worship of the earth and the dead and her conceptions of hierarchy and order were far from those of

Maurras and the *Action Française*. It is true that Weil shared with such authors their anti-liberalism and their preference for a spiritual over an economic revolution.[30] But the anti-liberalism was common to most sections of the Resistance and the spiritual revolution of French Fascism was based on a concept of military virility that was quite anathema to Weil, whose roots were not in the earth and the dead but in the supernatural. She was careful to point out that 'love of the past has nothing to do with any reactionary political attitude' (NR, p. 49). On the contrary, Weil's whole project was to recover from the past those spiritual weapons that would present a firm barrier to the reappearance of totalitarianism in the future.

The second 'Testament' does, nevertheless, represent a sharp shift of emphasis from the *Oppression and Liberty* of 1934. She is still profoundly interested in politics – indeed *The Need for Roots* contains more than *Oppression and Liberty* on the detail of how political power should be exercised. But she is now concerned to place this politics in the context of a new culture. She is still concerned with an order that will not fall victim to totalitarianism, still as opposed to any centralised state power, still advocating a strong liberty of choice with as few laws as possible, and still utopian in the sense of proposing measures whose realisation she did not think immediately possible. But she has modified her pre-war individualism, is less inclined to question the material bases of inequality, and has replaced talk of revolt with that of consent to an organisation of society based no longer on the enlightened goodwill of individuals but on contact with the supernatural and divine grace. *The Need for Roots* is about the preservation of the *metaxus* as bridges leading to the supernatural; 'the metaxus are the region of good and of evil . . . no human being should be deprived of these relative and mixed goods (home, country, traditions, culture, etc.) which warm and nourish the soul and without which, apart from sanctity, a human life is impossible'.[31] Her pre-war disgust with politics has now been replaced by a religious perspective that gives meaning and hope to political activity.

While she was completing *The Need for Roots*, Weil's health and morale were deteriorating. Nevertheless, for all that she worked and wrote with such grim intensity, she could still enjoy London and the company of her friends. On Sundays she would go to Hyde Park to watch the people listening to the speakers, 'the last remaining trace in any white country, and perhaps in the world, of the discussions in the Athenian Agora which Socrates frequented' (SL, p. 181). She went to see performances of *Twelfth Night* and *King Lear*. She was 'enchanted by the altogether special atmosphere of the pubs in working-class districts'. Indeed, she claimed that there was 'no break in continuity between Shakespeare's drinking scenes and the atmosphere of the London pubs today' (ibid.), one among several impressions of the power of tradition in England which reinforced her views in *The Need for Roots*. On Sundays, too, she would go to the Brompton Oratory with Schumann, but separated from him at the door as she wished to pray alone. She would then go on to have lunch with her friends the Rosins, German refugees with whom she had stayed in Switzerland in February 1934 when recovering from her stint at Alsthom. Professor Fehling, who was staying with the Rosins and had also met her in Switzerland, found that her rather extreme and forced attitudes of ten years earlier had disappeared: her life seemed more harmonious and she was more open to discussion. She would also visit the Closons, where she was friendly and affectionate, particularly with the children. But there was always the same refusal of almost any food, not, it seemed to Louis Closon, in a morbid or vexatious manner but simply because she could not do otherwise.[32] Her most constant companion was Simone Deitz, and they had some fun together. While Weil tried to teach her friend Tibetan so that she would be able to read Milarepa in the original, Deitz tried to teach Weil how to drive – with the disastrous result that her pupil's clumsiness and short-sightedness made only too predictable. Once they went camping near London in the grounds of a convent. It rained hard and the tent let water. Deitz accepted the hospitality of the nuns: Weil preferred to spend a cold, wet and sleepness night in the tent. On another occasion, they went boating on the Serpentine and Weil teased her friend so much by rocking the boat that they both fell into the water.

But such episodes were short and uncharacteristic. During March, Weil's physical well-being and her morale began an irreversible decline. She talked of a 'deadly chagrin' at ever having left Marseilles, and that is what it proved to be. When Jacques Kaplan came over from America, he found a very different person from the young woman he had got to know on the *Serpa Pinto*: 'She was worn out and tense; she seemed remote and it was impossible to make contact with her' (C, p. 236). She had doubts about whether what she was doing would have any effect whatsoever. 'Why', asked Philip, 'doesn't she tackle something concrete, such as trade union problems, instead of wallowing in generalities?' (P, p. 530). However much someone like Camus might think that 'it is impossible to imagine a re-birth of Europe which does not take account of the requirements laid down by Simone Weil',[33] it had little to do with the immediate preoccupations of Hill Street: Mounier was surely right in remarking about *The Need for Roots* that, 'if it ever got to its destination, one can easily see the knowing smiles with which it must have been greeted in the offices'.[34] When the Resistance did finally publish, in August, its Declaration of the Rights of the Individual and the Citizen, it incorporated many of the formulations that Weil had been at such pains to oppose.[35] Moreover she felt that she had arrived in London three years too late: she was ill at ease at having recently joined what was now the winning side, and disgusted with the petty rivalries and jockeying for position that went with it.[36] Even with her friends the Closons she avoided talk of Free French politics because it was too divisive.

It was now clear even to her that her *idée fixe* of the Front-Line nurses would never be accepted. She tried instead to get herself selected for some sort of sabotage mission inside France. As in New York, she turned to Schumann and wrote him a long letter appealing for his help to persuade the Bureau Central de Renseignement et d'Action, responsible for clandestine operations in France, to take her on. Pathetically, she rehearsed her tactics for resisting torture and her readiness to offer her life unconditionally for any service. But, as with the nurses project, it was not the practical side that was most important for Weil: life for her had never meant anything but a threshold to the revelation of truth, and 'a Christian knows that a single thought of love, lifted up to God in truthfulness, even though mute and without echo, is more useful even in this world than the most splendid action' (SL, p. 178). The attainment of truth through total sacrifice she felt to be no less than a command of God. She wrote, 'I have always had the fear of failing, not in my life, but in my death. This fear has never ceased to grow more and more intense' (ibid.). Her tone is desperate:

> I feel an ever-increasing sense of devastation, both in my intellect and in the centre of my heart, at my inability to think with truth at the same time about the affliction of men, the affection of God, and the link between the two . . . I am outside the truth; no human agency can bring me to it; and I am inwardly certain that God will not bring me to it except in that way. (Ibid.)

Schumann could get her to London, but he could not get her to France. The decision rested with Cavaillès, who spent a lot of time in clandestine work in occupied France (he was later shot by the Gestapo) and whom she had known from her time at the Ecole Normale, where he had taught philosophy. He refused to accede to her wishes, thinking such acts of gratuitous heroism, however noble, were entirely misplaced in the sort of work in which the Resistance was engaged. The last straw for Weil was when Simone Deitz was accepted for a mission. Although the mission was subsequently aborted, it demonstrated to her how impossible of realisation were her own deepest desires.

At the same time, Weil's personal preoccupation with religion was as strong as ever. She attended Mass almost daily at the Jesuit church in Farm Street near her office. For some time she had felt it an injustice on the part of the Church to refuse anyone the sacraments and she herself felt 'an intense and ever-increasing desire for Communion'. With her last letter to Schumann she enclosed an article she had written on 'The Theory of the Sacraments', which saw the presence of Christ in the consecrated bread as God's convention for bridging the gulf that would otherwise have existed between desire and reality (cf. WG, pp. 66ff). And she drew an explicit parallel between this and the only too evident gulf existing between her desire to go to France and the reality of her situation. Although she did not consider herself outside the Church as a source of sacramental life but only outside it as a social reality, her position in the Resistance was rather the reverse. In Farm Street her desires could become reality: in Hill Street they were beating in a void.

Probably the last thing Weil wrote before being hospitalised was a short statement of her religious position. She entrusted it to Simone Deitz to show to various priests of her acquaintance. The statement began: 'I believe in God, the Trinity, the Incarnation, Redemption, the Eucharist, and the teachings of the Gospel' (GaG, p. 72). What she meant here by belief, she continued, was that, 'through love, I hold on to the perfect, unseizable truth which these mysteries contain, and that I try to open my soul to it so that its light may penetrate into me' (ibid.). The Church, moreover, did not have the right to limit the operations of the intelligence or to insist upon the truth of what were only commentaries on the central mysteries; the only task incumbent on the Church was that of 'formulating judgements on a few essential points, but only as a guideline for the faithful' (ibid.). To baptise someone holding such views would constitute a profound rupture with seventeen centuries of tradition. Weil made it absolutely clear that she was not asking for baptism, but felt 'the need, not abstract but practical, real and urgent, to know whether, if I did ask, it would be granted or refused' (GaG, p. 74). Both her preoccupation with the question of baptism and her attitude towards its pre-conditions had remained unchanged since Perrin first broached the subject two years earlier in Marseilles.

The impossibility of her position in London weighed more and more heavily on Weil. She wrote to Schumann:

The work I am doing here will be arrested before long by a triple limit. First, a moral limit; because the ever-increasing pain of feeling that I am not in my right place will end in spite of myself, I fear, by crippling my thought. Second, an intellectual limit; obviously my thought will be arrested when it tries to grasp the concrete, for lack of an object. Third, a physical limit; because my fatigue is growing. (SL, pp. 177f)

Before long, her prediction was fulfilled. Sleeping only three hours a night, plagued by a return of her headaches, and eaten up by remorse (the feeling she dreaded above all others), she finally collapsed. On 15

April, Simone Deitz called in to see her at her office in Hill Street. Weil was not there and had also been absent the previous day. Going to Portland Road, Deitz found her unconscious on the floor. On being revived with a little brandy, Weil broke into tears: 'It's all over now. I'll be taken to hospital.' And the same day she was indeed taken into the Middlesex Hospital, off the Tottenham Court Road. She was diagnosed as tubercular in both lungs and was constantly feverish. After three days she consented to be moved to a private room, but only on being assured that she was contagious. The doctor predicted a recovery, given complete rest and adequate food. She was too weak to feed herself and had to be helped by the nurse. But she ate very little. Rations in Occupied France had been reduced even further that month and Weil, as usual, did not want to be an exception.

After a few weeks she recovered some strength and began to read the *Gita* in Sanskrit. And she had frequent visitors. Thérèse Closon came to see her two or three times a week. Simone Deitz, the Rosins and Mrs Francis came often. Closon and Schumann saw her when they were not abroad. She continued to write to her parents as regularly as before, pretending to be still living in her lodgings, at work in Hill Street, and enjoying the hottest early summer within living memory. She talked fondly of the London pubs, of roast lamb with mint sauce and roast pork with apple sauce as her favourite dishes and was careful to put the Portland Road address on the back of the envelope. Her writing was still as firm and regular as ever, which must have demanded great effort, given how weak is the contemporaneous handwriting in her notebook.

Soon after entering the hospital, Weil had asked to see a priest and Deitz brought her René de Naurois, who was Chaplain to the Free French. He visited her three or four times during May and June, staying about half an hour on each occasion. Weil feverishly and disjointedly rehearsed the points she had made so strongly in her *Letter to a Priest*, beginning with the question of the fate of non-baptised infants. De Maurois felt that there was an air of unreality to their discussions and found difficulty in coping with the style of her thought, which was

> highly abstract and abstruse, of a rapid dialectic, and very 'feminine', under which I could feel deep instincts and tacit decisions perhaps hardly reflected upon, and which appeared to me to be travesty, dressed up in 'rationalisation' (as the modern psychologists say); in short, a thought that was elusive and at the same time prodigiously rich, which could not manage to grasp and formulate itself satis-factorily, and which would not accept fixed starting points from which to advance (or retreat). (C, p. 340)

At the same time, he was struck by her complete humility and loyalty: 'The essential thing in my memory of her is the feeling, so strong and free of any admixture, which I had in her presence: the feeling of an extraordinarily pure and generous soul, to whom precisely because of its strength and rectitude the Lord had seemingly refused the tokens of Joy and Peace' (P, p. 523). Weil asked for a blessing; she did not ask to be baptised. To Deitz she said: 'If one day I am completely deprived of will and in a coma, then I should be baptised' (SWNYL, p. 71). Some time after de Naurois's visits Deitz did indeed take some water from the tap, pour it on her friend's head, and pronounce the baptismal formula.[37] Weil merely remarked: 'You can do it; it can't do any harm' (P, p. 498). Her attitude to her own baptism seems to have remained unchanged.

When she entered the hospital, the doctors had expected that she would be able to leave it in about two months. London, as she wrote to her parents, was covered in blossom. In April von Paulus had capitulated at Stalingrad and, with the capture of the remains of Rommel's forces in Tunisia in May, the way was open for the re-entry of the Allied Forces into Europe via Sicily in July. But, as victory for the Allies appeared on the horizon, Weil's prospects of recovery began to vanish. By mid-June she was no better than when she had entered the hospital and she asked her friends to help get her transferred to a sanatorium. She felt stifled in the atmosphere of the hospital and, although she got on well with the nurses, quarrelled with her doctor, who found her the most difficult patient with whom he had ever had to deal. The main cause of her decline was that she did not eat enough to arrest the advance of the tuberculosis. In a sense, of course, she had been killing herself all her life. But, in spite of the Coroner's eventual verdict, it would be wrong to call Weil's attitude suicidal in the strict sense. Up to a few days before her death she was envisaging that she might eventually be released from hospital and rejoin her parents (cf. P, p. 531). And none of her friends, except for Mrs Rosin, thought her suicidal. She herself had often condemned suicide (cf. FLN, p. 212). It seems probable that she had developed a disorder of her digestive system which made eating physically very difficult and painful. More fundamentally, she was unwilling to eat when, as she thought, so many in France were starving. Even this was not an act of deliberate privation but more a communion with France by natural abstention.[38] This was her kind of obedience and any outcome was equally welcome. As she had written a few months earlier:

The eternal part of the soul feeds on hunger. When we do not eat, our organism consumes its own flesh and transforms it into energy. It is the same with the soul. The soul which does not eat consumes itself. The eternal part consumes the mortal part of the soul and transforms it. The hunger of the soul is hard to bear, but there is no other remedy for our disease. (FLN, p. 286)[39]

At the end of July, Weil broke completely with the Free French. Resentful of their near-total neglect of her work, she was disgusted at the political manoeuvring in North Africa as de Gaulle sought for predominance there, and at what she saw as the emergence of a Gaullist political party. She asked her parents to tell Souvarine that 'I did not have, do not have, and, I hope, never will have (I'd rather sleep under bridges) any responsibility for anything – either for good or evil' (SL, p. 192). She resigned from her post with the Free French and confirmed her resignation in a long and passionate letter to Closon. Given that they refused to send her on any mission into Occupied France, 'I do not have, I cannot have, and I do not wish to have any direct or indirect or even very indirect, connection with the French Resistance' (P, p. 529f). Philip, she continued, had complained that he could not make use of her intellect. But

> all intellects wholly, exclusively surrendered and consecrated to the truth cannot be utilised by any human being, even by the person in which it resides. I myself cannot utilise my own intelligence; so how could I put it at Philip's disposal? It is my intelligence that utilises me, and it obeys without reserve – at least I hope that is so – what seems to be the light of truth. It obeys day by day, instant by instant and my will never has any influence on it. Such people, I believe, don't really have anything in common with Ministers, even Ministers like Philip. (P, p. 530f)

She added a postscript: 'I am finished, broken, beyond all possibility of mending, and that independent of Koch's bacilli. The latter have only taken advantage of my lack of resistance and, of course, are busy demolishing it a little further' (P, p. 531). When Schumann came to visit her at the end of July on his return from Algeria, her resentment spilled over and they quarrelled violently. She reproached him with the degeneration, as she saw it, of the Free French; in his radio broadcasts he was far too kind to the Soviet regime, simply because they were allies; above all, he had failed to get her into France. She would not forbid him to come and see her, but she would never talk to him again. And indeed their last meeting was a silent one: he had brought her Vercors's famous Resistance novel, *The Silence of the Sea*; she returned it without so much as looking at it.

She had now abandoned any *raison d'être*. She still concealed her whereabouts from her parents, asking for news of Sylvie and her 'sunny laughter' and sending them a marvellously acute and funny description of the 'pure cockney' cleaners. But in the last substantial letter that she wrote to her parents her bitterness and resignation were clearly revealed. 'I have a sort of growing inner certainty', she wrote, 'that there is within me a deposit of pure gold which must be handed on. Only I become more and more convinced, by experience and by observing my contemporaries, that there is no one to receive it . . . This does not distress me at all. The mine of gold is inexhaustible' (SL, pp. 196f). In one of her articles for the Free French she had written movingly about the 'folly of love' (EL, pp. 56f). Now to her mother she pointed out the essential affinity between herself and the fools of Shakespeare's tragedies:

> In Shakespeare the fools are the only people who tell the truth . . . there is a class of people in this world who have fallen into the lowest degree of humiliation, far below beggary, and who are deprived not only of all social considerations but also, in everybody's opinion, of the specific human dignity, reason itself – and these are the only people who, in fact, are able to tell the truth. All the others lie. (SL, pp. 200f)

The fact that she herself was reputed to be so intelligent only served to add irony to tragedy. This was her last message to a world that had failed to understand her.

By mid-August, it was arranged that she should be transferred to the Grosvenor in Ashford, Kent. The doctors at the Middlesex were only too pleased to see the back of such a recalcitrant patient. At first the Director of the Sanatorium, Dr Roberts, had refused to take her on the grounds that the sanatorium catered mainly for industrial workers and she would not feel at home there. Little did he know that here, at least, he was in a position to fulfil one of Weil's life-long desires. In the event, his French mother-in-law, Mrs Jones, who had come to visit Weil twice in the Middlesex, prevailed on him to take her. On 17 August Weil supervised the packing of her books – Plato, the *Gita*, Saint John of the Cross – and left for Ashford in an ambulance, accompanied by Thérèse Closon. Before leaving, she scribbled a short note to her parents: 'Very little time or inspiration for letters now. They will be short, erratic, and far between. But you have another source of consolation . . . Au revoir, darlings. Heaps and heaps of love' (SL, p. 201). She had only one week to live.

Once again the staff at the sanatorium tried to make her eat. She made every effort,[40] but could take very little and her thoughts wandered to the food of her youth. She asked Thérèse Closon when she came to see her to make her a potato puree like her mother used to. She also requested a bread-and-butter soup and a French roll, and even asked the sanatorium to hire a French cook. She knew she was dying. She was waiting for the instant of death, 'the centre and object of life . . . the instant when, for an infinitesimal fraction of time, pure truth, naked, certain and eternal enters the soul' (WG, p. 16). Her last visitor was Simone Deitz, to whom she said: 'Like me, you are a piece that God has cut out badly. But I soon will no longer be cut out; I shall be re-attached and united' (SWNYL, p. 86). When she first saw her room in the sanatorium, she murmured: 'What a beautiful place in which to die!' The room was on the first floor, with a view over a wide lawn and fields. Beyond the hills on the horizon lay Folkestone, the sea, and France.

Tuesday 24 August was a warm summer's day. As Simone Weil lay in her bed, her mind moved beyond the distant hills. She saw again the Paris in which she grew up, the cafes of the Boulevard St Michel, her paper-strewn room in the spacious flat of the rue Auguste Comte, with its view over Paris as far as the Sacré Cœur, at the Lycée Henri IV where she listened to the thoughts of Alain, and the Ecole Normale with its passionate political commitments. She saw again her school in quiet Le Puy, her little class in the summer house at Roanne, and the workers of Saint-Etienne with their red flag. She saw again the grinding factories of Alsthom and Renault, the miserable little room in the rue Lecourbe, and the joyful days of the Popular Front. She saw the Abbey of Solesmes beside its quiet river and heard the Gregorian chant. She saw the flat in Marseilles with the sound of the sea and the cries from the beach coming in through the open windows; soft-voiced Perrin weeping in his white robes and earthy Thibon philosophising among his vines. She saw New York and the Hudson River and her anxious, waiting parents. She saw London with its parks, its pubs, its telegrams, and its anger. And she saw Ashford with its trees and green fields on which the sun was declining. At half past five she fell into a coma. At half past ten her heart stopped beating and she died.

The inquest was held on 27 August and the Coroner's verdict was 'cardiac failure due to myocardial degeneration of the heart muscles due to starvation and pulmonary tuberculosis . . . The deceased did kill and slay herself by refusing to eat whilst the balance of her mind was disturbed'. The *Tuesday Express* of Ashford published a report on its front page, under the headline 'French Professor starves herself to death'. The *Kent Messenger*'s story ran with the title 'Death from starvation. French Professor's curious sacrifice'. There were nine people present at the funeral at Ashford New Cemetery on 30 August: Maurice Schumann, Simone Deitz, Thérèse and Louis Closon, Mrs Rosin and Professor Fehling, Suzanne Aron, Mrs Francis and Mrs Jones. Perhaps appropriately, the priest who had been asked to officiate missed the train and Maurice Schumann read the prayers, with Thérèse Closon giving the responses. Mrs Francis laid a bouquet of red roses tied with a tricolour in the grave. When she left home her son John noticed that the ribbon was the wrong way up: 'No, Mummy: *this* is the French side; don't put the English side up.' She was buried, again fittingly, in that part of the cemetery which formed the border between the Catholic and the Jewish sections. For fifteen years it remained an anonymous grave, without inscription. The inhabitants of Ashford considered it a pauper's grave.

Conclusion

'To believe in God is not a decision that we can make. All we can do is to decide not to give our love to false gods.' (SNL, p. 148)

When Simone Weil died in 1943 she had only a few published articles to her name and was only known in restricted circles: a handful of revolutionary syndicalists, the *Cahiers du Sud* circle in Marseilles, a few disciples of Alain. The unfinished and paradoxical character of her writings, together with the piecemeal nature of their publication, has meant that her subsequent reputation has been very varied. It was the appearance in the late 1940s of the first two collections of her writings that brought her to the attention of a wide public. These were Perrin's edition of some of her letters and articles written for him, entitled *Waiting for God* and Thibon's selection from her *Notebooks*, entitled *Gravity and Grace*. These collections very much reflected the inclinations of both editors and presented only a partial view of Weil's thought, since they concentrated on her dialogue with Catholicism. The letters and articles in *Waiting for God* come from the period when she was at her closest to Catholicism; and Thibon's selection reinforced the impression of Perrin's book by largely excluding Weil's extended meditations on Greek philosophy, on science, and on comparative religion. Thus the first guise in which Weil appeared to the world was as some sort of Catholic mystic, slightly *manquée*.

As such her influence on the Church around the time of the Second Vatican Council was considerable. Pope John XXIII was impressed by her writings. His biographer tells us that while, as Cardinal Roncalli, he was Nuncio in Paris,

> he wrote to her father with the idea of visiting the austere room – it had a sleeping bag but no bed – where she used to work. He read *La Connaissance Surnaturelle* and greatly admired it. He was moved by her final note which begins 'I believe in God, the Trinity, the Incarnation, the Redemption, the Eucharist and the Gospel . . .' but then explains why she must remain 'on the threshold of the Church'. Roncalli treasured this text, and gave a copy of it to Cardinal Augustine Bea before it was published in 1962.[1]

His successor, Paul VI, is said to have counted Weil, together with Pascal and Bernanos, as one of the three most important influences on his intellectual development.[2]

But as more details of her early life became known, Weil seemed less of a latter-day version of Saint John of the Cross than a contemporary follower of Tolstoy: the same urge to put evangelical principle immediately into practice, the desire to engage in manual labour, the attempt to reject privilege and share the lot of the poor, the yearning for a reactionary socialist Utopia. At the same time, the sharpness of her social analysis became clear. With the publication, under the editorship of Albert Camus, of some of her earlier political writings, Simone Weil emerged as a contemporary political theorist. In such works as *Oppression and Liberty* she appeared as the very prototype of the Révoltés so vividly portrayed in Camus's own book, *The Rebel*, the practitioner of a lucid and active pessimism. Her starting-point was the syndicalist movement which, according to Camus,

> started from a concrete basis, the living cell on which the organism builds itself . . . The revolution of the twentieth century, on the contrary, claims to base itself on economics, but is primarily political and ideological. Despite its pretentions, it begins in the absolute and attempts to mould reality. Rebellion, inversely, relies on reality to assist it in its perpetual struggle for truth.[3]

As such, Weil was the very opposite of any abstract, ethereal thinker. This firm anchorage in economic and social reality rather than political ideology enabled her to produce analyses of state socialism of the Soviet model and of Nazism that were to be the keystone of Arendt's *Origins of Totalitarianism*, as well as of the more contemporary reflections of such writers as Castoriadis. Her searching exposures of the psychological and material bases of power are akin to those of Foucault. And the relevance of her critique increases with the power of technocracy and the centralisation of the modern state.

Nevertheless Weil remains *peculiar*. This French version of Kafka, this cross between Pascal and Orwell remains unclassifiable. She is intellectually stateless, a prophet without any country in which she can be sure of honour. A Catholic Jewess who criticised implacably both traditions, she is a voice crying in the wilderness, an outsider, the patron saint of all outsiders. Many of the discussions of Weil have concentrated on the peculiarities of her life and particularly of her psyche, and tended to obscure her thought. Thought is, of course, inseparable from life and the context of Weil's writings (so many of which are *pièces d'occasion*) is vital for their understanding. But facile judgements of her character have often led to equally facile judgements of her work. The cruel (and inaccurate) skits on her in such novels as Bataille's *Le Bleu du Ciel* and de Beauvoir's *Le Sang des Autres* have left their mark. More seriously, to many she has seemed to suffer from some deep-seated psychological disorder. Weil has, for example, frequently been called anorexic; and it is true that hunger and nourishment are the dominant metaphors in her writings. But she showed none of the obsessive concern with her body that characterises anorexia; quite the reverse. As Robert Coles has well remarked, her hunger was for God, not for a slim waistline. Nor will it do to label her a masochist. She had her own perceptive comment to make about that:

> Believe that reality is love, while seeing it exactly as it is. Love what is intolerable. Embrace what is made of iron, press one's flesh against the metallic harshness and chill. This is not any kind of masochism. What excites masochists is only the semblance of cruelty, because they don't know what cruelty is. In any case what one has to embrace is not cruelty, it is blind indifference and brutality. (FLN, p. 260)

For Weil pain was neither an end in itself nor a means to produce pleasure. In the early part of her life she desired to share the sufferings of others by, for example, living on five francs a day like the unemployed, working in the factory, or fighting in Spain; and later she meditated long on the link between suffering and love. In her own words, 'I believe in the value of suffering, so long as one makes every (legitimate) effort to escape it' (FLN, p. 3). Her conception of what was legitimate in this connection was, it is true, extremely strict. But this did not make her into a gloom-laden dolorist. She was perfectly content to indulge herself in cigarettes, books and trips to Italy. And the witness of her friends and family show her considerable capacity for humour and gaiety. At the same time, she had a strong sense of her own peculiar vocation: 'I haven't in me the energy to undergo pain and to suffer except when an inner necessity drives me that I feel I cannot avoid without betraying myself . . . if I were so weak as to retreat before the harshness of the life that awaits me I know that I could then never do anything else' (P, p. 433). If Weil imposed an abnormally harsh life upon herself, it was not because she was in love with suffering, but because, she felt, the suffering would enable her to love.

It is also Weil's conception of love that puts her at odds with the dominant attitudes of our age and makes her appear abnormal. She was certainly no prude and remarkably tolerant towards the amours of others. But, as far as she herself was concerned, her rejection of sexual love and indeed of almost any physical contact was unyielding. She saw sex as bound up with passion that generated illusion and with power that precluded equality. As a woman, she felt handicapped in doing many of the things she wished to do – and minimised her femininity by adopting asexual garments. Again, it was, for her, a question of vocation. She wrote to one of her pupils: 'I can tell you that when, at your age, and later on too, I was tempted to try to get to know love, I decided not to – telling myself that it was better not to commit my life in a direction impossible to foresee until I was sufficiently mature to know what, in a general way, I wish from life and what I expect from it' (SL, p. 13). In the event, she held as firmly to chastity (together with poverty and obedience) as any in a religious order. This attitude was of a piece with the rest of her life, since 'every attachment is of the same nature as sexuality. In that, Freud is right (but only that)' (FLN, p. 287). Weil was simply not a joiner, whether of Party, Church or herself to anyone else. For friendship, on the other hand, she had the very highest regard and felt it to be a vital need. Friendship was, for her, one of the implicit forms of the love of God. She liked to quote the Pythagorean saying, 'Friendship is an equality made of harmony'. Here, too, she emphasised the importance of distance:

> All friendship is impure if even a trace of the wish to please, or the contrary desire to dominate is found in it. In a perfect friendship these two desires are completely absent. The two friends have fully consented to be two and not one, they respect the distance which the fact of being two distinct creatures places between them. Man has the right to desire direct union with God alone. (WG, p. 135)

It is noticeable that in her marvellous letters to her friends it is those of farewell that are the most expressive of her feelings.

With such an abnormal personality, it is inevitable that psychological factors should retain our attention. But, unless we are going to adopt a crude psychological reductionism, the more interesting question is the use which she made of such factors. It is her life, not her psyche, that is the essential counterpart to her thought. Weil feared, with some justification, that the peculiarities of her personality would obscure her message:

> If no one consents to take any notice of the thoughts which, though I cannot explain why, have settled in so inadequate a being as myself, they will be buried with me. The fact that they happen to be in me prevents people from paying any attention to them. It is a great sorrow for me to fear that the thoughts which have come down into me should be condemned to death through the contagion of my inadequacy and wretchedness. I never read the story of the barren fig tree without trembling. I think that is a portrait of me. (WG, p. 46f)

Here she is unduly pessimistic. Morbid and perverse to some, to those with a deeper sympathy her very intensity gives to her life and thought a kind of personal authority which commands respect. She had no time for hagiography. As she wrote to Schumann shortly before her death:

> I don't want you to do me the injustice of imagining that I affect saintliness. Above all I don't want at any price that you should think better of me than the truth allows. I can tell you very plainly my position as regards saintliness. It seems to me that saintliness is, if I dare say so, the minimum for a Christian. But by a conspiracy as old as Christianity itself, and stronger with each century, this truth has been concealed, along with several others equally uncomfortable. There exist in fact dishonest merchants, cowardly soldiers, etc., and also people who have chosen to love Christ but who are infinitely below the level of sanctity. Of course I am one of them. (SL, p. 175)

Whatever may be the case with regard to sanctity, the characteristic of Weil most often mentioned by those who knew her well is the lack of any gap between her thought and her action. The drama of her life, as of her thought, was her continual search for the absolute and her continual disappointment. This could lead her into absurd situations, such as some of her efforts at manual labour or her myopic soldiering in the Spanish Civil War. It could also lead to absurd intellectual conceptions, such as her idea that Christ must have delivered the Our Father in Greek, her insistence that the Jewish religion was necessarily allied to the politics of the Gush Emunim, or her fantastic account of the progeny of Noah. With her vertigo of the absolute, it is not surprising that she sometimes found it difficult to keep her balance on the ground. But such aberrations should not be allowed to divert attention from the central thrust of her work, or to obscure the fragmentary brilliance of her writings which illuminate so many areas of the human condition. Reversing Péguy's famous dictum, her *politique* ended in *mystique*. But, for her, contemplation was not a means of stopping a nauseating world and getting off, but of seeing the world in a different and truer perspective and, above all, of developing a sharp eye and ear for the traces of God in all human activity and experience. And, like all mystics, her last word was silence, the silence of God more real than any sound:

> I cannot conceive the necessity for God to love me, when I feel so clearly that even with human beings affection for me can only be a mistake. But I can easily imagine that He loves that perspective of creation which can only be seen from the point where I am. But I act as a screen. I must withdraw so that He may see it.

Appendix: Simone Weil, 'On Human Personality'

'You do not interest me.' No man can say these words to another without committing a cruelty and offending against justice.

'Your person does not interest me.' These words can be used in an affectionate conversation between close friends, without jarring upon even the tenderest nerve of their friendship.

In the same way, one can say without degrading oneself, 'My person does not count', but not 'I do not count'.

This proves that something is amiss with the vocabulary of the modern trend of thought known as Personalism. And in this domain, where there is a grave error of vocabulary it is almost certainly the sign of a grave error of thought.

There is something sacred in every man, but it is not his person. Nor yet is it the human personality. It is this man; no more and no less.

I see a passer-by in the street. He has long arms, blue eyes, and a mind whose thoughts I do not know, but perhaps they are commonplace.

It is neither his person, nor the human personality in him, which is sacred to me. It is he. The whole of him. The arms, the eyes, the thoughts, everything. Not without infinite scruple would I touch anything of this.

If it were the human personality in him that was sacred to me, I could easily put out his eyes. As a blind man he would be exactly as much a human personality as before. I should have destroyed nothing but his eyes.

It is impossible to define what is meant by respect for human personality. It is not just that it cannot be defined in words. That can be said of many perfectly clear ideas. But this one cannot be conceived either; it cannot be defined nor isolated by the silent operation of the mind.

To set up as a standard of public morality a notion which can neither be defined nor conceived is to open the door to every kind of tyranny.

The notion of rights, which was launched into the world in 1789, has proved unable, because of its intrinsic inadequacy, to fulfil the role assigned to it.

To combine two inadequate notions, by talking about the rights of human personality, will not bring us any further.

What is it, exactly, that prevents me from putting that man's eyes out if I am allowed to do so and if it takes my fancy?

Although it is the whole of him that is sacred to me, he is not sacred in all respects and from every point of view. He is not sacred in as much as he happens to have long arms, blue eyes, or possibly commonplace thoughts. Nor as a duke, if he is one; nor as a dustman, if that is what he is. Nothing of all this would stay my hand.

What would stay it is the knowledge that, if someone were to put out his eyes, his soul would be lacerated by the thought that harm was being done to him.

At the bottom of the heart of every human being, from earliest infancy until the tomb, there is something that goes on indomitably expecting, in the teeth

273

of all experience of crimes committed, suffered, and witnessed, that good and not evil will be done to him. It is this above all that is sacred in every human being.

The good is the only source of the sacred. There is nothing sacred except the good and what pertains to it.

This profound and childlike and unchanging expectation of good in the heart is not what is involved when we agitate for our rights. The motive which prompts a little boy to watch jealously to see if his brother has a slightly larger piece of cake arises from a much more superficial level of the soul. The word justice means two very different things according to whether it refers to the one or the other level. It is only the former one that matters.

Every time that there arises from the depths of a human heart the childish cry which Christ himself could not restrain, 'Why am I being hurt?', then there is certainly injustice. For if, as often happens, it is only the result of a misunderstanding, then the injustice consists in the inadequacy of the explanation.

Those people who inflict the blows which provoke this cry are prompted by different motives according to temperament or occasion. There are some people who get a positive pleasure from the cry; and many others simply do not hear it. For it is a silent cry, which sounds only in the secret heart.

These two states of mind are closer than they appear to be. The second is only a weaker mode of the first; its deafness is complacently cultivated because it is agreeable and it offers a positive satisfaction of its own. There are no other restraints upon our will than material necessity and the existence of other human beings around us. Any imaginary extension of these limits is seductive, so there is a seduction in whatever helps us to forget the reality of the obstacles. That is why upheavals like war and civil war are so intoxicating; they empty human lives of their reality and seem to turn people into puppets. That is also why slavery is so pleasant to the masters.

In those who have suffered too many blows, in slaves for example, that place in the heart from which the infliction of evil evokes a cry of surprise may seem to be dead. But it is never quite dead; it is simply unable to cry out any more. It has sunk into a state of dumb and ceaseless lamentation.

And even in those who still have the power to cry out, the cry hardly ever expresses itself, either inwardly or outwardly, in coherent language. Usually, the words through which it seeks expression are quite irrelevant.

That is all the more inevitable because those who most often have occasion to feel that evil is being done to them are those who are least trained in the art of speech. Nothing, for example, is more frightful than to see some poor wretch in the police court stammering before a magistrate who keeps up an elegant flow of witticisms.

Apart from the intelligence, the only human faculty which has an interest in public freedom of expression is that point in the heart which cries out against evil. But as it cannot express itself, freedom is of little use to it. What is first needed is a system of public education capable of providing it, so far as possible, with means of expression; and next, a régime in which the public freedom of expression is characterised not so much by freedom as by an attentive silence in which this faint and inept cry can make itself heard; and finally, institutions are needed of a sort which will, so far as possible, put power into the hands of men who are able and anxious to hear and understand it.

Clearly, a political party busily seeking, or maintaining itself in, power can discern nothing in these cries except a noise. Its reaction will be different according to whether the noise interferes with or contributes to that of its own propaganda. But it can never be capable of the tender and sensitive attention which is needed to understand its meaning.

The same is true to a lesser degree of organisations contaminated by party influences; in other words, when public life is dominated by a party system, it is true of all organisations, including, for example, trade unions and even churches.

Naturally, too, parties and similar organisations are equally insensitive to intellectual scruples.

So when freedom of expression means in fact no more than freedom of propaganda for organisations of this kind, there is in fact no free expression for the only parts of the human soul that deserve it. Or if there is any, it is infinitesimal; hardly more than in a totalitarian system.

And this is how it is in a democracy where the party system controls the distribution of power; which is what we call democracy in France, for up to now we have known no other. We must therefore invent something different.

Applying the same criterion in the same way to any public institution we can reach equally obvious conclusions.

It is not the person which provides this criterion. When the infliction of evil provokes a cry of sorrowful surprise from the depth of the soul, it is not a personal thing. Injury to the personality and its desires is not sufficient to evoke it, but only and always the sense of contact with injustice through pain. It is always, in the last of men as in Christ himself, an impersonal protest.

There are also many cries of personal protests, but they are unimportant; you may provoke as many of them as you wish without violating anything sacred.

So far from its being his person, what is sacred in a human being is the impersonal in him.

Everything which is impersonal in man is sacred, and nothing else.

In our days, when writers and scientists have so oddly usurped the place of priests, the public acknowledges, with a totally unjustified docility, that the artistic and scientific faculties are sacred. This is generally held to be self-evident, though it is very far from being so. If any reason is felt to be called for, people allege that the free play of these faculties is one of the highest manifestations of the human personality.

Often it is, indeed, no more than that. In which case it is easy to see how much it is worth and what can be expected from it.

One of its results is the sort of attitude which is summed up in Blake's horrible saying: 'Sooner murder an infant in its cradle than nurse unacted desires', or the attitude which breeds the idea of the 'gratuitous act.' Another result is a science in which every possible standard, criterion, and value is recognised except truth.

Gregorian chant, Romanesque architecture, the *Iliad*, the invention of geometry were not, for the people through whom they were brought into being and made available to us, occasions for the manifestation of personality.

When science, art, literature, and philosophy are simply the manifestation of personality they are on a level where glorious and dazzling achievements are possible, which can make a man's name live for thousands of years. But above this level, far above, separated by an abyss, is the level where the highest things are achieved. These things are essentially anonymous.

It is pure chance whether the names of those who reach this level are preserved or lost; even when they are remembered they have become anonymous. Their personality has vanished.

Truth and beauty dwell on this level of the impersonal and the anonymous. This is the realm of the sacred; on the other level nothing is sacred, except in the sense that we might say this of a touch of colour in a picture if it represented the Eucharist.

What is sacred in science is truth; what is sacred in art is beauty. Truth and beauty are impersonal. All this is too obvious.

If a child is doing a sum and does it wrong, the mistake bears the stamp of his personality. If he does the sum exactly right, his personality does not enter into it at all.

Perfection is impersonal. Our personality is the part of us which belongs to error and sin. The whole effort of the mystic has always been to become such that there is no part left in his soul to say 'I'.

But the part of the soul which says 'We' is infinitely more dangerous still.

Impersonality is only reached by the practice of a form of attention which is rare in itself and impossible except in solitude; and not only physical but mental solitude. This is never achieved by a man who thinks of himself as a member of a collectivity, as part of something which says 'We'.

Men as parts of a collectivity are debarred from even the lower forms of the impersonal. A group of human beings cannot even add two and two. Working out a sum takes place in a mind temporarily oblivious of the existence of any other minds.

Although the personal and the impersonal are opposed, there is a way from the one to the other. But there is no way from the collective to the impersonal. A collectivity must dissolve into separate persons before the impersonal can be reached.

This is the only sense in which the person has more of the sacred than the collectivity.

The collectivity is not only alien to the sacred, but it deludes us with a false imitation of it.

Idolatry is the name of the error which attributes a sacred character to the collectivity; and it is the commonest of crimes, at all times, at all places. The man for whom the development of personality is all that counts has totally lost all sense of the sacred; and it is hard to know which of these errors is the worst. They are often found combined, in various proportions, in the same mind. But the second error is much less powerful and enduring than the first.

Spiritually, the struggle between Germany and France in 1940 was in the main not a struggle between barbarism and civilisation or between evil and good, but between the first of these two errors and the second. The victory of the former is not surprising; it is by nature the stronger.

There is nothing scandalous in the subordination of the person to the collectivity; it is a mechanical fact of the same order as the inferiority of a gram to a kilogram on the scales. The person is in fact always subordinate to the collectivity, even in its so-called free expression.

For example, it is precisely those artists and writers who are most inclined to think of their art as the manifestation of their personality who are in fact the most in bondage to public taste. Hugo had no difficulty in reconciling the cult of the self with his role of 'resounding echo'; and examples like Wilde, Gide, and the Surrealists are even more obvious. Scientists of the same class are equally enslaved by fashion, which rules over science even more despotically than over the shape of hats. For these men the collective opinion of specialists is practically a dictatorship.

The person, being subordinate to the collective both in fact and by the nature of things, enjoys no natural rights which can be appealed to on its behalf.

It is said, quite correctly, that in antiquity there existed no notion of respect for the person. The ancients thought far too clearly to entertain such a confused idea.

The human being can only escape from the collective by raising himself above the personal and entering into the impersonal. The moment he does this, there is something in him, a small portion of his soul, upon which nothing of the collective can get a hold. If he can root himself in the impersonal good so as to be able to draw energy from it, then he is in a condition, whenever he feels the obligation to do so, to bring to bear without any outside help, against any collectivity, a small but real force.

There are occasions when an almost infinitesimal force can be decisive. A collectivity is much stronger than a single man; but every collectivity depends for its existence upon operations, of which simple addition is the elementary example, which can only be performed by a mind in a state of solitude.

This dependence suggests a method of giving the impersonal a hold on the collective, if only we could find out how to use it.

Every man who has once touched the level of the impersonal is charged with a responsibility towards all human beings: to safeguard, not their persons, but whatever frail potentialities are hidden within them for passing over to the impersonal.

It is primarily to these men that the appeal to respect the sacredness of the human being should be addressed. For such an appeal can have no reality unless it is addressed to someone capable of understanding it.

It is useless to explain to a collectivity that there is something in each of the units composing it which it ought not to violate. To begin with, a collectivity is not someone, except by a fiction; it has only an abstract existence and can only be spoken to fictitiously. And, moreover, if it were someone it would be someone who was not disposed to respect anything except himself.

Further, the chief danger does not lie in the collectivity's tendency to immolate himself in the collective. Or perhaps the first danger is only a superficial and deceptive aspect of the second.

Just as it is useless to tell the collectivity that the person is sacred, it is also useless to tell the person so. The person cannot believe it. It does not feel sacred. The reason that prevents the person from feeling sacred is that actually it is not.

If there are some people who feel differently, who feel something sacred in their own persons and believe they can generalise and attribute it to every person, they are under a double illusion.

What they feel is not the authentic sense of the sacred but its false imitation engendered by the collective; and if they feel it in respect of their own person it is because it participates in collective prestige through the social consideration bestowed upon it.

So they are mistaken in thinking they can generalise from their own case. Their motive is generous, but it cannot have enough force to make them really see the mass of people as anything but mere anonymous human matter. But it is hard for them to find this out, because they have no contact with the mass of people.

The person in man is a thing in distress; it feels cold and is always looking for a warm shelter.

But those in whom it is, in fact or in expectation, warmly wrapped in social consideration are unaware of this.

That is why it was not in popular circles that the philosophy of personalism originated and developed, but among writers, for whom it is part of their profession to have or hope to acquire a name and a reputation.

Relations between the collectivity and the person should be arranged with the sole purpose of removing whatever is detrimental to the growth and mysterious germination of the impersonal element in the soul.

This means, on the one hand, that for every person there should be enough room, enough freedom to plan the use of one's time, the opportunity to reach ever higher levels of attention, some solitude, some silence. At the same time the person needs warmth, lest it be driven by distress to submerge itself in the collective.

If this is the good, then modern societies, even democratic ones, seem to go about as far as it is possible to go in the direction of evil. In particular, a modern factory reaches perhaps almost the limit of horror. Everybody in it is constantly harassed and kept on edge by the interference of extraneous wills while the soul is left in cold and desolate misery. What man needs is silence and warmth; what he is given is an icy pandemonium.

Physical labour may be painful, but it is not degrading as such. It is not art; it is not science; it is something else, possessing an exactly equal value with art and science, for it provides an equal opportunity to reach the impersonal stage of attention.

To take a youth who has a vocation for this kind of work and employ him at a conveyor-belt or as a piece-work machinist is no less a crime than to put out the eyes of the young Watteau and make him turn a grindstone. But the painter's vocation can be discerned and the other cannot.

Exactly to the same extent as art and science, though in a different way, physical labour is a certain contact with the reality, the truth, and the beauty of this universe and with the eternal wisdom which is the order in it.

For this reason it is sacrilege to degrade labour in exactly the same sense that it is sacrilege to trample upon the Eucharist.

If the workers felt this, if they felt that by being the victim they are in a certain sense the accomplice of sacrilege, their resistance would have a very different force from what is provided by the consideration of personal rights. It would not be an economic demand but an impulse from the depth of their being, fierce and desperate like that of a young girl who is being forced into a brothel; and at the same time it would be a cry of hope from the depth of their heart.

This feeling, which surely enough exists in them, is so inarticulate as to be indiscernible even to themselves; and it is not the professionals of speech who can express it for them.

Usually, when addressing them on their conditions, the selected topic is wages; and for men burdened with a fatigue that makes any effort of attention painful it is a relief to contemplate the unproblematic clarity of figures.

In this way, they forget that the subject of the bargain, which they complain they are being forced to sell cheap and for less than the just price, is nothing other than their soul.

Suppose the devil were bargaining for the soul of some poor wretch and someone, moved by pity, should step in and say to the devil: 'It is a shame for you to bid so low; the commodity is worth at least twice as much.'

Such is the sinister farce which has been played by the working-class movement, its trade unions, its political parties, its leftist intellectuals.

This bargaining spirit was already implicit in the notion of rights which the men of 1789 so unwisely made the keynote of their deliberate challenge to the world. By so doing, they ensured its inefficacy in advance.

The notion of rights is linked with the notion of sharing out, of exchange, of measured quantity. It has a commercial flavour, essentially evocative of legal claims and arguments. Rights are always asserted in a tone of contention; and when this tone is adopted, it must rely upon force in the background, or else it will be laughed at.

There are a number of other notions, all in the same category, which are themselves entirely alien to the supernatural but nevertheless a little superior to brute force. All of them relate to the behaviour of the collective animal, to use Plato's language, while it still exhibits a few traces of the training imposed on it by the supernatural working of grace. If they are not continually revived by a renewal of this working, if they are merely survivals of it, they become necessarily subject to the animal's caprice.

To this category belong the notion of rights, and of personality, and of democracy. As Bernanos had the courage to point out, democracy offers no defence against dictatorship. By the nature of things, the person is subdued to the collectivity, and rights are dependent upon force. The lies and misconceptions which obscure this truth are extremely dangerous because they prevent us from appealing to the only thing which is immune to force and can preserve us from it: namely, that other force which is the radiance of the spirit. It is only in plants, by virtue of the sun's energy caught up by the green leaves and operating in the sap, that inert matter can find its way upward against the law of gravity. A plant deprived of light is gradually but inexorably overcome by gravity and death.

Among the lies in question is the eighteenth-century materialists' notion of natural right. We do not owe this to Rousseau, whose lucid and powerful spirit was of genuinely Christian inspiration, but to Diderot and the Encyclopedists.

It was from Rome that we inherited the notion of rights, and like everything that comes from ancient Rome, who is the woman full of the names of blasphemy in the Apocalypse, it is pagan and unbaptisable. The Romans, like Hitler, understood that power is not fully efficacious unless clothed in a few ideas, and to this end they made use of the idea of rights, which is admirably suited to it. Modern Germany has been accused of flouting the idea; but she invoked it *ad nauseam* in her role of deprived, proletarian nation. It is true, of course, that she allows only one right to her victims: obedience. Ancient Rome did the same.

It is singularly monstrous that ancient Rome should be praised for having bequeathed to us the notion of rights. If we examine Roman law in its cradle, to see what species it belongs to, we discover that property was defined by the *jus utendi et abutendi*. And in fact the things which the property owner had the right to use or abuse at will were for the most part human beings.

The Greeks had no conception of rights. They had no words to express it. They were content with the name of justice.

It is extraordinary that Antigone's unwritten law should have been confused with the idea of natural right. In Creon's eyes there was absolutely nothing that was natural in Antigone's behaviour. He thought she was mad.

And we should be the last people to disagree with him; we who at this moment are thinking, talking, and behaving exactly as he did. One has only to consult the text.

Antigone says to Creon: 'It was not Zeus who published that edict; it was not Justice, companion of the gods in the other world, who set such laws among men.' Creon tries to convince her that his orders were just; he accuses her of having outraged one of her brothers by honouring the other; so that the same honour has been paid to the impious and the loyal, to the one who died in the attempt to destroy his own country and the one who died defending it.

She answers: 'Nevertheless the other world demands equal laws.' To which he sensibly objects: 'There can be no equal sharing between a brave man and a traitor', and she has only the absurd reply: 'Who knows whether this holds in the other world?'

Creon's comment is perfectly reasonable: 'A foe is never a friend, not even in death.' And the little simpleton can only reply: 'I was born to share, not hate, but love.'

To which Creon, ever more reasonable: 'Pass, then, to the other world, and if thou must love, love those who dwell there.'

And, truly, this was the right place for her. For the unwritten law which this little girl obeyed had nothing whatsoever in common with rights, or with the natural; it was the same love, extreme and absurd, which led Christ to the Cross.

It was justice, companion of the gods in the other world, who dictated this surfeit of love, and not any right at all. Rights have no direct connexion with love.

Just as the notion of rights is alien to the Greek mind, so also it is alien to the Christian inspiration whenever it is pure and uncontaminated by the Roman, Hebraic, or Aristotelian heritage. One cannot imagine St. Francis of Assisi talking about rights.

If you say to someone who has ears to hear: 'What you are doing to me is not just', you may touch and awaken at its source the spirit of attention and love. But it is not the same with words like 'I have the right . . .' or 'you have no right to . . .' They evoke a latent war and awaken the spirit of contention. To place the notion of rights at the centre of social conflicts is to inhibit any possible impulse of charity on both sides.

Relying almost exclusively on this notion, it becomes impossible to keep one's eyes on the real problem. If someone tries to brow-beat a farmer to sell his eggs at a moderate price, the farmer can say: 'I have the right to keep my eggs if I don't get a good enough price.' But if a young girl is being forced into a brothel she will not talk about her rights. In such a situation the word would sound ludicrously inadequate.

Thus it is that the social drama, which corresponds to the latter situation, is falsely assimilated, by the use of the word 'rights', to the former one.

Thanks to this word, what should have been a cry of protest from the depth of the heart has been turned into a shrill nagging of claims and counter-claims, which is both impure and unpractical.

The notion of rights, by its very mediocrity, leads on naturally to that of the person, for rights are related to personal things. They are on that level.

It is much worse still if the word 'personal' is added to the word 'rights', thus implying the rights of the personality to what is called full expression. In that case the tone that colours the cry of the oppressed would be even meaner than bargaining. It would be the tone of envy.

For the full expression of personality depends upon its being inflated by social prestige; it is a social privilege. No one mentions this to the masses when haranguing them about personal rights. They are told the opposite; and their minds have not enough analytic power to perceive this truth clearly for themselves. But they feel it; their everyday experience makes them certain of it.

However, this is not a reason for them to reject the slogan. To the dimmed understanding of our age there seems nothing odd in claiming an equal share of privilege for everybody – an equal share in things whose essence is privilege. The claim is both absurd and base; absurd because privilege is, by definition, inequality; and base because it is not worth claiming.

But the category of men who formulate claims, and everything else, the men who have the monopoly of language, is a category of privileged people. They are not the ones to say that privilege is unworthy to be desired. They don't think so and, in any case, it would be indecent for them to say it.

Many indispensable truths, which could save men, go unspoken for reasons of this kind; those who could utter them cannot formulate them and those who could formulate them cannot utter them. If politics were taken seriously; finding a remedy for this would be one of its more urgent problems.

In an unstable society the privileged have a bad conscience. Some of them hide it behind a defiant air and say to the masses: 'It is quite appropriate that I should possess privileges which you are denied.' Others benevolently profess: 'I claim for all of you an equal share in the privileges I enjoy.'

The first attitude is odious. The second is silly, and also too easy.

Both of them equally encourage the people down the road of evil, away from their true and unique good, which they do not possess, but to which, in a sense, they are so close. They are far closer than those who bestow pity on them to an authentic good, which could be a source of beauty and truth and joy and fulfilment. But since they have not reached it and do not know how to, this good might as well be infinitely far away. Those who speak for the people and to them are incapable of understanding either their distress or what an overflowing good is almost within their reach. And, for the people, it is indispensable to be understood.

Affliction is by its nature inarticulate. The afflicted silently beseech to be given the words to express themselves. There are times when they are given none; but there are also times when they are given words, but ill-chosen ones, because those who choose them know nothing of the affliction they would interpret.

Usually, they are far removed from it by the circumstances of their life; but even if they are in close contact with it or have recently experienced it themselves, they are still remote from it because they put it at a distance at the first possible moment.

Thought revolts from contemplating affliction, to the same degree that living flesh recoils from death. A stag advancing voluntarily step by step to offer itself to the teeth of a pack of hounds is about as probable as an act of attention directed towards a real affliction, which is close at hand, on the part of a mind which is free to avoid it.

But that which is indispensable to the good and is impossible naturally is always possible supernaturally.

Supernatural good is not a sort of supplement to natural good, as we are told, with support from Aristotle, for our greater comfort. It would be nice if this were true, but it is not. In all the crucial problems of human existence the only choice is between supernatural good on the one hand and evil on the other.

To put into the mouth of the afflicted words from the vocabulary of middle values, such as democracy, rights, personality, is to offer them something which can bring them no good and will inevitably do them much harm.

These notions do not dwell in heaven; they hang in the middle air, and for this very reason they cannot root themselves in earth.

It is the light falling continually from heaven which alone gives a tree the energy to send powerful roots deep into the earth. The tree is really rooted in the sky.

It is only what comes from heaven that can make a real impress on the earth.

In order to provide an armour for the afflicted, one must put into their mouths only those words whose rightful abode is in heaven, beyond heaven, in the other world. There is no fear of its being impossible. Affliction disposes the soul to welcome and avidly drink in everything which comes from there. For these products it is not consumers but producers who are in short supply.

The test for suitable words is easily recognised and applied. The afflicted are overwhelmed with evil and starving for good. The only words suitable for them are those which express nothing but good, in its pure state. It is easy to discriminate. Words which can be associated with something signifying an evil are alien to pure good. We are criticising a man when we say: 'He puts his person forward'; therefore the person is alien to good. We can speak of an abuse of democracy; therefore democracy is alien to good. To possess a right implies the possibility for making good or bad use of it; therefore rights are alien to good. On the other hand, it is always and everywhere good to fulfil an obligation. Truth, beauty, justice, compassion are always and everywhere good.

For the aspirations of the afflicted, if we wish to be sure of using the right words, all that is necessary is to confine ourselves to those words and phrases which always, everywhere, in all circumstances express only the good.

This is one of the only two services which can be rendered to the afflicted with words. The other is to find the words which express the truth of their affliction, the words which can give resonance, through the crust of external circumstances, to the cry which is always inaudible: 'Why am I being hurt?'

For this, they cannot count upon men of talent, personality, celebrity, or even genius in the sense in which the word is usually employed, which assimilates it to talent. They can count only upon men of the very highest genius: the poet of the *Iliad*, Aeschylus, Sophocles, Shakespeare as he was when he wrote *Lear*, or Racine when he wrote *Phèdre*. There are not very many of them.

But there are many human beings only poorly or moderately endowed by nature, who seem infinitely inferior not merely to Homer, Aeschylus, Sophocles, Shakespeare and Racine but also to Virgil, Corneille and Hugo, but who nevertheless inhabit the realm of impersonal good where the latter poets never set foot.

A village idiot in the literal sense of the word, if he really loves truth, is infinitely superior to Aristotle in his thought, even though he never utters anything but inarticulate murmurs. He is infinitely closer to Plato than Aristotle ever was. He has genius, while only the word talent applies to Aristotle. If a fairy offered to change his destiny for one resembling Aristotle's he would be wise to refuse unhesitatingly. But he does not know this. And nobody tells him. Everybody tells him the contrary. But he must be told. Idiots, men without talent, men whose talent is average or only a little more, must be encouraged if they possess genius. We need not be afraid of making them proud, because love of truth is always accompanied by humility. Real genius is nothing else but the supernatural virtue of humility in the domain of thought.

What is needed is to cherish the growth of genius, with a warm and tender respect, and not, as the men of 1789 proposed, to encourage the flowering of talents. For it is only heroes of real purity, the saints and geniuses, who can help the afflicted. But the help is obstructed by a screen which is formed between the two by the men of talent, intelligence, energy, character, or strong personality. The screen must not be damaged, but put aside as gently and imperceptibly as possible. The far more dangerous screen of the collective must be broken by abolishing every part of our institutions and customs which harbours the party spirit in any form whatsoever. Neither a personality nor a party is ever responsive either to truth or to affliction.

There is a natural alliance between truth and affliction, because both of them are mute suppliants, eternally condemned to stand speechless in our presence.

Just as a vagrant accused of stealing a carrot from a field stands before a comfortably seated judge who keeps up an elegant flow of queries, comments and witticisms while the accused is unable to stammer a word, so truth stands before an intelligence which is concerned with the elegant manipulation of opinions.

It is always language that formulates opinions, even when there are no words spoken. The natural faculty called intelligence is concerned with opinion and language. Language expresses relations; but it expresses only a few, because its operation needs time. When it is confused and vague, without precision or order, when the speaker or listener is deficient in the power of holding a thought in his mind, then language is empty or almost empty of any real relational content. When it is perfectly clear, precise, rigorous, ordered, when it is addressed to a mind which is capable of keeping a thought present while it adds another to it and of keeping them both present while it adds a third, and so on, then in such a case language can hold a fairly rich content of relations. But like all wealth, this relative wealth is abject poverty compared with the perfection which alone is desirable.

At the very best, a mind enclosed in language is in prison. It is limited to the number of relations which words can make simultaneously present to it; and remains in ignorance of thoughts which involve the combination of a greater number. These thoughts are outside language, they are unformulatable, although they are perfectly rigorous and clear and although every one of the relations they involve is capable of precise expression in words. So the mind moves in a closed space of partial truth, which may be larger or smaller, without ever being able so much as to glance at what is outside.

If a captive mind is unaware of being in prison, it is living in error. If it has recognised the fact, even for the tenth of a second, and then quickly forgotten it in order to avoid suffering, it is living in falsehood. Men of the most brilliant intelligence can be born, live, and die in error and falsehood. In them, intelligence is neither a good, nor even an asset. The difference between more or less intelligent men is like the difference between criminals condemned to life imprisonment in smaller or larger cells. The intelligent man who is proud of his intelligence is like a condemned man who is proud of his large cell.

A man whose mind feels that it is captive would prefer to blind himself to the fact. But if he hates falsehood, he will not do so; and in that case he will have to suffer a lot. He will beat his head against the wall until he faints. He will come to again and look with terror at the wall, until one day he begins afresh to beat his head against it; and once again he will faint. And so on endlessly and without hope. One day he will wake up on the other side of the wall.

Perhaps he is still in a prison, although a larger one. No matter. He has found the key; he knows the secret which breaks down every wall. He has passed beyond what men call intelligence, into the beginning of wisdom.

The mind which is enclosed within language can possess only opinions. The mind which has learned to grasp thoughts which are inexpressible because of the number of relations they combine, although they are more rigorous and clearer than anything that can be expressed in the most precise language, such a mind has reached the point where it already dwells in truth. It possesses certainty and unclouded faith. And it matters little whether its original intelligence was great or small, whether its prison cell was narrow or wide. All that matters is that it has come to the end of its intelligence, such as it was, and has passed beyond it. A village idiot is as close to truth as a child prodigy. The one and the other are separated from it only by a wall. But the only way into truth is through one's own annihilation; through dwelling a long time in a state of extreme and total humiliation.

It is the same barrier which keeps us from understanding affliction. Just as truth is a different thing from opinion, so affliction is a different thing from suffering. Affliction is a device for pulverising the soul; the man who falls into it is like a workman who gets caught up in a machine. He is no longer a man but a torn and bloody rag on the teeth of a cog-wheel.

The degree and type of suffering which constitutes affliction in the strict sense of the word varies greatly with different people. It depends chiefly upon the amount of vitality they start with and upon their attitude towards suffering.

Human thought is unable to acknowledge the reality of affliction. To acknowledge the reality of affliction means saying to oneself: 'I may lose at any moment, through the play of circumstances over which I have no control, anything whatsoever that I possess, including those things which are so intimately mine that I consider them as being myself. There is nothing that I might not lose. It could happen at any moment that what I am might be abolished and replaced by anything whatsoever of the filthiest and most contemptible sort.'

To be aware of this in the depth of one's soul is to experience non-being. It is the state of extreme and total humiliation which is also the condition for passing over into truth. It is a death of the soul. This is why the naked spectacle of affliction makes the soul shudder as the flesh shudders at the proximity of death.

We think piously of the dead when we evoke them in memory, or when we walk among graves, or when we see them decently laid out on a bed. But the sight of corpses lying about as on a battlefield can sometimes be both sinister and grotesque. It arouses horror. At the stark sight of death, the flesh recoils.

When affliction is seen vaguely from a distance, either physical or mental, so that it can be confused with simple suffering, it inspires in generous souls a tender feeling of pity. But if by chance it is suddenly revealed to them in all its nakedness as a corrosive force, a mutilation or leprosy of the soul, then people shiver and recoil. The afflicted themselves feel the same shock of horror at their own condition.

To listen to someone is to put oneself in his place while he is speaking. To put oneself in the place of someone whose soul is corroded by affliction, or in near danger of it, is to annihilate oneself. It is more difficult than suicide would be for a happy child. Therefore the afflicted are not listened to. They are like someone whose tongue has been cut out and who occasionally forgets the fact. When they move their lips no ear perceives any sound. And they themselves soon sink into impotence in the use of language, because of the certainty of not being heard.

That is why there is no hope for the vagrant as he stands before the magistrate. Even if, through his stammerings, he should utter a cry to pierce the soul, neither the magistrate nor the public will hear it. His cry is mute. And the afflicted are nearly always equally deaf to one another; and each of them, constrained by the general indifference, strives by means of self-delusion or forgetfulness to become deaf to his own self.

Only by the supernatural working of grace can a soul pass through its own annihilation to the place where alone it can get the sort of attention which can attend to truth and to affliction. It is the same attention which listens to both of them. The name of this intense, pure, disinterested, gratuitous, generous attention is love.

Because affliction and truth need the same kind of attention before they can be heard, the spirit of justice and the spirit of truth is nothing else but a certain kind of attention, which is pure love.

Thanks to an eternal and providential decree, everything produced by a man in every sphere, when he is ruled by the spirit of justice and truth, is endowed with the radiance of beauty.

Beauty is the supreme mystery of this world. It is a gleam which attracts the attention and yet does nothing to sustain it. Beauty always promises, but never gives anything; it stimulates hunger but has no nourishment for the part of the soul which looks in this world for sustenance. It feeds only the part of the soul that gazes. While exciting desire, it makes clear that there is nothing in it to be desired, because the one thing we want is that it should not change. If one does not seek means to evade the exquisite anguish it inflicts, then desire is gradually transformed into love; and one begins to acquire the faculty of pure and disinterested attention.

In proportion to the hideousness of affliction is the supreme beauty of its true representation. Even in recent times one can point to *Phèdre*, *L'École des femmes*, *Lear*, and the poems of Villon; but far better examples are the plays of Aeschylus and Sophocles, and far better still, the *Iliad*, the book of Job and certain folk poems; and far beyond these again are the accounts of the Passion in the Gospels. The radiance of beauty illumines affliction with the light of the spirit of justice and love, which is the only light by which human thought can confront affliction and report the truth of it.

And it sometimes happens that a fragment of inexpressible truth is reflected in words which, although they cannot hold the truth that inspired them, have nevertheless so perfect a formal correspondence with it that every mind seeking that truth finds support in them. Whenever this happens a gleam of beauty illumines the words.

Everything which originates from pure love is lit with the radiance of beauty.

Beauty can be perceived, though very dimly and mixed with many false substitutes, within the cell where all human thought is at first imprisoned. And upon her rest all the hopes of truth and justice, with tongue cut out. She, too, has no language; she does not speak; she says nothing. But she has a voice to cry out. She cries out and points to truth and justice who are dumb, like a dog who barks to bring people to his master lying unconscious in the snow.

Justice, truth, and beauty are sisters and comrades. With three such beautiful words we have no need to look for any others.

Justice consists in seeing that no harm is done to men. Whenever a man cries inwardly: 'Why am I being hurt?' harm is being done to him. He is often mistaken when he tries to define the harm, and why and by whom it is being inflicted on him. But the cry itself is infallible.

The other cry, which we hear so often: 'Why has somebody else got more than I have?', refers to rights. We must learn to distinguish between the two cries and to do all that is possible, as gently as possible, to hush the second one, with the help of a code of justice, regular tribunals, and the police. Minds capable of solving problems of this kind can be formed in a law school.

But the cry 'Why am I being hurt?' raises quite different problems, for which the spirit of truth, justice, and love is indispensable.

In every soul the cry to be delivered from evil is incessant. The Lord's Prayer addresses it to God. But God has power to deliver from evil only the eternal part of the soul of those who have made real and direct contact with him. The rest of the soul, and the entire soul of whoever has not received the grace of real and direct contact with God, is at the mercy of men's caprice and the hazards of circumstance.

Therefore it is for men to see that men are preserved from harm.

When harm is done to a man, real evil enters into him; not merely pain and suffering, but the actual horror of evil. Just as men have the power of transmitting good to one another, so they have the power to transmit evil. One may transmit evil to a human being by flattering him or giving him comforts and pleasures; but most often men transmit evil to other men by doing them harm.

Nevertheless, eternal wisdom does not abandon the soul entirely to the mercy of chance and men's caprice. The harm inflicted on a man by a wound from outside sharpens his thirst for the good and thus there automatically arises the possibility of a cure. If the wound is deep, the thirst is for good in its purest form. The part of the soul which cries 'Why am I being hurt?' is on the deepest level and even in the most corrupt of men it remains from earliest infancy perfectly intact and totally innocent.

To maintain justice and preserve men from all harm means first of all to prevent harm being done to them. For those to whom harm has been done, it means to efface the material consequences by putting them in a place where the wound, if it is not too deep, may be cured naturally by a spell of well-being. But for those in whom the wound is a laceration of the soul it means further, and above all, to offer them good in its purest form to assuage their thirst.

Sometimes it may be necessary to inflict harm in order to stimulate this thirst before assuaging it, and that is what punishment is for. Men who are so estranged from the good that they seek to spread evil everywhere can only be reintegrated with the good by having harm inflicted upon them. This must be done until the completely innocent part of their soul awakens with the surprised cry 'Why am I being hurt?' The innocent part of the criminal's soul must then be fed to make it grow until it becomes able to judge and condemn his past crimes and at last, by the help of grace, to forgive them. With this the punishment is completed; the criminal has been reintegrated with the good and should be publicly and solemnly reintegrated with society.

That is what punishment is. Even capital punishment, although it excludes reintegration with society in the literal sense, should be the same thing. Punishment is solely a method of procuring pure good for men who do not desire it. The art of punishing is the art of awakening in a criminal, by pain or even death, the desire for pure good.

But we have lost all idea of what punishment is. We are not aware that its purpose is to procure good for a man. For us it stops short with the infliction of harm. That is why there is one, and only one, thing in modern society more hideous than crime – namely, repressive justice.

To make the idea of repressive justice the main motive of war or revolt is inconceivably dangerous. It is necessary to use fear as a deterrent against the criminal activity of cowards; but that repressive justice, as we ignorantly conceive it today, should be made the motive of heroes is appalling.

All talk of chastisement, punishment, retribution or punitive justice nowadays always refers solely to the basest kind of revenge.

The treasure of suffering and violent death, which Christ chose for himself and which he so often offers to those he loves, means so little to us that we throw it to those whom we least esteem, knowing that they will make nothing of it and having no intention of helping them to discover its value.

For criminals, true punishment; for those whom affliction has bitten deep into the soul, such help as may bring them to quench their thirst at the supernatural springs; for everyone else, some well-being, a great deal of beauty, and protection from those who would harm him; in every sphere, a strict curb upon the chatter of lies, propaganda, and opinion, and the encouragement of a silence in which truth can germinate and grow; this is what is due to men.

To ensure that they get it, we can only count upon those who have passed beyond a certain barrier, and it may be objected that they are too few in number. Probably there are not many of them, but they are no object for statistics, because most of them are hidden. Pure good from heaven only reaches the earth in imperceptible quantities, whether in the individual soul or in society. The grain of mustard seed is 'the least of all seeds'. Persephone ate only one grain of the pomegranate. A pearl buried deep in a field is not visible; neither is the yeast in dough.

But just as the catalysts of bacteria, such as yeast, operate by their mere presence in chemical reactions, so in human affairs, the invisible seed of pure good is decisive when it is put in the right place.

How is it to be put there?

Much could be done by those whose function is to advise the public what to praise, what to admire, what to hope and strive and seek for. It would be a great advance if even a few of these makers of opinion were to resolve in their hearts to eschew absolutely and without exception everything that is not pure good, perfection, truth, justice, love.

It would be an even greater advance if the majority of those who possess today some fragments of spiritual authority were aware of their obligation never to hold up for human aspiration anything but the real good in its perfect purity.

By the power of words we always mean their power of illusion and error. But, thanks to a providential arrangement, there are certain words which possess, in themselves, when properly used, a virtue which illumines and lifts up towards the good. These are the words which refer to an absolute perfection which we cannot conceive. Since the proper use of these words involves not trying to make them fit any conception, it is in the words themselves, as words, that the power to enlighten and draw upward resides. What they express is beyond our conception.

God and *truth* are such words; also *justice*, *love*, and *good*.

It is dangerous to use words of this kind. They are like an ordeal. To use them legitimately one must avoid referring them to anything humanly conceivable and at the same time one must associate with them ideas and actions which are derived solely and directly from the light which they shed. Otherwise, everyone quickly recognises them for lies.

They are uncomfortable companions. Words like *right*, *democracy* and *person* are more accommodating and are therefore naturally preferred by even the best intentioned of those who assume public functions. Public functions have no other meaning except the possibility of doing good to men, and those who assume them with good intentions do in fact want to procure good for their contemporaries; but they usually make the mistake of thinking they can begin by getting it at bargain prices.

Words of the middle region, such as *right*, *democracy*, *person*, are valid in their own region, which is that of ordinary institutions. But for the sustaining inspiration of which all institutions are, as it were, the projection, a different language is needed.

The subordination of the person to the collectivity is in the nature of things, like the inferiority of a gram to a kilogram on the scales. But there can be a scales on which the gram outweighs the kilogram. It is only necessary for one arm to be more than a thousand times as long as the other. The law of equilibrium easily overcomes an inequality of weight. But the lesser will never outweigh the greater unless the relation between them is regulated by the law of equilibrium.

In the same way, there is no guarantee for democracy, or for the protection of the person against the collectivity, without a disposition of public life relating it to the higher good which is impersonal and unrelated to any political form.

It is true that the word person is often applied to God. But in the passage where Christ offers God himself as an example to men of the perfection which they are told to achieve, he uses not only the image of a person but also, above all, that of an impersonal order: 'That ye may be like the children of your Father which is in heaven; for he maketh his sun to rise on the evil and on the good, and sendeth rain on the just and on the unjust.'

Justice, truth, and beauty are the image in our world of this impersonal and divine order of the universe. Nothing inferior to them is worthy to be the inspiration of men who accept the fact of death.

Above those insitutions which are concerned with protecting rights and persons and democratic freedoms, others must be invented for the purpose of exposing and abolishing everything in contemporary life which buries the soul under injustice, lies, and ugliness.

They must be invented, for they are unknown, and it is impossible to doubt that they are indispensable.

Notes

1 Paris: Childhood and Adolescence

1. B. Saint-Sernin, *L'Action politique selon Simone Weil* (Paris, 1988) p. 16.

2 Paris: Student Days

1. See F. Copleston, *A History of Philosophy* (London, 1975) ch. 9, pt. 2.
2. See further especially L. Lavelle, *La Philosophie française entre les guerres* (Paris, 1947) pp. 242ff.
3. Further on Alain, see the portrait in T. Zeldin, *Intellect and Pride* (Oxford, 1980) pp. 213ff. Also, G. Pascal, *La Pensée d'Alain* (Paris, 1946); G. Fiori, *Simone Weil: Une Femme Absolue* (Paris, 1987) pp. 30ff; and the collection *Hommage à Alain* (Paris, 1952).
4. See A. Bridoux, *Alain. Sa vie, son œuvre* (Paris, 1964) pp. 7f.
5. R. Colquhoun, *Raymond Aron*, London, 1985, vol. 1, p. 34. On Alain's wide influence, see further: J.-F. Sirinelli, *Génération intellectuelle* (Paris, 1988) ch. 13.
6. Quoted in J. Steel, *Paul Nizan: Un révolutionnaire conformiste?* (Paris, 1987) p. 29.
7. See further: D. Canciani, *Simone Weil prima di Simone Weil* (Padua, 1983) ch. 1 and A. Moulakis, *Simone Weil: Die Politik der Askese* (1981).
8. M.-M. Davy, *Simone Weil* (Paris, 1956) p. 13.
9. S. de Beauvoir, *Memoirs of a Dutiful Daughter* (London, 1959) p. 239. For further information, see S. Fraisse, 'Simone Weil vue par Simone de Beauvoir', *Cahiers Simone Weil*, vol. 8, no. 1, March 1985. For an interesting comparison of the backgrounds of Weil and de Beauvoir, see J. Hellman, *Simone Weil. An Introduction to her Thought* (Waterloo, 1982) pp. 7ff.
10. See further, T. Zeldin, *France 1848–1945* (Oxford, 1977) vol. 2, pp. 333ff.
11. P. Nizan, *La Conspiration* (Paris, 1938) p. 28. The whole of the second section of this novel contains a splendidly evocative description of the Panthéon quarter at this time.
12. Cf. S. de Beauvoir, *Memoirs of a Dutiful Daughter* (London, 1959) p. 310.
13. See J. and M. Alexandre, 'Notes concernant les *Libres Propos*', *Hommage à Alain* (Paris, 1952) p. 172.
14. Quoted in D. Canciani, 'Penser le travail: Simone Weil 1927–1934', *Cahiers Simone Weil*, vol. 9, no. 4, Dec. 1986, p. 346.
15. V.-H. Debidour, *Simone Weil ou la transparence* (Paris, 1963) p. 24. See also: H. Queffelec, *Un Breton bien tranquille* (Paris, 1978) p. 134.
16. If Alain is correctly reported, he had got the mark slightly wrong.
17. See pp. 165ff.
18. Cf. J. Chastenet, *Les Années d'illusion (1918–1931)* (Paris, 1962).
19. S. de Beauvoir, *Memoirs of a Dutiful Daughter*, 2nd edn (London, 1962) p. 197.
20. See further, J. Touchard, 'L'Esprit des années trente', in *Tendances politiques dans la vie française depuis 1789* (Paris, 1960); J.-L. Loubet del Bayle, *Les non-conformistes des années 30* (Paris, 1969).

21. E. Mounier, 'Réflexions sur le personnalisme', *Synthèses*, 1947, vol. 4, p. 25, quoted in Bayle, *Les non-conformistes*, p. 22.
22. P. Andreu, 'Les Idées politiques de la jeunesse intellectuelle de 1927 à la guerre', *Revue des Travaux de l'Académie des Sciences Morales et Politiques*, vol. 108, July 1957, p. 19.
23. See D. Caute, *Communism and the French Intellectuals* (London, 1964).
24. See S. Hughes, *The Obstructed Path. French Social Thought: the Years of Desperation 1930–1960* (New York, 1966) ch. 1.

3 Le Puy: Teacher and Anarchist

1. See P. Dujardin, *Simone Weil: Idéologie et Politique* (Grenoble, 1975) p. 75.
2. See, in general, H. Dubief, *Le Syndicalisme révolutionnaire* (Paris, 1969).
3. For similar difficulties encountered by Paul Nizan in Bourg-en-Bresse, see J. Steel, *Paul Nizan: conformiste révolutionnaire?* (Paris, 1987) pp. 93ff.
4. C. Claveyrolas *et al.*, 'Simone Weil professeur', *Foi et Education*, May, 1951, p. 171.
5. See G. Lefranc, *Le Mouvement syndical sous la troisième république* (Paris, 1967) p. 280.
6. S. Weil, 'Le Congrès de la CGT', *Libres Propos*, Oct. 1931, p. 476, quoted in Cabaud, p. 49.
7. J. Duperray, 'Quand Simone Weil passa chez nous', *Les Lettres Nouvelles*, April/May 1964, p. 92, quoted in Pétrement, p. 79.
8. See further G. Lefranc, *Le Mouvement syndical sous la troisième république* (Paris, 1967) pp. 53ff.
9. T. Zeldin, *France 1848–1945* (Oxford, 1977) vol. 1, pp. 243ff. More broadly on this disappointment, see U. Thévenon, 'Une Etape dans la vie de Simone Weil', *La Révolution Prolétarienne*, May 1952, p. 14/158.
10. See further the excellent article by D. Canciani, 'Penser le travail: Simone Weil 1927–1934', *Cahiers Simone Weil*, vol. 9, no. 4, Dec. 1986, pp. 349ff.
11. A. Thévenon, Preface to S. Weil, *La Condition Ouvrière* (Paris, 1951) p. 8.
12. A. Thévenon, 'Une Etape dans la vie de Simone Weil', *La Révolution Prolétarienne*, May 1952, p. 17/161.
13. Cf. A. Moulakis, *Simone Weil: Die Politik der Askese* (Stuttgart, 1981) p. 54.
14. See Arthur Koestler's vivid memoirs of the period in *The God that Failed*, R. Crossman (ed.), (New York, 1965).
15. See G. Leroy, Introduction to Simone Weil, *Oeuvres complètes*, vol. 2 (Paris, 1988) pp. 27ff.
16. Further on Souvarine and his circle, see C. Ronsac, *Trois noms pour une vie* (Paris, 1988) pp. 34ff.
17. See the similar analysis in F. Fried, *La fin du capitalisme* (Paris, 1932) pp. 144ff, to which Weil makes reference (OL, pp. 26f).
18. L. Trotsky, *Writings 1933–1934*, G. Breitman and B. Scott (eds) (New York, 1972) p. 114.
19. A. Reynaud, Preface to S. Weil, *Lectures on Philosophy* (Cambridge, 1978) p. 24.
20. J. Duperray, 'Quand Simone Weil passa chez nous', *Les Lettres Nouvelles*, April/May 1964, p. 94.
21. Ibid., p. 97.
22. See further H. Lottman, *The Left Bank* (London, 1982) pp. 76ff. This book contains a splendidly vivid account of the Parisian intellectual scene between the wars.
23. Cf. P. Rolland, 'Simone Weil et le syndicalisme révolutionnaire', *Cahiers Simone Weil*, vol. 3, no. 4, Dec. 1980, p. 255.

24. Cf. U. Thévenon, 'Une Etape dans la vie de Simone Weil', *La Révolution Prolétarienne*, May 1952, p. 18/162.

4 Oppression and Liberty

1. S. Weil, *Lectures on Philosophy* (Cambridge, 1978) pp. 133f.
2. See pp. 251ff.
3. See further, S. Pétrement, 'La Critique du Marxisme chez Simone Weil', *Le Contrat Social*, Sept. 1957; A. Birou, 'L'Analyse critique de la pensée de Karl Marx chez Simone Weil', *Cahiers Simone Weil*, vol. 7, no. 1, March 1984.
4. See further: H. Abosch, 'La critique du Marxisme par Simone Weil', *Cahiers Simone Weil*, vol. 8, no. 2, June 1985, pp. 151ff.
5. See, for example, N. Berdiaev, *La source et le sens du communisme russe* (Paris, 1963) pp. 181ff.
6. See, for example, R. Pierce, *Contemporary French Political Thought* (Oxford, 1966) pp. 108f; A. Moulakis, *Simone Weil: Die Politik der Askese* (Stuttgart, 1981) pp. 112ff.
7. See particularly, J.-P. Loubet del Bayle, *Les Non-conformistes des années 30* (Paris, 1969) pp. 282ff.
8. See also the similar contemporary critique by V. Serge, *Memoirs of a Revolutionary* (Oxford, 1963) pp. 281ff, whose views Weil much admired (cf. P, p. 196). On the information about the Soviet Union available in the France of that time, see B. Saint-Sernin, *L'Action politique selon Simone Weil* (Paris, 1988) pp. 52f.
9. Cf. L. Laurat, *Economie dirigée et socialisation* (Brussels, 1934) especially pp. 234ff on the critique of Soviet bureaucracy, and pp. 98ff and 167ff on technocracy, and the crisis of capitalist democracy.
10. Cf. K. Marx, *Capital* (Harmondsworth, 1976) vol. I, pp. 455ff.
11. For an interesting comparison of Weil and Sartre here, see B. Saint-Sernin, *L'Action politique selon Simone Weil* (Paris, 1988) ch. 21.
12. See p. 48 above.
13. Pétrement, p. 122. See also the passages from *Capital* (Harmondsworth, 1976) pp. 548f which Weil cites in *Perspectives* and elsewhere.
14. Quoted in: S. Dermen, 'Necessity, oppression and liberty: Simone Weil's thoughts on work', in E. Goodman (ed.), *Non-Conforming Radicals of Europe* (London, 1983) p. 173.
15. See further on this topic the fascinating book by M. Cooley, *Architect or Bee? The Human Price of Technology*, 2nd edn (London, 1987).
16. For contemporary versions of this thesis, see F. Fried, *La fin du capitalisme* (Paris, 1932) and A. Berle and G. Means, *The Modern Corporation and Private Property* (New York, 1932).
17. See further, for example, J. Ellul, *The Technological System* (New York, 1980).
18. See A. Giddens, *The Nation State and Violence* (London, 1985) ch. 7.
19. Cp. H. Marcuse, *One-dimensional Man* (London, 1968) pp. 120ff; *Soviet Marxism* (New York, 1958) pp. 248ff; J. K. Galbraith, *The New Industrial State* (Boston, 1967) pp. 59ff; C. Wright Mills, *The Power Elite* (New York, 1956).
20. S. Weil, *Lectures on Philosophy* (Cambridge, 1978) p. 138. See also pp. 133ff which contain in summary her ideas on liberty and society elaborated in *Oppression and Liberty*.
21. K. Marx, *Selected Writings*, D. McLellan (ed.) (Oxford, 1977) p. 569. Cf. OL, pp. 104ff.
22. Cp. S. Weil, *Lectures on Philosophy*, Cambridge, 1976, pp. 146f. Also the excellent article by R. Chenavier, 'Relire Simone Weil', *Les Temps Modernes*, vol. 440, March, 1983, esp. pp. 1704ff.

23. See further: S. Dermen, 'Necessity, oppression and liberty: Simone Weil's thoughts on work', in E. Goodman (ed.), *Non-conforming Radicals of Europe*, London, 1983.
24. A. Camus, *Introduction* to OL, p. 8.
25. Ibid.
26. See R. Chenavier, 'Civilisation du travail ou civilisation du temps libre?', *Cahiers Simone Weil*, vol. 10, no. 4, December 1987, pp. 416f.

5 Paris: Factory Year

1. See J.-L. Loubet del Bayle, *Les Non-conformistes des années 30* (Paris, 1969) p. 117.
2. See G. A. White, 'Simone Weil's Work Experiences: From Wigan Pier to Chrystie Street', *Cross Currents*, vol. 31, pt. 2, Summer, 1981.
3. S. Weil, *Lectures on Philosophy* (Cambridge, 1978) p. 139.
4. See the passage of self-examination, P. pp. 219f. and C. Ronsac, *Trois noms pour une vie* (Paris, 1988) pp. 129ff.
5. H. Arendt, *The Human Condition* (Chicago, 1958) p. 131.
6. Homer, *Iliad*, Bk VI, l.548.
7. Ibid. See also the vivid account in her later article 'La vie ouvrière', CO, pp. 161ff.
8. CO, p. 253. Weil has in mind here the proposals of R. Aron and A. Dandieu, *La Révolution nécessaire* (Paris, 1933).
9. See further: F. Rosen, 'Labour and Liberty: Simone Weil and the Human Condition', *Theoria to Theory*, vol. 7, 1973, pp. 37ff.
10. See, for example, the discussion inaugurated by H. Braverman, *Labour and Monopoly Capital. The Degradation of Work in the Twentieth Century* (New York, 1974).
11. Letter to Jacques Lafitte, 'Deux lettres de Simone Weil sur le travail et les machines', *Cahiers Simone Weil*, vol. 3, no. 3, Sept. 1980, p. 163.
12. Letter to Jacques Lafitte, p. 164.
13. See H. Arendt, *The Human Condition* (Chicago, 1958) pp. 79ff.
14. Cf. E. Goodman, *A Study of Liberty and Oppression* (London, 1963) pp. 151ff.
15. See A. Gorz, *Paths of Paradise* (London, 1985); R. Chenavier, 'Civilisation du travail ou civilisation du temps libre?' *Cahiers Simone Weil*, vol. 10, no. 4, Dec. 1987, pp. 408ff.
16. See further, J. Little, *Simone Weil. Waiting on Truth* (New York, 1988) pp. 112ff.

6 Paris: The Drift to War

1. J.-C. Dreyfus, 'Souvenirs et réflexions', *Cahiers Simone Weil*, vol. 9, no. 4, Dec. 1986, pp. 332f.
2. G. Orwell, *Homage to Catalonia* (London; Penguin, 1986) p. 8.
3. Ibid., p. 38. On this episode of the Civil War, see H. Thomas, *The Spanish Civil War* (London, 1986) pp. 316ff; also the famous description in *Homage to Catalonia*, ch. 4.
4. Quoted in S. Fraisse, 'Simone Weil, journaliste politique 1937–1940', *Cahiers Simone Weil*, vol. 10, no. 3, Sept. 1987, p. 262.
5. Cf. pp. 115ff. above.
6. See further S. Fraisse, 'Simone Weil, journaliste politique 1937–1940', *Cahiers Simone Weil*, vol. 10, no. 3, Sept. 1987, pp. 258f.

7. See further O. Huber, 'Une soulerie de statues grècques', *Cahiers Simone Weil*, vol. 6, no. 1, March, 1983, pp. 30ff.
8. See further: L. Allen, 'French Intellectuals and T. E. Lawrence', *Durham University Journal*, vol. 19, no. 1, December 1976, pp. 59ff.
9. Cf. J. Brezolles, *Cet ardent sanglot . . . pages de mon journal* (Paris, 1970) pp. 204ff.
10. For more detail, see the excellent Introduction by Simone Fraisse to Simone Weil, *Oeuvres complètes*, vol. 3 (Paris, 1989).

7 Paris: War and History

1. See, for example, the view that Israel originated from a revolt within Canaan itself, in N. Gottwald, *The Tribes of Jahweh* (Maryknoll, NY, 1981).
2. Introduction to Simone Weil, *Attente de Dieu* (Paris, 1950) pp. 29f.
3. Cf. *Notebooks*, 564ff on different concepts of Jahweh.
4. Cf. S. Pétrement, 'Sur la religion d'Alain, avec quelques remarques concernant celle de Simone Weil', *Revue de métaphysique et de morale*, vol. 60, 1955, pp. 319ff.
5. See, in particular, G. Bernanos, *Grands cimetières sous la lune* (Paris, 1938) Part Four.
6. See further F. de Lussy, 'Simone Weil. Confrontation avec deux grandes figures juives contemporaines: Martin Buber et Emmanuel Levinas', *Revue de la Bibliothèque Nationale*, vol. 20, Summer 1986, pp. 17ff.
7. It is interesting to compare the much more negative account of the Cathar conception of love as ancestor of the disruptive anarchy of modern sexual relations by Weil's contemporary, Denis de Rougemont, *Passion and Society*, 2nd edn (London, 1956) chs 6 and 7.
8. See further on this point: J. Pratt, *Simone Weil: Contributions Towards a Critique of Science*, PhD dissertation, Marquette University, 1985, pp. 74ff.
9. See her letter to Alain, *Bulletin de l'Association des Amis d'Alain*, vol. 58, June, 1984, pp. 37ff.
10. See J. Little, 'Society as Mediator in Simone Weil's *Venise Sauvée*', *Modern Language Review*, vol. 65, no. 2, April 1970.
11. See further: G. Fiori, *Simone Weil. Une Femme absolue* (Paris, 1987) pp. 78ff.

8 Marseilles: Life

1. For an over-harsh criticism of the position adopted by Weil in this letter, see R. Coles, *Simone Weil. A Modern Pilgrimage* (Reading, Mass., 1987) pp. 43ff.
2. L. Bercher, 'Un témoignage en forme de notes', *Cahiers Simone Weil*, vol. 9, no. 2, June 1986, p. 126.
3. Further on the *Cahiers du Sud*, see *Rivages des origines (Archives des Cahiers du Sud)*, N. Cendo (ed.) (Marseilles, 1981).
4. See also Lanza del Vasto's similar description in his book *L'Arche avait pour voilure une vigne* (Paris, 1978) p. 42.
5. Cf. 'Deux lettres de Simone Weil à René et Véra Daumal', *Cahiers Simone Weil*, vol. 11, no. 1, March 1988, pp. 1ff.
6. Cf. R. Gaillardot, 'A propos de la mort de Lanza del Vasto', *Cahiers Simone Weil*, vol. 4, no. 2, June 1981, p. 89.
7. Cf. J. Lambert, *Les vacances du cœur* (Paris, 1975) pp. 233ff.
8. Cf. J.-M. Perrin, 'Témoignage', in *Simone Weil: Philosophe, historienne et mystique*, G. Kahn (ed.) (Paris, 1978) p. 56.

9. Cf. J.-M. Perrin, *Mon dialogue avec Simone Weil* (Paris, 1984) p. 64.

10. R.-L. Bruckberger, 'Témoignage sur Simone Weil', *Cahiers Simone Weil*, vol. 2, no. 4, December 1979, pp. 179f.

11. Cf. her remark to Hélène Honnorat quoted in P, p. 441.

12. See further, R. Bedarida, *Témoignage Chrétien, 1941–1944* (Paris, 1977).

13. Cf. 'Simone Weil, la Résistance et la question juive', *Cahiers Simone Weil*, vol. 4, no. 2, June 1981, pp. 76ff.

14. Quoted in A. Freixe, 'A propos de la rencontre Simone Weil–Joe Bousquet', *Cahiers Simone Weil*, Vol. 10, no. 4, p. 400.

15. Quoted in M. Narcy, 'Visite à Joe Bousquet', *Cahiers Simone Weil*, Vol. 6, no. 2, June 1983, p. 114.

16. See also the *reprise* of these ideas in FLN, pp. 264ff.

17. See further, in particular, J.-M. Perrin, *Mon dialogue avec Simone Weil* (Paris, 1984) pp. 128ff. E. Springstead, *Christus Mediator: Platonic Mediation in the Thought of Simone Weil* (Chico, 1983) pp. 71ff.

18. See here also SL, pp. 102f.

19. Simone Weil–Gustave Thibon, 'Correspondance', *Cahiers Simone Weil*, vol. 4, no. 4, December 1981, p. 195.

9 Marseilles: Thought

1. See further, E. Ostier, 'La théorie des sacrements de Simone Weil', *Cahiers Simone Weil*, vol. 4, no. 1, 1981, pp. 16ff.

2. See, for example, C. Moeller, *Littérature du XXe siècle et Christianisme* (Paris, 1967) vol. 1, pp. 246ff; M. Murray, 'Simone Weil: Last Things', in G. A. White (ed.), *Simone Weil, Interpretations of a Life* (Amherst, 1981) pp. 57ff.

3. Cf. J.-M. Perrin, G. Thibon, *Simone Weil telle que nous l'avons connue* (Paris, 1952) p. 73.

4. For a reliable guide to the actual doctrines of gnosticism, see H. Jonas, *The Gnostic Tradition* (Boston, 1963).

5. See p. xiii above.

6. The best book in this area is M. Veto, *La Métaphysique religieuse de Simone Weil* (Paris, 1964). See also E. Springstead, *Christus Mediator: Platonic Mediation in the Thought of Simone Weil* (Chico, 1983).

7. See further, E. Springstead, *Christus Mediator*, pp. 85ff.

8. See p. 185 above.

9. M. Veto, *Métaphysique religieuse*, p. 148. For an insightful meditation on this aspect of Weil's thought, see I. Murdoch, *The Sovereignty of Good* (London, 1970) especially ch. 2.

10. These texts are assembled in *Intimations of Christianity among the Ancient Greeks* (London, 1957), pp. 74ff and in *Science, Necessity and the Love of God* (London, 1968) pp. 89ff.

11. See further M. Broc-Lapeyre, 'Simone Weil et son refus de Nietzsche', *Cahiers Simone Weil*, vol. 3, no. 1, March 1980, pp. 19ff.

12. See J. Little, 'Heracleitus and Simone Weil. The Harmony of Opposites', *Forum for Modern Language Studies*, vol. 5, no. 1, 1968, pp. 72ff.

13. Quoted in F. Heidsieck, 'Platon, maître et témoin de la connaissance surnaturelle', *Cahiers Simone Weil*, vol. 5, no. 4, December 1982, pp. 246f.

14. As in, for example, the work of A. Nygren, *Agape and Eros* (New York, 1953).

15. The passage in question is Ezekiel, ch. 28, vv. 12–15.

16. *The Upanishads*, trans. and ed. by S. Nikhilananda (New York, 1964) p. 115.

17. *Bhagavad Gita*, R. Zaehner (ed.) (Oxford, 1969) p. 59.

18. Ibid.
19. Further on Hinduism, see P. Bowes, *The Hindu Religious Tradition* (London, 1977) and the standard work of M. Hiriyanna, *Outlines of Indian Philosophy* (Bombay, 1976).

10   New York: Waiting

1. See IC, pp. 108ff and p. 206 above.
2. See above. p. 25.
3. Cf. J.-M. Perrin, *Mon dialogue avec Simone Weil* (Paris, 1984) p. 101.
4. Simone Weil, Gustav Thibon, 'Correspondance', *Cahiers Simone Weil*, vol. 4, no. 4, December 1981, p. 99.

11   London: Politics and Death

1. F.-L. Closon, 'Témoignage', *Cahiers Simone Weil*, vol. 5, no. 3, September 1982, p. 222.
2. See further here, H. Michel and B. Mirkine-Guetzévitch, *Les Idées politiques et sociales de la Résistance* (Paris, 1954) pp. 24, 88, n. 1.
3. On the radical nature of the documents from France, see H. Michel and B. Mirkine-Guetzévitch, *Idées*, p. 47 and H. Michel, *Les Idées politiques de la Résistance* (Paris, 1962) p. 72.
4. S. Weil, 'The Legitimacy of the Provisional Government', *Philosophical Investigations*, vol. 10, no. 2, 1987, pp. 88–9.
5. S. Weil, 'Legitimacy', p. 96.
6. Cf. J.-P. Azéma, *De Munich à la Liberation* (Paris, 1979) pp. 272f.
7. In fact, a lot of it is drawn from the various constitutions of the ancient Greek city states: see M. Finley, *Politics in the Ancient World* (Cambridge, 1983) ch. 4.
8. See H. Michel, *Idées politiques*, pp. 91ff.
9. See, for example, W. Rabi, 'La conception Weilienne de la creation: rencontre avec la Kabbale juive', in *Simone Weil: philosophe, historienne, mystique* (Paris, 1978) pp. 144f; R. Coles, *Simone Weil, A Modern Pilgrimage* (Reading, Mass., 1987) pp. 47ff.
10. See M. Marrus and R. Paxton, *Vichy France and the Jews* (New York, 1981) p. 190.
11. According to Schumann, Weil spoke to him in 1942 about the massacre of the Amalekites by Saul. 'How', she asked him, 'can we condemn one holocaust, if we have not condemned all the holocausts of the past?' See M. Schumann, 'Présentation de Simone Weil', in *Simone Weil: philosophe, historienne, mystique* (Paris, 1978) p. 18.
12. On the contrary views current in London, see H. Michel, *Idées politiques*, pp. 74ff.
13. This is Weil's finest essay and has been reprinted as an Appendix (pp. 273ff) to enable the reader to appreciate the sweep and beauty of her writing.
14. For a similar recent questioning of the concept of rights, see A. MacIntyre, *After Virtue*, 2nd edn (London, 1985) pp. 66ff.
15. See H. Michel and B. Mirkine-Guetzévitch, *Idées*, p. 13.
16. See pp. 167f, above.
17. A particularly striking example was the suicide, in November 1936, of the Minister of the Interior, Roger Salengro, who had been hounded by right-wing scandal sheets.

18. See further the perceptive comments in D. Meakin, *Man and Work. Literature and Culture in Industrial Society* (London, 1976) pp. 188ff.
19. See H. Michel, *Idées politiques*, pp. 72ff.
20. See further, J. King, 'Simone Weil and the Identity of France', *Journal of European Studies*, vol. 6, 1976, pp. 129ff.
21. See the good discussion in I. Malan, *L'Enracinement de Simone Weil* (Paris, 1961) pp. 100ff.
22. J.-M. Perrin and G. Thibon, *Simone Weil telle que nous l'avons connue* (Paris, 1952) p. 166.
23. See J. Pratt, *Simone Weil: Contributions Towards a Critique of Science*, PhD dissertation, Marquette University, 1985, pp. 76ff.
24. See the recent discussion in M. Midgley, *Wisdom, Information and Wonder* (London, 1989).
25. J.-M. Perrin and G. Thibon, *Simone Weil telle que nous l'avons connue* (Paris, 1952) p. 95.
26. E. Mounier, 'Une lecture de ''L'Enracinement'' ', *Cahiers Simone Weil*, vol. 5, no. 3, September 1982, p. 227.
27. See, for example, C. O'Brien, 'Patriotism and *The Need for Roots*: The Antipolitics of Simone Weil', in G. White (ed.), *Simone Weil: Interpretations of a Life* (Amherst, 1981) p. 96; P. Dujardin, *Simone Weil: Idéologie et Politique* (Paris, 1975) pp. 170ff.
28. For a negative view, see P. Milza, *Les Fascismes français* (Paris, 1987) ch. 4.
29. See J. King, 'Simone Weil and the Identity of France', pp. 139f.
30. Cf. R. Sovey, *Fascism in France: The Case of Maurice Barrès* (Berkeley, 1972) pp. 283ff. See also G. Lagowski, 'Simone Weil and Romantic Conservatism', *Reports on Philosophy*, vol. 5, 1981.
31. CS, p. 170, quoted in I. Malan, *L'Enracinement*, p. 148.
32. Cf. L. Closon, 'Témoignage', *Cahiers Simone Weil*, vol. 5, no. 3, September 1982, p. 224.
33. A. Camus, *Oeuvres complètes* (Paris, 1965) vol. 2, p. 1700.
34. E. Mounier, 'Une lecture', p. 298.
35. See H. Michel and B. Mirkine-Guetzévitch, *Idées*, pp. 283ff.
36. See, for example, G. Ferrières, *Jean Cavaillès* (Paris, 1982) p. 194.
37. See further on this rather distasteful subject, W. Rabi, 'Simone Weil ou l'itinéraire d'une âme', *Les Nouveaux Cahiers*, vol. 26, 1971, pp. 51ff.
38. See L. Closon, 'Témoignage', *Cahiers Simone Weil*, vol. 5, n. 3, September 1982 p. 224.
39. See further the sensible remarks of her brother in *GaG*, pp. 159f.
40. Thérèse Closon, 'Lettre à André et Eveline Weil', *Cahiers Simone Weil*, vol. 9, no. 4, December 1986, p. 329.

Conclusion

1. P. Hebblethwaite, *John XXIII, Pope of the Council* (London) p. 57.
2. Cf. P. Hebblethwaite, *The Year of the Three Popes* (London, 1978) p. 2.
3. A. Camus, *The Rebel* (London, 1953) pp. 264f.

Chronology

1872	Birth of Simone Weil's father, Bernard Weil, at Strasbourg	
1879	Birth of Simone Weil's mother, Selma Reinherz, at Rostov	
1905	Marriage of Simone Weil's parents	
1906	Birth of André Weil	
1909	Birth of Simone Weil, 3 February, at 19 Bvd. de Strasbourg, Paris	
1913	Weil family move to 37 Bvd. Saint-Michel	
1914 **August**	Weil family move to Neufchâteau	Outbreak of First World War
1915 **April**	Weil family move to Mayenne	
1916 **February**	Selma Weil and children return to Paris	
1917 **January**	Weil family move to Chartres	
September	Weil family move to Laval; attends Lycée	
November		Russian revolution
1919 **January**	Weil family returns to Paris	
October	Starts at Lycée Fénelon	
1920		Foundation of French Communist Party
1922		Mussolini's march on Rome
1924 **July**	Passes first part of *baccalauréat*	
October	Attends Lycée Victor-Duruy	
1925 **October**	Enters Lycée Henri IV	
1928 **October**	Enters Ecole Normale Supérieure	Kellogg Pact against war
1929 **May**	Weil family move to 3 rue Auguste Comte	Trotsky forced into exile
September		The Wall Street Crash
1930	Headaches begin	

July	Defends thesis on *Science and Perception in Descartes*	
1931 **July**	Passes *agrégation*	
October	Starts teaching at Le Puy	Efforts of French trade union movement to reunite
December	Involved with demonstrations of unemployed	
1932	Writes numerous short articles for trade union journals	
March		Death of Briand
August	Spends six weeks in Berlin	
October	Starts teaching at Auxerre; writes *Germany Waits* and *The Situation in Germany*	
November	First contact with Boris Souvarine	
1933 **January**		Hitler takes power
August	Holiday in Spain; writes *Are We Heading for a Proletarian Revolution?*	
October	Begins teaching at Roanne	
December	Meets Trotsky	March of the Saint-Etienne miners
1934 **February**		Stavisky riots in Paris
Autumn	Finishes *Oppression and Liberty*	
December	Begins work at Alsthom	
1935 **February**	Convalescence at Montana	
April	Begins work at Carnaud	
June	Begins work at Renault	
Aug./Sep.	Holiday in Spain and Portugal	
October	Begins teaching at Bourges	Italy invades Abyssinia
1936 **January**	Contacts with Bernard and Rosières factory	
March		Hitler re-militarises Rhineland
May		Victory of Popular Front in France
July		Beginning of Spanish Civil War
Aug./Sep.	Enrols in anarchist militia in Spain	Beginning of Moscow show trials
1937	Contacts with Belin, Mounier	

Jan./Feb.	etc; writes *Let Us Not Begin The Trojan War Again!*	
March	Stays in Montana	
April/June	Travels in Italy	
June		Fall of Blum government
September	Writes *The Workers' Condition*	
October	Begins teaching at Saint-Quentin	
1938 March		*Anschluss* in Austria
April	Visit to Solesmes	
May/August	Travels to Italy	
September		Munich agreements
November	First mystical experiences	
1939 March	Renounces pacifism in *Cold War Policy in 1939*	Hitler enters Prague
September	Writes *Some Reflections on the Origins of Hitlerism* and *The Iliad: Poem of Force*	Outbreak of Second World War
1940 Spring	Reads *Bhagavad Gita*; drafts project for front-line nurses	
June	Weils leave Paris	Fall of France; establishment of Vichy regime; de Gaulle reaches London and broadcasts appeal for resistance
July	Weils stay in Vichy; writes *Venice Saved*	
September	Weils arrive in Marseilles; contacts with *Cahiers du Sud*	
1941 January	Begins *Notebooks*	
Spring	Writes *Science and Ourselves*	
June	Meets Perrin	Germany invades Russia
August	Works for Thibon at Saint-Marcel d'Ardèche	
September	Works in wine harvest at Saint-Julien-de-Peyrolas	
October	Returns to Marseilles	
December		Pearl Harbor
1942 Jan.–April	Writes two articles on the Languedoc, most of *Waiting on God* and of *Intimations of Christianity*	
March	Meets Joe Bousquet in Carcassone	
Easter	Goes to En Calcat; conversations	

	with Jacob and others	
May	Leaves for America; stops in Casablanca; finishes texts on Pythagorean thought	
July	Arrives in New York	
September	Birth of Sylvie Weil; writes *Letter to a Priest*	
October	Writes *New York Notebook*	Battles of El Alamein and Stalingrad
November	Leaves for England	American troops land in North Africa; Germans occupy Free Zone in France
December	Arrives in London	
1943 **Jan.–April**	Writes *The Need for Roots* and various articles, including *Human Personality*	
15 April	Enters Middlesex Hospital	
July	Resigns from Free French	
17 August	Enters Grosvenor Sanatorium, Ashford	
24 August	Death of Simone Weil	
30 August	Buried in New Cemetery, Ashford	

Bibliography

Simone Weil published little during her lifetime and the haphazard posthumous publication of her writings has produced a confusing jumble. The relatively brief bibliography below is designed to help the reader who wishes to have access to works by or about Simone Weil. Those who wish further information should consult the exhaustive bibliography by J. P. Little (1973) *Simone Weil. A Bibliography* (London: Grant and Cutler (Supplement 1979)) and also J. Cabaud (1964) *Simone Weil. A Fellowship in Love* (New York: Harvill) pp. 364–85.

Works by Simone Weil: French Originals

Book Collections

Attente de Dieu (1950, Paris: La Colombe). (Letters to, and articles written for, Perrin.)

Cahiers, 3 vols (1951, 1953, 1956, Paris: Plon). (The Marseilles *Notebooks*. A second edition containing important new material was published in 1970ff.)

Ecrits de Londres et dernières lettres (1957, Paris: Gallimard). (Writings from the last six months of her life.)

Ecrits historiques et politiques (1960, Paris: Gallimard). (A large collection of shortish articles on historico-political themes.)

Intuitions préchrétiennes (1951, Paris: La Colombe). (Contains writings on Greek philosophy from the Marseilles period.)

La Condition ouvrière (1951, Paris: Gallimard). (Factory journal and later relevant articles.)

La Connaissance surnaturelle (1950, Paris: Gallimard). (Contains New York *Notebooks*.)

La Pesanteur et la grâce (1947, Paris: Plon). (Selections made by Gustave Thibon from the Marseilles *Notebooks*.)

La Source grècque (1953, Paris: Gallimard). (Contains essays on the *Iliad*, on Greek tragedy, and on Plato.)

Leçons de philosophie de Simone Weil, A. Reynaud (ed.) (1959, Paris: Plon). (Notes on Simone Weil's classes in Roanne by one of her pupils.)

L'Enracinement. Prélude à une déclaration des devoirs envers l'être humain (1949, Paris: Gallimard). (Her long essay designed as a contribution to the reconstruction of postwar France.)

Lettre à un religieux (1951, Paris: Gallimard). (New York letter to Couturier on the deficiencies of the Catholic Church.)

Oppression et liberté (1955, Paris: Gallimard). (Contains the long article 'Reflections on the causes of Oppression and Liberty' and several smaller ones on the same theme.)

Pensées sans ordre concernant l'amour de Dieu (1962, Paris: Gallimard). (Articles from the Marseilles period.)

Sur la science (1966, Paris: Gallimard). (Contains her student thesis on Descartes, letters to her brother, and later articles on scientific themes.)

Poèmes, suivis de 'Venise sauvée' (1968, Paris: Gallimard). (Contains her play and other poetry.)

Articles
(This is an alphabetical list of Weil's articles with date of publication or composition and reference to the collection in which they can be found. For abbreviations, see list at the front of the book.)

'Allons-nous vers la révolution prolétarienne?' (1933) *Révolution Prolétarienne,* no. 158, August, pp. 3–11, OL, pp. 9–38.
'A propos de la question coloniale dans ses rapports avec le destin du peuple français' (1943) EHP, pp. 364–78.
'A propos du "Pater"' (1941/2) A, pp. 215–28.
'Cette guerre est une guerre de religions' (1943) EL, pp. 98–108.
'Condition première d'un travail non-servile' (1941) CO, pp. 261–73.
'Dernier texte', (1943) PSO, pp. 150–8.
'En quoi consiste l'inspiration occitanienne?' (1942) *Cahiers du Sud,* vol. 20, Autumn, pp. 150–8, EHP, pp. 75–84.
'Esquisse d'une histoire de la science grècque' (1941) IPC, pp. 172–180.
'Etude pour une déclaration des obligations envers l'être humain' (1943) EL, pp. 74–84.
'Examen critique des idées de révolution et de progrès' (1937) OL, pp. 178–85.
'Expérience de la vie d'usine' (1941) CO, pp. 241–59.
'Faut-il graisser les godillots?' (1936) *Vigilance,* nos 44 and 45, October, p. 15, EHP, pp. 48–9.
'Formes de l'amour implicite de Dieu' (1942) A, pp. 122–214.
'Idées essentielles pour une nouvelle constitution' (1943) EL, pp. 93–7.
'Journal d'Espagne' (1936) EHP, pp. 209–16.
'Journal d'usine' (1934–5) CO, pp. 35–107.
'La Condition ouvrière' (1937) CO, pp. 233–9.
'L'Agonie d'une civilisation vue à travers un poème épique' (1942) *Cahiers du Sud,* vol. 20, Autumn, pp. 99–107, EHP, pp. 66–74.
'L'Amour de Dieu et le malheur' (1942) PSO, pp. 85–131, A, pp. 98–121 (first half only).
'La Personne et le sacré' (1943) EL, pp. 11–44.
'La rationalisation' (1937) CO, pp. 215–32.
'La Situation en Allemagne' (1932/3) EHP, pp. 146–94.
'Le Christianisme et la vie des champs' (1941/2) PSO, pp. 21–33.
'Légitimité du gouvernement provisoire' (1943) EL, pp. 58–73.
'Les Trois Fils de Noé et l'histoire de la civilisation méditerranéenne' (1941) A, pp. 229–46.
'Lettre à Georges Bernanos' (1936) EHP, pp. 200–4.
'Lettres à Auguste Detoeuf' CO, pp. 181–95.
'Lettres à Joe Bousquet' (1942) *Correspondance Simone Weil – Joe Bousquet* (1982) J. Silberstein (ed.) (Lausanne: L'Age d'homme).
'Lettres à un etudiant' (1937/8) *Cahiers Simone Weil* (1987) vol. 10, no. 2, June, pp. 103–32.
'Lettres à un ingénieur directeur d'usine' (1936) CO, pp. 125–59.
'L'Europe en guerre pour la Tchecoslovaquie?' (1938) *Feuilles Libres de la Quinzaine,* vol. 4, no. 58, May, pp. 149–51, EHP, pp. 273–8.
'L'*Iliade* ou poème de la force' (December 1940 and January 1941) *Cahiers du Sud,* vols 19 and 20, pp. 561–74 and 21–34, SG, pp. 11–42.

'Luttons-nous pour la justice?' (1943) EL, pp. 45–57.

'Méditation sur l'obéissance et la liberté' (1937) OL, pp. 186–93.

'Méditations sur un cadavre' (1937) EHP, pp. 324–9.

'Ne recommençons pas la guerre de Troie' (1937) Les Nouveaux Cahiers, April, no. 2, 8–10 and no. 3, 15–19, EHP, pp. 256–72.

'Note sur la suppression générale des partis politiques' (1943) EL, pp. 126–48.

Projet d'une formation d'infirmières de première ligne' (1942) EL, pp. 187–95.

'Quelques méditations concernant l'économie' (1937) EHP, pp. 319–23.

'Réflexions à propos de la théorie des quanta' (1942) Cahiers du Sud, vol. 19, December, pp. 102–19, SS, pp. 187–209.

'Réflexions concernant la technocratie, le national-socialisme, l'U.R.S.S. et quelques autres points' (1933) OL, pp. 39–44.

'Réflexions en vue d'un bilan' (1939) EHP, pp. 296–312.

'Réflexions sans ordre sur l'amour de Dieu' (1941/2) PSO, pp. 35–45.

'Réflexions sur la barbarie' (1939) EHP, pp. 63–5.

'Réflexions sur la guerre' (1933) La Critique Sociale, no. 10, November, EHP, pp. 229–39.

'Réflexions sur le bon usage des études scolaires en vue de l'amour de Dieu' (1942) A, pp. 85–97.

'Remarques sur le nouveau projet de constitution' (1943) EL, pp. 85–92.

'Remarques sur les enseignements à tirer des conflits du Nord' (1936/7) CO, pp. 197–205.

'Réponse à une question d'Alain' (1936) EHP, pp. 244–7.

'Sur les contradictions du marxisme' (1937?) OL, pp. 194–204.

'Théorie des sacrements' (1943) PSO, pp. 134–47.

'Un Soulèvement prolétarien à Florence au XIVe siècle' (1934) EHP, pp. 85–101.

'Y a-t-il une doctrine marxiste?' (1943) OL, pp. 169–95.

Works by Simone Weil: English Translations

Book Collections

First and Last Notebooks (1970) trans. R. Rees (Oxford: Oxford University Press). (Contains the pre-war notebook from *Cahiers*, vol. 1, 1970 and *La Connaissance surnaturelle*.)

Formative Writings, 1929–1941 (1987) trans. D. McFarland and W. Van Ness (London: Routledge & Kegan Paul). (Contains diploma thesis on Descartes, articles on Germany, factory journal and later articles.)

Gateway to God (1974) D. Raper (ed.) (Glasgow: Collins). (Contains selected *pensées*, *Lettre à un religieux*, and essays from *Pensées sans ordre*.)

Gravity and Grace (1952) trans. A. Wills (New York: Putnam). (*La Pesanteur et la grâce*.)

Intimations of Christianity Among the Ancient Greeks (1957) trans. E. C. Geissbuhler (London: Routledge). (*Intuitions pré-chrétiennes* and most of *La Source grecque*.)

Lectures on Philosophy (1978) trans. H. Price (Cambridge: Cambridge University Press). (*Leçons de philosophie de Simone Weil*.)

Letter to a Priest (1954) trans. A. Wills (New York: Putnam). (*Lettre à un religieux*.)

The Need for Roots (1952) trans. A. Wills (New York: Putnam). (*L'Enracinement*.)

The Notebooks of Simone Weil (1956) trans. A. Wills, 2 vols (New York: Putnam). (First French edition of *Cahiers*.)

On Science, Necessity and the Love of God (1968) trans. R. Rees (Oxford: Oxford University Press). (Contains essays on science, on Plato from *La Source grecque*, and from *Pensées sans ordre*.)

Oppression and Liberty (1958) trans. A. Wills and J. Petrie (London: Routledge & Kegan Paul). (*Oppression et liberté.*)

Selected Essays, 1934–1943 (1962) trans. R. Rees (Oxford: Oxford University Press). (Contains political essays of the 1930s, the long essay on Hitler, the two articles on the Languedoc, and *La Personne et le sacré.*)

Seventy Letters (1965) trans. R. Rees (Oxford: Oxford University Press). (Contains the most important letters to friends and family.)

Simone Weil: An Anthology (1986) Sian Miles (ed.), (London: Virago). (Contains many of the major essays in full.)

The Simone Weil Reader (1977) G. Panichas (ed.) (New York: David Mackay). (A lengthy and comprehensive anthology.)

Waiting for God (1951) trans. E. Craufurd (New York: Putnam). (*Attente de Dieu.*)

Articles

'Cold War Policy in 1939', SE, pp. 177–94.

'Concerning the "Our Father"', WG, pp. 143–53.

'Critical Examination of the Ideas of Revolution and Progress', OL, pp. 134–40.

'Draft for a Statement of Human Obligations', SE, pp. 219–27.

'East and West: Thoughts on the Colonial Problem', SE, pp. 195–210.

'A European War Over Czechoslovakia?', FW, pp. 264–8.

'Factory Journal', FW, pp. 155–226.

'Forms of the Implicit Love of God', WG, pp. 79–142.

'The Great Beast: Reflections on the Origins of Hitlerism', SE, pp. 89–140.

'Human Personality', SE, pp. 9–34.

'The Iliad, Poem of Might', IC, pp. 24–55.

'Is There a Marxist Doctrine?', OL pp. 169–95.

'Last Text', GaG, pp. 72–4.

'The Legitimacy of the Provisional Government' (1987) *Philosophical Investigations*, vol. 10, no. 2, April, pp. 87–98.

Letter to Georges Bernanos, SE, pp. 171–6.

'Letters to Auguste Detoeuf', SL, pp. 55–64.

'Letters to Joe Bousquet', SL, pp. 136–42.

'The Love of God and Affliction', WG, pp. 61–78; GaG, pp. 87–102.

'A Medieval Epic Poem', SE, pp. 35–43.

'The Next World War' (1938) *International Review*, vol. 3, no. 1, pp. 7–11.

'A Note on Social Democracy', SE, pp. 150–3.

'On the Contradictions of Marxism', OL, pp. 147–55.

'The Power of Words', SE, pp. 154–71.

'Prospects: Are We Heading for the Proletarian Revolution?', OL, pp. 1–24.

'Reflections concerning Technocracy, National-socialism, the U.S.S.R. and certain other matters', OL, pp. 25–9.

'The Romanesque Renaissance', SE, pp. 44–54.

'Rome and Albania', SE, pp. 140–2.

'The Situation in Germany', FW, pp. 97–147.

'Theory of the Sacraments', GaG, pp. 65–72.

'The Three Sons of Noah and the History of Mediterranean Civilization', WG, pp. 155–69.

'A War of Religions', SE, pp. 211–18.

Commentaries

English
ALLEN, DIOGENES (1983) *Three Outsiders: Pascal, Kierkegaard, Simone Weil* (Cambridge: Cowley).
ANDERSON, DAVID (1977) *Simone Weil* (London: SCM).
BLUM, LAWRENCE and VICTOR SEIDLER (1989) *A Truer Liberty. Simone Weil and Marxism* (London: Routledge & Kegan Paul).
CABAUD, JACQUES (1965) *Simone Weil: A Fellowship in Love* (New York: Harvill).
COHEN, ROBERT (1964) 'Parallels and the Possibility of Influence between Simone Weil's *Waiting for God* and Samuel Beckett's *Waiting for Godot*', *Modern Drama*, February.
COLES, ROBERT (1987) *Simone Weil. A Modern Pilgrimage* (Reading, Mass.: Addison-Wesley).
DAVY, MARIE-MAGDELENE (1951) *The Mysticism of Simone Weil* (Boston: Beacon Press).
DIETZ, MARY (1989) *Between the Human and the Divine: The Social and Political Thought of Simone Weil* (New Jersey: Rowman & Littlefield).
DUNAWAY, JOHN (1984) *Simone Weil* (Boston: Twayne).
EATON, JEFFREY (1984) 'Simone Weil and the Problem of Analogy', *Theology*, vol. 87, January.
ELIOT, THOMAS (1952) Preface to *The Need for Roots* (New York: Putnam).
FIORI, GABRIELLA (1989) *Simone Weil. An Intellectual Biography* (Atlanta: University of Georgia Press).
GOLLANCZ, VICTOR (1953) *More for Timothy* (London: Gollancz) pp. 83–126.
GOODMAN, EDWARD (1975) *A Study of Liberty and Revolution* (London: Duckworth).
HELLMAN, JOHN (1982) *Simone Weil. An Introduction to Thought* (Waterloo: Wilfrid Laurier University Press).
HARDWICK, ELIZABETH (1984) *Bartelby in Manhattan* (New York: Random House) essay entitled 'Simone Weil'.
KING, PAUL (1975) 'The Social and Political Thought of Simone Weil', PhD dissertation, UCLA.
LICHTHEIM, GEORGE (1973) 'Simone Weil', *Collected Essays* (New York: Viking).
LITTLE, JANET (1970) 'Society as Mediator in Simone Weil's "Venise sauvée"', *Modern Language Review*, vol. LXV, 2.
LITTLE, JANET (1988) *Simone Weil. Waiting on Truth* (Oxford: Berg).
McFARLAND, DOROTHY (1983) *Simone Weil* (New York: Ungar).
MERTON, THOMAS (1968) 'Pacifism and Resistance in Simone Weil', in *Faith and Violence: Christian Teaching and Christian Practice* (Notre Dame: University of Notre Dame Press).
MILOSZ, CZESLAW (1981) *The Emperor of the Earth: Modes of Eccentric Vision* (Berkeley: University of California Press) pp. 85ff.
PANICHAS, GEORGE (1983) 'The Christ of Simone Weil', *Studies in Formative Spirituality*, 4 (2).
PERRIN, J.-M. and G. THIBON (1953) *Simone Weil As We Knew Her* (London: Routledge & Kegan Paul).
PÉTREMENT, SIMONE (1976) *Simone Weil: A Life*, trans. R. Rosenthal (New York: Pantheon).
PEYRE, HENRI (1964) 'Simone Weil', *Massachusetts Review*, vol. 6.
PHILLIPS, LEON (1982) 'Simone Weil: A stranger among her own', *Encounter*, 43 (2).

PIERCE, ROY (1966) 'Simone Weil: Sociology, Utopia and Faith', *Contemporary French Political Thought* (Oxford: Oxford University Press) pp. 89–121.

REES, RICHARD (1966) *Simone Weil: A Sketch for a Portrait* (Oxford: Oxford University Press).

ROSEN, FRED (1973) 'Labour and Liberty: Simone Weil and the Human Condition', *Theoria to Theory*, vol. 7, pp. 33–47.

ROSEN, FRED (1979) 'Marxism, Mysticism & Liberty. The Influence of Simone Weil on Albert Camus', *Political Theory* 7 (3) August.

SPRINGSTEAD, ERIC (1983) *Christus Mediator: Platonic Mediation in the Thought of Simone Weil* (Chico: Scholars Press).

SPRINGSTEAD, ERIC (1986) *Simone Weil and the Suffering of Love* (Cambridge: Cowley).

TAUBES, SUSAN (1955) 'The Absent God', *The Journal of Religion*, vol. xxxv, January, no. 1.

TEUBER, ANDREWS (1982) 'Simone Weil: Equality as Compassion', *Philosophy and Phenomenological Research*, vol. 43, no. 2, December.

TOMLIN, ERIC (1954) *Simone Weil* (New Haven: Yale University Press).

WALL, E. (1955) 'Simone Weil and Metapolitics', *Religion and Life*, xxiv.

WHITE, GEORGE (1981a) 'Simone Weil's Work Experience: From Wigan Pier to Chrystie Street', *Cross Currents*, 31 (2).

WHITE, GEORGE (ed.) (1981b) *Simone Weil: Interpretations of a Life* (Amherst: University of Massachusetts Press).

WINCH, PETER (1989) *Simone Weil. The Just Balance* (Cambridge: Cambridge University Press).

French and Other

BATAILLE, GEORGES (1949) 'La Victoire militaire et la banqueroute de la morale qui maudit', *Critique*, vol. v, no. 40, September, pp. 789–803.

BLECH-LIDOLF, LUCE (1976) *La Pensée philosophique et sociale de Simone Weil* (Bern: Herbert Lang).

BUGNION-SECRETAN, PAULE (1954) *Simone Weil: itinéraire politique et spirituel* (Neuchatel: Messeiller).

CABAUD, JACQUES (1957) *L'expérience vécue de Simone Weil* (Paris: Plon).

CANCIANI, DOMENICO (1983) *Simone Weil prima di Simone Weil* (Padova: GLEUP).

CANCIANI, DOMENICO *et al.* (1984) *Simone Weil: la passione della verita* (Brescia: Editrice Morcelliana).

DANIELOU, JEAN *et al.* (1964) *Réponses aux questions de Simone Weil* (Paris: Aubier).

DEBIDOUR, VICTOR-HENRY (1963) *Simone Weil ou la transparence* (Paris: Plon).

DEL NOCE, AUGUSTO (1968) *Simone Weil, interprete del mondo di oggi* (Torino: Einaudi).

DUJARDIN, PHILIPPE (1975) *Simone Weil. Idéologie et Politique* (Grenoble: Presses Universitaires de Grenoble).

EPTING, KARL (1955) *Der geistliche Weg der Simone Weil* (Stuttgart: Friedrich Vorwech).

FIORI, GABRIELLA (1987) *Simone Weil: Une femme absolue* (Paris: Editions du Felin).

FLEURE, EUGENE (1955) *Simone Weil ouvrière* (Paris: Fernand Lanore).

GINIEWSKI, PAUL (1978) *Simone Weil ou la haine de soi* (Paris: Berg).

GOLDSCHLAGER, ALAIN (1982) *Simone Weil et Spinoza. Essai d'interprétation* (Scherbrooke: Naaman).

HAUTEFEUILLE, FRANÇOIS DE (1970) *Le Tourment de Simone Weil* (Paris: Desclee de Brouwer).

HEIDSIECK, FRANÇOIS (1967) *Simone Weil: Une Etude avec un choix de textes* (Paris: Seghers).

HOURDIN, GEORGES (1989) *Simone Weil* (Paris: La Découverte).

KAHN, GILBERT (ed.) (1978) *Simone Weil, philosophe, historienne, mystique* (Paris: Aubieu).

KEMPFNER GASTON (1960) *La philosophie mystique de Simone Weil* (Paris: Vieux Colombier).

KROGMANN, ANGELICA (1970) *Simone Weil* (Hamburg: Rowohlt).

KUHN, ROLF (1980) 'Le Monde comme texte. Perspectives herméneutiques chez Simone Weil', *Revue des sciences philosophiques et théologiques*, 64 (4) pp. 509–30.

KUHN, ROLF (1983) 'L'Inspiration Religieuse et Philosophique en Grèce, vue à partir des mystères d'Eleusis (Eléments d'une philosophie religieuse chez Simone Weil)', *Revue d'histoire et de philosophie religieuse*, 63 (3).

MALAN, IVO (1960) *L'Enracinement de Simone Weil* (Paris: Didier).

MOELLER, C. (1967) 'Simone Weil et l'incroyance des croyants', *Littérature du XXe siècle et Christianisme*.

MONSEAU, MARCEL (1958) 'L'humanisme de Simone Weil dans *La Condition ouvrière*', *Revue de L'Université Laval*, vol. xii, no. 5, Quebec.

MOULAKIS, ATHANASIOS (1981) *Simone Weil: die Politik der Askese* (Alphen aan den Rijn: Sijthoff).

NARCY, MICHEL (1967) *Simone Weil: Malheur et beauté du monde* (Paris: Centurion).

OTTENSMEYER, HILARY (1958) *Le thème de l'amour dans l'œuvre de Simone Weil* (Paris: Lettres Modernes).

PERRIN, JOSEPH-MARIE (1984) *Mon Dialogue avec Simone Weil* (Paris: Nouvelle Cité).

PÉTREMENT, SIMONE (1955) 'Sur la religion d'Alain avec quelques remarques concernant celle de Simone Weil', *Revue de Métaphysique et de Morale*, vol. 60, July–Oct., pp. 306–30.

PÉTREMENT, SIMONE (1973) *La Vie de Simone Weil* (Paris: Fayard).

PICCARD, E. (1960) *Simone Weil. Essai biographique et critique, suivi d'une anthologie raisonnée des œuvres de Simone Weil* (Paris: Presses Universitaires de France).

SAINT-SERNIN, BERNARD (1988) *L'Action politique selon Simone Weil* (Paris: Cerf).

SAVINEL, P. (1960) 'Simone Weil et l'hellénisme', *Bulletin de l'Association Guillaume Bude*, March.

SCHLETTE, HEINZ and ANDRÉ DEVAUX (eds) (1985) *Simone Weil: Philosophie, Religion* (Frankfurt: Verlag Josef Knecht).

SCHUMANN, MAURICE (1974) *La Mort née de leur propre vie – Péguy, Simone Weil, Gandhi* (Paris: Fayard).

VETO, MIKLOS (1971) *La Métaphysique religieuse de Simone Weil* (Paris: Vrin).

VICKI-VOGT, MAJA (1983) *Simone Weil. Eine Logik des Absurden* (Bern: Paul Haupt).

Name Index

Abraham, 149, 151
Aeschylus, 203, 282, 285
Alain (Emile Chartier), 1, 12ff, 16, 18,
    20, 23f, 29, 37, 42, 48, 51, 78, 81,
    91, 106, 119, 124, 133f, 136, 153,
    170, 191, 197, 202, 217, 222, 239,
    266, 268, 289
Alexander the Great, 15
Alexandre, Jeanne, 21
Alexandre, Michel, 21
Angrand, Alice, 110, 112
Antheriou, Simone, 39f
Antigone, 279f
Appian, 145
Aquinas, Thomas, 288
Archimedes, 146
Arendt, Hannah, 95, 108, 269
Aristotle, 30, 168, 207, 211, 281f
Arjuna, 214ff
Aron, Raymond, 14, 20f
Aron, Suzanne (née Ganchon), 9, 266
Atares, Antonio, 164
Aubigné, Agrippe d', 253, 255
Augustine of Hippo, 30, 195, 224
Aurelius, Marcus, 210

Bach, Johann Sebastian, 129, 132
Bacon, Francis, 30
Ballard, Jean, 164, 166, 170, 181
Balzac, Honoré, 83, 134
Barrès, Maurice, 257
Basch, Victor, 24f
Bataille, Georges, 94, 269
Bea, Augustine, 268
Beauvoir, Simone de, 1, 18, 32, 136,
    269, 289
Beethoven, Ludwig v., 131
Belin, René, 115f, 125
Bell, Charles, 137f
Belleville family, 111
Benda, Julien, 255
Bentham, Jeremy, 30
Bercher, Louis, 171f, 224
Berdiaev, Nicholas, 77
Berger, Gaston, 168
Bergson, Henri, 12, 14, 21, 30, 39, 167,
    256

Berkeley, Bishop, 30
Bernanos, Georges, 120, 153, 268, 279
Bernard, Monsieur, 112ff, 118, 136
Blake, William, 275
Blum, Léon, 114, 119, 124, 133
Bonaparte, Napoleon, 79, 147, 230
Boticelli, Sandro, 130
Bouglé, Célestin, 25, 31
Bousquet, Joe, 181, 189, 210, 221
Briand, Aristide, 25, 31
Brion, Marcel, 167
Broglie, Louis de, 132, 178
Brosselette, Pierre, 236
Bruckberger, Raymond-Leopold, 172
Brunschvicg, Léon, 14, 26, 29
Burnham, James, 81

Caesar, Julius, 145
Camus, Albert, 91, 259, 269
Cancouet, Lucien, 19, 44
Canguilhem, Georges, 39
Castoriadis, Cornelius, 269
Cavaillès, Jean, 260
Cazamian, Jacqueline, 17
Ceresone, Pierre, 22
Chamberlain, Neville, 135
Chaplin, Charles, 35
Charbit, François, 58
Charles, V., 252
Château, René, 18, 20, 22, 24, 160
Chateaubriand, Francois, 144
Chiappe, Jean, 25
Claire, Rene, 35
Claudel, Paul, 32
Clausewitz, Karl von, 238
Cleanthes, 113
Closon, Louis, 234, 236, 259, 262, 264,
    266
Closon, Thérèse, 262, 265f
Cocteau, Jean, 33
Coles, Robert, 270
Comte, Auguste, 30
Conrad, Joseph, 108
Copeau, Edwige, 9
Corneille, Pierre, 6, 282
Coulomb family, 111
Couturier, Edouard, 226, 232

308

Subject Index